Sept 22, 2007

To Bill & Sue,
      How wonderful to have friends
over a span of 30 plus years.
A lot of memories from that time,
and hopefully many more to come
We always love to see you.
            Love
               Margret

Sarah ~ Her Story

The Life Story of
Sarah Parker Rice Goodwin,
Wife of Ichabod Goodwin,
New Hampshire's Civil War Governor

Based on her
Pleasant Memories,
Journals and Other
Goodwin Family Correspondence

Margaret Whyte Kelly

Margaret Whyte Kelly

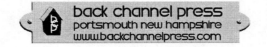
back channel press
portsmouth new hampshire
www.backchannelpress.com

SARAH ~ HER STORY
Copyright © 2006 by Margaret Whyte Kelly
ISBN-10 0-9767590-7-1
ISBN-13 978-0-9767590-7-2

BACK CHANNEL PRESS
170 Mechanic Street
Portsmouth, NH 03801
editor@backchannelpress.com
www.backchannelpress.com

Printed in the United States of America

Cover and book design by Nancy Grossman

Library of Congress PCN 2005911211

Second Printing August 2006

Acknowledgements

My thanks to Funi Burdick, former head of the Education Department at Strawbery Banke, now President of the American Independence Museum in Exeter, NH, for suggesting that I write this book. Also thanks to Dennis O'Toole, former President of Strawbery Banke, for his approval and support for the project.

Much appreciation for my co-workers at Strawbery Banke, whose encouragement, suggestions, historical input and editing skills were invaluable in preparing this book for publication. In particular, I thank Caroline Chase and Charles Librizzi for sharing their editing skills and knowledge, while Nancy Pempey, Polly Brown, and Joan Haskins gave me valuable suggestions and wonderful encouragement. Many other friends at Strawbery Banke also encouraged me to stay the course and get this book published. Thank you all for caring and helping to bring this project to completion.

I also want to thank Tara Webber, current Librarian, and Roberta Ransley Mattheu, former Librarian of Strawbery Banke's Thayer Cummings Library; Nicole Cloutier, Special Collections Librarian, and Richard Winslow, City Historian, Portsmouth Public Library; Barkley Feather, archivist, Milton Academy Library; Sharon Lee, Archivist from CEL Regional Library in Savannah, GA; Cynthia Cooper, Librarian, Peotone, IL, Library; my cousin Timothy Whyte of Brunswick, ME, for gathering research material for me; and various other librarians and archivists in Concord, Cambridge and Boston, MA, whose names I do not have, but they all have my deep appreciation for their kind help.

In addition I am thankful for the work of other New Hampshire historians both past and present whose works have benefited me in my effort to reconstruct the city of Portsmouth as it was during the nineteenth century.

Dedication

This is book is dedicated to my family, particularly my husband Patrick Kelly who has always encouraged me in my writing and all of my pursuits. Also, my daughters Katheryn and Elizabeth Kelly, and Patricia Kelly Wachsmuth; my granddaughters, Meghan and Patricia Kelly of Wells, ME; and my three grandsons, Benjamin, Connor, and Patrick Wachsmuth of Bow, NH, all of who give me inspiration and make my life much richer because they are part of it.

Contents

ILLUSTRATIONS

PREFACE

The earliest extant records of the Goodwin family in New England indicate that several branches of the Goodwin family arrived there sometime between 1630 and 1650. It is known that William and Ozias Goodwin were living in Hartford, Connecticut by 1632, and at about this same time Christopher and Richard Goodwin settled in Charlestown and Gloucester, Massachusetts respectively.

Daniel Goodwin came from Suffolk, England to settle in what was then known as Quamphegan. This was a part of early Kittery, Maine, which became the township of Berwick and eventually South Berwick.[1] It is not certain when Daniel Goodwin arrived, but records show he signed the act of submission in 1652, agreeing to abide by the laws of the Kittery Township.[2]

Daniel was active in his new community and at various times he was town commissioner, constable, and sergeant in the local frontier force. In addition he was one of the founders of the First Congregational Church. For many years he served as deacon, as well as church elder for this congregation. After his first wife, Margaret Spencer, died he married Mrs. Sarah Sanders, a wealthy widow. All in all he sired nine children.[3]

Town records indicate that Daniel was a surveyor, an innkeeper, and for many years he kept a public house, both with and without license. It was apparently a rowdy establishment, as he was often hauled into court for running a disorderly pub. At one point his oldest son Daniel, a surveyor of highways and a town selectman, was also taken into court for "being overtaken with drink."[4]

From these mixed and somewhat inauspicious beginnings the Goodwin family grew and prospered in Berwick. Many of Daniel's descendants became prominent citizens, who played leading roles in the early settlement of Berwick and surrounding towns. During the French and Indian Wars Captain Ichabod Goodwin along with his son and namesake, Major General Ichabod Goodwin served the country with distinction. The eldest was a member of the Massachusetts Court when Maine was a district of Massachusetts. His son became a member of the Provincial Congress, and was Major General of the 6th Division Massachusetts Militia during the American Revolution.[5]

Years later another Ichabod Goodwin brought honor and distinction to the Goodwin family name. Born on a farm in North Berwick in 1796, he was the oldest son of Samuel and Nancy Gerrish Goodwin. His mother was the daughter of Col. Joseph Gerrish, a member of the family that first settled Gerrish Island in Kittery, Maine, and a prominent Harvard graduate of the class of 1752.[6]

Samuel was a farmer in the area now known as North Berwick, and his son Ichabod grew up in modest circumstances. Family legend recalls him taking over the management of his step-grandmother's farm in South Berwick when he was just twelve years old. While there he enrolled in Berwick Academy for a few short years.

At age sixteen Ichabod Goodwin moved to Portsmouth, New Hampshire to work in the counting house of Samuel Lord, a prominent Portsmouth merchant. He was related to the Lords through marriage, and resided in their home on High Street as a member of their family while he became established in the area. Goodwin must have impressed the Lord family with his innate business acumen and leadership qualities, as when he was just twenty-two years old he was made supercargo of the *Elizabeth Wilson*, then the largest ship in Portsmouth Harbor.

It was unusual for someone his age to be named to this position. The supercargo on a ship was vested with the power to make all business decisions when the ship was at sea. Goodwin determined what to buy, sell or trade, and for what price. After two ocean voyages Goodwin became adept as a navigator, and Lord made him the ship's captain as well as the supercargo. These two positions were seldom combined or held by someone so young. Within a few years Goodwin was a part owner of his first ship.[7]

By the time he met his future wife, Sarah Parker Rice, the daughter of a wealthy Portsmouth merchant, he was established in the city. They were married in 1827, and had two sons and five daughters. Through the years Goodwin was prominently involved in local, state, and national politics. When he was sixty-five years old he was elected Governor of New Hampshire in 1859 and in 1860 at the start of the Civil War.

In business, as in politics, he was quite innovative, and at the forefront of many significant changes in Portsmouth during the nineteenth century. For over fifty years Goodwin was one of Portsmouth's leading citizens. Much of the credit for his success in life can be attributed to the estimable lady who stood by his side during these years, Sarah Parker Rice Goodwin, who traced her family lineage back to the city's founding fathers

INTRODUCTION

Sarah Goodwin was born in Portsmouth, New Hampshire in 1805 at the dawn of the nineteenth century, and lived there until her death in 1896. During her long lifetime Sarah witnessed great changes in the world around her, especially in the city of Portsmouth. Therefore when she turned seventy she decided to write down her memories of the town and her childhood for the sake of her grandchildren as well as others who were unfamiliar with the history of the area.

Sarah called her memoirs *Pleasant Memories.* For the most part she remained faithful to the title since it was her intent they be left as a legacy for her grandchildren. Starting with her memories of the Portsmouth of her youth, she wrote down her earliest impressions of the society that set the cultural mores of the city during the early 1800s, recalling:

> *There are records & traditions of elegant women & courtly men on the Piscataqua~ There was great punctilio & etiquette~*[8]

For the next fifteen years Sarah worked on her memoirs, which she wrote in a large legible script variously in pencil or pen on unlined paper. Upon her death they were left in the care of her oldest daughter. As she had wished these papers were passed down through several generations of grandchildren.

In the 1960s her family generously donated her writings to Thayer Cummings Library at Strawbery Banke Museum in Portsmouth, New Hampshire. This collection includes *Pleasant Memories*: a series of vignettes on her life in Portsmouth, and the places and people who made up her community, four of her "common daybooks," and letters both to and from her. In addition there are letters from various other family members and friends all of which fill in her story.

Sarah's common daybooks are quite eclectic. They range in style and topic matter from brief notations on the weather to short essays on the spiritual beginnings of the world. That she had varied interests is particularly clear from a reading of these daily jottings. She loved her garden, and kept copious notes on the progress of her plantings as well as her grove of trees, which she called "Tanglewood." She was given to flights of poetical musings especially about nature.

> *Oh trees! Trees! Big trees, bright trees, symmetrical trees! What would life be without them?*[9]

Sarah commented on family happenings, and expressed her opinion on a variety of subjects. She held strongly defined ideas and beliefs on subjects such as child rearing, marriage, personal conduct, religion, and the need to face life with a firm philosophical foundation. Her convictions on such matters were noted in her journals, sometimes quite tersely.

Gone the one word that applies eternally~
Understand what you read even if your have time for only six lines~

Always look to the bright side of your husbands character and never expose
his faults to any being~

Some people are so dependent on excitement that they are afraid of their
own company~

Society should be the recreation not the purpose of life~[10]

She was a curious and prolific reader, who filled her journals with notations from her readings. Favorite authors included Whitman, Emerson, Thoreau, Hawthorn, Thomas Hardy, Charles Dickens, George Elliot, and eventually Tolstoy. She also jotted down nostrums, recipes, maxims, conundrums, and witty sayings or jokes from the newly popular ladies' journals of her day.

Which is the strongest day in the week?
Sunday, because all the rest are weak days

When rain falls does it get up again?
Yes in dew time~

What length ought a lady's crinoline be?
A little above two feet~

When is a storm like a beer?
When it is brewing~[11]

These she may have used later as conversational tidbits to entertain her guests. Sarah was often called upon to entertain her friends and neighbors, as well as prominent politicians and business associates of her husband. She apparently was a wonderful hostess. One former neighbor recalled her as:

A woman of such intellectual and social gifts, that if her lot had been cast in
less obscure regions she would have without effort have proved herself one
of the most memorable American hostesses of her century.[12]

Sarah was well educated in the liberal arts at a time when most women fortunate enough to receive an education were schooled primarily in the feminine arts such as sewing and cooking. She attended private schools in Portsmouth and went to public school for one year. At age fifteen she entered Miss Willard's School for Young Ladies, and there she received a wonderful education under the tutelage of Mary Willard, whose own father was President of Harvard College for many years. Miss Willard instilled in Sarah a love of learning, which she retained for the remainder of her life.

She was a perfect teacher & a perfect lady...my dear friend & teacher Miss Mary Willard...If I have a taste for books it is owing to her influence...[13]

Sarah possessed the imagination and creative abilities found in many writers, and left behind at least one poem, as well as a short children's story she wrote for her grandchildren. As did many Victorians, Sarah loved nature, art and music. She played the piano from the time she was quite young. Blessed with a beautiful singing voice, Sarah sang in the church choir and was a member of the Handel and Haydn Society for many years.

No one could count the number of waves of sound that go to make up a musical note...I don't know anything of the science of music, but I am all alive to the essence of it~ That is I have great feeling of for it, a great enjoyment~[14]

A religious woman with a great faith in God, Sarah was a life long spiritual seeker. She sought deeper meaning to the many mysteries of life from her readings. She was curious, in particular about mystical sects or religions based on pacifism, such as Buddhism, Gnosticism, and the Quaker faith. Her common daybooks were filled with notations on the doctrines and practices of these religious groups.

The philosophical movements that arose during her day such as spiritualism, transcendentalism, and Theosophy also intrigued her. At one point she noted in her journal with some perplexity:

My late reading in the Theosophical doctrine of cycles makes clear to me some things heretofore inexplicable~ I am led to think I did not begin life in 1805 & that sometime I may come again~ I don't want to but I must~ I hope I shall be a better woman then~[15]

The wife of a politician, Sarah found politics interesting, and she believed women should be more involved in the political process. She was interested in the women's suffrage movement of her day. Her writings express indignation at the political inequalities that existed between the sexes. Sarah not only believed women should have the vote, but was convinced of their innate moral superiority. Writing down her sentiments on the subject she expressed these feelings.

"The...symbol of moral power ~ the Declaration of Independence ~ was intended to cover the whole human race."

I think it is the mission of women to lift man (in the great future) out of the bestial condition in which he mostly lives~[16]

Sarah volunteered her time to charitable organizations, and was quite active in the Mount Vernon Association, a group dedicated to preserving the home of the country's first president. She was active in the Women's Humane Society, and the New Hampshire Society for the Prevention of Cruelty to Animals, which her husband helped to found.

All in all Sarah Goodwin was a true Renaissance woman, with a curious open mind who eagerly sought knowledge from diverse disciplines. She wrote with equal zest about the alms house residents who sometimes called at her home, or her grandmother's slaves, Dinah and Boston, as she did about the President of the United States, who dropped in for breakfast one day, or the Chief Justice of the United States Supreme Court, who called on the family during the Civil War.

I first became acquainted with Sarah's memoirs when I was chosen to portray her in an ongoing historical reenactment at Strawbery Banke, a ten-acre outdoor museum in Portsmouth, New Hampshire. This museum is dedicated to teaching almost four hundred years of social history as it has evolved in one neighborhood known as Puddle Dock. Although the Goodwin home was originally built at least a half a mile from this site, it was moved there in 1963. Now the home and the story of the Goodwin family are used to present the many changes that took place in the overall social structure of the community during the nineteenth century.

In my role as Sarah Goodwin, these memoirs became a wonderful teaching tool. Her stories became my stories, and I was able to instruct as well as entertain visitors of all ages through her remembrances. I have put these memoirs together with other extant letters and writings in response to an overwhelming show of interest by the many visitors to the museum who asked if they had been published. And if not, why?

One reason the memoirs weren't published earlier was that more background information was needed about Sarah and her family to fill out the history and circumstances surrounding her stories. Although a lot of information pertaining to Ichabod Goodwin's business and political career was readily available, there was not a great deal of published information regarding his wife and children.

I set about to correct this inequity several years ago, and have since managed to compile enough information on the family to fill in the gaps and piece together a coherent story of Sarah's life. During this time I visited historical societies, museums, town halls, probate courts, and libraries throughout New England where I dug through old town records and other relevant material in search of information on the family. In addition there were quite a few occasions when I walked the streets of Portsmouth, New Hampshire, as well as Boston, Cambridge, and Concord, Massachusetts, just to stand for a few moments in front of an old home or building where a family member had once lived or worked. I've even visited the burial sites of some family members.

The search turned into an interesting journey. Like all researchers, I've felt the small thrill of triumph when some small nugget of information confirmed my speculations, and great discouragement when no treasure was found at the end of the trail. I came to look upon my research as a fascinating attempt to reconstruct the pieces of a large jigsaw puzzle. Unfortunately, after a century and a half, many of the pieces have been permanently misplaced.

Sarah's stories are not always presented here in their original format. In an attempt to tell her story in a chronological narrative I have taken the liberty of melding together some of her writings, particularly in cases when she wrote twice on the same subject, and I have interspersed journal notes, as well as excerpts from extant letters, with the memoirs to assure that her whole story is told as much as possible in her own words.

I believe Sarah's intent was to not only leave behind a record of her own life and those of her family, but to also leave an anecdotal history of the people and localities of the town of Portsmouth. Though her stories of the town and townspeople are not as numerous in number, they are similar to Charles Brewster's, *Rambles,* two volumes of anecdotal town history first published just about the time Sarah began writing her memoirs. Sarah often refers her grandchildren to his works, and I too have relied upon his work, as well as the writings of other Portsmouth historians, both past and present, in an attempt to recreate the Portsmouth that surrounded her during the nineteenth century. It is my hope that Sarah's reminiscences combined with the stories of others will inform and enlighten those who are interested in Portsmouth history.

Sarah's life roles as daughter, student, wife, mother, friend, and eventually grandmother all defined her, as they do most women, and I knew it would be impossible to fully understand her story without including the story of her husband as well as other family members. In addition to presenting her personal story, I have used her memories as a vehicle to explore the ways in which the technological advances of her time impacted both the male dominated world of business, industry, and politics, and the female sphere of the home, family and caretaker.

At the same time I have attempted to look at a number of reform movements and new schools of thought that arose during the nineteenth century in order to highlight the many ways, both dramatic and subtle, that they may have altered Sarah's world-view. However, it was not her intent, nor is it mine to present her writings as scholarly treatises and they should not be viewed as such. Rather the focus on this compilation of her writings should be on the unique perspective every woman's personal stories can bring to the study of history.

In preparing these memoirs for publication my major hurdle was how to organize such a diversity of subjects and interests. While Sarah's eclecticism was one of her primary charms, this wide range of subject matter presented a challenge as to how to best organize her writing. For the most part I have attempted to present her writings in a chronological order. The book begins with her writings on the early history of her family and town, and continues through the years when she and her husband were actively involved in their community and family affairs.

I have also written about the changes within the community of Portsmouth throughout the years, particularly in areas that would have concerned Sarah, because I believe this might be of interest to the readers. I have included an epilogue at the end with a brief account of her children's lives after her death, as well as what information I was able to gather about that first generation of grandchildren to whom she had so lovingly dedicated her *Pleasant Memories.*

TRANSITIONS DURING
THE NINETEENTH CENTURY

Sarah Goodwin lived through a time of tremendous change in America. When she was born the nation was just a quarter of a century old, and the manners, beliefs, and social customs prevalent then were not very different than those of the first English settlers. But by the time Sarah began writing her memoirs, the world had changed in ways few people could have ever envisioned at the start of the nineteenth century.

During her lifetime the very pace of everyday life quickened. The way that people thought, worked, traveled, and communicated with each other changed drastically, and basic beliefs and life styles were altered permanently for large segments of the society. In her writings Sarah looked back on the multitude of changes, which had occurred in work and living patterns as well as customs.

> *It was the New England custom to have a whole salt codfish cooked on Saturday with the accompaniments of boiled potatoes, beets, onions, liquid port with the scraps, & eggsauce~ Beef steak followed & then apple pie & cream~*

> *Plated or silver candlesticks were in great demand before a party & people borrowed from relations & neighbors for the occasion~ Cut papers of bright colors were put tastefully around the lower part of the candle & the effect was very pretty~*

> *Ladies who were very delicate looked beautiful by candlelight~ My father used to say "Never choose ladies or linen by candlelight~"*

> *Every lady liked to look delicate~ A good complexion was esteemed almost more than good features~ Ladies laced very tight~ A small waist was thought a great beauty~ People did not know as much about the laws of health as they do now~*[17]

> *Forty years ago in the United States there were long parallel tables in the dining rooms, behind which files of waiters were marched up & down like soldiers~ They were drilled to set down the dishes with a simultaneous bang from end to end~ The small tables & quiet service now are an immense improvement~*[18]

The America of her childhood expanded from the established eastern cities on the Atlantic Coast to those western territories along the Pacific Coast, that were for so many years home to a large number of Mexican missions, villas, and haciendas. In between it embraced vast areas of previously unexplored and undeveloped prairie land and mountain wilderness.

> *The wildest imagination could not have dreamed of provisions from California or Chicago ~ indeed Chicago was not~*[19]

> *San Francisco had to be reached by way of Cape horn~which took months & friends had to wait a long time for news~ Now there are four railroads across the continent~*[20]

Then the northern and southern sections of the country split apart, dividing into separate governments. For four long years, these two regions engaged in a terrible battle, which almost destroyed the nation Sarah's ancestors had fought to build.

> *The war of the rebellion was brought about by southern women & Presbyterian ministers & encouraged by northern democrats for their own advantage & aggrandizement~*[21]

During the first half of the century river power was harnessed, and then the steam engine was adapted to power factories. These factories in turn made life more comfortable, yet much more difficult at the same time. As a result of these new technologies a variety of material goods once considered luxuries, became accessible to large segments of the middle class.

Fashions did not often change in any part of the world in those days~ there was a great deal of wise economy & a good thing was expected to last~ A Dunstable straw or a velvet bonnet would be made over year after year~[22]

In my childhood & middle age the dresses were hooked or buttoned behind~ Only old women fastened their gowns in front~ Old women wore horrid caps & black hair front pieces~[23]

Ladies embroidered muslin a good deal but worsted work came up later~ People mended a great deal in those days & clothes were passed down from one to another in families~

It is wonderful how crockery & glass lasted~ A dozen cut glass tumblers (called double flint) were in use at my father's forty years~ In fact it was expected that nothing would be broken~ American servants were very poor but they valued suitably what they had, as their English ancestors had done from time immemorial~[24]

However, the factories brought drastic changes in the living and working patterns of much of the population. This was especially true in the cities, which experienced substantial increases in population due to an influx of rural workers and immigrants needed to run them. Sarah recalled how life had been for the average worker.

Pins & needles were made by hand~ Men swung the scythe day after day & women sewed day & night & made linen shirts with ruffles for a dollar apiece~

There were a great many poor people in the first half of this century~ A great many poor widows who were glad to go out as nurses or to do sewing~ A dollar was looked at twice before it was spent & people talked a good deal about what they had~[25]

Steam powered engines were also adapted to power new and faster modes of travel making possible steamships and railroads. These enabled, indeed encouraged, young people to venture outside of their own regions to explore and develop other parts of the country.

A visit to Boston was a rare & great occasion to most people~ Two accommodation stages & one mail stage ran from here to Boston every day & they seldom were full~[26]

And then the <u>dear old Ferry</u>~ how lovely it was to cross our beautiful river with perfect confidence in the ferryman~ It was a thousand times more poetic than a railroad car or any other carriage~[27]

Many young people moved to new areas great distances from their places of origin to settle and raise their children, leaving behind their childhood families and traditions. Once there most of them embraced new concepts and outlooks along with the social mores prevalent in their adopted communities, while in turn introducing their own family customs and intellectual perspectives to their new neighbors. Over the course of a few decades this exchange of ideas and traditions brought about a homogenous blending of the American culture.

Dinner parties were not uncommon & the Russian style had not come in~ A tall glass pyramid with Jellies & creams occupied the centre of the table & the top cloth was removed~

Every lady made a great many preserves~ jellies, almond custards, lemon creams, whipped cream in tall glasses, blancmange & preserves with cream, were served among other delicacies on large trays & carried round by a man at parties~ Tea & coffee were passed three times & cake of several kinds, four times~

Ladies called upon one another a good deal especially when they had anything new ~ Before a party came off everybody to be invited was called upon ceremoniously~ This gave time for revision of toilets though I never heard this spoken of~[28]

Science transformed the world around Sarah with new inventions and ideas. These not only changed the outer world, but also challenged such basic concepts as the origin and supremacy of mankind. Forty years after Darwin's treatise On the Origin of the Species was first published, Sarah commented in a letter to her daughter-in-law Molly Buttrick:

"We talk glibly of heredity, but how few perceive what a terrible power it may be and what a burden to carry"[29]

The telegraph and eventually the telephone further transformed Sarah's world, by changing the ways she and the rest of the world communicated. Gaslights and then electricity replaced candles and kerosene or whale oil lamps used to illuminate homes. At the same time wood burning hearths were replaced by coal stoves and furnaces.

The railroad, the telegraph, telephone, & ocean steam ships were unknown... The Astral Lamp followed by the Solar Lamp came in just before gas was introduced~ Air tight stoves, double sashes, and stoves in houses about 1830 and furnaces still later~[30]

These inventions and new modes of travel brought conveniences and comforts to the average home Sarah could never have envisioned in her childhood.

> *But Oh it was cold all about the house in winter in my childhood & youth~*
> *No hall stoves~ no furnaces! Water froze where it dropped except in kitchen*
> *or parlor~*
>
> *Housewives did not rejoice in the sewing machine until they were safely in*
> *Heaven where they can still be glad for those who came after them~*[31]
>
> *Shades for windows were not in use before 1850~ Curtains or blinds of some*
> *sort were used to cover the window~ Shutters were an inside appendage to*
> *windows in all good houses in the olden time they were usually in three*
> *parts & folded back with hinges~ There were close sliding shutters also~*[32]

Given all the changes within her own lifetime it's no wonder she was interested in preserving the history of her town through her memories of the people and customs which reigned in Portsmouth during her youth.

> *Whittier's "Snow Bound" described the effect of the Alms House teams*
> *after a deep snow as they passed through the streets breaking the paths~*
>
> *Families cured all the corn beef & hams necessary for their use & many*
> *large families raised the pork for home consumption~ The squealing of a*
> *pig was by no means an unusual sound~*
>
> *But after all is said people were satisfied ~ They did not dream of these*
> *times~*[33]

Sarah loved history and realized that she had lived through a lifetime of great change. She also knew that everyday details, as well as the stories of ordinary people, made up the history of the town. So she wrote down her stories to preserve them for future generations, so they would know about life in nineteenth century Portsmouth.

TOWN HISTORY

Sarah wrote a brief overall history of Portsmouth. She then scrawled at the top of this section in large bold print *"Read This First."* She went on to explain:

> *I have sometimes been surprised by the remarks of persons who have taken up their residence in Portsmouth within thirty years in relation to style, manner &c~ The families who led Society previous to that period were for the most part born here & were familiar with the antecedents of the place… So many families have come in… who know little of the antecedents…that I feel constrained to leave these notes for the sake of my grandchildren if not for others~ Portsmouth is a grand old town unlike any other….*[34]

Following this Sarah inexplicably wrote: *"It's proverbial that Boston people have bad manners~"* Then apparently changing her mind about this ungracious comment concerning the residents of the similar but larger coastal city less than fifty miles to the south, she crossed it out with a large loop like scrawl. The most logical explanation for Sarah's reference to Boston at the outset of her treatise on Portsmouth history is that she was tempted to compare these two cities.

This would have been understandable as the cities historically shared much in common. Both were former English colonies and port cities, closely connected by trade for many years. In 1623 Portsmouth was the first of the two cities to be settled by the English, when a small settlement began in the area of Ordione Point. The Pilgrims had settled in Plymouth, Massachusetts by then, but the Bay Colony that was later called Boston was not yet established.

In each town the majority of the settlers earned their livelihood from seafaring industries. However, Boston was founded by people seeking religious freedom, while those who came to Portsmouth came to earn a living off the bounty of the fish, game, and timber earlier explorers had discovered flourishing in this region.

Sarah was a descendent of several of the first English families sent to the Piscataqua region in the 1630s by Sir Ferdinando Gorges and Captain John Mason of England. These men divided a grant from King James I giving them ownership to all the lands between the Kennebec and Merrimack Rivers. Mason claimed the area between the Merrimack and Piscataqua, named New Hampshire and Gorges the area between the Piscataqua and Kennebec called the Province of Maine.[35]

These settlers landed near Portsmouth Harbor, in the spring of 1630 and called their new settlement Strawbery Banke, indicating that they found wild strawberries growing along the banks of the Piscataqua. A second group followed in 1631. They first built a Great House, located on about one thousand acres of marsh and meadowland near the corner of the present day Court and Marcy Streets, and lived in a communal society until they became established. Eventually they settled on both banks of the river, calling those portions in Southern Maine,

Piscataqua Plantation.[36]

Mason died in 1635 and left his holdings to his grandson Robert Tufton on the condition that he take the name Mason. However, Robert was only six months old, too young to fight for his inheritance. Mason's former servants and their families soon seized the lands that they had settled in his name.[37]

That same year King Charles I appointed eleven councilors to oversee all the lands of American Plantations. Sir Gorges was officially appointed Governor of New England. The region between the Piscataqua and Kennebec Rivers was named New Somersett, and Gorges nephew, William Gorges, became governor of that province.[38]

A few years after Mason's death the Massachusetts Bay Company, disputed the interpretation of the original charter. They claimed that all portions of New Hampshire and Maine settled by the heirs and agents of Mason and Gorges belonged to Massachusetts.[39] Eventually residents of both states consented to Puritan rule. New Hampshire became incorporated into Massachusetts from 1641 until 1679, and during this time Strawbery Banke was renamed Portsmouth. Maine joined Massachusetts in 1652, five years after Sir Gorges died.[40]

In 1679, more than twenty-five years later, it was determined that the original boundaries had been correct. Maine was then sold back to Massachusetts by the grandson of Sir Gorges. It remained part of Massachusetts until 1820.[41] Massachusetts offered to buy New Hampshire from Mason's grandson, but he refused to sell. For a number of years he pursued his claim to no avail. Those who had originally settled the lands once owned by Mason refused to give them up.[42]

With the exception of the years from 1686 to 1692, when the colonies from New Jersey to Maine were joined during the Dominion of New England, New Hampshire remained a royal province. For a while New Hampshire and Massachusetts shared a governor, but in New Hampshire the lieutenant governor held primary authority.[43]

> *There are records & traditions of elegant women & courtly men on the Piscataqua~ The Governors appointed by the crown copied the fashions of the English court circle & their dress & entertainments were modeled as closely after them as was possible under the circumstances~ There was great punctilio & etiquette~*[44]

In 1717, John Wentworth of Portsmouth, a member of the King's Council, was appointed lieutenant governor of New Hampshire. The Wentworths were prominent members of the English aristocracy for many generations. The branch that first came to the New Hampshire seacoast in the 1600s eventually formed a royal dynasty that reigned in Portsmouth throughout the greater part of the eighteenth century.[45]

In 1742 Wentworth's younger brother Benning came from England and was appointed royal governor of New Hampshire. He built a mansion in Little Harbor, and his reign as governor lasted twenty-five years. Under his administration corruption, misplaced power, greed, and nepotism were rampant.[46]

Older and widowed, Benning scandalized the more staid residents of the city, when he wed a former tavern wench, twenty-year-old Martha Hilton. She was his housekeeper when he impulsively proposed and married her on the same night. This took place in his parlor in the presence of several astonished dignitaries and friends. Henry Wadsworth Longfellow memorialized this occasion in a poem entitled *Lady Wentworth*.[47]

Sarah was familiar with the story of this scandal, as well as others that took place amongst the wealthy families of old, as they were related to her in her youth by a woman who made her living preparing and delivering pastries to the prominent families in town. According to her account it would seem that the young bride had anticipated the impulsive proposal.

> *She kept a little shop on Pleasant street~ but made a variety for herself by making Pastry & cakes for the great families~ Once a week she went to Little Harbor to get up desserts for Gov. Benning's great weekly dinners~*

> *It had been noticed by the servants, that the Immortal Patty was putting on airs, & that she had treated herself to a new flowered calico gown & also a new silk which was scarcely more valued, & they were not at all surprised, on this particular company day, at the wedding that came off ~[48].*

Benning eventually made enough enemies on both sides of the Atlantic that he fell into disfavor with the king, and in 1766 his nephew, John Wentworth, a native of Portsmouth and a Harvard graduate was chosen to replace him. By all accounts John was quite handsome and charming, and he won the approval of the majority of the townspeople. He settled into a residence on Pleasant Street, and soon became immersed in his own personal scandal when he married his cousin, Francis Wentworth Atkinson, ten days after her husband Thomas Atkinson succumbed to a debilitating illness. Francis was an old flame Wentworth had courted before he left for England. Upon his return it was noted that the two were often seen alone together. The reason for the hasty wedding soon became apparent when a child was born to the newlyweds three to four months after the wedding.[49]

> *Of course the ideas and manners of the English Aristocracy gave the tone to the circle in which the crown appointed Governors moved and reigned~[50]*

In spite of this personal scandal, John proved to be a good governor. However, his rule was destined to end after nine years, due to changing allegiances. As the Revolution drew closer Wentworth was caught between two factions in town, the Royalists and the Patriots. His final downfall came in 1775 when he made arrangements to hire New Hampshire men to build British barracks in Boston.

Once this became public knowledge an angry crowd broke down the door to his Pleasant Street mansion demanding that he release a Royalist he had harbored there. Wentworth fled out the back to safety at the British fort in nearby New Castle. For a while he attempted to govern from the Isle of Shoals, but was unsuccessful. Soon after that he and his family sailed to England. This ended the long reign of the Wentworth family in Portsmouth.[51]

Boston's royal families also had their share of scandals, and they too were eventually driven out of power, and in many cases out of the country. During the Revolution Portsmouth and Boston both played an important role in freeing the country from the tyranny of the Royal Crown.

At the start of the Revolution each city was the seat of government for their province. Boston continued to be the capital of Massachusetts. However, New Hampshire's central government was moved to nearby Exeter during the Revolution, because it was thought that its close proximity to the sea made it more vulnerable to attack.[52]

The populace of each city was quite cosmopolitan and many of the residents in both Boston and Portsmouth were well traveled, well educated, and sophisticated. There was a great deal of intercourse between the two cities, both social and economic. Each city also had their share of English loyalists, content with English culture and customs. They did not wish to change their allegiances to England. On the opposite side both cities had a large number of Patriots, dissatisfied with the oppressive taxes and tyrannous laws of the mother country. They were willing to fight for their country's independence.

One well-known Boston Patriot, who traveled to Portsmouth often when he was a young lawyer, was John Adams. On those occasions he always made it point to call upon his fellow classmate and good friend, Governor John Wentworth. One time he bypassed the city by following a new route, and afterward wrote in his journal he would have to make amends to Wentworth, as they were friends. However he noted that had he followed the regular route, he *"should have seen enough of the Pomps, Vanities and Ceremonies of that little World, Portsmouth…"*[53]

Other notable Boston Patriots who visited Portsmouth were Benjamin Franklin and John Hancock. Franklin was credited with installing Portsmouth's first lightening rod in the home now known as the Warner House. [54] Also, John Hancock owned a warehouse in nearby York, Maine, and was a frequent visitor to the area.

Numbered amongst the Portsmouth Patriots were William Whipple, a signer of the Declaration of Independence, John Langdon, a member of the Continental Congress, and Tobias Lear, George Washington's personal secretary. Hunking Wentworth, the leader of the Patriot's Committee of Safety was a member of the Wentworth family, which formed Portsmouth's royal dynasty.

> *Col. Lear of Portsmouth was a graduate of Harvard college & brought great prestige by his marriage with a niece of Gen Washington & by being chief of staff & private secretary to the Gen. for thirty years~ He lived in the family & on the death of the General's niece he married a niece of Mrs Washington~ The house in which he was born & in which his mother died is still in good preservation~*[55]

In both cities the residents engaged in acts of disobedience against the tyranny of the English rulers. People in Portsmouth were so vehemently opposed to the Stamp Act passed in 1765, that when the stamped paper did arrive in Boston no agent dared to claim it for Portsmouth. In March of 1766, following a demonstration against the tax, the residents hoisted a large flag with the words "Liberty, Property and no Stamp" over the swing bridge in the Puddle Dock neighborhood of town. After this the bridge was always known as the Liberty Bridge.[56]

As in Boston, Portsmouth citizens protested the royal tax on tea. Some ships carrying tea to Portsmouth met with a certain degree of violence before they could be diverted to Nova Scotia. Then the British government banned the importation of gunpowder to the colonies, and on December 13th of 1774 Paul Revere rode to Portsmouth to warn the local Sons of Liberty that a British warship was headed to Portsmouth to seize all of the ammunition in the area.

This culminated in a raid on the Royal Crown's Fort William and Mary, then known as the "Castle," led by John Langdon and Thomas Pickering, both respected sea captains at the time. The following day approximately 400 area men rallied in Market Square and marched to the water's edge where they rowed to nearby New Castle. At the island they took about a hundred pounds of powder and returned the next day to take sixteen cannons and sixty muskets as well as other weapons. Although this was a clear act of treason against the British Crown, no one was hurt and no arrests were made. These were part of the stores used against the British forces in the battle of Bunker Hill five months later[57]

Five of the ships built by the Continental Navy during the Revolution were built on a small island in the Piscataqua River overlooking the city of Portsmouth. It was originally known as Withers' Island, named after its first proprietor, Thomas Withers, Sarah's paternal great-great-great-grandfather. By the time of the Revolution it was called Langdon's Island, and is currently called Badger's Island.

Two of the most memorable ships built there were the *Raleigh* and the *Ranger*. The latter was the first navy ship to be copperclad. It sailed out of Portsmouth in November of 1777, under the command of John Paul Jones. The *Ranger* became famous, as did its captain, in part because it was honored that following February with a nine gun salute from a French warship. This salute marked the first official recognition of the American flag from another country.[58]

During the next war with Great Britain in 1812, another local patriot rose to national fame. Daniel Webster was a resident of Portsmouth when the war began. He and his wife set up their first home there and he opened a law practice in the city. Sarah was no more than twelve when he was her neighbor on nearby Vaughan Street.

> *Perhaps the grandest jewel in the crown of Portsmouth was Daniel Webster~ He came to Portsmouth in 1807~ His bride found her first home in Portsmouth & all their children were born here~*
>
> *I believe he was appreciated from the beginning & he soon rose to eminence at a bar where Joseph Story, Samuel Dexter & Jeremiah Mason were at the height of their fame~*[59]

Daniel Webster was a United States Representative at the time of the War of 1812, and was purportedly amongst the local ranks of Portsmouth and Rye men defending the harbors from the British. Following this war Webster moved to nearby Boston where he set up his law practice. There in the larger city his fame as a speaker grew to legendary proportions.

> *In the early times the rich families were few & the poor were many~ the grand people were much looked up to & rank was as much respected as in the mother country~*
>
> *Almost every gentlemen had a farm somewhere in the neighborhood of the town to which he took his family for recreation, once or twice a week~ Butter, milk, vegetables, apples &c were brought frequently to the house in town~ Many who drive on our beautiful roads know little of those who once owned the various farms & loved to visit them~*[60]

Around the time of the Revolution Portsmouth was the tenth largest city in the country, with proportionally more liveried servants and fine carriages in relation to population than any other city.[61] It seems clear that despite the many similarities between Portsmouth and Boston, Sarah believed the smaller city was superior when it came to fine manners and breeding. Many of the wealthiest families, which Sarah names as ones that set the social tone in those years, were related to Sarah either directly or through marriage. This was true of the Sherburnes and Langdons.

> *One hundred and fifty years ago, the Sherburnes, Wentworths, Moffats, Warners, Scheafes and others rode in grand coaches and lived luxuriously~*
>
> *All the leading families had from two to four servants and almost everybody kept a horse chaise & sleigh~ Spans & fine carriages were owned by the James Scheafes, Masons, Woodbury's, Rundlet's, Shaw's & others~*[62]

John Langdon, who entertained both George Washington and the Marquis de Lafayette at his home during their visits to Portsmouth, helped to draft the Constitution of the United States, and was one of the signers of this document. Sarah, who was distantly related to him by marriage, recalled her childhood impressions of him when he was an elderly man.

> *Gov Langdon lived in great style~ His pew at the north church was curtained around with green stuff & was next to the pulpit~ I can just remember him as he walked feebly up the broad aisle leaning on the arm of his valet~ The Langdons "came up" with the Revolution & they were very important & elegant people~*[63]

FAMILY HISTORY

The Langdons weren't the only ones who *"came up"* during the American Revolution. Many of the leading families of Portsmouth, including Sarah's family, made their fortunes during this war and the War of 1812 through investments and activities connected to privateering. Privateering was a lucrative enterprise in which privately owned and manned vessels were outfitted for war. During the Revolutionary War there were approximately one hundred privateering vessels sailing out of the Piscataqua region, and a roster of their investors/owners included men from the wealthiest and most respected families in the area.[64]

In 1775 the Continental Congress enacted laws regulating privateering. Privateers were required to obtain the permission of Congress by first posting bond and agreeing to honor international maritime laws. Those that did so were issued letters of marque and reprisal, giving them legal permission to capture British and many non-British merchant ships suspected of carrying contraband to aid the enemy.

Under the new laws all captured prizes were brought into an official American port where they were libeled, tried, and condemned before they could be sold at auction. Admiralty courts were set up just for the purpose of rendering judgment on these captures. Once condemned the contraband was sold at public auction, and the profits divided between the ship's investors, captain and crew. Of course a certain percentage was set aside to pay for the court trials and the auctioneer.[65]

Privateering was considered a patriotic enterprise, as well as a profitable one. Indeed it did inflict a lot of damage to the British economy through the loss of merchandise, shipping vessels, sailors, and resultant prohibitive insurance rates. These privateers often intercepted ships carrying supplies to the British navy, and diverted the supplies to Washington's army. Such captures of course directly impacted on the Revolution, benefiting the Patriots and creating hardships for the British.

In Sarah's family men on both her paternal and maternal sides engaged in and profited from privateering. Her mother, Abigail Parker, was the daughter of Robert Parker and Sarah Sherburne.

> *My mother's mother was Sarah Sherburne for whom I was named~ She had like my grandmother Rice twelve children~*[66]

The Sherburnes were one of the leading families in Portsmouth at the time of the Revolution. The first Sherburne in Portsmouth was Henry, a nobleman from Stonyhurst, England who came to America with the Mason settlers in 1631. He married Rebecca Gibbons, the daughter of Ambrose Gibbons, Mason's steward.

Sherburne was the proprietor of the first licensed tavern in Portsmouth, called an "ordinary" in the vernacular of that day. It was located on the site of today's Prescott Park near the Grand House built by those first settlers. His grandson, Henry, a Provincial Councilor, married the sister of Lieutenant Governor John Wentworth.[67]

Sarah's maternal grandmother was the daughter of Ephraim Sherburne. He had gone into the ship building business with his father in law, John Shillings, many years before the Revolution. The two men were quite successful and owned shipyards in both Kittery and Portsmouth.[68]

> *I have been thinking about My grandfather Parker & what a good benevolent man he was~ His father was a shipmaster who died when Robert was an infant~ Robert learned to build boats at Kittery where all his people lived~ His mother was a Miss Moore whose father was a shipmaster & who taught his daughters navigation saying they should have as much education as he had~ She lived In Kittery & there were no schools there then~*

> *I like to think that perhaps I have in me the blood of Sire Thomas Moore~ Robert chose the sea for a profession & was a shipmaster many years~ When he became tired of the sea he staid at home & built ships~*[69]

Thomas Moore was listed as one of the original Mason settlers, but it was his son John Moore of Star Island who was Robert Parker's grandfather. John moved to the vicinity of Spruce Creek in Kittery in 1668 and married Sarah Cutt, daughter of Robert Cutt, a shipbuilder in Kittery, and one of three prominent brothers who settled in Portsmouth before the 1640s.[70]

When John Moore married Sarah Cutt he received a grant of thirty acres in the Spruce Creek area, where he built their home. In 1702 their daughter Abigail Moore married Nathum Parker, a shipmaster from England who settled in Portsmouth sometime during the early 1700s. Together they had five children. Their youngest son, Robert Parker, was born in 1735, just seven years before Nathum died in 1742.[71]

When Robert Parker married Sarah Sherburne, once again a father and son-in-law joined together in the shipbuilding business. According to Sherburne family information, Ephraim was extensively engaged in the privateering business with Robert Parker during the American Revolution. Parker profited from the privateering enterprise and he also contributed to the Revolution.

> *Robert chose the sea for a profession and was a shipmaster many years~ When he became tired of the sea he staid at home and built ships~*[72]

In 1776 he was captain of the schooner, McClary, which captured the British ship *Hero*, with 500 hogshead of rum aboard; when he presented one to General George Washington, he became somewhat of a local hero.[73] He also captured an American ship trading at enemy ports.[74] In 1777 he received permission to use the Portsmouth as a privateer armed to engage the "enemies of the states of America."[75]

A shopkeeper as well as a ship's captain, Parker used his trading contacts to obtain needed gunpowder for the Revolution from a Frenchman at St. Pierre, Martinique Harbor. In the summer of 1777, ignoring an embargo against privateering vessels instituted by the New Hampshire Assembly, Captain Parker sailed to the West Indies during the height of the hurricane season. At the time, the Committee of Safety had forbidden ships carrying valuable cargo from sailing from the Port of Portsmouth whenever it was determined there was a high risk of capture.

Parker had heard that the natives of Martinique were low on necessary supplies, and he convinced the committee that the risk of capture was low since few ships traveled to the West Indies seas during these months. He held out the promise of trading cod and lumber for needed guns, powder, and woolen supplies for the Continental Army, and he was able to deliver. On this journey he captured three vessels, which yielded 5,700 stands of arms along with a large amount of food supplies intended for the British navy.[76]

That fall Parker joined nine other prominent Portsmouth men, including John Langdon, to form a privateering syndicate. These ten men invested a total of ten thousand pounds to fund this venture. Joshua Wentworth headed it, and Parker, who was appointed as agent, was instructed to oversee the construction of the brigantine *General Sullivan*. It was a very profitable venture, and each investor made a great deal of money from her successful voyages.[77]

While privateering promised thrilling adventures on the high seas, and the chance for a quick and substantial profit, great risks were inherent in the profession. Robert Parker's oldest son and namesake was lost at sea in 1778. He was just seventeen and was probably engaged in privateering with his father at the time of his death.[78].

Parker was a master carpenter, and he oversaw the construction of the barracks built on Pierce Island to house the American army. He was also put in charge of the fire rafts needed to defend Portsmouth harbor. While Parker was a loyal Patriot, he was first a businessman and once refused to sell rum to the state for the use of the Continental Army. It seems the price wasn't right. However, the Committee of Safety, the local authorities during the Revolution, wouldn't accept Parker's refusal and ordered the sheriff to confiscate four hogsheads of his rum.[79]

Sometime before the Revolution Robert Parker moved most of his family from Portsmouth to Lee, New Hampshire. He was active in the Patriot movement in both communities, but it was in Lee that he signed the Association Test swearing to oppose the British to the utmost of his power in 1776.[80]

> *While going about the country after timber he fell in with a tract of land at Lee which pleased him very much~ It reminded him of English scenery & he bought it~*[81]

> *Before the Revolution he...built a fine large house with double pitch roof, dormer windows, & large hall & staircase~ He was very ambitious about his farming & had the largest outbuildings in this part of the country~*[82]

The outbuildings were probably part of a shipyard Robert Parker set up on his farm in Lee, five miles from the nearest body of water. It was here that he built the brigantine *General Sullivan.*[83]

> *There was a front yard with great trees on each side & a splendid lawn reaching down half a mile in front & skirted by a dense wood~ The road between the front yard & the lawn was very broad & the walls were all of what was called faced stones~ That is, stone selected & carefully laid~*[84]
> *[he]...took his wife & her father & mother & his own mother to live with him there~ Two of his daughters were married & there were three single~*

These last refused to go into the country~ They had a pleasant home near the river on Market St & they were very attractive & had a lot of beaux & their father could not bear to oppose them & for some years he had to support several families~ The three old people were over ninety when they died~

By & by the girls concluded to go to Lee & there they had a house full of company~ Mrs John Parrot, Mrs EGPM at Greenland & my mother were married at Lee~[85]

Mrs. EGPM was her Aunt Susanna who married Enoch Greenleaf Parrott. Their first home was in Portsmouth at the site of today's Kearsarge Hotel. They moved to Greenland at a later date. She was widowed in 1828. Enoch's brother, Captain John Fabyan Parrott, married her sister Hannah. Both men were involved in a number of profitable business enterprises with Sarah's father. In his later years John Parrott was elected to the United States Senate. Her Aunt Sarah was married to Captain Samuel Briard, and her Aunt Elizabeth to Captain John Flagg. These men were all prominent merchants or ship captains in Portsmouth, and all of them were engaged in some aspect of the privateering trade either during the Revolution and/or the War of 1812, as was Sarah's own father.[86]

My grandfather was one of the most genial & delightful of men~ He dearly loved young company & music & all beautiful things in nature & art~ The china and pictures he brought from abroad are in my keeping & I hope my grandchildren will always value them~ He married twice after my grandmother's death, which did not please his children very well~[87]

It is not surprising his family disapproved of his subsequent marriages. Sarah Sherburne died in 1804, when Robert Parker was sixty-nine years old. He wed Hannah Chelsey of Durham within the year.[88] When she died he married Ann Pendergast also of Durham. This last marriage took place in March of 1814.[89]

Ada Parker, author of the letters, was the daughter of the third wife~ One son of the third marriage survives ~ Robert Parker of Woburn, Mass~[90]

The ages of the brides are not known, but Parker was seventy-nine the year he married for the third time. The following January his son Robert Whipple was born, followed within a year and a half by another son, John Flagg. His last child Adaline Rice was born when he was eighty-four. He died shortly after her birth. Ada became a well-known schoolteacher.[91]

I cannot forget my grandfather's kindness to me~ He used to call me "Sally dear~".... Just before his death on his last visit to P__he stayed at my father's & after tea I asked him to sing me a song~ He at once sang "Oh when shall I see Jesus" as well as a younger man could have done and with great feeling although he was then eighty-four years old~ He died shortly after of lung fever ~[92]

At the time lung fever was a common term for what was later called consumption, and now is known as tuberculosis. When her Grandfather Parker died, Sarah and her father traveled to Lee ahead of the rest of the family to make funeral arrangements. Her Grandfather Parker died in 1819, and although Sarah recalls her age at the time as ten, she would have actually been closer to fourteen.

> *Two or three days before his funeral my father took me to Lee to be of use I suppose as the rest of the family did not go up until the day of the burial~ If I was not useful, I fully took in what was going on & as funerals in the country were then conducted very differently from what they are now, I was in a continual state of surprise & amusement at what I saw~ I dearly loved my grandfather but I was only ten years old & soon forgot my grief~*

> *Extra help was brought in & the bushels of donuts that were fried, the ovens full of pies that were baked, the geese, turkeys, chickens & beef that were roasted amazed me~ Piles of cooked food stood round the great kitchen & on the day of the funeral a long table was set in the largest front parlor & liquors of all sorts abounded~*

> *People came from Barrington, Madbury, Nottingham, Durham & Dover, for my grandfather was well known & much beloved & everybody ate & drank~ On the return of the procession the mourners went upstairs & seated themselves in a front chamber~*

> *Presently a solemn looking man with a cue appeared bearing a great waiter full of wineglasses, containing each madeira wine, a lump of loaf sugar & a tea spoon~ The effect of the whole was so military, so like bayonets & the man's face so funeral that I had the greatest difficulty in restraining my laughter~[93]*

> *Since then I have been two or three times at the place in a picnicking way but the farm was sold to Mr Wm Hale of Dover Soon after my grandfather's death & we could not stay there anymore~ The widow of Gov Smith lived there many years & her son the Judge is the present proprietor~[94]*

The Rice family also came from Kittery. Sarah's ancestor Thomas Withers was about twenty-five years old when he arrived in America in 1631 with the Mason Company.[95] He settled on the side of the Piscataqua River nearest to Maine in what is now known as Kittery, and is numbered amongst the town's original proprietors.

> *Sir Ferdinando Gorges made a grant of 640 acres of land in Kittery to my ancestor Thomas Withers in 1643~ When Thomas Withers settled near the water with his wife & three daughters, there was not a house in what is now Portsmouth~ They called the opposite shore Strawberry Bank~[96]*

In 1643 Withers received a grant from Sir Fernando Gorges for four hundred acres of land bordering the river. At this time he also received two islands to the south and southwest of this land, which gave him around two hundred and eighty more acres. He was then told to choose another four prime acres anywhere on Spruce Creek. The four acres he chose were in the area known as Eagle Point.[97]

In March of 1644 Richard Vine, an agent for Sir Gorges, sold Withers six hundred more acres at the head of Spruce Creek for ten pounds. The land ran from Eagle Point on one side of the creek and Martin's Cove on the other and was joined at Pine Point. Then the town gave him another hundred at Eagle Point and one hundred more at Martin's Cove. All in all Withers owned approximately fifteen hundred acres.[98]

In Kittery Withers was elected to several town positions. In 1644 he was named Commissioner and in 1656 he was Deputy to the General Court. At another time he held the office of Councilor.[99] Withers owned a farm and a sawmill at Eagle Point, and a farm on the bank of the Piscataqua overlooking Withers' Island.[100] Other records state that he also had a home near Braveboat Harbor.[101] Like many of the area's most prosperous men Withers may have engaged in the export of lumber to Europe, since he owned a sawmill. It is known that he was a skilled builder, and one source indicates he was a shipbuilder. In addition, a number of land transactions in the town records show that he frequently sold smaller parcels of his land to new settlers in the area.[102]

It is not known when Withers married his wife Jane, and there is no record of her family name in Kittery town archives. It is known that they were definitely married by 1651, about twenty years after he first arrived in America. For a young man to remain single during those years was uncommon. A wife was a valuable commodity during this time, needed for more than companionship or to do domestic chores. Women helped clear the lands, build the cabins, run the farms, and tended the sick.

The birth and marriage dates of his children suggest that Jane was twenty to thirty years younger than Thomas. They had three daughters. Their oldest, Sarah, married John Shapleigh in 1671, at which time Thomas deeded her half of the house and land where he lived. This may have been the home at Eagle Point. Their second daughter, Elizabeth, was first married to Benjamin Berry in 1688, and then to Dodvah Curtis in 1702. She was given a portion of the land near Spruce Creek.[103] Mary, their youngest daughter, married Thomas Rice. He was a seaman who came to Kittery about 1674. They wed in 1675 when she was sixteen years old. The same year Withers gave half of the house to Sarah he deeded Withers' Island to both Mary and Elizabeth. When Mary wed Thomas Rice he deeded the land behind it to them.

When Withers died in 1685 at age eighty, the long strip of land that went to Eagle Point at Spruce Creek was given to Thomas Rice and John Shapleigh. The northeast portion went to Rice and remained in the family for two hundred years. The other half went to Shapleigh. It was divided and sold throughout the years.[104]

Six years after Withers died his widow wed her neighbor William Godsoe, who was forty-six years old at the time of their marriage. Her age at the time is unknown. Mary and Thomas Rice eventually had at least five children, and their son Thomas inherited their portion of the island. This second Thomas is credited with starting the ferry between Withers' Island and Portsmouth sometime during the early 1700s.[105]

The ferry was built for the first Rice for a son~ This Rice, Thomas built a house on the rise between the graveyard & the bridge~ Richard Rice his

son, the third generation from Thomas Withers, built the one story house at
the corner~ He was my great grandfather~ Cousin Ann used to tell me that
the "Ferry House" was the oldest in Kittery~[106]

Kittery town records indicate that the General Court gave the first ferry license to John Woodman in 1692. He operated the first ferry from Braveboat Harbor. Then in 1699 he came into possession of land in Kittery that had belonged to Withers. This land abutted the Rice land on the southeast side directly above Withers' Island. Sometime after that that a partnership was formed between the second Thomas Rice and Woodman to start a second ferry between Withers' Island and Portsmouth. This ferry was located on the Rice family section of Withers' Island.

The Rice family's future share in the ferry was assured when John Woodman's daughter, Mary, and Thomas's son, Richard, were wed. Together the younger Rices ran the ferry from both locations and further developed the land behind the island known as the Rice farm.[107]

After Mary died Richard married Mary Pope. They had two sons, John and Samuel. John died at sea in 1750, and Samuel was a sailor who sailed out of Boston. He married Elizabeth Manson from Boston. They settled on the family property in Kittery and raised a family of twelve children. Their youngest son, William Rice, was Sarah's father. Sarah wrote down some of the history surrounding her paternal grandparents' courtship and subsequent marriage.

> *My Grandmother Rice's maiden name was Elisabeth Manson~ She was*
> *born in Boston, somewhere near where the Revere House stands now, &*
> *next door to Gov. Bowdoin~ Her father was a Scotsman & commanded a*
> *regular trader between Boston & Glasgow~*[108]

The Revere House was in Bowdoin Square located in the Back Bay area of Boston. This was a prestigious section of town, indicating that Elizabeth Mason's family was well to do.

> *My grandfather would go to sea & leave his poor widowed father (who had*
> *no other child) all alone with an old housekeeper whose name was Marget*
> *Ball~ He did not care to sail from the Bank as P_ was called then, but*
> *thought there was a better chance in Mass~*
>
> *He sailed with Capt Manson several voyages & then proposed for his*
> *daughter Elizabeth, who was very handsome~ The mother objected, as she*
> *would never consent to her daughter marrying a sailor~ So the young man*
> *concluded to give up the sea, took the bride on a pillion & in a weeks time*
> *arrived at Kittery~*[109]

Before leaving together for Kittery on a pillion, (a second seat behind the saddle of a horse) Samuel and Elizabeth were married at King's Chapel in Boston. The exact date of their wedding is not known but it was in the early 1750s. Back in Kittery Samuel became half owner of the ferry, which he and his wife ran along with the Rice farm.

During the Revolution Samuel went back to sea as a privateer. It may have been from the profits of this enterprise that the Rices built Rice Tavern in 1777. The tavern was quite successful, drawing a steady clientele from the ferry passengers.[110] All in all they thrived, and the Rices and their descendents became prosperous and respected members of the early Kittery community.

> *The Rice family were among the builders & first members of the Kittery Point Church & my grandparents attended on the ministrations of Mr. Newmarch first & then on those of Dr Stephens~*[111]

There was an early meetinghouse at Kittery Point and it is possible that Thomas Withers built it. In 1674 he presented the town with a bill in the amount of twenty pounds for the land and materials to build the second meetinghouse. The third meetinghouse at Kittery Point was built in 1727. It burned down in 1730, and was replaced immediately with another structure.[112]

The Reverend Newmarch was Kittery's first ordained minister. He graduated from Harvard in 1690 and came to the town of Kittery in 1695. Newmarch was not officially ordained as a minister until 1714 when the Congregational Church was organized at Kittery Point. Original members of the church covenant included Mary Rice, Mary Rice Jr., and Elizabeth Rice. Portions of the Shapleigh land abutting the Rice land were sold to Newmarch, and this is where he was buried.[113]

> *Parson Newmarch preached at Kittery Point & lived near the Rice's on the river~ He was buried on the Rice estate & a monument of some kind marks the grave near the navy yard road, erected by Mrs Ann Rice & Dr Chase~ The house in which he lived was near the Ferry house, on the other side of the road~ He was succeeded by Dr. Stephens the father in law of Dr. Buckminister, who married Sally Stephens in the house in which Parson Newmarch lived~This was pulled down when I was a child~ In those days the Rices went to Kittery Point Church by water~*[114]

> *They were obliged to go by water as there was no bridge in those days~*[115]

There was no bridge connecting New Hampshire to Maine when Sarah was quite young, and a visit to her relatives meant a ride on the ferry then run by her Uncle Alexander Rice.

> *Ferry boats of all kinds plied regularly between Kittery & the opposite shore~ the landing on the Portsmouth shore being just north of the stone stoor~ My relations were good to me & I could go anywhere among them & be welcome~*

> *I used to love to go to Kittery & when my mother was living, my father used to take her & such of the children as could go & cross the river in the Ferry boat & drink tea with his mother~*

> *She was then very aged but was very erect, had red cheeks & the perfect possession of her mental faculties~ She loved these visits and loved to take my father's head in her lap & comb his hair~ He was the youngest of her twelve children~*[116]

The Ferry right was relinquished (by my Uncle Rice) to the proprietors of the Portsmouth bridge company when I was about seventeen years old~ I liked the boat better than the bridge~ I have somewhere else described that ideal Kittery home & the delightful people who were so kind to me there~ They are all gone now~[117]

Ferrymen used poles or paddles to guide the ferries across the rivers. In some cases ferries were pulled across the rivers by ropes. Sarah's confidence in the ferryman was probably well deserved as it would have taken a great deal of skill to maneuver a ferryboat across the swift moving currents of the Piscataqua several times a day.

All my ancestors on the Rice side lived some distance from the water~ The house near the water was built originally to accommodate the Ferry Privilege & some son or nephew usually occupied it...My uncle Alexander Rice the father of cousin Ann & the Major lived in the house near the water~[118]

The ferry was discontinued in 1819 after a group of prominent Portsmouth businessmen, including Sarah's father William Rice, formed a corporation to build a toll drawbridge to connect the state of Maine to New Hampshire.[119] Alexander Rice received $4,000 taken from the bridge tolls to compensate him for the loss of his ferry business. After that he established the Eastern Stagecoach route between Portland and Portsmouth.[120]

My Aunt Rice was a wonderful woman for ambition, energy & thrift~ Her husband represented the town of Kittery twenty consecutive years in Boston when Maine was a district & his wife not only sent her children to the best schools but took charge of the Ferry, the Farm, which was a large one & the stage interest between Kittery & Portland~ My Uncle with Mr. Paine of Portland (the father of Capt John Paine of the Navy) established the first stage route between Portsmouth & Portland~[121]

Alexander's wife was Sally Adams of Kittery. Her ancestor Christopher Adams first settled in the area around 1650. A native of England, he had originally settled in Braintree, Massachusetts, and was said to be a relation of President John Adams.[122]

I used to think very much of my visits there ~ The cousins were mostly many years older than I & the ladies had been at boarding school in Boston & Portland and had a library & a mineralogical cabinet & a piano (an English one as there were no others then) & although I had a home where the creature comforts abounded (for my father was famous for his larder) yet I was very much impressed by the educated tone of conversation & manners ~ and really felt as if we had nothing in comparison~[123]

In addition to Alexander's service as a district representative he was a member of the Massachusetts General Court from 1807 to 1808. He served as a member of the Maine

State Senate in 1820, when Maine was first admitted to the Union. He was Kittery's town selectman during the years 1811 through 1815, and in 1823. [124]

The sea played an important role in the lives of most members of the Rice family. William's sister Elizabeth married William Badger, a well known shipbuilder from Kittery. When she died another sister married the bereaved husband. William's oldest brother, Samuel Jr., was the commander of the *Fancy, the Humbird,* and the *Retaliation*, privateering ships that operated out of Maine during the American Revolution.[125] Samuel moved to Portsmouth sometime after the Revolution. His son Robert became one of Portsmouth's wealthiest merchants. [126]

All of these family connections helped William to become established in Portsmouth, and to prosper from the sea. He joined his brother Samuel in Portsmouth during the 1790s, and was at first a shipmaster with a license to engage in privateering.[127] He began to invest in ships, and eventually became a merchant, with a counting house on Scheafe's Wharf in Portsmouth.[128]

William Rice, circa 1840, Sarah Goodwin's father.

Childhood Streets

*The streets of Portsmouth in my childhood were for the most part flagged
with large granite stones~ Market Street was paved with brick & by way of
special distinction it was called "Paved Street~"*[129]

At the turn of the century Portsmouth was a busy maritime seaport. For the first few decades after the Revolution Portsmouth remained for the most part a port town dependent on activities and commerce related to the sea. Across the ocean the French general Napoleon Bonaparte, intent on capturing all of Europe since 1792, remained at war with the British. This distant conflict had a positive effect on the American economy, as each of the warring countries needed American ships and products.

The years between 1793 and 1805 were very prosperous for Americans involved in shipbuilding and foreign trade, and for port cities like Portsmouth. During 1800 alone twenty-eight ships, forty-seven brigs, ten schooners, and one bark engaged in foreign trade sailed from the Port of Portsmouth. Also, in that year seventeen vessels destined for foreign trade were built in the local shipyards.[130]

During these prosperous years the Portsmouth Pier Corporation was formed by a group of local investors. In 1795 they built the Portsmouth Pier wharf, which extended more than three hundred feet out into the harbor from the corner of present day State and Marcy Streets. The first level of the building divided into fourteen stores, which sold molasses, rum, Madeira, sugar, coffee, crockery, and dry goods brought in by the merchant vessels. A sail loft filled the next level, and on the third was a counting house. North of this was a three-story building split into two more stores, and at the western end stood the New Hampshire Hotel, a large two-story brick building.[131]

Market Square, once known as the Parade, was where the militia had drilled in earlier years. In 1800 the town's fathers built a combination brick market place and town hall in Market Square, right near the old State House. It was a large two level brick structure, supported by sixteen brick arches that divided the area below into ten stalls. The roof was covered with tar and gravel to protect it from fire.[132]

The area above the market was used as a town hall. It was a building of many uses. This is where the townspeople held their public dinners, town meetings, political events, Fourth of July celebrations, musical recitals, collations, and band or choir practices and voted. When the hall first opened in November of 1800, it was called Town Hall, but the name was soon changed to Jefferson Hall in honor of the country's new president. [133]

Thomas Jefferson was elected president in 1800, and by the time Sarah was born, his purchase of the French owned province west of the Mississippi known as the Louisiana Purchase had doubled the size of the country. By 1812 seventy-five thousand Americans had immigrated to the West to settle the southern part of this new territory.[134]

The city of Portsmouth, although enjoying a period of prosperity from sea related enterprises, was also undergoing a period of growth and expansion in other areas during these years. Fortunately, Portsmouth's city fathers at that time had the foresight to prepare for inland growth. A syndicate called 'The Proprietor's of the Piscataqua Bridge,' built the Piscataqua Bridge in 1794. It was a half-mile long, wooden bridge, painted white, which spanned the Great Bay connecting Portsmouth to Durham and Dover.

The center arch of the bridge was two hundred and forty-four feet high to allow for passage of tall sailing ships. At the time it was the highest arch in America, and many knowledgeable men opined that the bridge was the finest in the country. It cost a total of $62,000 to build, and it was paid for by tolls, which ranged from 2 1/2 cents for walkers to 40 cents for four wheeled wagons or carriages.[135]

Two years later a group of Portsmouth businessmen formed the New Hampshire Turnpike Authority. They constructed a toll road, four rods in width, which connected Portsmouth to Concord.[136] Within the decade transportation inland was further enhanced, when local entrepreneurs formed the Portsmouth Livery Stable to provide transportation within and without the city for reasonable rates.[137]

> *Two accommodation stages & one mail stage ran from here to Boston everyday & they seldom were full~ People went to the stage house the previous evening to Book their names~ A visit to Boston was a rare & great occasion to most people~*
>
> *Oh what a great flourish & blowing of horns when the stage with four horses swept around to the stage house door~ The driver was a great character in those days, for had he not just come from Boston or Concord?*[138]

Sometime during these early years in Portsmouth William met and married Abigail Parker. By 1806 he was the owner of the ship *Agenoria*, and eventually owned a considerable number of ships.[139] One of these was named the *Robert Parker* in honor of his father in law.[140] The young couple set up housekeeping in a home near the corner of Market and Deer Streets. It sat directly across from what is known today as the Moffat-Ladd House.

> *My mother's two first babies were born in the house opposite to the large house now occupied by Mr. Alexander Ladd~ The house was two stories front & four stories on the back~ It was burnt in 1802~ Madame Whipple lived in the large house~ She was an excellent friend to my mother~*
>
> *My father was at sea when the house was burned & my mother took her children & went to Lee~ She remained with her father until her husband returned & bought the house on Deer St where I was born~*[141]

Madame Whipple was the widow of General William Whipple, who died in 1785. Her father Captain John Moffat built the house at 154 Market Street. When Sarah was young Alexander Ladd, a prosperous merchant, lived in the house.

The fire Sarah wrote of started at four o'clock on Sunday morning, December 26th, 1802. Its cause was not known, but it quickly spread, and wiped out a large portion of downtown Portsmouth. It destroyed the Rice home along with many other residential and commercial buildings, including all of those on the eastern side of Market Street up to the corner of Bow Street, and those on the western side south of the Whipple home.[142]

Many of the merchants in the city lost all of their merchandise as well as the buildings. The tar and shingle roof of the new Brick Market caught on fire, and the roof as well as the interior of the building was destroyed. It stood in the center of town in ruins for two years before it was rebuilt in 1804 with a fireproof tin roof.[143]

This was the first of three great fires, which would drastically alter the face of Portsmouth's market district during the early part of the nineteenth century. The second occurred on December 24th 1806, in a large wooden building on Bow Street. On one side of this structure the neighboring buildings were wooden, and they all burned. On the opposite side a row of buildings were constructed of brick, and only one of these was destroyed.

Many of the wooden frame buildings, which had been destroyed in 1802 and rebuilt just four years before were again leveled. A spark from the fire on Bow Street flew over the embankment on the corner of Chapel to ignite the steeple of Queen's Chapel. Despite a valiant effort to save it, this small wooden structure, that had once hosted the country's first president, was totally destroyed by the fire. However, parishioners managed to retrieve some valuable artifices from the burning church, and within a year the Episcopalian congregation had rebuilt the church.[144] The structure that currently stands on the same site was dedicated on St. John's Day, June 24th 1807 as St. John's Church.[145]

The worst of these fires started on December 22, 1813 at about seven in the evening. Sarah was eight years old at the time. Surprisingly she makes no mention of this dreadful fire, which began in a barn on the corner of Church and Court Streets. This fierce fire spread so fast there was little time for residents to save their valuable possessions. One resident from that era recalled seeing a high arch of flames form over the center of Buck Street, and watching it grow until it traversed its entire length while the fire roared down this narrow path destroying wooden structures lining each side. When it reached the harbor's edge it was fueled by the large casks of rum stored in the nearby warehouses, and loud explosions added to the terror of the scene. It was finally contained at the water's edge, but not before it destroyed the Pier Wharf buildings and the New Hampshire Hotel.[146]

It came perilously close to the North End neighborhood where Sarah lived before it was finally contained at five o'clock the following morning. This fire spread over fifteen acres, and destroyed one hundred and eight homes, one hundred barns and sixty-four businesses.[147] The total property loss was valued at $300,000.[148]

There were at one time six fire societies in Portsmouth. Insurance companies originally formed fire societies to aid policyholders. The first one in the country was formed in Boston in 1717. The first in Portsmouth was the United Fire Society formed in 1719, and the second was the Federal Fire Society formed in 1789. Members of Sarah's family were amongst the earliest members of this society. Ichabod Goodwin joined in 1832, and was president in the 1870s.[149] Sarah noted in 1889:

> *The centennial of the Federal Fire societies dinner comes off today~ Just one hundred years since the Constitution of the United States was accepted by some of the states~ The society was initiated by Federalists~ The object was two fold brotherly & patriotic~ Two of my uncles, Briard & Flagg were among the originators~* [150]

Membership in these societies was limited to twenty-five members and new members joined by invitation only. The primary reason for keeping membership to a minimum was that in each of the societies the members were told where their fellow members kept their valuables so they could help to rescue them in the event of fire. Distinctive leather buckets that bore the insignia of the society as well as the name of the family indicated membership. Inside were linen bags used to carry the valuables to safety and a wrench to dismantle beds.

During the time of these three great fires the town was divided into fire wards. Most fires were fought by volunteer fire departments, aided by these societies. Also helping during these fires were the crews on the ships docked in the harbor, as well as crews from the Portsmouth Naval Yard. At the time of these fires Portsmouth had three hand pumped fire engines.[151] An aqueduct company, formed in 1797 to deliver fresh spring water to a limited area of the city through hollowed logs of wood, supplied some of the water needed to fight these fires, but the main source came from the river or the millponds.[152]

After the fire of 1813 a town ordinance, known as the Brick Act of 1814, was put into place. It called for any new building of more than one story constructed in the commercial part of Portsmouth to be made of brick. This was to prevent future fires from spreading unchecked throughout the downtown. However, it was not well received in the community, as the cost of brick buildings was higher than wooden.[153]

The last two fires occurred during a period of economic downturn in Portsmouth, due to the Embargo of 1807 and the War of 1812. These national events combined with the restrictive building code made the cost of rebuilding prohibitive. So a good portion of the city's commercial area was not rebuilt until after 1820, when the Brick Act was rescinded in response to continued protest.[154]

Despite the setbacks encountered from fires and distant wars many other successful new business ventures began in Portsmouth around this time. Banks, insurance companies, and other innovative enterprises all added to the city's growing prosperity during these years when Sarah's young parents were establishing themselves within their home and community. William Rice, along with other members of his family, was at the forefront of many of these new developments, and together he and his family prospered and grew along with the city of Portsmouth as it embarked upon the nineteenth century.

CHILDHOOD FAMILY

It was around 1875, at the age of seventy, Sarah began her memoirs. Underlining the title *Pleasant Memories* at the top of the first page, she began by addressing her intended audience.

> *My dear Grandchildren,*
>> *I was born in a two story house on the north side of Deer Street on the 15th of May, 1805~*
> *The house has three dormer windows (for it still stands) & a large hall & a delightfully easy flight of stairs, with what was called a broad stair or landing with a large deep window, circular at the top, & a seat for a cusheon~ The window once had a very large, full green worsted damask curtain & the effect from below, I used to think quite grand~*[155]

The house was a large, high styled, hip roofed, Georgian home built in 1756 by Samuel Hart. It was originally located at 95 Deer Street in Portsmouth's North End. William Rice purchased it in 1804.[156]

Sarah was born there a year later, the middle child in a family of seven children. Her three older siblings were named Elizabeth, William, and Robert, the younger three were Samuel, Susan, and Adeline. By her own admission, Sarah was an inconsequential child who often got into trouble during her youth.

> *I was a very funny & mischievous child & required a great deal of watching~ Up to my tenth year I had a trick of running away & I particularly delighted in the boats and wharves & in wading into the water after sea urchins & starfishes & horseshoes~ Everything in the water interested me even the pebbles & mussels~*
>
> *At that time the wharves & shores at the north end were clean & there were no foreigners, only our own people, whose ancestors had been here for generations & there was nothing to annoy~*
>
> *The gondolas & other boats, were always at the wharves in numbers & it was my delight, to sit alone in them & look into the water~ I was missed nearly every day & then my brother William four & a half years older than I, was sent to look me up & I was taken home in disgrace~ But I was very mercurial & my tears were soon forgotten…*[157]

The town harbor would have been a fascinating place for a young child to explore. Watercraft of all types and sizes abounded on the Piscataqua in those days. Ships from exotic countries unloaded their bounty alongside the smaller craft of local fishermen who brought in their daily catch to sell to the nearby fish market. However, it would be a mistake to think that the young Sarah sat serenely in elegantly carved Italian gondolas docked alongside the wharves in Portsmouth Harbor, such as those that one might see floating in the canals of Venice.

"Gondola" was a common local spelling in Portsmouth for the gundalows that were so numerous there during the nineteenth century. Gundalows were rough square ended barges built narrow enough to go past bridges and low enough to carry heavy loads in shallow water. Recent historians use the alternate spelling of gundalow, also in common use during Sarah's lifetime.[158]

Sarah continued to dispel the notion that children were always obedient and well behaved almost two centuries ago, or that parents adhered to the adage "spare the rod and spoil the child." In fact Americans at that time, influenced by the earlier writings of John Locke and Jean-Jacques Rousseau, did develop somewhat of a laissez faire attitude towards their children.

> *My Father never scolded me, on the contrary I have seen him many a time have difficulty in looking displeased~ He thought I was very funny~ He did undertake punishment twice~ Once he had sent me to bed in the middle of a midsummer afternoon with the sun pouring in at a western window at the foot of my bed~ I thought the sun would never set & it was a most unhappy experience~*[159]

There was less emphasis on restriction or protection of children in America at the start of the nineteenth century than there had been prior to the Revolution, or would be in Victorian times when Sarah became a mother herself. [160]

> *At another time I was put into a room & told to stay there~ There was a great meal chest in the room, with three compartments~ one for corn meal, one for rye & the third for bran~ I did not mean to do anything wrong but in looking about for something to do (being an active child) I thought how nice it would be to mix the three, so I got up in a chair, put the cover against the wall & found full employment for an hour or more, for there were bushels to fix~*
>
> *Then I shut down the cover & said nothing about the matter to anybody~ Next day when the great oven was being heated & the great loaves of rye and indian were about to be made the family was aghast at the disclosure of Sarah's doings & the right proportions were with difficulty made out~*[161]

The room to which Sarah was sent was a grain room where the various types of grains needed for the weekly baking in the brick hearth oven of all of the breads and pies needed to feed a household of eight were kept. The grain room was probably located right off to the side or back of the kitchen, and would have been a dark and dreary place in which to confine a child. The "Rye and Indian" bread was made of three-quarters rye and one quarter cornmeal.

When I was a child the great brick oven was heated every Saturday and a great wooden trough of rye & indian bread was made which filled iron pans, besides skillet & spider~ Also several great loaves of yeast bread & at the mouth of the oven a few large flat cakes, made of milk, eggs & flour were dropped on the cleanly swept bricks & did we not enjoy them at tea time?

The great loaves made toast at tea & breakfast nearly all the week but we always had Johnny cake at breakfast, split & buttered most generously~ These cakes were corn meal scalded with a little salt, spread on tin sheets & upheld before the open fire by a flatiron or brick~ When brown on one side, they were slid off & turned most dexterously by the cook ~[162]

In those days, long before furnaces were invented, the kitchen and the family parlor, both warmed by open-hearth fires, were where families congregated to eat and visit. This was particularly true during the long, cold, New England winters.

But Oh it was cold all about the house in winter in my childhood & youth~ No hall stoves, no furnaces! Water froze where it dropped except in kitchen or parlor~

Every family ate in the setting room in cold weather and many a time have I left the breakfast table to heat the handles of my knife & fork at the open parlor fire~ (But we were healthy~ I never had a cold until after I was thirty)[163]

When Sarah turned seven, the country was once again embroiled in a war with the British. However, in the Rice family other more personal and tragic events overrode the war news. What Sarah remembered most vividly about that year was the loss of her mother. Abigail Parker Rice was thirty-nine years old when she died that August. Sarah recalled this sad time in the Rice family.

In the summer of 1812 we as a family had not only the war to distress us but our dear mother & and my playmate brother were taken from us by death~[164]

I lost my mother when I was seven years old & had a rather rough time of it after she was gone~ My father was very good to me. My eldest sister used to say that I was his favorite~ That was not so but he seemed to pity me, because I came between two boys & the other girls were either too old or too young to play with me~[165]

Robert, Sarah's nine-year old brother also died that year. But the local journals note only that Abigail Rice died after a short illness. There are no extant death certificates for either Abigail or her son. While it is not certain that they died at the same time Sarah implies it. The cause of their deaths is not known. There were a number of trained physicians in

Portsmouth by this time, and at least one botanist.[166]

Most Portsmouth residents were inoculated against small pox during the late eighteenth and early nineteenth centuries at one of the inoculation hospitals set up on Shapleigh's, Henzell's, and Pest Islands. There is no record of an outbreak of either yellow or typhoid fever in Portsmouth that year, but cases of dysentery were common during the summer months and often fatal.[167]

Both the *New Hampshire Gazette* and the *Portsmouth Oracle* published tributes to Abigail Rice expounding on her generous nature, as well as her exemplary character. The *Portsmouth Oracle* noted the great loss to entire community.

> It is seldom we are called to notice the death of a person so deeply and universally lamented. Mrs. Rice, with the greatest propriety might be said to be an ornament to her sex. She was a good wife, a good mother, and a neighbor. She was benevolent and kind to all. The poor have always called her blessed for her hand was ever open to relieve the needy. She opened her mouth with wisdom, and her tongue was the law of kindness... There are none who had the pleasure of being acquainted with her but loved her.[168]

At this time in America women were not allowed to own property, go into business, or sign legal documents, and it was believed their greatest fulfillment was found within the confines of the traditional roles of wife, mother, and caretaker. However, more and more women like Abigail, began to reach out into their communities acting as unofficial guardians of the town's welfare who oversaw the care of their less fortunate neighbors.

Sarah memorialized her older brother in a short vignette.

A Reminiscence~

A deep snow lay on the little garden which was heavily encrusted with ice~ The ice looked brilliant in the moonlight & the two brothers, nine & eleven years of age with their sleds & the little seven year old sister made quite a pleasant group~

In a moment of impatience the elder called his brother a fool~ "Don't say that, was the reply~ Don't you know that whosoever calls his brother a fool will be in danger of hell fire?" He died the next year beloved & regretted by all who knew him~ He was my playmate but that admonition is my chief memory of him~ He was very white with golden hair & large blue eyes~[169]

William Rice was able to raise his six remaining children with the help of his niece Elizabeth Rice, the oldest daughter of his older brother Samuel who had died in 1803.[170]"Cousin Betsy," as she came to be known, went to live with her uncle's family soon after Abigail died. She was thirty-nine the year she moved to the Rice home on Deer Street. It can be assumed there were servants in the household, and that Cousin Betsy acted in the capacity of mistress of the home, overseeing the day-to-day household operations as well as the care of the children.

One time Sarah's inconsequential behavior was unintentionally directed at Cousin

Betsy and the incident brought great disgrace upon the young Sarah, but years later it made a delightful childhood tale.

> *Another time Cousin Betsy, my Father's housekeeper, bought a large parasol, for which she paid a great price~ It was of green silk lined with white silk & trimmed round with a heavy green fringe~ She put it in the best parlor (the other being called a sitting room) for safe keeping~*
>
> *It was Sunday afternoon, midsummer, too warm to go to church, or meeting, as it was called & I thought how nice it would be to take that Parasol & call on some child in the neighborhood & go up to Cutt's orchard for the walk & to get a few summer apples~*
>
> *Just as I had filled my parasol with the delicious yellow fruit, a thunder storm broke upon us & as I was without bonnet or other outside protection I dumped the apples & with parasol over my head made the best of my way home~*
>
> *Before I arrived I saw the green from the silk dropping over me & at a glance saw ruin~ I know not how I got through the back gate & kitchen into the parlor but the parasol was put in its place~ A few days after when Cousin Betsy was in her "best bib & tucks" all ready for visits she went in for her sun shade & Oh! Oh! that was all she could say at first & I did not stop to hear any more at that time~*
>
> *Of course every body knew who did it & the disgrace of it laid heavily on me for a long time~ I don't think I ever meant to do wrong but I was wholly inconsequent~*[171]

William Rice never remarried. Sarah appreciated his sacrifice, and the devotion he gave to his family. She was very fond of her father and often reminisced about him in both her memoirs and common daybooks.

> *I have been thinking of my dear good father~ How well he understood the laws of health & how implicitly he obeyed them~ how careful for his children & how unostentatious yet how generous & hospitable~*
>
> *He literally lived for his children from 1812 until 1851 when he died~ How careful for his children~ He would not bring a stepmother to his children~*
>
> *He never used tobacco in any form & never exceeded his two glasses of what he called "toddy"...a small quantity of Old Jamaican with French Brandy filled with water & several lumps of loaf sugar~*
>
> *In regard to health he was careful to observe whatever disagreed with him & avoid it~ During the last thirty years of his life he never drank water*

unless it had been boiled & he always took a full bath in the morning summer & winter~[172]

When Sarah was young daily bathing was just starting to become fashionable for members of the upper class. It is known tubs for bathing were available in Portsmouth by 1806, as a local tinsmith advertised them for sale or rent.[173] Also about the time Sarah was born a bathhouse opened on Bridge Street.[174]

However, William Rice, like most people, probably relied upon sponge baths, washing only his face, neck, and hands on a daily basis until the 1820s. What bathing was done generally took place in the privacy of one's room or in the case of children in the kitchen area where water could easily be warmed on the stove.

Cousin Betsy remained with William for the next forty years, long after the children had all left home. Looking back Sarah fondly recalled her older cousin, and marveled at the wonderful care she had given to her father.

> *In this connection I would speak of Aunt Betsy's unequalled ability as a nurse~ She had every requisite for healing and comforting~ No one could lift a sick patient as she could~ It was a luxury to feel her touch~ She had a faculty of suiting and amusing my father which was marvelous~ His clothes and his bedroom were all under her care, & woe be to any child who interfered or disturbed her arrangements~ Her way of doing things was all her own & though it looked amazingly like prose in those days, it now has all turned into poetry~*

> *In winter, as soon as the tea table was cleared she would go to the closet & take down the "Farmer's Almanac" which she kept hanging on a nail & then she would take a seat opposite my Father by the fire & read to him about the rising or setting of the moon & all about the tides, particularly as to the time of high tide & then from that to all the recorded events that ever took place on that particular day of the present month & so on ~*

> *Then if not interrupted she would go on & call up memories of some of the strange, picturesque people of Kittery whom she knew or of whom she had traditions & as she had a good memory & a knack at mimicry & telling a story, she furnished my father with never ending amusement & he was never tired of hearing her stories over again~*

> *My Father bought for me when I was about ten years old "The Arabian Night's," entertainment & she would sit up into the small hours reading the stories & then she would tell him all about it at breakfast which they had to themselves quite early as, we children were all lazy & great sleepers~*

> *She used to talk a great deal about "Weem's Life of Washington" & Eliza Wharton & Dr. Buckminster & "Coelebs in Search of a wife" & " Dorcas Sheldon" by a lady of Exeter & "Julia of the illuminated Baron" written by a lady of York & "Think's I to Myself" by I don't know whom~*

> *In her last twenty years she read the Bible more than any thing else & never*
> *swerved from her life long belief in the infinite goodness of God~*[175]

Another book the family read together was *Explorations on the Columbia River*, the story of the "Corps of Discovery," expedition. an exploration party of fifty men led by Meriwether Lewis and William Clark between the years of 1804 to 1806. These men were authorized by President Jefferson to find the best passage West, and to gather economic, botanical, and geographical as well as other scientific knowledge relating to the land west of the Mississippi. Aided by Native Americans, they followed the Missouri and Columbia Rivers all the way to the Pacific.[176] The tales of their adventures in this unexplored wilderness fired the imagination of all Americans at the start of the nineteenth century, even that of a young girl from a small coastal city in New England.

> *Lewis and Clark Explorations on Columbia River, a large work was the*
> *delight of readers in my childhood~ My brother William read it aloud in the*
> *evening to my father & the family~*[177]

AUNT FLAGG

S arah had an extended family on both sides of the Piscataqua and they always made her feel welcome. One of her favorite places to visit was the home of her mother's older sister, Elizabeth, who lived nearby on the corner of Deer and Vaughan Streets. She was married to Captain John Flagg, a privateer who was once listed as an "enemy of the people" during the Revolution, after he loaded his ship with fresh fish to trade in the West Indies in defiance of an injunction by the Provincial Congress against carrying valuable cargo on the open seas.[178] Flagg was also the captain of the *Mentor,* the vessel that carried the scourge of yellow fever to Portsmouth in July of 1798. In those years knowledge of this disease was limited, and it was not known how it was spread. However, within weeks of his return from the isle of Martinique with two sick crewmen aboard, there were fifty-five deaths in town attributed to yellow fever, and for a few frightening weeks the entire North End was forcibly quarantined by armed guards.[179]

I am going to write about a very good woman~ She was my aunt, an elder sister of my mother's~ I shall not say much about my uncle, her husband, because though an exceedingly sensible & good man, his life is less interesting to me than hers~

They lived in a large gambrel roofed house with two parlors & a dining room, two kitchens & eleven finished bedrooms~ The house had passageways & closets innumerable & was very convenient~

The inner kitchen had a great open fireplace, with crane & pothooks & all the roasts were done in a tin~kitchen before the fire~ The outer kitchen had a Rumford apparatus~

It occupied nearly one side of the room, was built of bricks & mortar & had several small fireplaces with iron doors~ One fireplace was under the copper wash boiler~ Other fires under other kettles, & there were two or three ovens~

The chief recommendation of the Rumford Work, was the possible economy of fuel, as one small fire would boil a kettle, or the several fires would cook a large dinner & boil the clothes beside~ The inventor was Count Rumford the great scientist who was born in Massachusetts~[180]

Count Rumford was Sir Benjamin Thompson, a physicist who first established the principle that heat is a form of motion. He was born in Woburn, Massachusetts, but lived in Rumford, (now Concord) New Hampshire during the Revolution.[181]

There was a stable with a horse & cows, a garden that produced the most

*wonderful head lettuce, beets, carrots, & parsley~ There was a well of
clear, cold water on the line shared by a neighbor~ Then there was a front
yard with three tall poplars & two great snow ball bushes & masses of
crimson Peonies in the grass~*

*I was very much in & out of that house in my early childhood & preferred
the kitchen to any part of the house~ I remember one day, when the servant
girls tried what they called a "Project," to ascertain who their husbands
were to be~*

*One girl threw a ball of yarn into the cellar, keeping the end & as she
wound it in her hand, saying "Oh my true love who my true love is to be,
Let him come & stop this ball for me~" The ball stopped & I ran home
terrified~*[182]

It is not surprising that this incident frightened Sarah, as she was quite superstitious
throughout her lifetime. Notes written later in her life indicate she believed in omens or
portents.

*There were two women servants & a Dutchman named Eric, whom my
uncle had brought from abroad~ There was a great wooden washing
machine, worked by two women who did the laundry work of the family~
My Aunt was busy & bustling and moved with such impetus, that her cap
border was always flying back, as if she was going against the wind~*[183]

There were a number of washing machines on the market by this time. Waterproof
wooden boxes that set up on legs, they operated somewhat like a churn with paddles and
rollers that agitated the clothes. They were hand-powered and none too efficient. However,
to many housekeepers they may have seemed preferable to washing clothes with a scrub
board and tub.[184]

*She was very sweet tempered, only she liked to look after everything herself
& yet strange to say she originated the remarkable adage "What the eye
does not see the heart does not rue~"*

*There was a vast amount of cleaning done in that house & the labor
accomplished by all female servants, was much greater than now~
Furniture had to be rubbed with wax, brush & soft cloths, to the last degree
of polish~ Brasses were cleaned two or three times a week with rottenstone
& oil which was hard & disagreeable~ Then white floors & kitchen tables
had to be kept white with soap & sand & housekeepers urged very much the
importance of what they called "elbow grease", which would have come
under the head of "correlation of Forces"~*

*My Aunt always insisted that one parlor was enough for everyday life & so
twice a year, after the "best room" as it was called had been thoroughly*

cleaned, it was shut up until something pleasant or terrible happened to necessitate its being opened~

There were two children a son & a daughter whose lives were made exceedingly happy by every reasonable indulgence~ And now I must tell of my Aunt's benevolence & self sacrifice which came out so nobly, when she began to be in middle life~

How that when her eldest sister, became a widow she gave her the pleasantest room in the house, though she had ample means to live elsewhere~

Then a little neice of her husband's becoming motherless, was sent for & accepted as her own & then there came something sadder still, for her husband's brother a charming & accomplished man, fell in love with a most attractive young girl in Charlestown S.C. & with the impetuosity characteristic of him married in haste~

They had not lived together many days, when he discovered that his bride was a confirmed inebriate~ In his anguish he wrote to his brother & sister for advice~"Bring her to me" wrote my aunt & I will reclaim her" She became a member of their family but she was never reclaimed~[185]

To reclaim a person during these times meant to save them from the evils of drink. Apparently this attempt failed, but the bride was accepted despite her shortcomings. It was at Aunt Flagg's that Sarah first met her future husband. At the time the meeting made very little impression on them, as she was six and he sixteen.

It was the custom with my Aunt & her sisters to entertain one another, with their families, on Thanksgiving days~ On Thanksgiving day of (I think) 1811, my Uncle & aunt entertained all the brothers & sisters & their children~

Among the guests was a school fellow of the son, at a distant Academy~ His name was Ichabod Goodwin~ He was sixteen & I was six, & we dined together without being conscious of each others presence~

After dinner there came a dispatch from my Uncle John Parker summoning my aunt to attend his dying bed in Salem, Mass~ My Uncle took his wife in a close carriage & they traveled post haste arriving early in the next morning~ The grief & confusion among the sisters, who had come to a house of feasting, was terrible as he was a dearly loved brother~ I well remember my mother's distress for a long while after~

The dying man was spared just long enough to receive from my aunt a promise to adopt his motherless child, a little daughter~ they returned to

P___ the next day with his remains, which lie beside my mothers at the cemetery~

The little girl was a most beautiful creature resembling two lovely cousins, (who also are gone) Sarah Parrott & my own Sadie~ This little girl became the care of the two young ladies & she remained in P___ until the daughter of the house was married & took her away to a distant city~[186]

Her Uncle John was buried at Proprietor's Cemetery, now known as South Cemetery. The following year Sarah's mother was buried at the same cemetery. Two years later Sarah's Aunt Flagg was widowed, when her husband, Captain John Flagg died just two days before Christmas of 1814.[187]

Then my uncle died & the son went away in pursuit of business & my aunt broke down in health & not being happy without her daughter left her affairs in my Father's care & became a member of her family where she endeared herself to her grandchildren & made their home the sweeter for her presence~

About forty years after her death an old house at the corner of Deer & Vaughan Sts was moved back almost into the front year of the Flagg house & so spoiled its outlook~ It once had a field in front~[188]

THE WAR OF 1812

*My father was a Jeffersonian Patriot but never a politician~ I was an
observant child & very little that went on escaped me~*[189]

Although Portsmouth's commercial interests began to embrace new areas of industry and commerce during the long period of prosperity following the Revolution, shipping and related industries such as shipbuilding remained the primary source of wealth for the town. Still there were many dangers awaiting American merchant ships sailing out of the Port of Portsmouth into international seas. Off the coast of North Africa Barbary pirates regularly terrorized American ships, and privateers from both France and England did the same.

When the French Revolution started in 1789, France declared war on England, Holland, and Spain. The British and French navies began to terrorize American ships found heading towards the enemy's port, and the British pressed Americans into service aboard their ships. At the time British law gave this power to their navy during time of war, and as they had been during the American Revolution, Americans suspected of being of British birth were forced to fight their own country.

American seamen started traveling with papers of citizenship to prove they were indeed American citizens. The country tried to stay out of the conflict between the French and the English. What Americans wanted was to establish the principle of freedom on the seas, and maintain a neutral stance that allowed them to trade with all countries. Instead both France and England turned against the young country.

The British believed their former colony should be loyal to their cause, and the French believed America's loyalty rightly belonged to the country that had helped them gain their independence. In 1795 the Jay Treaty between Great Britain and America brought some peace from British seizures, and eased restrictions on American trade with the West Indies. Not all were happy with the treaty when it was first signed, as it seemed to favor English interests over American.[190]

In Portsmouth feelings against the treaty ran high. Senator John Langdon of Portsmouth voted against it, while the state's other senator, Samuel Livermore, a former Portsmouth resident, approved. In Portsmouth a town meeting in July gave a vote of thanks to Langdon for his stance against the treaty, and a letter was drafted to President Washington expressing the community's disapproval.[191]

Most of the merchants in town disagreed with the terms of the treaty, especially the limitation of tonnage allowed for vessels trading with British colonies to seventy. But Federalists such as Jacob Scheafe felt it was their duty to support President Washington. When Scheafe and other merchants met in private he circulated a petition to that effect, signed by thirty-nine Portsmouth merchants.[192]

Those of the Republican persuasion held their own meeting near Liberty Bridge and demanded that Scheafe turn over the petition. He refused, but gave them a copy. At the meeting they planned a parade, and that evening wooden effigies of Livermore and John Jay, the author of the treaty, were carried throughout the town in an open carriage. This drew a large crowd to Warner's wharf, where they were burned. Some mob violence took place, mainly at the homes of prominent Federalists.[193] However, when the treaty went into effect trade increased between the two countries. Within a few years America was England's best customer, while the British bought more exports from America than from any other country. However, the new alliance between England and her former colony angered the French. In retaliation for what the French viewed as disloyalty and a refusal to live up to the terms of 1778 Treaty of Alliance, French vessels were ordered to attack any American merchant ship carrying supplies to the British. This situation created an international crisis for America, and brought about the Quasi War with France.[194]

It also prodded Congress into increased defense spending. Appropriations were voted to pay for the stockpiling of ammunition, as well as the building of new ships for a navy. Colonel James Hacket built four navy vessels commissioned during this period in Portsmouth. Three of these vessels, the *Scammel,* the *Portsmouth,* and the *Congress* were all ordered to the West Indies to patrol the seas and protect American merchants from French marauders. Then in 1800 the *Portsmouth* was sent to Le Havre to escort peace commissioners negotiating in Paris back home. While there it was involved in an exchange of naval salutes with the French.[195]

The fourth was the *Crescent,* a thirty-two gun frigate given as a gift from the American government to the Dey of Algiers in 1799, as an inducement to honor a treaty with America.[196] However, the country's problem with the Barbary pirates persisted until 1805, when a peace treaty was signed following a two year long naval blockade of Tripoli under the command of Lieutenant Stephen Decatur.[197]

The government vessels built in Portsmouth were constructed on Withers' Island, by then called Langdon's Island. Then in 1800 the federal government purchased the nearby Dennett's Island for a Federal Naval Yard.[198] The following year an agreement was reached with the French government to reimburse American merchants for the estimated fifteen million dollars lost to the French privateers. Of seventeen hundred American vessels captured forty were Portsmouth vessels.[199]

Naval hero Stephen Decatur II. His descendant, Stephen Decatur IV, will marry Sarah Goodwin's granddaughter, Mabel Storer, in 1884.

By the time Sarah was born in 1805, Thomas Jefferson was President of the United States, the British navy controlled the continental seas, and Napoleon Bonaparte was intent on capturing all of Europe. Neither France nor England could strike directly at one another, so they tried to disrupt each other's economy by resorting to commercial warfare. The two countries instituted so many rules and imposed so many duties and fees upon the continental merchant ships. Their actions were viewed as an organized form of extortion against American merchants.[200]

Once again Americans were at the mercy of both the French and English governments and their privateers. Between 1803 and 1807 both countries seized hundreds of American merchant ships, and once again the British, who still refused to honor the American flag, began to press American seamen into service upon their vessels. Joseph Whipple, the collector of customs in Portsmouth at the time, issued a large number of papers to local seaman that vouched for their status as American citizens.[201]

The English were impressing our seamen, taking them out of our ships by force & compelling them to serve in their navy~ Every young sailor had to be furnished with papers, suitably drawn up & signed called "Protection papers"~[202]

Sarah was just two when the USS *Chesapeake,* still within the boundaries of American waters outside of Norfolk, Virginia, was shot at by a British frigate that demanded the right to search it for deserters. When the captain refused, the British opened fire and killed three Americans, wounded eighteen, and impressed four sailors. Three of these were American citizens. In response President Jefferson closed American ports to the British, invoked the Non-Importation Act, and enacted the Embargo Act of 1807. This stopped the sale of exports to all countries, and virtually eliminated the import trade, causing a rise in illegal smuggling activities. [203]

Mr Jefferson ordered an Embargo & our ships were laid up at the wharves or up the river to rot~ Well I do remember the sorrows of that time as Portsmouth was dependent on the shipping interest~[204]

The impact on the American economy was catastrophic, especially in communities such as Portsmouth that were reliant upon the sea. A mass meeting held there shortly after the *Chesapeake* incident brought about a patriotic response to Jefferson's actions, and ended with a unanimous resolve to support the President. However, by the following year, after the value of exports from the port had dropped to one-sixth of what it had been in 1806, and customs revenue dropped by one-fifth, everyone in Portsmouth was anxious to see the end of the hated embargo.[205]

A depression followed in Portsmouth and throughout all of New England, which was heavily dependent on the shipping commerce. Ships sat idle in dock, merchants were forced into bankruptcy, and Jefferson fell out of favor with many. There was a great division in Portsmouth over the merits of this war. Most New Englanders were Federalists, and since this embargo struck directly at the economy of this region, there was serious discussion of secession from the rest of the country.[206] However, not all agreed with the Federalist stance. Such prominent citizens as William Rice and John Langdon, governor of New Hampshire at the time, were Republicans and felt it was their patriotic duty to support Jefferson's policies.[207]

Some approved & others were filled with dismay~ Families were divided Society was more or less dislocated~ Men calling themselves gentlemen fought in the streets~

Then in 1812 Mr. Madison declared war against Great Britain~ The Federalists were bitter~ The Jeffersonians were jubilant~ I believe we gained one point by the war & that was relief from impressment~ [208]

By 1812 James Madison was president of America. France and England remained at war, and Napoleon Bonaparte seemed to be well on his way to conquering all of Europe. Relations between America and England grew quite tense over these years. After the failed

Embargo Act was repealed, the Non-Intercourse Act was invoked, but it too failed. By the time the war began, an economic depression in England was leading to a change in British policies regarding American ships and their crews, However, before these were finalized America declared war against Britain, even though most Americans concurred that the bigger threat was Napoleon.

> *Bonaparte, as they called him was regarded with terror by everybody~ The French were taking our ships on every sea, not being able to distinguish us from the English~*[209]

Locally a meeting of concerned citizens from Rockingham County formed a committee of fifteen men to write a letter to President Madison presenting their grievances against the war. In it they noted that the continuation of the war would in all probability inflict greater harm upon New England shippers and the regional economy than English privateers or the English government ever had in the past. They also expressed their suspicion that Madison's ulterior motive was to aid France while sacrificing New England's economy.[210]

> *During the last war with England there were Continual alarms about the enemy having landed somewhere or other & my Father thought as a British fleet was cruising on our coast that he had better send Sarah, Susan & Adeline to Lee under the care of Aunt Briard, my mothers eldest sister~*
>
> *We were there many weeks & my perfect delight was to go out with my grandfather after breakfast to feed the sheep with corn meal dough~ He had a large flock of them & they were very fond of him~*[211]

A British squadron of seven ships of war blockaded the coast between Portsmouth and Boston throughout 1814. One or more of these ships often patrolled right outside Portsmouth Harbor, making it impossible for ships to enter or leave. Their bold presence caused great alarm. Local history recalls that many families moved women, children and valuables further inland during this period.[212]

Commodore Hull, the Naval Yard Commander, feared the British planned to attack the Yard and destroy the USS *Washington*, a 74 being built during this time by William Badger, Sarah's uncle by marriage. The Commodore relied upon the local militia, a group of about sixty men of various ages and professions, for aid in the event of attack. The signal to rally them was to be three cannon shots. The shots came one night, and the militia formed, many of them armed with fowling guns. At the Yard, they found the alarm had been sounded too hastily when some fishing vessels were mistaken for the enemy.[213]

One clash with the British occurred on May 30th of that year when a barge from one of two warships anchored off of Rye on Gunboat Shoal Harbor chased a schooner that coasted into Rye Harbor. However, the invaders were fended off by a company of local men hidden behind a stonewall fortress on Little Neck. They exchanged gunfire with those on the raft, and eventually bested the British in this battle that became known as "The Battle of Rye Harbor." The coasting schooner safely sailed into Portsmouth Harbor that evening. This exchange was viewed by a large group of townspeople who remained at a safe distance from the exchange of gunfire. To this day it remains New Hampshire's only recorded naval battle.[214]

Less than two months later the Portsmouth Revenue Cutter captured the tender of the British warship *Tenedos*, and within a week the officers of the *Tenedos* arrived at the Isle of Shoals with a flag of truce and some American prisoners to exchange for the crew of the tender.[215]

There are several other stories in the annals of Portsmouth that are similar, to the above, though they differ in detail. However, they all serve to demonstrate the ways local shipmasters relied upon their Yankee ingenuity to outwit and outrun the British navy during this war.

> *Fort Constitution was put on military footing & seemed very formidable~*
> *the Drum & fife might be heard at all hour~*[216]

There was increased military activity at Fort Constitution in New Castle during these years, and voluntary militias known as the Sea Fencibles were ready to fend off any attempt by the British to invade their former fortress, known as Fort William and Mary before the Revolution. There was also a great deal of activity on Portsmouth's Fort Washington. It is said that United States Representative Daniel Webster gave an eloquent speech during an emergency town meeting and urged the residents to act rather than talk by first repairing the town forts and preparing themselves to defend them. He then set an example for all to follow when he took up a spade and helped to shore the walls of Fort Washington. He was also a member of the local militia.[217] The British never did land on the shores of Portsmouth or surrounding towns during this war, but if they had the local militia was prepared to fight.

> *He came to Portsmouth in 1807... Mr. Webster served two terms in*
> *Congress from this District, was living here during the whole period of the*
> *war with England & removed to Boston in 1816~*[218]

The truth was that America was ill prepared to fight this war in every way. The country had a population of eight million vs. twenty million British. They fell far behind in necessary resources such as fighting forces, financial assets, and equipment. The United States Navy had just sixteen ships, while the British had eight hundred and thirty.[219]

Even though Portsmouth had a naval yard, very few vessels were available to protect this area. Therefore much of the fighting was conducted by privately owned merchant ships commissioned by the government to operate as privateers. Sailing out of Portsmouth alone there were approximately twenty privately owned ships involved in this profitable enterprise.[220]

The most successful of the privateers to sail out of the Port of Portsmouth during these years was the schooner *Fox*. Built in Portland, Maine by Richard Moulton it was commissioned as a Portsmouth privateer on September 12, 1812, with William Rice, and William Flagg acting as her agents. There were in total eighteen owners of the *Fox*. Sarah's father was one of them, as were both Uncle Parrotts.[221] The *Fox* at 208 tons, sported clipper lines, and a flush deck with a considerable sheer. Her name came from a fox head carving in the stern, and she was painted white. One source remembered her as "ugly but fast." She was built to accommodate sixteen guns, although the number varied from cruise to cruise.[222]

Like her armament, the size of her crew varied from cruise to cruise, generally staying within the range of eighty to ninety men. During this time she had three different captains, Elihu Brown, Samuel Handy, and John Winkley.[223] All were successful. The *Fox* left on her maiden cruise within three months of the declaration of war, and went out on seven cruises in all. She brought in many prizes, and came to be known as a "million dollar privateer."

During her first year out the *Fox* captured the *Stranger,* a British six-gun, headed to Canada with a full cargo of ammunition, cannons, and guns for the British. Records note that the wives and children of the British officers aboard ship were sent to Salem, but no mention is made of the officers and crew.[224] They may have been taken for ransom. One source indicates the *Fox* once captured seventy-four British prisoners for whom the English government paid a bounty of close to $4,000.[225]

During her fifth cruise in May of 1814 the *Fox*, after escaping the *Tenedos* one of the fastest British ships around, came upon a convoy of British merchant vessels traveling out of Cork to Halifax. They took one named the *Beliese* for a prize. Her cargo of dry goods on board netted her crew and owners between $300,000 and $400,000. A catalogue of prize goods auctioned off from the *Beliese* listed clothe, knives, wigs, blankets, flannels, iron harps, knives, spoons, and quills.[226] There was a rumor that the cargo also contained enough copper to sheath the bottom of the 74 *Washington* launched from the Naval Yard in 1813. There were also several dozen tomahawks found on the *Beliese*. The local speculation was that the latter were intended to arm the Canadian Indians so they would aid the British in the war.[227]

Shortly after this William Rice held a "calico party" at his Deer Street, and invited all the lady relatives and friends of the family to come and cut out as many patterns as they could carry home. [228] This bounty was probably from the *Beliese*. Cloth was quite an expensive item at the time as most fabric was either woven at home or manufactured in England. The first power loom in America had been set up in nearby Waltham, Massachusetts just a year before.[229]

All in all privateering brought over two and a half million dollars in prizes into Portsmouth during the war of 1812. This was not pure profit. The owners had to split the bounty with the crew, the auctioneer, the courts, and the customhouse, which put two percent of the net prize money into a fund for disabled privateers, their widows and children. The majority of those involved in privateering were Jeffersonian Republicans like Sarah's father. However, some Federalists such as Major Larkin, the auctioneer who sold off the majority of the prizes in Portsmouth, also profited from this lucrative enterprise.[230]

> *In 1813 a Packet Ship arrived bringing the latest news of Bonaparte~ He was in Russia fighting his way to universal monarchy~ My dear old grandfather Parker was on a visit to us~ He exclaimed to my father, "My God Sir we shall have him over here"*
>
> *"Oh no said my father we have nothing that he wants over here~" "Sir" said my grandfather, "He will never be satisfied until he conquers the world"~ I was not taken into the account but I thought I saw him coming...[231]*

Captain Brown of the *Fox* carried news of Napoleon's defeat to Portsmouth in May of 1814. That August the *Fox* left on another cruise, slipping out of the harbor under the cloak of night, as most privateers must have done whenever the British were close to Portsmouth Harbor.[232] She returned that November, and left on what was to be her last cruise in January of 1815.

The Treaty of Ghent had been signed on Christmas Eve of 1814, so the war was over by then, but no one in Portsmouth knew this. The *Fox*, unaware of the peace treaty continued to fight and plunder British merchant ships in the name of patriotism and free enterprise until the following April. During her last cruise she captured two British ships. The British *Antiqua* was the last prize she took. It sold for $30,000. [233]

The *Fox* earned close to a half million dollars pure profit for its owners during the war.[234] William Rice's portion of the prizes insured his family's financial well being for many years to come. After the war he continued to prosper in Portsmouth through investments in banking, insurance, shipping, and factories. Along with John Parrott, he founded the Union Insurance Company, and became a director and president of the New Hampshire Union Bank about this time. It is safe to assume many of the new enterprises and business ventures started in Portsmouth during the first quarter of the nineteenth century were funded by profits from the *Fox,* and other successful privateers that sailed from the Port of Portsmouth during the War of 1812.

> *But after all everybody was glad when the news of <u>Peace</u> came & a great Ball was given~*[235]

ASSEMBLY HOUSE

It is almost certain the ball thrown to celebrate the end of the war was held at the Assembly House. This hall, built in 1750 on Vaughan Street in the North End of Portsmouth was the cultural center of the city during Sarah's youth. She recalled the importance it played in the lives of Portsmouth's elite during its hey day.

> *There were when I was young & had been for a hundred years or more regular assemblies~ Every autumn certain gentlemen met & balloted for members & often persons were blackballed ~*
>
> *They were conducted with great regard to etiquette, the gentlemen appearing in small clothes & silk stockings & the ladies in full dress~[236]*
>
> *They were very exclusive, care being taken to offer the subscription paper to certain gentlemen only~ Every gentleman must appear in the prescribed costume, which was as follows, knee britches, silk stockings, pumps, blue coat with bright buttons & white kid gloves~*
>
> *The assemblies had two managers, who with powdered head and chapeau under left arm looked the personification of power and dignity~*
>
> *Almost every family gave a large party once a year, besides smaller entertainments but our Assemblies were the chief glory of the place~ Both Washington and Lafayette had an opportunity to witness the elegance & grace present on those occasions~[237]*

George Washington visited Portsmouth in 1789, and subsequently recorded his impressions of the city in his journal. Although an artillery salute, welcoming crowds, and numerous odes warmly received him; his impressions of the city of Portsmouth were not totally flattering. He wrote in his personal journal that he found Portsmouth homes "unimpressive," making an exception for the home of John Langdon on Pleasant Street. However, he wrote that the Assembly House was, "one of the best I have seen anywhere in the United States."*[238]*

> *The ladies wore feathers (three a la Prince of Wales) & low dresses of silk, satins and velvet & everything was conducted with great state & propriety~[239] Ostrich feathers were very much worn in the hair & it was not unusual to see them arranged after the fashion of the Prince of Wales~*
>
> *Silks satins & what was known as Italian crape over satin & trimmed with the satin were much worn though nothing was so much admired by*

the gentlemen as white muslin with white Kid slippers~ White kid gloves reaching to the elbow were universal~[240]

Every lady was taken into the ball room by a manager, & seated~ At the appointed moment, the numbers were called for the draw dance~ After that the cotillions, which were voluntary~ A manager took the eldest lady present, or a bride if one was present, and led down the first dance with her~[241]

Sarah made several notations in her journal indicating her disapproved of the way older women were expected to dress in the 1870s and 1880s during the reign of Queen Victoria, when modestly high necklines, long sleeves, and unflattering bustles were in fashion for mature ladies. She wrote that she found the styles for older ladies *"almost distressing,"* when compared to the prescribed dress for those dignified ladies of her youth. When she was young the Empire gown with its elegant romantic style and slimmer lines was in fashion, and decidedly more flattering to women of all ages.

Elderly ladies of whom there were many & all middle aged ladies wore satins~ Low necks & short sleeves were universal~ When I was young there were thirty or forty ladies from forty to sixty who danced & gave dignity & prestige to such occasions~[242]

These Assemblies were eight in number occurring once a fortnight & followed by a Ball on Washington's Birthday the 22 Feb~ They were conducted with great regard to etiquette, the gentlemen appearing in small clothes & silk stockings~the ladies in full dress~ The managers wore powder & carried their chapeaux under the arm~[243]

Anybody who would pay five dollars could attend this ball but the outside world did not care much about it~ Court was sitting about this time and the Ballroom was thickly sprinkled with lawyers~[244]

The annual Washington's Ball, in honor of the first president's birthday, was a traditional day of celebration all over America throughout the nineteenth century. It is a holiday unique to America that is still celebrated as President's Day. During these early years it was considered almost equal in importance to Thanksgiving or Fourth of July, both also strictly American celebrations.

At the Assemblies sandwiches of ham & tongue & biscuit, with coffee & chocolate were passed around about ten o'clock & at twelve precisely the managers dismissed the music~

At the Washington Ball a great fruit cake was placed in one corner of the room & served around by the gentlemen after which they, the gentlemen, had a hearty supper~[245]

It would seem the ladies were dismissed at this point of the evening while the gentlemen gathered for a supper that probably included drink and political conversation deemed unfit for the gentler sex. Sarah attended the Assembly Balls for many years, first at the Assembly House and later at Franklin Hall. For the edification of her grandchildren, she left behind a description of her first ball gowns.

> *I attended the Assemblies many winters before & after I was married & it may be interesting to the young people to know that my first two Ball dresses were a white, wrought India Muslin & a blue Italian crape trimmed with white satin~ Long white Kid gloves, and white Kid slippers, of course~*[246]

The Assembly House was quite grand according to Sarah's memories of this Georgian style building. Its ballroom was sixty feet long, and it was embellished with unique wooden carvings of every possible style and description both within and without. Years after it was gone she recalled its former splendor.

> *If the old Assembly House were still in being, what a treasure of art & memories it would be in these days of Centennial excitement & interest~*

> *It was built by a Mr. Whidden who must have been a real artist & a remarkable man~ I can remember him very distinctly as he appeared in his nineties when I went to the dancing school~ He was a little, florid looking man in a white linen skull cap, something like what is worn by masons at their work~*[247]

The Whidden family produced a number of master joiners. Michael Whidden II, noted for his carving skills, built the Assembly House. His father, Michael Jr., was one of the first builders to introduce the Georgian architectural style to Portsmouth; his son, Michael Whidden III, built the Governor Langdon mansion in the 1780s.[248]

> *The house was long & large & painted white~ There were three great square parlors & a kitchen & an immense hall & staircase~ The Assembly Room took the whole front in the second story and was about sixty by thirty feet~ Back of it were the two dressing rooms for ladies and gentlemen~*

> *Perhaps the most remarkable feature about the Assembly House was the abundance and variety of wood carvings~ The Facade was decorated in festoons of flowers over the windows & every imaginable figure, proper to external ornamentation, was there~*

> *The cornices and mantles were beautifully carved and in all the rooms & in the Assembly room, the carving was richly gilt~ There were three chandeliers for wax candles & branches from the walls for candles in the same style~*

> *As you opened the great heavy front door you looked down the Hall and*

out upon the Summer House, which was on a rise in the garden~ It was an octagon with large glass windows & of two stories~

The garden had a broad central walk, but all the rest was clover and very sweet~ How many bouquets of clover blossoms I have gathered there to my great delight~[249]

Before Sarah came of age to attend these dances, she attended other cultural events at the Assembly House that would have appealed to audiences of every age.

The first time I was in that house I went to see Ramo Samee, with his company of Hindoo jugglers~ He swallowed a sword and pulled yards of ribbon out of his nostrils~

Every summer for many years, the Boston stock company had theatrical entertainments in the Assembly room~ Mr & Mrs Duff & Mr & Mrs Pelby & Mr Addison, a famous comic singer & others played five nights in the week to the elite of the town~ The ladies went without bonnets, usually with a large rich vail thrown over the head, the border coming over the forehead~[250]

When I was a little girl I attended dancing school two seasons in this house~ I was also a member of a Handel & Hayden Society presided over by Mr Brierly & attended by many music loving ladies and gentlemen who held their meetings in this ball room~[251]

Plays, operas, and other theatrical fare were offered in Portsmouth by 1769. These first performances took place in local taverns such as the Earl of Halifax Tavern. Because it was fashionable for ladies to adorn their hair with large head dressings at this time, advertisements for theatrical affairs often warned the ladies to wear less obtrusive head coverings so as not to obscure the view of those in the back.

The first great oil painting that I ever saw was exhibited in the back room of that house & covered one side of the wall~ It was by Granet & represented a Capuchin chapel with the monks at their devotions~ I went twice to see it & the perspective was so good that I could not get out of the building~ The moment I entered the room I was in the chapel~

The picture made a great impression on me & curiously enough, when we were first in our own house Mr Goodwin bought the engraving of it in New York, with its companion picture, "A nun taking the veil," without knowing how I felt about the original~ Above every other engraving, I would have desired that~ The original painting was destroyed by fire in St Petersburg~[252]

Francois Marius Granet (1775-1848) was a French landscapist of the neoclassical school. For a number of years he lived and worked in a Capuchin convent, and his paintings are reflective of that period of his life.[253]

In the 1820s Langley Boardman, a master cabinetmaker and real estate mogul who built a number of fine homes in Portsmouth during this time, built Franklin Block. Located within the block was Franklin Hall, a newer and larger assembly hall that came to replace the older one as the cultural center of Portsmouth. It was destroyed in 1879 by a fire[254]

> *About 1820 Mr. Langley Boardman built Franklin Hall & then all the dancing was transferred to that place~ The new hall was grander than the one on Vaughan Street, but not half so beautiful~[255]*

Much to Sarah's dismay the Assembly House was dismantled in 1838, the upper level cut away, the hallway taken out, and the southern section moved down eight feet. What remained were two small houses that sat on each end of Rait's Court. These nondescript cottages stood there for another century, conspicuous only because of a plaque hanging in commemoration of President Washington's visit to the Assembly House that he had once deemed one of the best in the United States.[256]

> *When the house was sawed in two preparatory to being moved away, the bits of carving & gilding were scattered about the street to the delight of the children~ It was clear, sheer vandalism & there is nothing so beautiful now~*
>
> *Rait's Court occupies the sacred ground~ During the demolition, or what Mr. Rait styled the improvement, he removed a young thrifty Apple tree which he presented to Mr. Goodwin~ It is a valuable memento of the place inasmuch it bears excellent apples~ It stands near the entrance to the Field & the blossoms are a perennial joy~ 1870[257]*

In her recollections of the Assembly House Sarah noted that both George Washington and the Marquis de Lafayette, the French nobleman who volunteered in 1777 to fight for the American cause with him, were familiar with the Assembly House. It is known Lafayette visited Portsmouth twice. The first time was in 1782 when he made a brief visit to his fellow French officers lodging at Stavers Tavern on Court Street. He may have paid a visit to the Assembly House during this visit, but it is not a matter of record. He came again in 1824 and received a triumphant welcome during his day's long visit to Portsmouth on the first of September. A public dinner was given in his honor at Jefferson Hall, and that evening a ball attended by over three hundred of the city's most prominent citizens was held. Sarah would have been nineteen at the time of his visit, and surely would have attended the ball in his honor.[258]

Sarah ~ Her Story

THE DRESSMAKER

The beautiful ballroom gowns in which Sarah and other ladies graced the Assembly balls were designed, fitted, and hand sewn for them by dressmakers, as were their everyday garments. Likewise gentlemen relied upon tailors for their evening finery, as well as their everyday wear.[259] The dressmaker employed by the Rice family was an attractive young lady named Sally Shoors, she was greatly admired by the young Sarah for her beauty, her many ardent suitors, her high spirited singing, and her outspoken theological convictions.

> *A person of rare individuality, was much of her time tailoress, dressmaker & seamstress, in our family in the first third of this century~ Almost all are gone who were interested in her at that period & all are gone about whose feelings there need be any delicacy~ We children adored her & in my earliest childhood, she delighted me by her singing & her enthusiasm~*

> *She was brought up by her grandmother who must have been a very useful woman~ She too had a career~*

> *She inherited from her Father a powerful physique & great mental ability~ In her youth she was anointed handsome~ Her blue eyes, long flaxen curls & pretty feet & ankles were very killing to the young mates of vessels, from abroad, who were very plenty in those days, as the shipping interest of P__ was large & in the Autumn, the freighting vessels all came home making a perfect forest of masts at our wharves~*

> *There was also a large West India trade & now & then an east india man arrived with dinner & tea sets, teas, coffee &c~ Our heroine was very attractive to the first mates (second mates being of no account)~[260]*

There was a large import trade in Portsmouth when Sarah was young, and the largest percentage of the ships coming into port entered from the French West Indies carrying molasses, brown sugar, and rum. Other ships came from the Dutch West Indies, England and other ports bringing Madeira wine, coffee, tea, hardware, and other specialties for Portsmouth merchants to sell. However, the West Indies trade was sharply curtailed during the Embargo of 1807 and the War of 1812. Although it resumed to a small degree after the war it was never again as strong as it had been.[261]

> *She was often perplexed by the number of her suitors & she was at one time engaged to two of them, a situation very embarrassing, when they both happened to be around at the same time, causing jealousies & bitter heart burnings~*

But the thing was settled for her, by one of them dying abroad, his chest being sent to her address, followed by a visit from his Father & Mother, from the lower part of Maine who came as in duty bound to condole with her~

She was at work for us when the summons came to go home & receive them~ She accepted the situation & they went back satisfied taking the chest with them & ever after regarded her as a daughter~

Once she saw an advertisement for a wife in some newspaper~ She sent a description of herself and to her horror & affright the man appeared & a very becoming man too & she had a great deal of trouble getting out the affair~

But the most thrilling of her experiences, was tragic also, for her own cousin, a young Englishman, out of his hopeless love for her, shot himself in Boston, leaving a letter telling how he had always loved her but dared not aspire to her hand~

She sang a great many old fashioned love songs & with cloth pinned to her knee & the tipless thimble ever stitching, her clear ringing voice could be heard all through the day, as she always sang at her work~

She delighted in Dibden's sea songs, which were very popular in those days~ "Black eyed Susan," she sang with great effect. ...~[262]

Charles Dibdin was an English actor, author, and self taught musical composer, who produced eight operas, wrote over a hundred plays, and fourteen hundred songs, as well as a few novels. He became famous for his sea songs, which he composed, sang, and played the musical accompaniment in one-man entertainments. His sea songs were very popular in America at the turn of the nineteenth century.[263]

She was very accomplished in Theological controversy, as indeed every body was in that day, and could talk as glibly, of Free will & Fate, as the ablest divine, or so we children thought~

She would expatiate for hours on St. Paul & quote from memory almost the whole of his writing~ Justification by Faith, as illustrated by the thief on the cross, was her pet theme~ She was always in ready sympathy with the Methodists & Baptists & vibrated from one to the other as a revival sprang up in either sect~[264]

There were two major revival movements in America, known as the First and Second "Great Awakenings," they revolved around the rise of evangelical religions. This brand of religion appealed to the emotional nature of their followers rather than their rational side as the established religions did.

In the 1740s the First Awakening was started by George Whitehead, an itinerate preacher from England, who came to America to spread the word of his Methodist faith. He attracted many followers in New England. He was in Portsmouth by 1740, but his impact on Portsmouth was not as great as it was in many communities.

When Whitefield first preached in the city, he wrote in his journal that the residents were so unconcerned that he questioned if he had been speaking to "rational or brute creatures." When he next spoke there he received more response, and wrote that he felt that there was reason to believe he was "preaching to living men."[265] Whitehead's firebrand style of preaching drew large crowds whenever he spoke. By 1754 when he once again visited Portsmouth, such a large group came out to meet him he was overcome with joy. [266] He attracted young people, as well as unschooled country folk, often isolated from the center of their communities and established churches. They came seeking a personal as well as emotional religious experience. [267]

In New England many other preachers began to imitate Whitehead's religious fervor with its revivalist emphasis on emotional immersion and direct contact with the Holy Spirit. Preachers who followed his style, along with their converts, became known as "New Lights." Those who remained with the ruling religions that relied on scripture and established church teachings became known as "Old Lights." There was great conflict between them; traditional ministers railed against the upstarts.[268]

> *She gloried in a revival & the way she followed up the meetings & sang the hymns, was wonderful~ How we loved to hear her sing~*
>
> *She was always on hand at baptisings which took place at Christian Shore where the water was pure & clear & where Deacon Dearborn rolled out the Bass, to the delight of the crowd, for half a mile around~*[269]

To meet the challenges of the new style of ministry, many traditional churches began to compete for members by bringing New Light ministers into their churches. By the time of the Revolution about one-third of the ministers in New Hampshire town churches were part of the New Light movement. [270] Eventually traditional churches gained back their dominant positions in the communities, while the New Lights were relegated to the outlying districts where they established independent churches.

At the start of the 1800s the country underwent the Second Awakening. As before the appeal was emotional and attracted mainly young, unschooled, but passionate converts such as Sally. This awakening took place largely out West, as more and more young people moved there.[271]

However, its effects were also felt in the East. About the same time Sally Shoors was vacillating between the theologies of the Baptists and Methodists, New Hampshire had on record eleven established religions.[272] Eventually these religious movements in America brought about a spirit of tolerance for religious diversity, and opened the way for new denominations.

Sally Shoors was just as passionate about her country, as her various religions. She came of age when Americans once again fought to retain their independence from England, and as always she expressed her feelings in song. Sarah recalls one favorite ditty popular during the War of 1812 that Miss Shoors sang.

If her Religion was earnest & sincere, so was her Patriotism~ The last war with England drew powerfully on her memory~ one song had thirty verses of eight lines each & began in this way

> *"Ye mariners of England*
> *Ye Lords & Commons too,*
> *Remember well what you're about, and what you're going to do~*
> *You are at War with Yankees,*
> *I'm sure you'll rue the day,*
> *In fighting those sons of Liberty*
> *In North America"*

And then in the boastful spirit of those days there, came a recapitulation of our naval successes~ a sample of which I will give you~

> *"The Essex in the South Sea,*
> *Will put out all your lights,*
> *The Flag she wears at her masthead,*
> *Free trade & sailor's rights,*
> *The next the Macedonian*
> *No finer ship could swim,*
> *Decatur took her gilt works off,*
> *And then he sent her in,*
> *The next you sent your Boxer,*
> *To box us all about*
> *We had an Enterprising brig,*
> *That beat your Boxer out,*
> *We boxed her up to Portland*
> *And moored her off the town,*
> *To show the sons of liberty,*
> *The Boxer of renown"*[273]

Miss Shoors and Sarah kept in touch throughout their lives, and the exploits of her childhood seamstress continued to delight Sarah. She eventually married well, and according to Sarah became a *"house holder & owner of bank stock."* Years later she embraced the Adventist faith, and was as vocal about it as she once was the Baptist and Methodist sects of her youth. She was also as forceful in her denunciations of the spiritual movement popular America at that time, as she had been against the British Empire during the War of 1812.

NORTH END NEIGHBORS

There were others living in the lively North End neighborhood of Portsmouth during the early part of the nineteenth century who made enough of an impression on the young Sarah to live on in her memories. Sarah recalled her frequent visits to the home of Captain Nathaniel Kennard, and his family. He was a retired ship's captain and commander of the revenue cutter in Portsmouth when she was young.

There lived next door east of my Father's, in a rather small two story house, a family by the name of Kennard~ They were a little different in their way of living, from their neighbors, adhering to transmitted customs, and in no wise carried away by the fashions of the day~

The entry was very small ~ On one side was the best Parlor and on the other the sitting room~ The Parlor had a carpet woven in one piece which did not quite cover the floor, some good chairs & a pair of spindle legged card tables~

But the gem of this house was the kitchen! There sat Aunt Kennard, in her mob cap & spectacles & who was an immensely large woman & there the table was three times a day spread with the best of food~

They were perfect old fashioned cooks & thrift, order & comfort reigned~ Aunt Kennard was never allowed to do anything except perhaps to darn a stocking or something of that kind & when in the afternoon she sat in the sun by the kitchen window asleep, for she napped a good deal, & the cat laid asleep in the chair by her, it was the most perfect picture of comfort that can be imagined~

There were dressers in this kitchen & the crockery & pewter on them shone & there were large quart mugs, turned down as covers over cup cake & dried orange peel or some other dainty~ Or perhaps~ indeed always, one large mug was full of cider & very good cider too as I well know & this was carefully covered –

But what took the shine from all these splendors was a Buffet, called by them a beaufat, which held some really beautiful things~ There were a set of little old fashioned real china cups & saucers~ A great superb china platter which Miss Nancy the eldest daughter afterwards gave to me, two great silver gravy spoons, that would weight two pounds apiece and many other nice things~

The sitting room where Miss Nancy sat at a window with her needle work, was always sanded~ When the sand was first put on, which might be once a fortnight it was wet & dropped in some pattern, a diamond perhaps, or a square, & after this order was broken a hemlock broom was gently used, to draw the sand into waves~ Short curtains covering the lower panes, were at the windows~[274]

It was common in those days to clean whitewashed wide board pine floors with coarse white sand, which acted as an abrasive cleaning agent that scoured the surface of the floor when spread across the top by a broom. After this treatment a thin layer of clean white sand was applied to the freshly scrubbed floor, where it remained to absorb moisture and spills. It was commonly arranged in fanciful patterns.[275]

East of this room & opening out of it, was what they called the shop, where they never sold anything, but where they took in country produce & where Miss Eliza, the younger daughter, delighted to be & to lounge over the lower half of the shop door & talk to the passers by~[276]

The shop that Sarah recalls in the Kennard home may have sold rum at one time as well as produce. Although Kennard never set himself up as a merchant in Portsmouth, during his years as a sea captain it was customary for him to import anywhere from 100 to 300 gallons of rum on each of his voyages. He then sold this rum for personal profit, not an uncommon practice amongst the ship captains in Portsmouth who often supplemented their captain's pay in this manner.[277]

Adjoining that was the covered shed, a passage from the street to the yard & back door and which uncle Kennard as I liked to call him, always used, instead of any other entrance~ Look out when you would Uncle K__ was either coming out of the shed or going in~

They had a garden with all sort of vegetables in it, in the summer & the most glorious damask rose bush for size & fragrance that I have ever seen~ [278]

Then they kept a Pig! & such a pig! There was nobodies pig like uncle Kennard's ~ He was scrubbed with pails of water & broom every day by Uncle Kennard's own hand & fed on the daintiest meal & potatoes~ & as to the floor of his sty it was a marvel of whiteness~

Well there is another side even to the rose leaf & Uncle Kennard's Pig once a year, had to be killed~ When the fatal day arrived I always tried to be out of the way but we always had pork steaks for breakfast next morning, sent in as a present~[279]

It was not unusual to find a pig or even a cow in that neighborhood during Sarah's childhood. Her father owned a cow and almost every home had a garden.

*Once for some reason, I became disgusted with my home (I was then
about six years old) & I told my father that I wished I could go into uncle
Kennard's to live~ "Well go along said he, I have no objection"~ So I went
to the bureau where my things were mostly kept & made up a bundle &
started~*

*I walked through to the kitchen just as they were sitting down to dinner &
told them that I had come to live~ They gave me the heartiest welcome &
put me up to the table at once & never shall I forget the baked beans & the
Indian Pudding! What a dinner I made!*

*So far so good~ I sympathized with the clearing away & with the dish
washing & taking care of the remains of the dinner, smoothed Nancy's hair
as she sewed at the front window~ rejoiced in aunt Kennard's repose as in
that of the cat but when the work was all done & Eliza had gone upstairs
for a change of toilet & a nap & nobody took notice of me~ I crept upstairs,
got my bundle & left them to wonder what had become of me~*[280]

Kennard had quite a colorful history, according to historian Ray Brighton, and it bears
looking at as it lends a new dimension to Sarah's rendition of one of her favorite neighbors
of old. In his early twenties, Kennard spent a year during the Revolutionary War fighting
with the Continental Army troops outside of Boston, and afterward he tried his hand at
privateering. However, his ship was subsequently captured, and he spent the next two years
in England's Mill Prison. In 1799 he was exchanged for English prisoners, and was sent to
France where he enlisted on the *Bon Homme Richard*, commanded by John Paul Jones.

After they captured a British ship he was assigned to sail on board this prize, but it was
soon re-captured by the British, who impressed him into service in the Royal Navy. While
serving on the HBM *Unicorn,* he managed to escape in Jamaica. He eventually returned to
America, where he became a shipmaster and trader.

In his early sixties Kennard returned to sea for one more sea journey in the ship *Watson*.
On the return voyage from LeHavre, France, they ran into a gale, which destroyed the ship's
masts. The crew was rescued, but the *Watson* was lost at sea. [281]

During his last years Captain Kennard was a customs inspector. He died in 1823, at
sixty-eight years of age.[282] Sometime after that the Kennard house was sold and removed to
a nearby location on Deer Street.

*He was in the Revenue Service during his last years & capt of the Revenue
Cutter~ In early & middle life he had been a shipmaster & this place in the
Revenue was given him, as proof of the esteem in which he was held by his
fellow citizens~*

*Many years after that when some had died & others gone from Portsmouth,
my Father bought the place, took away the house & threw the lot into the
garden~*[283]

Other neighbors she thought worthy of observation were the Misses Slade and the

Misses Hart. There were three generations of Harts living on Deer Street from 1702 to 1830. The Misses Hart were probably members of the same family who built and sold the Deer Street home to William Rice.

> *When I was a child I used to think a great deal of the three Misses Hart & the two Misses Slade~ They were all probably in their forties when I first observed them~ Every evening about dusk Miss Polly & Miss Susan went down Deer Street to visit the Misses Hart~*[284]

> *They were tall, thin, pale ladies & in summer evenings wore cardinals or short cloaks of pale blue satin trimmed with a swans down~ Their father said when he gave them those Cardinals "Lord love ye gals if these don't get ye husbands nothing else will,"~ When the Misses Hart returned their visits I do not know, but probably they whipped down the garden walk round Betsy Walker's corner & through School St~*

> *The Misses Slade lived on Vaughn St~ next door to the house Daniel Webster once lived in & their brother Sam was the acknowledged head of the family~ He was a tall, narrow, dried up bachelor, who sold vinegar on Spring hill~*[285]

Spring Hill Market was a popular market place located near the wharves just below where Bow intersects Ceres Street. Its name came from a natural spring that flowed there without interruption, providing all who came with a supply of pure fresh water. For years this structure, which jutted out about twenty feet over the edge of the wharves at the town harbor was the primary market place in the city. It was open on three sides and covered with a huge, sagging, wooden awning.

This was where fresh fish was sold right off the fishing boats, along with other provisions brought in by barges from nearby farms. During Sarah's childhood fleets of twenty or more canoes traveled down the Piscataqua each Saturday morning, manned mainly by women from small surrounding Maine towns, and laden down with baskets of fresh vegetables, fruits, berries, and ciders to sell.[286]

> *There was another brother, Jacob, who went to parts unknown, made a fortune & never came home, but one day there came a rumor that Jacob Slade had married a very rich & very highly connected lady & that they were coming in their own coach to visit the family in Vaughn St~*

> *The whole North End was in a fever of excitement & expectation~ Dinah said that, the Whiddens said that the preparations were enormous! & one day they came~*

> *Where the coach & horses were kept I do not know but I do know that the next Sunday they all appeared at the Old North Church in very great style & not much attention was paid that morning to the Calvinistic sermon of the Rev Israel Putnum~*

Jacob Slade in the course of his journeying picked up the story that there was a great estate waiting in England for the next Slade heir & why he did not look it up I do not know but Sam & the sisters thought so much about it that it was determined to raise money & send some competent person out to take care of their right~

After a while one Jos Which was fixed upon as just the man~ He was a handsome dashing fellow, a lawyer & a great Mason ~ I knew him well & he was very civil to me~ He went to England & it was said got hold of property in consequence, of which he was either transported or hanged, nobody ever knew which but he never came back~

Now for the Misses Hart! Miss Sally was the eldest, a woman of remarkable understanding, presence & dignity~ Then followed Miss Mary full of honest indignation & spirit, when her rights were interfered with & then Miss Betsy full of benevolence & good will~ They were all very nice ladies & their home was a delightful place to go to~

The house, an old fashioned double one, two stories, fronting on Russell St. but the family & everybody else preferred the entrance on Deer St~ A gate & a flagged walk made the entrance to the house easy & agreeable~

On each side of the walk were long narrow beds full of everything~ There were no such roses and carnations, anywhere else & as the garden sloped to the South & had the sun all day, everything was earlier than elsewhere~

But to my youthful imagination there was nothing about these ladies so impressive as their shawls~ When I was a child there came up a new style of shawl called French cashmere~ the material was partly silk & partly indian cashmere wool~ They were woven in beautiful patterns & cost from twenty to forty dollars~

When the three Misses Hart came out one Sunday in their three forty dollar "French Cashmere" long shawls, the old three Decker became alive with curiosity & excitement~ Never shall I forget my sensation as I saw them looming at the top of the rise on High St.! At the corner of School they would stop & have a few last words & handshaking with the Misses Slade, though these ladies always went to church by the way of Vaughn~[287]

The "old three Decker" Sarah referred to above was a nickname for the North Meetinghouse that stood in the center of Market Square.

The father of the Misses Hart was somewhat eccentric~ He became a widower when his children were very young & he never got over his great loss~ Whenever he heard that anyone was dying he always went to see them

& sent his love to his wife~
He had been in the Slave trade when that traffic was not thought wrong &
my grandmother Rice bought Boston of him~ Dinah & Boston were brother
& sister~

Two of Mr. Hart's daughters were married & one of them died leaving a
boy baby who was most tenderly cared for by the grandfather & aunts~The
daughter of this child now owns & lives at the old place & everything looks
fresh & respectable as in other days~1878

Dinah and Boston were slaves at her grandmother's farm in Kittery, and Sarah was very fond of them both. Captain Thomas Hart was a merchant ship captain involved in the triangular trade route out of Portsmouth around the time of the Revolution. He also imported a few slaves. Captain Hart was at one time the town moderator, and was apparently a rather pious man. He once reported a fellow captain to the magistrate for setting sail on Sunday, and then reported him for the second time for cursing after the man confronted him for filing the first report.[288]

DINAH & BOSTON

My grandmother had two slaves, Boston & Dinah & two better people never lived~ Boston was a man of great dignity & good sense~ He had one of the noblest foreheads I ever saw ~[289]

It is not known if Boston and Dinah were born in Portsmouth or if they arrived in the area on one of Captain Hart's ships during the 1760s when the slave traffic was at its peak in New England. Although there was never a large number of slaves in New England, legal documents such as wills indicate there was a small amount of African slavery in Portsmouth as early as 1645. [290]

By 1727 Portsmouth's slave population was only fifty-two, but by 1776 there were one hundred and eighty-seven slaves in the city. [291] Statistics as to the amount of slavery in Kittery during this time are not as widely available as in Portsmouth. However, even though these two communities were in different states, they shared much in common including connections between prestigious families.

The majority of black slaves in Portsmouth during this time came from the coast of Africa with New England ship captains involved in the importation and exportation of miscellaneous cargo. Captain Thomas Hart fit into this category and slaves were just one of a variety of imported goods in which he dealt. Ships such as Captain Hart's first sailed to the West Indies with merchandise, and then continued on to Africa to buy slaves. After this they returned to the West Indies, and then journeyed to the southern colonies where the majority of these slaves were sold. The remaining slaves came to New England. [292]

The preferred sex was male, as they were considered to be physically stronger in general. The majority of slaves in Portsmouth ranged in age from nine to early adolescence. Although slaves as young as nine were not ideal, they were generally strong enough to work, yet malleable enough to train for the particular needs of individual families or businesses. [293]

My first recollections of Kittery are associated with Dinah~ My Grandfather Rice bought her about 1760, when she was eighteen years old & she remained faithful & devoted to the family until 1825 or 6~[294]

Dinah and Boston fit these profiles. Sarah indicates that Dinah was eighteen when she first came to the Rice farm in Kittery in 1760, where she worked in the capacity of a house servant, and although Boston was her brother they were apparently purchased at different times, indicating he was younger. Their mother was also a slave in the area, perhaps for Captain Hart's household.

My father was the youngest of my grandmothers twelve children & she was exceedingly fond of him~ He always took tea with her on Saturday afternoons & his family often went with him~

> *As soon as Dinah saw us coming up the road, she would arrange the bowls of bread & milk on the kitchen dresser & as we always made a rush for the kitchen, the bread & milk were taken as a matter of course & dispatched accordingly~*[295]

Female slaves were not valued for their fertility, as it was not the custom to breed slaves in New England, because promiscuous sexual relationships between the slaves were looked upon as immoral. Therefore the slave owners encouraged marriage between slaves, complete with religious and official sanctions. When the bride and groom belonged to different households the marriage was performed just to legitimize sexual relationships. Slaves received no surname at the time of marriage. Children born of these unions were considered the property of the owner of the female, and they could be sold into bondage or given to a relative or neighbor. Sarah indicates this was the fate of at least one of Dinah's children.[296]

> *In her twenties, she had married a very fine looking Negro, who played the violin at parties~ My grandmother gave her a very handsome wedding to which all the Portsmouth colored people were invited, & all my grandmother's family beside~ The Colored people were served first & the dancing was kept up all night~*
>
> *There were two children born to them, one of whom was brought up by my Aunt Dennett~ When I came to know Dinah she was a widow her husband having been dead some years~*[297]

It was not uncommon in New England for slaves to work alongside family members in places of business. Many were skilled workers, such as Prime Fowle who worked as the pressman of *The New Hampshire Gazette*, the state's first newspaper, for many years. Caesar, the slave of Richard Hart, became a skilled joiner and was credited for finishing the Hart family parlor. [298]

> *I remember that Dinah, who assisted the Whiddens at those times used to tell a great deal about the sandwiches & how long they boiled the chocolate which had spice in it~*[299]

Some slaves were contracted out to work for others in the community, and it was not unusual to find slaves working on the docks or on board ships. Dinah often worked for the Whidden family preparing and serving the refreshments at the Assembly House balls. While Cuffee Whipple, a slave belonging to William Whipple played the fiddle at these balls looking down at the proceedings from his perch in the orchestra loft that hung over the ballroom entrance.[300]

In Portsmouth, as in most New England communities, slaves were taught to read and write. This was done in order to teach them to read the Bible and thus convert them to Christian beliefs. This was in direct opposition to the practice of the southern states where teaching a slave to read and write was prohibited by law. By the eighteenth century the majority of Portsmouth slaves could read, and had been converted to Christianity. They were expected to attend religious services along with the families who owned them, but were segregated from the white congregation.[301]

By this period in time slaves were identified by their given names as well as the surname of the family that owned them. This was true with Dinah and Boston who went by the name of Rice. During the eighteenth century Africans in Portsmouth created a sub-community that existed alongside the greater one. Within this black community some of the city's wealthiest families were represented, and the social status of these slaves was proportional to that enjoyed by their owner.

The leaders of this community set up their own government, and each June during a slave holiday elected their own "king." They also elected a sheriff and deputy. This mock election was generally followed by a parade, and their elected "king" led slaves dressed in their owner's finest castoffs. This procession ended up in Portsmouth Plains, where a daylong celebration, filled with games, bonfires, dancing, and fiddle or drum music was held.[302]

This annual ritual was practiced all over New England. In most other communities governors were chosen rather than kings, but Portsmouth was a community with royal leanings. Although these elected positions did not confer real power within the provincial courts, they did allow the slaves to control the fate of members of their own community accused of breaking the law. They not only sat in judgment and carried out their own sentencing; they also oversaw all punishments.[303]

When the Revolution began New Hampshire offered to give slaves who enlisted to fight for three years the same bounty as whites. This sum was large enough to purchase their manumission papers, and many slaves earned their freedom this way.[304] When the war began William Whipple was appointed Brigadier General of the First New Hampshire Regiment, and he expected Prince, one of the two royal brothers owned by him, to join him in battle. However, when Prince objected to fighting for the liberty of others while he remained enslaved, Whipple immediately granted him his freedom on the condition that Prince agreed to fulfill his "duty" to his country. He did fight for the country's liberty, and following the war Prince was a free man.[305]

Many other slaves joined the fight against the British, and most that did so in the North believed a victory for America would bring their freedom as well. Some New England slaves sought a legal victory before the Revolution ended. In 1773 four blacks from Boston sent a petition the Massachusetts's legislature requesting that slaves be granted their freedom. This petition was followed by a similar one in 1779 presented to the New Hampshire legislature from a group of twenty slaves who lived in the seacoast area.[306] Similar petitions came from other parts of New England. While none of these petitions received the positive response for which they had hoped, they helped to pave the way for eventual legislative action that freed the slaves all over New England. [307]

In Vermont slavery was abolished in 1777.[308] The Massachusetts Constitution and Bill of Rights signed in 1783 clearly stated that all men were born free and equal. The New Hampshire Constitution and Bill of Rights that followed a year later was modeled closely after this, indicating equality for all men. However, for many years there was much confusion and debate over the true meaning of this phrase. By 1790 Massachusetts had confirmed that their Constitution did indeed abolish slavery in that state, but this clarification took an act of legislation. This ruling was inclusive of Maine, then part of Massachusetts, where Boston and Dinah resided. In 1790 the first official United States census listed no slaves in Kittery, Maine, but in Portsmouth it listed 36 slaves and 26 free Negroes as residents of the city.[309]

It would seem that the New Hampshire Constitution of 1784 never clearly abolished slavery to the satisfaction of all, and many legal scholars have argued both sides of the question.[310] But following the spirit of the times the majority of New Hampshire slave owners freed their slaves after this date, as did the rest of the New England states. However, as late as 1840 the New Hampshire census still listed one slave. [311] Of course the argument over slavery in New Hampshire was definitely settled following the Civil War when the Thirteenth Amendment was finally ratified. However, the legality of slavery was a moot point by then at least in New England.

Many freed slaves remained at the homes of the families that had owned them, where they continued to work in the capacity of servants. Some remained out of a sense of loyalty. While others, especially older slaves who had no place else to go stayed out of economic necessity. It would seem that both Dinah and Boston remained at the Rice farm until the death of Sarah's grandmother.

> *After my Grandmother's death Dinah came to town to live with her mother, who was very aged & who required her care~ They lived in half of a very small house in Green Street~ & old Dinah was the oldest & most dreadful looking Negro that I ever saw~ She was imported by a Portsmouth man & his family always provided for her ~*[312]

> *After my grandmother died he* [Boston] *came to Portsmouth & set up a horse & truck~ He died of consumption, when he was about fifty years old~ His home was with my Aunt Dennett in Daniel St~*[313]

In 1821, about the time that Dinah lived in Portsmouth, the *Portsmouth City Directory* listed twenty-eight "Coloured Persons" living in the city; neither her name nor Boston's is listed.[314]

> *Dinah Rice as she was called had the most remarkable way of mending her clothes~ She would tack on a piece of cloth above a hole, which so long as she was quiet, did not draw attention, but when out in the wind the flutter and display were wonderful to behold~*[315]

Slaves or former slaves such as Dinah and Boston relied upon others to supply them with cast off clothing or new clothing that was generally quite plain and simple. It is possible that Dinah's tendency to adorn her clothing with patches of cloth was not a botched attempt at mending, as Sarah seemed to imply, but rather an effort to embellish her plainer, worn out clothing with patterns of the bright colors traditionally favored within the culture of the African community.

> *As the quarters with her mother were very narrow, she might be seen any hour in the day drifting from house to house over all the North End~ She had the entree at every house and was popular everywhere ~*

> *She averaged three visits a day at my Father's & usually made a Bee line for the cider cellar where she emptied one mug & filled another & after foraging the Pantry, (she took her meals standing) she would depart for*

"pastures new"~

She had all the harmless gossip of the neighborhood and was the most good natured & kindest person alive~ She was the first to call me Miss Sarah & this before I felt any claim to such consideration~

She had intuitive reverence for the white race & was very proud of the family to which she belonged~ She always spoke of them as "High Folks"~

She was very fond of taking little children into Betsy Ward's Shop and treating them to two or three cents worth of walnuts~ If she had contented herself with nuts at Miss Ward's, she would have lived many years longer but three cents worth of Rum taken one awful evening in the winter, probably caused her death~ She was found dead on the ice early next morning~

Dear old Dinah! I have often said there would be no Heaven for me if Dinah were not there & if I do not meet her it will not be owing to any superior claim on my part~[316]

Betsy Ward's was apparently a grog shop, where a small amount of rum could be purchased like the penny candy sold to the neighborhood children. Within two years of Dinah's death, the *Portsmouth City Directory* indicated a significant increase in the number of blacks since 1821. Although they were still listed under the "Coloured Persons" section, at the back of book, the black population had increased by more than a third.[317] Slavery had literally died out in Portsmouth, and a new generation of free native African Americans emerged.

ALMSHOUSE RESIDENTS

*There was no alms house on the Piscataqua until about eighty years ago &
the old & homeless poor wandered about from house to house, sitting on
the kitchen settee by day & sleeping as they might by night~*[318]

Sarah recalled other lost souls who roamed the streets of Portsmouth during her
childhood. The poor, the physically or mentally handicapped, the aged, and the
infirm were not totally isolated from the greater community during the early part of
the nineteenth century. Before 1850 there were very few institutions in Portsmouth
other than the town almshouse and a few private charities to assist those in need.

From the beginning the poor laws in America were based on English heritage and
reflected the policies of the poor laws in England, designed to contain or control the
indigent population, as well as to provide basic sustenance for those unable to provide for
themselves.[319]

At first the needs of the poor in most New England towns were met by farming out
the paupers to local families. Portsmouth may have followed the custom of auctioning off
their care to the lowest bidder at town meetings. Payment varied depending on the ability of
the pauper to work. Some were paid up to sixty cents a week, while others received as little
as two cents a week. The town generally paid for clothing, medical care, and burial when
necessary.[320]

Shelter and food provided for the needy at these homes were often substandard, and
the sleeping quarters inadequate. It would not have been unusual to bed these unfortunates
in unheated attic garrets, barn lofts, or nothing more than temporary bedding placed by the
hearthside at night.

*There was old Ross who tired the families out by turns on both sides of the
river~*

*There was old Crosswell who had been all winter at one house & slept by
the kitchen fire~ As spring drew near, a son of the family & a wag, went to
the top of the great wide mouthed chimney & called down at twelve o'clock
at night, in solemn tones, "Crosswell, Crosswell" "Yea Lord thy servant
heareth," said Crosswell, "Crosswell take up thy staff & travel toward
Newington, for brother Nutter hath need of thee there"*

*Yea Lord was the response & in the morning the family had the satisfaction
of hearing him announce his intention to depart having been commanded
by the Lord~* [321]

In return for these accommodations the recipients were expected to work to earn their
keep when able. By taking in these town wards families gained not only a stipend from the
town, but when possible a free work hand or kitchen helper. In the case of young children

taken from their families or orphans, the providers received an apprentice bound to them for an undetermined time. Some arrangements worked out well and became permanent, but more often than not they were temporary, and the indigent moved from family to family never really finding a place within the society.

Sarah contradicted her earlier assertion that there was no almshouse in Portsmouth eighty years before, and stated correctly that Portsmouth had one of the first shelters for the indigent in the country. Built in 1716, it was located on the corner of Chestnut and Porter Streets, where the Music Hall now stands. Her contemporary, and fellow author and historian, Charles Brewster, claimed this was the first workhouse for the poor in America and Europe.[322]

> *The first alms house built in Portsmouth was a small house in Prison Lane*
> *(now Chestnut St) where the music hall now stands~ Rebecca Austin kept*
> *this house thirty years~*[323]

However, Brewster's claim was not entirely accurate. Boston built an almshouse in 1660, and another in 1682 when the first was destroyed by fire. These first almshouses housed the "vicious poor" alongside those deemed to be the "worthy poor," and acted as prisons as well as homes for the poor.[324]

When Portsmouth built this first almshouse it was in response to a large jump in the number of poor all over New England. Many more people applied for town relief around this time, and because of this welfare became more institutionalized.[325] These institutions were for the most part paid for by taxpayers not eager to spend their tax dollars taking care of slackers, and there were no frills. Although the town did not want to pay for their care, the almshouse residents didn't always have the option of leaving, as the secondary purpose of welfare was to keep vagrancy under control for the common good.[326]

> *The next house was on Court St~ Very long of one story~ It had a southern*
> *exposure & a fine view of South Pond~ The yard was very large & sunny*
> *& I liked when a child to go there and see Judge Sherburne's peacocks &*
> *talk with the funny people who were always out round the back door~ Polly*
> *Beck, Nabby Clear & Johnny Tilton were my perfect delight~ The paupers*
> *were always at work picking oakum or hair for furniture or mattresses~*[327]

In 1756 a new Portsmouth almshouse was erected on Jaffrey Street, which is now Court Street. It was a large facility built on the site of the present fire station with room for city offices, the town library, and the union hall. The mentally ill or handicapped were housed there alongside the poor and physically disabled. All were expected to earn their keep.[328] When Sarah was a child she came to know some of the residents when she went to visit her relative, Judge Sherburne, who lived nearby.

> *There was Johnny Tilton who was in the Alms House & carried the corn*
> *to be ground twice a week & wore peacock feathers in his steeple crowned*
> *hat~ He sang as he went & was wiser than he looked~*
>
> *One day the miller asked him what he knew~ "I know says Johnny that*

miller's hogs grow fat~ And what don't you know Johnny "I don't know whose corn they grow fat upon"~ Another time someone asked him if he could fly~ Yes, says Johnny but it hurts me to light~

I must tell of Mistress Molly James who usually sat in the door of her house of one room, at the crossroads interrogating every passerby who, when she saw her nephew coming up the road, put the smoking meat on top of the chest of drawers & invited him to "cabbage but no meat, MARK"~

She had lent her mourning bonnet so many times for funerals, that at last when it came home tattered, she exclaimed that "My God! This will never take another high poll"~

There was Sally Blank too, who after refusing assistance many times, said finally "Yes I will take it, for if I do not receive, how can people have the luxury of giving"~

There was Sally Hunt who told me I was her garden angel~

There was Tommy Mars, who used to drop in at meal times & always refused the first invitation to eat but would finally sit up to table & clear off everything, with the remark that he had no appetite, but somehow one mouthful had <u>driv</u> down another![329]

The mentally ill were also housed in these early almshouses. In Portsmouth's second almshouse some rooms were set aside for the mentally afflicted, along with funds to pay physicians and nurses to pay for needed medical treatment.[330]

I had been married several years when the brick alms house was built~ Many insane people were placed there in those days as there was no asylum in any state until a later period~ Mass excepted~[331]

In the 1820s and 30s the welfare population had increased substantially in Portsmouth. The second almshouse was very overcrowded and the medical facilities were considered unsanitary. After much discussion as to how best care for and contain this population, a new almshouse was built in 1834. It was built on land near North Mill Pond, where a one hundred and sixty-five-acre farm owned by Thomas Scheafe had stood for many years.[332]

After the city purchased it in 1833, they built a large brick work farm complex along the section that eventually became known as Myrtle Street. It was designed to accommodate two hundred and fifty people. Not a great deal is known about the hospital facilities, but in 1849 Dr. Samuel Coues, the son of Goodwin's longtime business partner, was appointed to the position of Almshouse Physician.[333]

The plan was for the residents to farm the land, and it was hoped that eventually the facility would become self-sustaining. However, that never happened as many of the poor that were capable of laboring stayed away from the town "Poor Farm," as it came to be known. Of those that remained about eight percent suffered from various forms of mental illness, and some were quite elderly. The population reached only about fifty percent occupancy during the time it was in existence.[334]

One resident of the almshouse who had several generations of service with Sarah's family, and one with whom she took a personal interest, was Esther Benson.

There was a beautiful girl who lived with my grandparents & my mother whose name was Esther B__[335] *When my grandfather Parker bought the estate at Lee & built a fine house & outbuildings upon it (which was about twenty years before the Revolution) he removed the elder members of the family to Lee leaving his daughters in town~ These elder members consisted of my grandmother, her Father & Mother (Mr. & Mrs. Ephraim Sherburne) & Mrs. Parker my grandfather's mother~ These last three were more than eighty years of age and very infirm~*

My great grandmother Sherburne could not leave her chamber & a little girl named Esther Winkley was brought from Kittery to wait on her~ She also assisted my grandmother in the care of the other older people and remained until they had all died~

After that she lived with my mother in town & assisted her in the care of her children~ She afterward lived some months with me & had the care of one of my babies~ So it will be perceived that she lived as a nurse with four generations~[336]

When about twenty~five years old she married a man by the name of Benson and had many children~ Benson was one of the worst men that ever lived and the scene of her wretchedness was the house now called the Haliburton house~ The house has been more than once enlarged, in fact two or three times & it must have been a mere den in her day~[337]

Her husband treated her brutally, turned her out of doors & in this forlorn condition she took to drink & to wandering & for twenty years found refuge where she might all over New England & even in the city of New York~ Occasionally she turned up in her native town with disheveled hair, miserably clad & followed by a troop of boys~[338]

She had fallen as low in drunkenness as it was possible for anyone to do...an outcast from all decent society & yet she had been one of the most beautiful persons in features, complexion & figure that could be found~[339]

When I was young once in two or three years, she would seem to have broken loose from some foreign almshouse, for she traveled on foot several times to New York & other states & then the cry would go up "did you know that Esther Benson is round again?" The boys always called her Esther & people were afraid of her & shunned her~

She finally came out of it all, to find her husband dead & her children dead or scattered~ She had become once more a sober woman and was living in our almshouse, when she came to me and asked me to let her come & take care of my baby~ It was my fourth, my Georgie & I took her & she proved a real comfort~[340]

She was more than seventy but retained something of beauty in the clearness of her eyes & the whiteness of her neck & arms~ In three months she was tired and glad to go back to the alms house where she could pass her days without care or work~

She told me that nothing could exceed the poverty she endured with her husband, that she & her many children were always hungry, that her husband often beat her but that the blow which broke her spirit and drove her to drunkenness & the streets was bringing in a strange woman to share their only bed~[341]

Because of the dreadful conditions that existed in most workhouses when Esther was young, many of these unskilled and unschooled women with no families to turn to for help, turned instead to prostitution to support themselves. Often women, like Esther, also turned to drink in a futile effort to gain temporary comfort and solace from their problems. In 1817 about the time Esther was in her middle years, the Portsmouth Society for the Suppression of Vice did a study which determined that fifty-six percent of welfare recipients in town fell into the category of those made "Poor from Vice," a common euphemism for alcoholism at the time.[342]

She found refuge in our new brick alms house, came & assisted me in the care of one of my babies & died much respected by the inmates of the house~ She had served five generations of my family very faithfully~[343]

Sarah's contact with Esther continued after she left her employment for the last time. Sarah recalled with dismay how the older woman talked her out of a treasured keepsake by taking advantage oF her trusting nature and playing upon her emotions.

But though she had become sober in her last years~ She had not become a saint, as a little incident will show~

She came a year or two before her death to ask for tea, sugar &c as was her wont, and with tears in her eyes begged me, if I had any garment once belonging to my mother, that I would give it to her, that she when death came, might be surrounded by something associated with early & happy days~

Now I had treasured several things that once belonged to my mother & among them a white Dimity gown, open in front & ruffled all around, everywhere~

I had seen my mother wear it and thought it looked beautiful, indeed it was the last dress in which I remembered her & for that reason I had cherished it, but Esther wept so in speaking of her and there seemed so few left to speak so feelingly that my heart softened & I gave her the gown~

The next week she was met by one of my daughters in Market Street, with black alpaca skirt, white gown blowing open and black crape bonnet~!!! [344]

Another resident of the Alms House, a life long friend as well as a relative, was her cousin Phebe. It is not known what Phebe's last name was, but Sarah made it clear Phebe was always welcomed into the Goodwin home.

I had an old friend who from a severe fall had the misfortune to have intervals of insanity~ Had there been asylums for the insane in her youth she might have been cured but for such at that time there were only bars & chains or the Alms House~

About half the time she was incarcerated, the other half she was a refined delicate woman who loved dearly to visit her friends & adorn herself with such odds & ends of finery as came in her way~

She was decidedly pretty and at sixty looked scarcely thirty~ As long as her mother lived she was confined during her insane periods in a barred & bolted room but after her mothers death there was no place for her but the Alms House~

Three or four times a year, she would spend a day with us & she distributed these favors pretty equally among her friends~ All were kind to her & not averse to her visits, though gentlemen not so much interested, could have dispensed with her company saying that she had the odor of the Poor House, but I knew she was clean & that it was only a fancy & so would receive her & make her welcome~

Her table manners were exceptionally dainty~ She ate slowly & used her knife & fork after the most approved rules~ Indeed she was never in haste & all her movements were calm & dignified~

She learned a great many songs in her youthful days and loved to sing them~ When she came to visit me I always asked her to sing~ She was sure to give us "The Starling" & "Sweet Lass of Richmond Hill," her two favorites~

She usually took an early leave after tea but not until with many whispers she had asked for tea, sugar, cake, dried fruit, pins, needles, tape, cord &c &c when she would depart with a fancy bag a yard long, full of all she wanted~ This bag was made of bits of lace & muslin & all white & very narrow with a string at the top~ A happier woman there was not than she, when the bag was filled & she was ready for her walk home~

Her entire freedom from envy was perhaps her most remarkable trait~ All her cousins were independent & so far as she could see, happy, & she rejoiced in their prosperity~ She would often say to me "How thankful I am for so many friends~You are all so good to me"

Once a fashionable man, a stranger was to dine with us & Phebe arrived~ There was some discussion as to Phebe's fitness but I was firm~ She was my relation & I would take the consequences & she was presented~

Our guest was delighted~ He was informed before dinner as to her belongings & to the state of the case pro & con, & seemingly eager for enlightenment, asked her all manner of questions, about the "Institution" & her associates or inmates as she called them~

In the course of years the happiness of meeting her at our table was often repeated & he enjoyed it thoroughly~

Once when he came back to tea he remarked that he had waited on Phebe home~ That he had met her at the Creek, stemming a stiff northwester, but he thought the northwester had the worst of it~ It was not true but it gave him a chance to be facetious~[345]

On another occasion Phebe was presented to five or six fashionable ladies visiting from New York. To Sarah's delight Phebe also charmed them.

Another time when she was passing the day with us six or eight fashionable young friends, mostly, from New York, who were spending the summer in South Berwick, arrived to tea, Phebe & I were in the parlor & they were shown into another~

What is to be done about Phebe? I thought~ anyhow she must be presented~ So after a while I said "Have you young ladies ever read Cowper's Kate "She begs an idle pin from all she meets" And then she would sit & weep at what a sailor suffers~ Oh yes some of them said –Why?

Because said I, I have her here in this house & she sings charmingly, don't you want to see to see her? They sprang to their feet & became enthusiasts for the pleasure & then I presented them as if she had been a princess, & she actually made all the pleasure of their visit~ They gathered around her & she became inspired & sang all her songs for them & they were delighted~[346]

Sarah always acknowledged and welcomed into her home her less fortunate cousin who resided at the town almshouse during much of her adult life.

> *She was very much respected & admired among the "inmates" & had their warmest pity & sympathy~ One day the news came that Phebe was free! No more Alms House! No more incarceration for the gentle spirit!*[347]

The Goodwin family was involved in charitable enterprises for the relief of the poor in Portsmouth throughout the nineteenth Century. In the Portsmouth area Ichabod Goodwin was for many years the president of the Howard Benevolent Society, a charitable organization that helped the poor to heat their homes during the winter. He was also a founding member of the Portsmouth Marine Society, a nationwide organization that paid for the medical care of indigent seamen. In Portsmouth these men were cared for at the Seaman's Home on Market and Bow Streets.[348]

Ichabod was also one of the founders of the New Hampshire chapter of The Society for the Prevention of Cruelty to Animals; an organization credited with opening the way for child protection laws in the United States. Some, and perhaps all of the Goodwin daughters, along with Sarah were members of the Ladies General Charitable Society in Portsmouth, which offered relief to the "deserving poor."[349]

In the 1880s, long after Esther Benson and Phebe had died, the almshouse was closed. The poor remained in Portsmouth, as did the town's obligation to care for them. However, by that time it was clear that giving pensions to those able to live alone was the most beneficial and economical way to care for the poor.

The land where the town farm stood was sold to Frank Jones the brewer. By the turn of the century Irish immigrants settled in that area known as the Creek.

SCHOOLS

In many New England towns, especially those settled under Puritan rule, schools were opened shortly after the first settlers arrived. This was done in order to teach all children to read and write, so they could read the Bible, and understand the religious principles underlying the laws of the state.[350] However, town records indicate the first public classes in Portsmouth were not held until 1696, and they were quite sporadic, and open only to males whose parents could split the costs with the town.[351]

The first Latin Grammar School of New Hampshire opened in Portsmouth around 1713.[352] This was supported, in part by the town, as they agreed to pay the schoolmaster's salary.[353] At the time most grammar schools in New England were private schools of higher learning for middle to upper class boys destined for a professional life as a minister, barrister, or other professions fit for gentlemen.[354]

During the Revolution education was nearly forgotten in most New England towns, when many grammar schools were closed to save expenses. By the time the Revolution ended, the majority of Latin Grammar Schools had evolved into free academies for male scholars.[355] Around this time the question of educating young women in Portsmouth received some attention.

In 1780 a Mr. Dearborn, an auctioneer and an inventor, opened a private school for young ladies in his home, located in the vicinity of Market Square. The first year his school attracted just six students, as most people thought it unnecessary to educate girls. However, within a year his classes were flourishing, but after two more years business took him to Boston and the school closed.[356]

Dearborn's classes had been so successful that in 1784 the town agreed to educate the female scholars at town expense. Existing accounts indicate the teacher chosen to teach that first group of young ladies was superior. However, this teacher left Portsmouth after the first year, and his replacement was a duller sort, who failed to attract enough students to fill a classroom, and eventually Portsmouth's first public school for women was discontinued.[357]

When Sarah was young she attended a series of small home schools. At that time there was a public academy in town, but enrollment was limited to male children who had already mastered reading and writing. Education for females was limited to private schools, or for those able to attend the summer sessions two hours a day, between six and seven in the mornings and five and six in the evenings.[358]

For the youngest children, both male and female, there were dame schools generally run by spinsters or housewives, many of whom were not qualified to teach school. These were often combinations of nursery school and kindergarten where the children learned basic skills such as the alphabet, Biblical maxims, recitation, and deportment. They were both public and privately funded. Due to the cost of heating and difficulty of travel in the winter, dame schools were held during the summer.

From Sarah's description of her first school, it seems to fit into this category. Sarah may have been as young as three or four when she attended this school, as there was no official age when children first entered the school system at that time. Rather school attendance, which was not mandatory, depended on many factors such as convenience, family income, location, and the child's readiness. [359]

> *My first school was under Marm Plaisted~ She sat in the middle of the room in an arm chair, her husband's big cane resting against it~ About twenty children usually attended & they were all very much afraid of her cane~*
>
> *She had sharp black eyes & wore large round spectacles & a mob cap~ When she dismissed school she would say "Elizabeth Ham, courtesy & go" "Sarah Rice courtesy & go" Daniel Ham bow & go" "John Boardman bow & go" & so on until the whole were dismissed~*
>
> *My next school was to a Miss Sally Hart~ I did not like that school so I shall not tell anything about it~*[360]

It was not uncommon for young children to attend sewing schools. Many of these "accomplishment schools," which focused on teaching one skill, were private. They fell into the category of dame schools, and were primarily attended by girls sent to learn the feminine arts of sewing, quilting, needlepoint, lacing, or crocheting.

> *Then I went to a Mrs. Williams in Mark Lane & there I accomplished my first triumph in linen shirt making~ My father put on his spectacles & examined buttonholes & stitching pronouncing it all <u>good</u>~*[361]

Young boys also attended these schools, and often teachers taught these boys to knit and sew just to keep them orderly and quiet. However, this was not always a successful tactic, and then teachers were forced to rely on other modes of discipline.

> *There was one boy at that school so active that he had to be fastened to a staple in the floor by the side of the teacher~ He was always opening his mouth & gnashing his teeth & pretending to bite flies like a dog~ The teacher supplied him with pieces of silk to ravel out but he was regularly tied as soon as he came in~ He made a very useful & respectable man~*
>
> *Then I was sent to Mrs. John Briard in the same room~ She was an Irish woman of some education & devoted to making pillow lace & pearling~ I don't think I learned anything there~*[362]

Privately run religious schools were common. At these the students received religious instruction, along with basic skills of reading and writing.

> *After that I went to a Mrs. Richards whose father had been a Universalist minister~ The school room was at the corner of Court & Middle near the reservoir~ We had good times there & there was a show of learning~*

During these years the free public academy in Portsmouth was the Old Latin Grammar

School on State Street that had opened in 1735. However, during the fire of 1813 all but the walls of the brick building was totally destroyed. For a while classes for the young male scholars were conducted at Jefferson Hall until the schoolhouse was restored.

Then in 1815 there was a complete overhaul of the town's public school system. Eight district grammar schools were opened and the brick schoolhouse was closed. These schools, which provided for the education of girls as well as boys, offered equal seating and instruction to all scholars in Portsmouth who were eight or older.[363]

However, equal seating still meant separate classrooms. Sarah, who turned ten that year, indicates that a male instructor oversaw the education of the boys while a female instructor taught Sarah and her all female classmates. This was not an uncommon practice at the time, and it was one that continued for many years.

> *Then I went to the Academy which at that time had a full board of trustees with Preceptor & Preceptress~ I was in the fifth class with five or six girls about my own age but the Preceptress was bordering on insanity & very melancholy & kept me in strokes a whole year & often carried me to her boarding house as a punishment for not getting my lessons ~ & such dreadful lessons for a little girl ~ every day a column of spelling & definitions in Walker's Dictionary~ a whole page in Cumming's geography & a page in Murray's grammar~ Well poor soul in one year she was sent to some asylum & I was relieved~*[364]

Some of the teachers of that time were quite competent and qualified, but many were very young, often as young as sixteen. These teachers received little training; many didn't possess the necessary skills to cope with the demands of teaching. Unable to maintain order by reasoning with their students, they sometimes relied upon harsher methods of corporal punishment to control their young charges. For the most part parents did not object to harsh discipline in the classroom during this time.

> *Then I was sent to Mr Blake & Miss Olney! Such a pretender as she was~ It was all prayers, bible reading, fears & nonsense~ Miss Francis afterward Mrs Lydia Maria Childs, was assistant to Mrs Olney & she was by no means appreciated~*[365]

Lydia Maria Childs, the teacher Sarah wrote so disparagingly about, later authored a popular book entitled *The Frugal Housewife*, which instructed other women on the finer arts of housekeeping and childrearing.

> *After that Mr. Austin & his sister, Miss Sarah, opened a rare seminary for young ladies & gentlemen~ I learned all I wanted to there & for three years had a grand good time~*
>
> *By this time I was fifteen years old, & as Miss Willard's school for young ladies was in great repute I went there, (Mr Austin having removed his sisters & mother into the country)~*[366]

Mary Willard the daughter of the Rev. Joseph Willard, President of Harvard College, and Mary Scheafe, a native of Portsmouth, moved to Portsmouth in 1817 with her recently widowed mother and her sister Lucinda. She opened a school for young ladies in the North End, and although she was there less than a decade she attracted a large following of young female scholars during those years. Sarah entered her school in 1820, at age fifteen.

Betsy Walker's house removed to give place to new school house corner of High & School Streets~ The large two story home where lived & kept school my dear friend & teacher Miss Mary Willard~[367]

At Miss Willard's I found everybody in advance of me~indeed I found that I knew almost nothing~ I was very much ashamed of my ignorance & resolved it should not be my fault if I did not come up with the rest before many months~ I studied hard ~ taking notes of everything & looking them over constantly~ By this means I arrived at the head of one class after another & when there I generally staid~

Miss Willard was a perfect lady~ She was the eldest daughter of President Willard of Harvard College & her Father had taken great pains with her education~

She was quiet & dignified & had the improvement of her scholars greatly at heart~ I was three years at her school & always felt the strongest motives to learn~

Three mornings in the week, she read one hour in Plutarch's Lives & on Friday morning one hour in Bonicastle's Astronomy~ She expected us to take notes & on one day in the week questioned us in relation to her readings, as well as to our other studies~[368]

Clara Pearse & I took lessons in stenography (shorthand) we wrote each other notes continually by way of practice~ The vowels were represented by the dots & the consonants by other characters~[369]

We studied aloud & talked aloud except during reading or recitations~ I think it was the most perfect school I had ever known anything about~ Every body learned or almost everybody~ Every body was happy & revered & loved the teacher~[370]

A letter from Mary Willard posted on July 26th 1817 to her brother Joseph offers some insight into her impressions of Portsmouth. Some of her comments indicate she wasn't overly impressed with the intellectual offerings of the city.

There is a dearth of communicable matter here at present; indeed we are generally in a pretty vapid state as you know; the President's visit of which you heard enough or too much probably produced considerable excitation;

but the calm the ennui, that succeeds such excitation, depresses the heart below its common level.[371]

President James Monroe visited Portsmouth on July 12, 1817 as part of a grand tour of the northeastern states. The town turned out in grand style to greet the President who was escorted into town by the cavalry.[372] The President stayed at the home of one of the Wentworths, and one evening he dined at the State Street home of Jeremiah Mason, an influential political acquaintance.[373]

The following day was Sunday, and the President paid a call on former Governor Langdon, an old acquaintance. He attended two church services that day. In the morning he went to St. John's Episcopalian Church on Chapel Street, and in the afternoon to the North Congregational Meeting House in Market Square, where he sat in the same pew George Washington had once occupied in 1789.[374] The Willard sisters attended the Congregational service, and later Mary wrote to her brother describing the special attentions shown them by the president.

> *There was one circumstance connected with the President's visit of particular interest to us; when the head of the Nation was entering Portsmouth Saturday, whom should we spy in the first or second carriage in the train, with hat off and spectacles on and look of full importance, but our dear friend Dr. Waterhouse...the next day whom should Miss Polly {Mary Willard} be called down to see but Dr. Waterhouse...he proposed accompanying us to Meeting... .*
>
> *As it was rather late before we set off we met throngs of people, greater numbers being out than usual in the hope of seeing the President...I thought that people stared at us very much...little did I think with how much honor we were looked up to. We afterwards learned it was noised abroad that the President was waiting upon the Miss Willards to meeting. Happy, happy, happy, fair!!!*[375]

Another letter in the Willard family collection, posted from Portsmouth on November 21st of 1821, from Lucinda Willard to her brother Joseph, contained a reference to the school, and less than flattering comments about Portsmouth.

> *I think Mary will continue to do a great deal of good here and must inevitably contribute to lessen the frivolity and love of riches in the town by giving her pupils treasures within~*[376]

Miss Mary Willard did indeed give Sarah "treasures within" and Sarah developed a deep love of learning that stayed with her throughout her life.

> *I owe Miss Willard a great deal she inspired me with a great desire for useful information~*[377]

Shortly after Sarah completed her education, many New England states began to require teacher certification. As a result three normal schools opened in the region about then, offering a free education to those willing to teach in public schools. [378]

THE OLD "THREE DECKER"

*My mother's family had been worshippers at the North Church from the
time it was built in 1714~ My father whose religious faith was of the most
liberal character, having great love for God and full of gratitude toward
him yet determined to take his family to the old church as their mother
would have wished~*[379]

The North End Meetinghouse played a significant role in Sarah's life as well as the life of the community throughout the years. Known as the old "Three Decker," it was the town's meetinghouse prior to the building of a town hall. During the Revolution this was where Portsmouth's "tea party" was held on December 16th of 1773, when concerned townspeople gathered there to plan the best course of action to take against the onerous tea tax the Royal Crown had placed upon her colonies.[380]

This was not Portsmouth's first house of worship. An Episcopalian Church, built in 1638 on the southeast corner of the town Glebe, today's Pleasant Street, predated all the others. The parcel of land known as the Glebe land was fifty acres of cornfields and meadowlands given to the church by the town just prior to the start of Puritan rule.[381] When the town came under Puritan rule in 1640 the Congregational Church became the official community church, and inherited the rights to the Glebe land. The Episcopalian Church on Pleasant Street then became the first Congregational meetinghouse in Portsmouth.[382]

In less than two decades the town outgrew this small building, and in 1657 they built a new meetinghouse at the fork of Marcy and South Streets, at the time convenient to the homes of the majority of worshippers. As the years went by the population grew, and expanded into the North End of Portsmouth. By the start of the eighteenth century the congregation was so large that it was clear a bigger meetinghouse was needed. However, a controversy arose over the location of this new structure, which eventually divided the congregation.

Residents of the North End, by then the majority of the parishioners, voted to build the new meetinghouse on the northeast corner of the Glebe right in the center of today's Market Square at the site of the present North Church. Most of the South End members were unhappy with this location. So in 1711 they split away from the main body of the congregation and voted to remain at the old South End meetinghouse, which survived until 1863.[383]

The North End Meetinghouse, completed in 1712, was an imposing wooden structure, with three stories, two galleries, and three tiers of small diamond shaped windows with lead sashes. There were entrances on the north, south, and east sides of the meetinghouse. At the top was a bell tower with an open belfry. A one hundred and fifty-foot steeple was added soon after, and a cross-shaped vane topped the peak of the steeple by 1732.[384]

*I remember a great deal about the "old three decker" as people were fond
of calling it~ Two galleries surrounded the north, east & south sides~ The
pulpit on the west side with its great dark sounding board both of solid oak*

looked very solemn & impressive~[385]

A heavy pulpit stood in the western end of the meetinghouse surrounded by the large sounding board, and the plaster ceiling that rose above the two galleries was painted blue when Sarah was young. It was common during those years to paint church ceilings sky blue to subtly suggest the heavenly realm of Paradise from which God looked down upon his congregation gathered below.

> *The old three decker was painted deep sky blue & the roof was so high that it seemed to me like the sky~ There were wooden pegs over the seats for the mens hats & when I was first taken to meeting at four years of age I began aloud during the sermon to count the pegs over Mr. Ackerman's pew~ My brother had me under the seat in a trice & I never repeated the offense~*[386]

There were strict rules of conduct to follow in meeting at that time, and for twenty-five years the church sexton who maintained perfect order as the tithing man, was an elderly gentleman named William Vaughan. Sarah recalls how quick he was to march rude little boys firmly to the pulpit steps where they were made to sit throughout the entire service with the disapproving eyes of the congregation upon them. In addition, stoves were not allowed in the meetinghouse, nor was there an organ at that time. [387] All of these rules made it difficult for a young child to sit through the lengthy services that went throughout the morning.

> *People dressed very thin & there were no stoves in the churches earlier than 1820 ~ but we suffered terribly through the long services~ Even the theology had no effect on the young people~ I used to sit on one foot at a time to warm it & sometimes it would get asleep & that was awful when it began to wake up~*[388]

> *Children were baptized & candidates for admission to the church had the articles of the covenant read to them previous to the sermon~ I pitied them very much & thought I could never do it~*

> *They had Tithing men in those days & never can I forget seeing the Tithing man come out from somewhere & take a little boy out of a pew in the broad isle & land him on the upper step of the pulpit stairs~ Poor boy I suppose he had been catching flies & there he sat under the ministers frown & the whole congregation staring at him~*[389]

Although propriety was required in the meetinghouse then, it was apparently all right for well-behaved animals to attend services with or without their owners.

> *I am reminded of a dog owned by my father that always accompanied him by day & night~ He regularly attended church with him & my father was a most conscientious church goer~ One Sunday he was confined to bed with a cold & after the morning service a friend came in who had occupied a seat in my father's pew~*

Where is Fidel? Someone said~ He is all right said our friend, he came when the bells rang, stood up in prayer time, listened to the sermon & left with the rest of the Congregation~[390]

It was customary for families to purchase private pews in houses of worship during this time period. There were pews of varying sizes and shapes, as well as pit, wall, gallery, and aisle pews. Less affluent families sat in the gallery pews, and some rented rather than bought pews.

I remember distinctly by whom most of the pews were occupied and the intricate windings among the pit pews~ The pews were painted dark green & those who had cushions had them green also ~ except one ambitious individual in the broad isle who lined & cushioned with red~

At that time our pew was on the north side next to the corner pew occupied by Dr. Goddard & his numerous family~ Soon after my father bought a pew on the south side, which had belonged to Mr. Joseph Whipple~[391]

The Rice family pew was originally located on the north side of the meetinghouse. After his wife died, William Rice bought a pew on the south side, it might have indicated a step up to a more prestigious section of the meeting, particularly since it was right next to the spacious southeast corner pew occupied by former Governor John Langdon, and just a few seats away from Daniel Webster.[392]

Gov Langdon's pew was a wall pew on the south side of the pulpit~ The governor was screened from observation by a curtain~ When he had become very old & infirm he passed slowly up the broad isle leaning on the arm of his man servant~[393]

Governor Langdon's manservant, Cyrus Bruce, was of African descent. It is not clear if he was a freed slave or if he had always worked in the employ of Langdon as a servant. In the North the terms servant and slave were often used interchangeably in referring to household slaves. If Bruce had originally been a slave, by the time Sarah observed him he would have worked for Governor Langdon as a servant

It was said that Bruce was one of the city's most dapper dressers, second only to Governor Langdon in elegance. Charles Brewster, recalled Bruce's personal attire featured a long gold chain, seals, fine black or blue broadcloth coats, smart knee britches, silk stockings, silver shoe buckles, carefully plaited linens, and pressed ruffles. All of which spoke to his impeccable taste in gentlemen's fashions.[394]

Cyrus Bruce may have attended meeting in the Langdon family pew, but he was an exception to the rule. Although no longer considered slaves, blacks in New England were subject to segregation at this time. It was common in most New England congregations for blacks to attend the same service as the rest of the community, but as in the North Meetinghouse they were relegated to the upper gallery, along with the residents of the Alms House.

*I was an inconsequent & busy kind of a child & one Sunday I was seized
with an irrepressible desire to be initiated into the mystery of the communion
service & while the congregation was passing out I slipped upstairs into the
upper gallery where the colored people worshipped & took my place on a
line with the pulpit where I could see everything~*

*The family were much disturbed at my absence & when I appeared wanted
to know what I had to say for myself~ When I told them what I had done
my eldest sister began to look very severe but a good bachelor cousin who
happened to be present interposed and said 'Now tell me about it~ what
did you see? I replied I did not like it~ they had coffee without any cream &
bread without any butter~*[395]

The North Meetinghouse was one of Portsmouth's two houses of worship honored
during the 1789 visit from the country's first president. President Washington was a member
of the Episcopalian faith, and on the Sunday morning of his stay in Portsmouth he attended
the service at Queen's Chapel. That afternoon he did the same at the North Meetinghouse.
Both houses of worship were purportedly filled to capacity during these historical occasions.
Washington was said to have appeared quite presidential during his visits to the churches,
dressed in a complete suit of black velvet, coat, vest, black silk stockings, and black shoes
adorned by "brilliant" silver shoe buckles.[396]

Washington sat in the wall pew next to the pulpit on the south side that belonged to
William Whipple.[397] The minister at this time and also during Sarah's early childhood was Dr.
Joseph Buckminister, who came to the North Congregational Meetinghouse in Portsmouth
upon his graduation from divinity school in 1779. He was twenty-eight years old the year he
gave a sermon to the country's first president.[398]

It is not known if Buckminister was a graduate of Harvard Divinity School, but it
is quite likely that he was, as that was where most New England's Congregational clergy
trained at this time.[399]

*My cousin, Sarah Parrott, a very noble woman, whose pew was next to
Daniel Webster's told me that when the theology became very terrible the
expression on Mr. Webster's face was more awful than could be described~*

*My father once shook his head at the minister & we children would have
been glad to drop into the cellar we were so ashamed~ My father could not
bear to hear God abused~*[400]

Dr. Buckminister became quite ill in the spring of 1812, and was persuaded to seek
a health cure in Vermont. On his way there he died on June 10, 1812, and was buried in
Bennington. He was sixty-one years old at the time of death, and had spent his last thirty-
three years as the minister of the North End Meetinghouse.[401]

The congregation mourned his passing by draping the pulpit, the chandelier and both
galleries in black cloth.[402] This black draping remained for many weeks. It was still in place
when Abigail Rice died in August of that same year.

Our minister was the great Dr. Buckminister~ When he died the parish showed it's deep respect & sorrow for his loss by draping the galleries & pulpit with black broadcloth~

My mother died on the same week & when we were taken to church or meeting as it was called then, I thought all the gloom of it was on account of my mother~ Susan was three & a half & I was seven but according to the custom of that day we were both put into deep mourning~[403]

Abigail Rice had been a member of the church choir, and Sarah had apparently inherited her mother's fine singing voice. Her father encouraged Sarah's singing.

He was very fond of sacred music & he had me instructed every opportunity in that branch of music~ We always had singing & the piano on Sunday evenings~ My mother when a girl had been one of the choir & my father was anxious that I should follow her lead~ Of course he was highly gratified by my receiving a note from Mr Henry Jackson the leader asking me to join the choir~

I was eleven years old & not much accustomed to receiving notes from grown people & my reply was after this fashion "Mr Henry Jackson Sir "It is with pleasure I shall take a seat in your singing seats" Sarah Parker Rice~

I hid the note under a corner of the parlor carpet meaning to carry it myself after school~ Judge of my disgust when I found a member of the family standing up on a chair reading it amidst peals of laughter~

The next Sunday I took the lowest seat with five older ladies~ They were Miss Mary Rogers, Miss Ann Goddard & the three Miss Hills~ There were a large number of men in the choir & some of them played on the flute & base viol~ There was no organ at the time~

Dr. Buckminister always lead the Doxology before the benediction~ He looked very grandly as he sang
"To God the Father, God the Son, And God the spirit, three in one, Be honor praise & glory given By all on earth & all in Heaven"
Sung to the tune of Old Hundred[404]

The North Congregational parish remained Calvinistic and Trinitarian in its theology throughout the years. The parish of the South Church under the leadership of Reverend Nathaniel Parker embraced the new Unitarian theology in vogue throughout New England during the first half of the nineteenth century.[405]

A great schism occurred between the two congregational churches in Portsmouth during my youth~ Dr Parker determined to avow Unitarian views which he had held for some time~ He made a statement of his opinions to his people & the thing was submitted to a vote~ They were all in sympathy and sustained him~ Mr Putnam was a rank Calvinist & he took occasion to state to Mr Parker that he could no longer exchange with him~ This led to a correspondence or controversy which lasted a year & which afterward was handed about from family to family for the edification of anybody that had patience to read –[406]

Since the turn of the century this new liberal wing of the Congregational denomination had gained steadily in popularity. The Calvinistic beliefs preached in Sarah's childhood began to lose favor amongst many Congregationalists, while this new religion, often referred to as the "Boston religion," was particularly popular in New England.[407]

My husband was a member of Dr Parker's parish & as I could understand his theology & was in sympathy with it I left the "old three decker" for the Stone church~ 1890[408]

The congregation of South Church built a new parish church on State Street between 1824 and 1826. It was an impressive large stone and granite structure fronted by a Greek revival portico with four Doric columns. This has been known throughout the years as the "Stone Church."

I must allude to the change I made, when I was married, from the Calvinistic, orthodox church to the Unitarian under the charge of Dr. Parker~ My Father's family though they attended the Kittery Point church were strong Universalists but my Mother's family had been members of the North Parish in Portsmouth for generations & so after my mother's death, my Father continued to go there until all his children left him for other churches.

I had never understood Calvinism & after I went to Dr. Parker's I began to read the New Testament in earnest & came out from conviction a "Conservative Unitarian" & I believe now that "Conservative Unitarianism" is the grandest religion the world has seen~[409]

In 1827, when the Goodwins wed, they donated to the South Church a wrought iron fence brought from England to Portsmouth on the *Marion.* Nearly two hundred years later it still surrounds this stately stone building on State Street.[410] The old "Three Decker," underwent extensive renovations about this time. The smaller sash windows were replaced by three large round-topped windows, rising up all three levels. Only the door on the west side of the building remained of its previous three. Its function changed as well; it was transformed from a meetinghouse into a church at this time. In 1854 the historic structure was demolished and the church that now stands in Market Square was built.[411]

MARRIAGE AND WEDDING JOURNEY

B lessed with a good singing voice, Sarah's musical talents were not confined to singing with the choir at the North Meetinghouse. She also took piano lessons from a widow in town.

> *When I was a child there stood on the sideboard a very large glass pyramid for the center of a dining table & it was my delight to stand in a chair & drum on it as an accompaniment to my voice~*

> *My father seeing that I had a taste for music bought a piano for me & sent me to take lessons of Mrs Champney, a widow of small means & some accomplishments & who was a daughter of Mr Boyd whom Mr Brewster celebrates in his rambles~*[412]

Her music teacher was Mary Champney the daughter of Col. William Boyd. He was a Royalist, who sailed to England in 1774 leaving behind a wife and ten children, including Mary Champney.[413]

> *I had good times under her tuition & as she took very little pains to give me a knowledge of the rules of music & put me into tunes at once & such tunes as I liked, I did not have that experience of drudgery in music, which most young people have to go through~*

> *She wore a turban & usually had a pinch of snuff between the thumb & forefinger of her left hand while she occasionally helped me with the right~ I very soon learned tunes enough to be able to sing & play for the entertainment of my eldest sister's friends~ So that I was very convenient to her~*

> *She finished her education at a famous boarding school kept by a Mrs Saunders & Miss Beach at Dorchester, Mass~ She was a great beauty & belle & had crowds of lovers~ I was six years younger & had scarcely grown up when she was married~*[414]

Her oldest sister was Elizabeth Mary. The school Elizabeth attended, Mrs. Saunders' and Miss Beach's Academy in Dorchester, Massachusetts was primarily an ornamental painting and needlework school. These design schools were very popular, for young women, and they flourished in America during this time. Elizabeth married Issac Parsons, a well to do Portsmouth merchant.[415]

When Sarah was older, probably in her late teens, she joined the local Handel & Haydn Society. This society was founded in Boston in 1815, to promote the music of the two well-known eighteenth century composers, German born George Frederic Handel, and Austrian, Franz Joseph Haydn. Branches of this society spread throughout the New England communities in the early 1800s.[416]

> *At one time Mr. Brierley, & Major Larkin organized a musical society composed of a large number of ladies & gentlemen, called the Handel & Hayden Society~*
>
> *His society met two afternoons in the week at the Assembly room where Mr Brierley as President wielded the baton with great dignity & precision~*
>
> *Miss Ann Larkin & the elder Miss B__ assisted by turns at the Piano & several gentlemen played on Flutes & the violin~ I was fortunate enough to be one of the members, & the meetings were very much enjoyed~*[417]

Pianos were just starting to be made in America around this time, as were clarinets, and viols. Organs, violins, and flutes were available as early as 1788. With her father's encouragement Sarah continued to train her voice. Singing was a popular pastime for young people during the early 1800s, and local newspaper advertisements of this time indicate that there were a number of singing schools in the area.

> *My father was very anxious that I should excel in sacred music & sent me to the singing school every winter for years~ A very handsome young man by the name of Cyrus P. Smith, a graduate of Dartmouth College, came to Portsmouth when I was about sixteen to teach sacred music~*[418]
>
> *He was the very soul of music & was endowed with almost super human energy in teaching classes here & in the neighboring towns~*[419] *He had three or four schools & I attended one kept in the afternoon~*
>
> *He had an oratorio in the old North church or three decker as some people called it, because it had two galleries & I sang the solos in "Strike the Symbols" & "Miriam's song"~ The audience was large & the tickets a dollar! & I don't know how I did it~*[420]
>
> *I knew him quite intimately & he was often at our house~ I attended an afternoon class & sometimes disturbed the gravity of the school by my levity~*
>
> *One day Mr Smith said "Will one of you ladies name some hymn that she would like for us to sing~ All were silent till I, moved by a spirit of mischief, broke out 'I should like "How shall the young secure their hearts"~ the first line in a well known hymn~*
>
> *It was the more trying to him, as a scandalous paper published at that time accused the girls of running after him~ He was much admired &*

wonderfully handsome~[421]

I was very intimate with my teacher & we corresponded after he left Portsmouth~ He is now & has been for a long time one of the first men in Brooklyn, NY~[422]

Cyrus Smith was five years older than Sarah, and a native of Brooklyn, New York. In 1839 he was Mayor of Brooklyn, a position he held for three years. He was also in the New York State Senate for a number of years. Smith died in 1877.[423]

Well the years rolled on & when I was twenty two our minister the Rev Israel Putnum was invited to perform the marriage ceremony at my wedding, which took place in Deer St in the house in which I was born~[424]

Sometime after Smith left the Portsmouth area, Sarah became engaged to marry Ichabod Goodwin. When they wed she was twenty-two and he was just a month short of thirty-three. By then Ichabod, a native of Berwick, Maine had lived in Portsmouth for approximately sixteen years. Although they had first met many years before at her Aunt Flagg's, it is not known when they first became acquainted as adults, as Sarah failed to leave behind an account of this meeting. However, Ichabod Goodwin and William Rice would have known each other through common business ventures.

Under the patronage of Samuel Lord, one of Portsmouth's most prominent ship owners and merchants, Ichabod became well established in town at an early age. By the time he and Sarah married he was a ship's captain, as well as a ship's investor and a partner in Goodwin and Coues Counting House. The counting house was located first on Fore Street in the Cushing Building, then at 82 Market Street for many years.

His partner Samuel Coues, another up and coming young Portsmouth businessman, had an interest in scientific theories, and he once wrote a treatise refuting Newton's theory of gravity. Later in his life Coues served in the Patent Office in Washington, DC. At one point he was the President of the American Peace Society.[425]

Together the two young men invested in the shipping trade, insurance and shipbuilding. Salt was their major import, along with coal, hardware, crockery, and other desired English exports.[426]

A portrait of Sarah painted by Joseph Cole about the time of her wedding, attests to her beauty at that age. A portrait of Goodwin of uncertain vintage, but done during his middle years depicts a good-looking man with a gentle mien. The match must have met with the approval of both families and friends. Sarah mentions several bridal parties that were given to the couple prior to their wedding.

The fashion of giving parties to brides was universal~ Many were given to me, among them, one in the Governor Langdon house, by Col & Mrs Decatur & one in the Elwin House by Mr & Mrs Enoch Parrott~ Music & dancing at both~[427]

Home weddings were quite common at the time, and they weren't very elaborate affairs. Sarah left her grandchildren a wonderful description of their wedding day.

At weddings only cake & wine were served~ Ice cream & oysters were not common at parties much before 1830~[428] Such wedding cake as is not seen now was made at home & baked in the great brick oven, one of which was in every house ~[429]

Ichabod Goowin, circa 1820s. Portrait painted about the time of his marriage to Sarah Parker Rice.

SarahParker Rice Goodwin's wedding portrait, painted by Joseph Cole circa 1828.

On the morning of Sept. 3, 1827 I was married~ The morning was delicious & we were accompanied on our wedding journey by my sister Susan & my cousin Marcia Rice, afterward Mrs Richardson & the mother of Mrs George Treadwell~. We were absent a month & we saw no rain during the first fortnight~[430]

On my marriage morning as soon as we took our carriage, guns were fired & colors were hoisted, on all the vessels in the harbor~ At that time Portsmouth was dependent on the shipping interest & a large number of fine ships & vessels of every class were owned by our merchants and were usually at the wharves in the Autumn~ As there were a large number of shipmasters at home, at that time, we were indebted to their politeness, for firing of guns & the hoisting of colors~[431]

It was common for sisters or close companions to accompany brides on their wedding journey. Sarah wrote that they first stayed in Boston. However, there were no railroads at that time. Only the stagecoach traveled the Old Post Road between Boston and Portsmouth, and since it was a two-day journey to Boston by stage, it is likely they spent the first evening in Newburyport or Ipswich, Massachusetts.

We spent two or three days in Boston at Mrs. Lecain's in Pearl St~ the most fashionable boardinghouse in the city~ Mr Tudor the projector of the ice business was one of the privileged boarders~ He was very kind to me~[432]

Boston, by the time of their visit, was a fairly large city compared to Portsmouth. The boarding house where they stayed was in the heart of Boston's commercial center overlooking the city's busy harbor. Pearl Street is now part of that city's financial district.

Frederick Tudor, a flamboyant bachelor at the time Sarah met him, would have been celebrating his forty-fourth birthday when they stayed at Mrs. Lecain's establishment. A native of Boston, he was known as the "Ice King," because of the successful business he had developed by shipping ice to tropical climates such as Martinique and eventually Calcutta. The ice for the tropics first came from ponds and lakes in Boston and eventually nearly every village in New England.[433]

> *There was not a railroad in the world then & so we traveled by stage to Albany, taking it very leisurely~ Then we took a steamer down the north river to Catskill, or Pine orchard as it was called & spent a week at the Mountain House, which was opened the first time that year~* [434]

The Mountain House was the very first of the many large resort hotels that were eventually built to accommodate the large number of tourists who flocked to the Catskills during the spring, summer, and fall months throughout both the nineteenth and twentieth centuries. This magnificent wooden structure, built in the fashionable Greek revival style of the time, was large enough to accommodate approximately three hundred guests. It was painted white and graced by a wide piazza, which was supported by a row of elegant Corinthian columns along the front. Although Sarah notes that it opened for the first time in 1827, it apparently opened at least one year earlier than that, as an essay written by an unnamed author who visited this same hotel appeared in one of the 1826 Boston papers.[435]

It took about five hours to reach the summit. The carriage ride was twelve miles long, and the first eight miles took them over mountainous hilltop elevations and woodlands, while a breathtakingly beautiful broad valley spread before them. The actual ascent up the mountain was about three miles. This was Rip Van Winkle country, and about two miles from the top the local legend seemed to come alive when travelers reached a shanty built into the mountain ledge. This hut was the home of an elderly hermit, who claimed both ancestry and the name of the legendary Rip Van Winkle. It was his habit to greet weary travelers with offers of fresh water that flowed from a nearby mountain spring.[436]

> *Very few persons were there but among them were Dr Storer of New York and Mr Paine of Portland, whose family we knew~*[437]

Dr. Storer was probably originally from Portsmouth or related to the Storer family of Portsmouth, one of the city's oldest and most respected families. Mr. Paine from Portland may have been her Uncle Alexander's partner in the stagecoach enterprise between Portland and Portsmouth or one of his relatives.

> *We met at Catskill another wedding party of four persons, dressed just like ourselves in grey pongee~ They were New Yorkers & our interest in one another has continued to this day~*[438]

Gray pongee is a soft silk fabric, usually kept in its natural tan color. It must have been fashionable for both men and women to wear it in gray that year. It is not surprising that the Goodwin party made friends while there, as the guests were encouraged to mingle during socials in the hotel's elegant, well lit, and fashionably furnished parlor. The entertainment centered on the piano. Each day throughout the late afternoon and early evening guests gathered there to take part in group sing alongs, or to promenade around the room to the rhythm of the fashionable tunes of the day.[439]

> *About twelve, one day when the sun was shining brightly overhead & the sky a delicious blue, the landlord came into the parlor & invited us out to see a thunderstorm beneath us~ It was about half way down the mountain & I have never seen so grand a sight~*
>
> *The whole prospect was obscured & the rush of the waters, the pealing of the thunder & the zig zag darting of the lightning was most grand~ I have been once since at Catskill & I enjoy it better than anything I have ever seen~[440]*

The prospect from the ledge of the Mountain House became legendary as the popularity of Catskills grew. On a clear day one could see all that was visible within a radius of fifty miles. The view encompassed over a hundred small towns, hills, woodlands, and valleys. The Hudson River, dotted with steamboats that looked like miniature toys from that great distance, wound through it all.[441]

During the day the party might have explored the thickly grown forest groves nearby, or ventured over the footpath to the Cauterskill Falls located in a glen about a mile and a half away from the hotel. The glen, which was about fifty-feet wide and two to three hundred feet in depth, was fed with water from a nearby lake. Whenever the gatekeeper could be persuaded, by the payment of a small token, to open the sluice to the lake's gate, the rushing waters tumbled down into a magnificent double level waterfall into the valley basin beneath. This was a spectacular show that never failed to delight those who visited this wondrous mountain retreat.[442]

The next part of their journey took them by steamboat down the Hudson River to New York City, where they spent ten days. In 1827 New York was much smaller, and less frenetic than the New York of today. It was home to the upper echelons of American society at that time. Entry into some of the finer homes would have required good credentials, and in some cases proper letters of introduction. Sarah's memories provide an interesting glimpse back at New York City during the first half of the nineteenth century.

> *Well then we went down to New York & stayed there about ten days & were shown a great deal of attention by your grandpa's correspondents & other friends~[443]*
>
> *On my wedding journey I saw New York for the first time~ Bunkers was the only fashionable Hotel~ The ladies promenaded on the Battery every pleasant afternoon and Bunker's Hotel was very near~ It was a large square brick house with perhaps a dozen good rooms~[444]*

Battery Park overlooked the river harbor at the southernmost tip of Manhattan Island. This was where British forts once stood to protect the city from invaders. But by the time Sarah visited there it was where the stylish ladies of the city gathered to promenade. Nearby was the fashionable Bunker Hotel. No finer promenade than Battery Park existed in any city in the world, according to the English commentator Mrs. Trollope who visited New York City about this time, and wrote of her observations of American society. [445]

> *We expected to stay there but fell in at the Hotel on the top of Catskill (called Pine Orchard) with Dr Storer who told us that his Father had been unfortunate & that his Mother had opened a large boarding house just above Bunker's on the other side of Broadway & would be glad to have us stay with her~*[446]

Broadway was a wide sunny street lined with fashionable homes, as well as exclusive little shops covered with neat awnings. The streets of Broadway bustled with throngs of fashionable men and women who strolled along the walkway, or rode down the wide boulevard in richly appointed horse-drawn carriages. Several handsome buildings fronted by trees and grass, and a well-kept park, surrounding the old City Hall, added to the overall favorable impression of the area. [447]

Broadway stretched nearly four miles across the length of Manhattan Island, but in 1827 only the upper part was developed. Just beyond the Bowery, Broadway turned into a country road that ran past park gardens or undeveloped farmland.

> *In Mrs Storer's dining room there was one very long table, long enough to seat forty or fifty ladies and gentlemen & Mrs Storer sat at the head~ Dishes of meat & vegetables were placed all along the table & gentlemen carved & helped their immediate neighbors~ In those days people did not mind asking those near them, in a polite way, to hand them anything~*[448]

The guests at Mrs. Storer's entertained themselves, much as they had at the Mountain House, by socializing in the parlor where they all gathered round the piano to join in singing the popular tunes of the time.

> *At Mrs. Storer's we met Mrs Gen Scott & many other well~known people, who talked very agreeably~ and gave us good music on the piano & some Comic Songs~*[449]

Mrs. Scott was the wife of General Winfield Scott, later a hero of the Mexican American War and a one time presidential candidate. When the Goodwins socialized with his wife in 1827, Scott was forty-two years old and already a major general.[450]

> *We were invited out a good deal while in New York~ Our friends were mostly in Broadway but we took tea in Canal St. & also in Chamber St. both of which streets were called up town~ We dined with old Mrs Sherrod in Broad Street who was said to be very rich~ Her husband had been an east india captain & had brought home all sorts of beautiful things~*[451]

A great deal of wealth came into New York from the shipping trade with the Indies in New York's early history, and Mrs. Sherrod's fashionable Broad Street address indicates she was indeed quite wealthy. At the time of Sarah's visit both Canal and Chamber Streets were considered quite fashionable addresses where the city's elite shopped or lived.[452]

Mrs. Trollope was impressed with the wealth of upper class New Yorkers, and particularly by the rich furnishings found in their stately homes. As a general rule she noted that silks and satins adorned the furniture, rather than chintz, and well-carpeted floors were found throughout the houses. Her only complaint was the uniformity of the exterior of the homes. The majority of them lacked balconies, were laid out in the same design, with red brick facades, neat green shutters, and fashionable wrought iron fences. Although flowers were generously found in decorative displays throughout the interior of the homes, she felt the displays of flowers in the external gardens were not nearly as impressive as those found in Paris or London. [453]

She also noted with dismay that mixed dinner parties of ladies and gentlemen were somewhat rare in the city, and that evening parties were geared towards the young. It seems they tended to rely on conversation in New York, rather than music or cards as in England. However, she conceded the society was worth cultivating.[454]

There were three theaters in New York City at that time. The most fashionable, the Park on Broadway, would have been the one the Goodwin wedding party attended. The theatre in the Bowery was of a superior style, in Mrs. Trollope's opinion, but it was not in fashion with the right people. The Bowery became even less than fashionable in later years. The third theatre was the Chatham, and in 1827 it was a rough place filled with common people, according to Mrs. Trollope." [455]

> *We went to the theatre (not the Bowery) but the Broadway & saw Madame Celeste & a large company of French dancers, who appeared for the first time that evening~[456]...French dancing, then something new to the New Yorkers~[457]*

> *I did not know what I was to see & not knowing anything about tights, thought they were only in their skins & was afraid to look but when I saw everybody else looking, I took courage and was much astonished at what I saw~ [458]*

The appearance of French dancers at the fashionable Park Theatre on Broadway indicates that even in the first quarter of the nineteenth century, New York theatre fare was much more avant-garde than that offered in Portsmouth. Shopping in New York was also an adventure. Just as the theatres provided the latest offerings in the entertainment world, the stores carried the latest in ladies fashions long before they reached Portsmouth. Sarah mentions several items made from barege, a sheer fabric woven of silk, cotton or wool, in fashion at the time. It was imported from Bareges, France.

> *A.T. Stuart had already established himself on Broadway & had the finest store in the City~ I bought there beautiful scarves & pink & yellow barege, palm leaf kerchiefs which were much worn at that time~[459]*

I bought a leghorn hat trimmed with black & gold colored ribbon & a dress of pink barege trimmed with black satin, or rather the trimming of the same which was very elaborate was edged with cross way black satin~ This style of mixing black with colors was all the rage then & when I came home I astonished the natives~[460]

Located at Ninth and Broadway, the store was owned by Alexander Stewart, an introverted and eccentric bachelor who catered to the city's fashionable elite. It eventually became one of the largest retail stores in the world

I also went to Grant Thornburn's famous seed store & indeed I believe I saw all the things best worth seeing at that time~[461]

The full name of the store was Grant Thornburn, Seedsman & Florist. Thornburn was from Scotland. He bought a farm in New Jersey to grow plants and seeds for resale, and opened his first store in 1802. Eventually Thornburn branched out to include catalogue sales, and was very successful.[462]

After ten days the wedding party left New York City. They returned to Portsmouth by way of Boston. Ichabod and Sarah then settled into to a suite of rooms at a boarding house located near her father's home on Deer Street.

We came home by way of Long Island sound & again stayed a few days in Boston~ On our return rooms were ready for us at Mrs Adams" in Deer St in the house called the Martin House where we boarded three month's~ We had a parlor & bedroom & took breakfast & tea in our own room~

Your grandpa' had all the gentlemen in town to a collation prepared by Mrs Adams & I stayed home a week or two to receive my lady friends & give them cake & wine~ [463]

After our return from our wedding journey many Large & elegant parties were made for us & on the whole, few couples were more gaily launched on the career of matrimony than ourselves~[464]

Ichabod Goodwin remained at home during this time, and when it was time for him to return to sea, he took along his new bride to introduce her to his business associates in the South as well as in England.

In January we left two feet of snow on the ground & with a spanking breeze sailed for Savannah in the good ship Sarah Parker named for me~[465]

According to extant records the official purchase of this ship, which was bound for the cotton trade between Savannah and Liverpool, took place on January 28th of 1828. Therefore the Goodwins must have sailed to Savannah on the *Sarah Parker's* maiden voyage within a few days of her purchase as Sarah indicates that they sailed from Portsmouth in the month of January.[466]

I had a colored woman the wife of the steward to wait on me & my quarters were very fine~ I had a large state room with high post bedstead & curtains & a chair with supporters for the head (which I still have), screwed to the floor, at the foot of the bed~[467]

In Savannah they visited George Cummings, a prominent young bachelor in that city. Cummings was also an associate of Coues and Goodwin. These men jointly owned several ships and these mutual ships were used in the triangular trade. Cummings arranged for the purchase of the cotton, much of which came out of Savannah and Mobile, Alabama.[468]

It was like fairy land in Savannah~ the flowers were blooming and all seemed like our mid summer~ I was very much interested as we went up the river to see the alligators basking on the river banks & thought how dreadful it would be if I were to fall in~ We stayed at the Hotel now called the Pulaski then called Mrs. Battie's~[469]

The Hotel Pulaski was located on the corner of Bull and Bryan Streets in Johnson Square. This was the heart of downtown Savannah with the shopping district on one side and the banking and mercantile district on the other. A stone's throw away was the busy shipping harbor where ship's captains from all over the world were attracted by the city's flourishing cotton trade. The original building was built in 1795. The Pulaski was four stories high, and built of the now valuable old gray bricks, known as Savannah "grays." From the start it became an important landmark, one that figured prominently in the city's history.[470] It became the Hotel Pulaski by 1838, just ten years after Sarah's first visit. Old newspaper accounts indicate that it was one of the finest hotels in the South with "cuisine not excelled outside of New York."[471]

By the time of the Civil War this southern hostelry was already legendary. Its clientele included some of the most prestigious names in the South including General Robert E. Lee, who was a frequent guest. John Wilkes Booth and other well-known personages in the theatrical world of that time were also included in the roster of famous visitors[472]

In the hotel's basement there were cells with iron bars, and mesh net covered some of these dank cubicles. In the center was a large brick fireplace. Tradition recalls that these cells were used to house the slaves of wealthy northern traders, as well as slaves of wealthy rice planters traveling within the vicinity.[473]

There was an elegant dining room with a moss covered exterior, and a "ladies' entrance" as well as a "ladies' parlor." Sarah's account of her first evening at the hotel indicates that she and other ladies were seated in the hotel's upper parlor while the gentlemen, including her new husband, were socializing in a room or rooms on a lower level.[474]

The first evening after we arrived at the hotel, as the evening was warm, the parlors were only lighted by the lamp in the Hall~ I saw curious shadows flitting over the carpet, & while I was wondering I felt something making free with my legs~ As I was among strangers I merely said with an uneasy movement, "I wonder what is the matter with me?"

"It is only the cockroaches," said Mrs. Battie, & then such a scream as I

gave! It brought twenty gentlemen at least from the room below, & then lights were brought & the roaches hurried to their homes under the wash boards~

The rooms were kept lighted after that & I saw few roaches though I did take a very large one in my hand one night in taking out my comb to go to bed~[475]

In Savannah, George Cummings entertained the newly weds, and introduced them to the local society. He was a bachelor at this time and this would explain why they did not stay at his home. Sarah mentions that she formed a friendship with a lady from New York, whose husband was a ship's captain. In letters Sarah wrote to her husband during their first few years of marriage, she refers to this lady on several occasions and was apparently very fond of her.

In Savannah I made the acquaintance of Mrs George Davis a young married lady from New York & we saw much of each other~ Our acquaintance ripened into friendship & she visited me afterwards, the first year of my housekeeping~ She was a most beautiful woman & good as she was beautiful~ She has been dead several years~[476]

However, she soon grew disenchanted with the South, and longed for the active life she was accustomed to in Portsmouth.

I felt very much pent up in Savannah as there were only two drives to "Thunderbolt" & Bonaventure~ The latter was once the seat of the Tatnall family~

There are acres of gigantic Live Oaks disposed in rows with broad avenues between~[477]

Thunderbolt and *Bon Adventure* were island bluffs overlooking the Savannah River. Many prominent families built plantations on these bluffs, and the gardens of Savannah were world famous primarily because of the large beautiful formal gardens that were set off by the long lines of stately oak trees, draped in Spanish moss.[478]

Commodore or rather Admiral Tatnall was the rebel Admiral conquered by Farragut~ He once took tea with us & I thought him an elegant gentleman~ [479]

When the Civil War began Captain Josiah Tatnall, a member of one of Savannah's oldest and most prestigious families enlisted in the Georgia State Navy. He was the flagship officer of the fleet of wooden ships that was routed from Port Royal by the Union Navy at the start of the war.[480]

I made some very pleasant acquaintances in S ~ but in May when we were ready for sea I was glad to leave~[481]

In the spring the captain and crew of the *Sarah Parker* set out on the second step of their journey. They sailed for Liverpool, probably carrying a cargo of cotton to trade for salt, and coal. More importantly they brought the captain's new bride to introduce to his business associates.

> *Our passage to Europe was in the month of May & the weather was delightful~ Your grandpa built a house round the companionway as entrance to the cabin with six windows & two doors, so that I could sit with my book or wool & look in any direction~*
>
> *The most delightful evening of my life was on this passage when after seeing a most glorious sunset & the setting of the evening star, the moon rose in the east, the Aurora borealis, gorgeous & shooting to the Zenith, the water still & the sea full of whales & porpoises, spouting all about us & giving life & animation to the scene~ I did not go to my berth until a late hour & went reluctantly then~*
>
> *In going up the channel to Liverpool we were obliged to tack constantly which gave me an opportunity to see the round castles on the coast of Ireland~ I was much interested to see them as their history & their builders are unknown~*
>
> *In Liverpool the going into dock was something new to me & I witnessed the operation of docking with some trepidation~ There were only two or three docks then~ There are miles of them now & they have cost vast sums of money~*[482]

There are a large number of ancient castles in Ireland, made of stone and often round in design. Some historians speculate that the first Viking settlers built the oldest castles. At this time Liverpool was England's largest port with four docks forming two miles of quays. By the 1880s, when Sarah was writing her memoirs, more docks had been added and Liverpool was the center of seven miles of quays on the Mersey River.[483]

Goodwin had been sailing to Liverpool for over a decade by then, and he had established many business friends and acquaintances in the region. It would seem these English acquaintances were quite anxious to extend a warm welcome to the newlyweds.

> *We went to board at Mrs Richards, a boarding house kept with great regard to etiquette~ It was a dinner party every day & I enjoyed it very much~ Your grandpa's old friends came to see us & we dined out several times~*
>
> *The next day after we arrived your grandpa', said to me if Mrs Grayson calls on you & invites you, be sure to be engaged~ That day Mrs Grayson came & invited me for the next evening~ I was engaged~ then for the next & the next until I was ashamed to refuse~ So we were engaged four days off ~*

Well we went~ Four tables at whist~ the ladies in full dress & feathers~ At twelve I rose to take leave~ What before supper? I sat down again & about half past twelve supper was announced~

A long table I on the right of the host & your grandpa' on the right of the hostess at the other end~ Course followed course as at a dinner, & then came speeches~ Mr G__made a complimentary speech to us as Americans & your grandpa' responded~ then all the gentlemen made speeches & then Mrs Grayson made a speech addressed to me & I was called on~

My tongue clove to the roof of my mouth~ I looked imploringly at your grandpa' & he got up & said that I had not been accustomed to make speeches & then he branched off into 4th of July & the American Eagle & they were satisfied~

By this time they had had enough of me & I had had enough of them & a day or two after I made the party call & that was the last I saw of them~[484]

The party call was a requirement of proper etiquette in which the guest, generally the lady of the family entertained, paid a daytime call on their hostess to express their thanks for an enjoyable evening.

Mr William Brown (afterward Sir Wm) & his wife were very attentive to us & very kind~ They dined us & took us to drive & to church &c~ Mrs Richards invited a very famous minister to dine with us, on my account & he took me into dinner~ I have forgotten his name~[485]

The Romans built the ancient wall surrounding the city of Chester in the first century as a fortress. Almost a thousand years later the Normans restored the structure, and it remains intact to this day. By the time Sarah visited the city, the walls of this ancient structure were no longer needed for defense, and had been turned into a two-mile circuit of walkway over which visitors could traverse the entire city.

We joined a party & went to Chester~ We walked around the old Roman Wall which is entire, visited a Cathedral & drove to Eaton Hall two miles distant which made me feel like Aladdin~ The suites of rooms, the furniture & pictures, the library, music room, old tapestry & chapel filled me with wonder~[486]

There are several old cathedrals in Chester. The most historic cathedral is St. John the Baptist, built in the classic style of Norman cathedrals during the thirteenth century. Surprisingly it was built outside the protective walls of the city. There was also Chester Cathedral, built within the walls[487]

Sarah was the most impressed with Eaton Hall in Chester. This magnificent stone castle, surrounded by impressive grounds and gardens, had been the ancestral home of the Grosvenor family since 1440.[488]

Then the grounds ~ the park with Pheasants & deer ~ the rockeries ~ conservatories, gardens & what delighted me extremely the river Dee running through the Park & spanned by one arch of iron~

Aunt Briard used to sing to us children "Jamie the glory & pride of the Dee" & it was a real, realization that ever I should see Jamie's river! Eaton Hall is the property of the Marquis (Duke) of Westminster, one of the richest noblemen in the kingdom~ It was said to be one of the finest places in England at that time~[489]

Sarah would have also crossed over the old Dee Bridge that spans the Dee River. This ancient bridge first constructed of wood by the early Romans and replaced during the twelfth century with a stone bridge, is distinguished by a series of seven unequal arches. It was originally a drawbridge with towers. It was widened in 1826. [490]

The Goodwins were invited by a business acquaintance to spend one day sightseeing in a small village of Childwall near Liverpool.

Mr Shiply a partner in the Brown's house invited us to spend a day with him at a small hotel at Childwall six miles from Liverpool~

There was a castle or Abbey there belonging to the Marquis of Salisbury, & the view from the tower was the finest in that part of the country~ I have forgotten how many castles & Parks & villages, even countries, could be seen from that tower but the view was wonderful for beauty as well as extent~[491]

Childwall Hall, the home of the Second Marquis of Salisbury, who married into the Gascoyne family and thus inherited this castle, was where they visited. There is a tall tower on one side that overlooks a magnificent prospect of villages and parks, which so delighted Sarah.

We went to Manchester for a day or two & visited a very old church there~ I brought away a piece of the crumbling stone from the crypt which I have now~ I did not much like Manchester, but I spent an evening with the Brierley family, relations of your Uncle Dwight, who had removed from Portsmouth~

Capt Graham accompanied us on this trip~ His son married a daughter of Mr George Brown of Baltimore~[492]

At the time of her visit Manchester had over five hundred cotton mills operating within the city limits. It was overcrowded with mill workers, who lived in substandard housing with inadequate sewerage disposal.[493] The Brierleys were relations of William Dwight, who married her youngest sister, Adeline, and may have been related to the president of the Handel and Haydn Society to which Sarah belonged. The old church might have been Manchester Cathedral, a Gothic stone cathedral built by Henry the Fifth in the fifteenth century.

In July they set sail for America.

I was in England the whole month of June the finest month in the year to be there~ The sun was absent from the sky very few hours & I could have read at almost any hour in the night without other light~

We had a sixty three days passage to Philadelphia~ nothing but head winds & calms~ I suffered a good deal from sea sickness and was very tired of the sea~[494]

One day when the weather & water were very clear we found ourselves on the Banks of Newfoundland, the great fishing ground~ We could see bottom & fishes swimming about~ The cabin boy & I begged that we might "lay to" & fish, as we were out of fresh provisions & my appetite, after recovering from seasickness, was very good~

So " the Capt" gave orders to "lay to" & all hands went to fishing~ About eighty large cod were taken & in less than an hour one was ready for the table~ Shall I confess it? I ate with vigor~ I could not do so now~

When we were in sight of the capes of Delaware we were becalmed three days~ The weather was very hot & the sea was covered with scum & straws but the dolphin were in great numbers about us, all the time, like a thousand rain bows, or "sun bows" as Georgy Dewey would call them~

The fourth day we took a Pilot & off New castle (about half way up the river) we sent ashore & bought some freshly baked crackers & some new butter~ I sat down by the pillow case of crackers & the cabbage leaf of butter & stayed so long, that your grandpa' had to take them away from me~

I forgot to mention that we had a lady passenger, very highly educated in Germany, though of Irish birth~ She was on her way to a Moravian institution in Penn. & was to be a teacher ~

She was very jealous & irritable & as her clothes gave out at half passage, borrowed of me & then sent them to me to be washed~ She got very angry with me one day because I spoke of the letter A~ She insisted that the first letter in the English alphabet was R~ She apologized afterward~[495]

Moravians were members of a Protestant sect that broke away from the Catholic Church in Bohemia during the fifteenth century. The center of their American missionary work was in Bethlehem, Pa. where they ran a mission for Indians.[496]

Well, we arrived at the city at last & as soon as the ship struck the wharf, my cousin, by marriage, Mr James Dow came on board, to our great delight &

told us that there had been great anxiety about us~ He took us directly to his house where we stayed three weeks~ We came home from Phil. by land & were received with open arms by all the family~[497]

The Goodwins returned by stage to Portsmouth. The *Sarah Parker* returned to Savannah to prepare for her second voyage under the command of another captain.[498]

CHILD BIRTH

A few months after their return from their wedding journey, Ichabod Goodwin sailed to Liverpool. This time Sarah remained behind at her father's home on Deer Street to await the arrival of their first child. Based on the custom of the time as well as extant letters, it can be assumed she was confined to the home for a period of approximately six months. This confinement would have begun about the fourth or fifth month of pregnancy when changes in her body became evident and lasted up to two months after the birth. [499]

A letter from Liverpool, England written in the early hours of New Year's Day in 1829 expresses his love and concern for her.

Liverpool 1st, Jany 1829
It is to me my dear Wife a source of happiness that it is in my power to devote a small portion of my time at the commencement of the new year to the dearest object of my earthly affections, and I will commence with the trite and common salutation of the season by wishing you a happy new year, may it indeed be happy and to you could this salutation be impressed with a kiss or even a touch of the hand it would make <u>me</u> happy indeed, in fact I could not find words to express the joy it would give me, happiness such as I have found thus far in life seems not to be a proper phrase. I think I can before hand with you in my new year's wish, as for our differences of longitude, you at this moment are probably comfortably in your bed asleep, if well which I hope and pray may be the case
We can not be too thankful my dear to the giver of all our comforts for the many blessings and enjoyments which were bestowed upon us during the past year,... . This is a fit time for us to take a retrospective view of our feelings and our thoughts and doings for the past year and where in we can find anything wrong let us amend and commence aright with the new year. I calculate upon a long passage home at this season of the year... You must not be the least anxious about me if you should not hear of me so soon as you may expect, recollect I have as good a ship as ever floated~
Your dear interesting and affectionate letters of the 28th and 4th were brought here by the packet of the 8th. I need not tell you how happy they made me, I have read them over and over. I daresay you will laugh to hear I have not been without one of your letters about me since the first one was received, indeed, I almost begin to believe them a fortunate talisman and think some misfortune would attend me if I had not their magical charm about me, I do not expect to hear from you again before my departure, but hope to have the pleasure of my dearest being in the course of 50 to 60 days.
Mrs. Richards had a large party last evening, they danced out the old year and in the new. I left the party at half past ten and returned to my chamber

and realized more pleasure there in thinking of your dear self than I did among the gay. Lpool is very gay at this time during the holidays. I have had constant invitations to dinner parties, card parties &c most of which I decline
Remember me to all your family….
Make my regards to Mrs Parrott and family and believe me your ever devoted husband.

Ichabod Goodwin~[500]

The Sarah Parker, ship purchased by Goodwin and Coues in 1828, following the Goodwins' wedding. Named in honor of the new bride, Sarah Parker Rice Goodwin.

Abigail Rice Goodwin arrived on February 19, 1829, just fifty days after this letter was written. She was named in honor of her maternal grandmother. Unfortunately the *Sarah Parker* ran into adverse conditions on the return trip home, and the journey lasted seventy-one days.[501]

Even if he had been able to make it back to Portsmouth in time for this occasion, Goodwin would probably not have been present at the actual birth, as husbands were traditionally excluded from participating in the birth process. Instead they were relegated to the sidelines to await the news of their child's arrival.

Abby was born the Feb following at my father's & became the idol of grandpa' & the aunts~ My sisters & aunt Elisa each worked a dress & cap & other friends embroidered for me~ All these pretty things I have now~[502]

Then, as always, the birth of a child was a social event as well as a private one, and Sarah's sisters and aunts all participated in the process before, during, and after the birth. Throughout the long months of her pregnancy they each sewed, knitted, laced, embroidered, or crocheted to provide the new mother with a proper layette. It is not surprising that Sarah still possessed these garments nearly a half a century later. Layettes were often treasured as family heirlooms that were passed on to other children as well as grandchildren.

Sarah's aunts, sisters, and female friends would have gathered at the home to help attend her when the birth of her child was eminent. However, before that time came, preparations were always made to feed those friends and relatives who helped.

Before every confinement a great batch of plum cake was baked in the great brick oven~ After being put to bed as (as the term was) the Doctor & such friends as were being useful & near had a feast of good things down stairs~[503]

When a woman went into labor it was said she was "put to bed." This term was used for many years to denote the start of the birth process, even during the previous centuries when most births took place on a birthing stool or on a chair placed near the bed. Then she was confined to her room. What these euphemisms had in common was the connotation that the woman suffered from an illness or handicap that required her to be set apart or hidden away from the rest of society for a period of time.

In New Hampshire midwives served the rural populace of the state throughout the first half of the nineteenth century. However, about the time Sarah gave birth to her children it was becoming increasingly fashionable, amongst upper class women in America, to turn to one of the male physicians who had entered the field of midwifery in increasing numbers since the beginning of the century, and this was true in Portsmouth as well.[504]

These early male physicians were often not well prepared or adequately trained within this field. They were hindered by the cultural emphasis on purity and modesty, which made it nearly impossible for them to receive practical training, or to properly care for their patients. Physicians were taught to avert their eyes from the patient's body and rely upon touch rather than sight to examine the patient or deliver a child.[505] Despite these obvious drawbacks, childbirth gained more respect in the hands of male doctors, and obstetrics came to be thought of as a science rather than simply a natural process.[506]

When Sarah gave birth to her children there was no way for physicians to ease the pain of childbirth. That panacea came along in the form of ether and chloroform within a few decades. This relief was sought by increasing numbers of women, but at first doctors administered these anesthetics selectively. However, when Queen Victoria insisted upon using chloroform in 1853 it became more widely accepted.[507]

When Sarah's children were born she followed the fashion of the day and employed a male physician to attend her during their births. Her physician was Charles Cheever, a Harvard graduate and a native of Boston, who moved to Portsmouth in 1816. He was politically and socially active in Portsmouth, a member of the Federalist-Whig fraction of town, as was Goodwin. Like most physicians at the time he was not a specialist, but he was noted for his surgical skills.[508]

Even though there was an increased reliance upon physicians, the births of most children were still attended by female friends and relatives. Sarah's sisters and aunts also gathered around her to help when her children were born. These women were probably more necessary than ever, as they helped not only in the preparation of the mother and the birthing chamber, but they also helped to ease the waiting period by walking with and attending to the mother's varied needs.[509]

As was the custom, after giving birth Sarah was more closely confined than before, moving from confinement within the home to the more restricted perimeters of the bedchamber and nursery for a month or two following the birth of each child. Although this long period of confinement was customary for a woman of her class, not all women were afforded the luxury of such a lengthy period of convalescence, and the lying in period varied according to the social station of the woman.

During these times in the Goodwin home a monthly nurse was always hired, in addition to the other servants. Her job was to oversee the nursery and take care of the baby, as well as attend to Sarah and the other children in the home. Child nurses were paid just a little above the general domestic help, but their duties were numerous and varied and included sleeping in the nursery with the child.

> *During my confinements, my monthly nurse ironed & pleated the shirts, washed & ironed my clothes & bedding and everything soiled by the baby & when confined with my four first children, cake & wine were passed by her to all who called on the fourth & fifth weeks~*

> *She also kept the baby & myself in elegant toilets, & waited on all the company upstairs & to the street door~ Oh how anxious she was in those hours when she had to be down in the laundry & left the baby & me to the occasional care of the second girl~*

> *The nurse had the baby in another bed but from one cause & another she seemed to get little sleep~ Dear mammy Leighton! What hard times she sometimes had!*

> *Another faithful nurse Mammy Ferguson had her labors increased after the birth of my fifth child by the breaking out of whooping cough among the other four~*

> *For my first confinements I had white flannel wraps trimmed down the front & all round with broad white satin ribbon~ for one occasion my wrap was trimmed with broad blue satin ribbon & blue tall bows on my cap~ I used to receive in dear aunt Dennett's great easy chair & I hope she knew how much I enjoyed it~*

> *Mammy Hall was with me in my last two confinements and she had the wisdom to strike for less work & more pay~ She would do no washing except for the baby & cake & wine were exploded~ Dr Cheever broke up that fashion~ He pronounced it an unsanitary custom~*[510]

It is not known if Sarah nursed her own babies, or if the monthly nurse she employed was also a wet nurse. Like pregnancy, breast-feeding was a subject that most women avoided talking about directly. The subject of breast-feeding versus bottle-feeding was a controversial one for centuries. It was the one maternal duty that many women of the upper class might have shunned at that time. As eminent a mother as Queen Victoria relied upon wet nurses to feed her infants, as she found the concept of breast-feeding distasteful. This was not an uncommon outlook amongst women of Sarah's class, but the mortality rate of "hand fed" infants, as babies raised on the bottle were called, was much higher than that of breast fed infants.[511]

However, Sarah did touch on the subject briefly in one of the early letters to her husband when she sympathized with her friend Marcia who was too sickly to nurse her own infant. From this remark it could be reasoned that Sarah was indeed in favor of nursing.

LETTERS FROM THE
EARLY YEARS OF MARRIAGE

Aletter written in June of 1829 from Savannah indicates Goodwin's pleasure at the new addition to the family, as well as his continued devotion to his bride.

Savannah 16 June, 1829

My Dear love,
As one of the packets is to sail this morning for New York and wind fair with a prospect of her having a short passage I cannot neglect so good an opportunity of letting you hear from me, although I have nothing of interest to communicate, but flatter myself that however uninteresting my letters might be to an indifferent reader, to you they may be a source of some pleasure, If I may judge from my own feelings in perusing your affectionate and interesting letters.
I wish I could get them more frequent, but I must acknowledge you have been very kind and that I ought not to complain if you have not written as much as once a week. I can well imagine that little Abigail occupies much of your time as well as thoughts~ I was made very happy a couple of days ago by the receipt of yours of the 29th with postscripts from our little girl, I shall not forget her but fear she will not keep me enough in remembrance to recollect that there is such a being as her father in existence.
I shall write again before sailing ~ fear my last letter will not reach you so soon as if it had been simply mailed and that you may be making yourself unhappy fearing something is the matter, the wind has been from the eastward most of the time since the vessels departure
I should write your father if I had anything written to communicate that would interest him~ I was pleased to hear of the safe arrival of the Lucy and that his spirits were better...tell him I hope he will now get the Lucy insured as she has arrived and safe should suppose there should be no difficulty in getting it effected...give my kind regards to all the family, kiss little Abigail Rice over and over again for me, does she grow prettier or otherwise and who does she look like I suppose by now a likeness may be discerned. It is now past six I must bid you good morning.
I am my dear Wife with every sentiment of affection; I am your devoted.
Ichabod Goodwin-

What shall I bring from France~ Is there anything wanted~ I am glad you decided on our old pew instead of Mr. Havens~ I hope some of your family will now sit with you~[512]

That fall when Goodwin returned from his European voyage they moved into her Uncle Flagg's gambrel house on Deer Street, the very same house she had loved to visit as a child.

> *When Abby was eight months old I went to housekeeping in the gambrel roofed house now occupied by Capt Godfrey~ What is now a restaurant was my barn~ There were two parlors, a dining room & eleven chambers~*
>
> *Your Aunt Hope was born in this house, "The Flagg house" it was called & belonged to my uncle Flagg~*[513]

The Goodwin's second daughter Hope was born in this house on September 23rd of 1830. Ichabod Goodwin was at home when she was born, but he left a little more than a month later to return to the sea. There are ten letters dated between October 30th 1830 and February 14th 1831 written by Sarah to her husband that trace his route from Portsmouth to New York City, Mobile, Alabama and finally on to Liverpool, England.

Unfortunately his correspondence to Sarah during this period is missing. However, the existing letters from Sarah are quite informative and excerpts from them provide a glimpse into the early years of their marriage, and Sarah's first years of motherhood.

The letters contain a number of references to Hope's health within the first few months of her life. Curiously in many of the letters there are notations or postscripts purportedly written by Abby written in a very childish scrawl. However, Abby was between eighteen months and two years of age when these letters were written, and the first reference to these postscripts is found in one of her father's letters when she was just four months old. It is not likely Abby was capable of writing at such a young age. It is, however, probable that Sarah held her young daughter's hand while guiding the pen and composing the notes from daughter to father herself.

For the most part the letters are chatty, filled with gossip about the town, social events and visits from friends and family. They also speak to the loneliness Sarah endured during his absence, and the difficulties she encountered while caring for two young children despite ample help from others. The first letter was written just a month after Sarah gave birth to Hope. It is addressed to Mr. Ichabod Goodwin care of Wm. G. Slater City of New York.

Portsmouth October 30th 1830

> *I suppose my dear husband you have been expecting a letter from me two or three days by the time you receive this & believe me I should not have delayed writing until the fifth day after your departure had not the <u>worrysomeness</u> of Mys <u>Hope</u> prevented. I have just put her into the cradle & hope she will stay there long enough to let me finish my letter. Little Abby is quite well and talks a great deal every day about you her continual song and theme is "Pa done," "Pa done in chaise", but this morning she heard the front door open & ran directly to the entry crying out "Pa tum" "Pa tum" but the poor child was doomed to be disappointed & probably will be many times before she can realize the joy of seeing you. The morning you left, Susan turned the house topsy turvey by moving me into my winter*

quarters & from that time we have eat, drank and slept altogether in them & compared with what I had anticipated they are very cheerful & pleasant.

Pa was over about an hour the evening before last & Aunt Wells has passed an afternoon with me, Adeline & Eliza too have been over frequently so that I have felt less of the void which must ever be produced by your absence than I shall probably feel hereafter, as I shall undoubtedly see less of them when the season becomes colder.... I am now expecting a letter from you every day supposing that you wrote directly upon your arrival at N. York~ Adeline even asked if it was not singular that you did not write from Boston, but I told her that you were not so much the ardent lover, as all that might seem to amount to. I hope while you are absent that you will not fall into the mark of some married men in regard to writing me, but that you will write often, even if sometimes but a line~ as it should be remembered that in your absence my highest pleasure is derived from these communications. I feel desirous to hear what sort of a journey you had to the city..., I want to know who you saw, what you said & all about it~ My hand is very weak, tremulous & tired but the heart is willing, let this suffice.

    Yours affectionately ever,
    Sarah P. Goodwin[514]

The next letter was written a few weeks later and despite the help from her sisters and others, the arduous chore of mothering a newborn and a toddler seemed to have taken its toll upon her.

Portsmouth Nov 2~1830
Dear husband
 Much tired with the exertions of the day, for indeed they have been many, I attempt this evening that which I wished to have done two or three days since, namely writing to you~ It seems to me that to no other being could I address one line, for really my ideas have been so scattered today by my innumerable cares above stairs, that it seems almost impossible for me to concentrate them sufficiently to make any communication interesting~

    I am writing completely in a hotbed of excitement and interruptions for setting aside the usual noises of the nursery I had not been seated five minutes when Abby reached on to the table & before I could prevent, caught the pen knife by the blade quite tightly in her hand~ I screamed for I was really frightened & this frightened her into opening her hand instantly when I found she was not hurt, not two minutes after she caught the ink stopper & daubed her frock & tire, not to speak of fingers most provokingly ~ then by the time I had got a little composed & pen in hand again I heard her choking out by the window & arrived just in time to find her pulling a pin from her throat, for which I thought it proper to give her a good scolding, at any rate a sufficient one to make her bring to mind the protection afforded by her dear father in similar cases, when at home, for she also immediately began with "I want Pa" "I want to see Pa" To which I replied I should write to her Pa to tell him what a naughty girl she had

*been. She is now crying "up a diddy" and I tell her not now but directly she
shall write a Postscript.*

*Today I have been reading a tract on the blessings of the sanctuary, left
here a day or two ago by Mrs. J Goddard~ It seems the orthodox societies
in this town have united in forming a tract society, the object of which is
to supply every family in Portsmouth with the means of salvation, <u>through
tracts</u>, which are to distributed monthly by individuals selected from the
different churches~ I believe Mr. Putnam and Mr. Waterbury are more
active than any others. This tract is a very excellent one, I think the best I
have ever read & I hope they all may effect the object they intended and
desired.*

*Capt Appleton's death is a most melancholy one, I am told the family are
uncommonly distressed in fact inconsolable, in a letter received the same
day the news came (which was through W. Langdon) Capt A__ mentions to
his family that it is his birth day, that he is going that day to Monte Video
& that he was very adverse to going, God knew his reasons, he would tell
<u>them</u> when he came home, that day he was drowned~ he also mentioned
that he should leave the vessel at Havana and quit the sea entirely. Abby
insists upon her turn & I must stop for the present for her~*

*I received yesterday a demijous of brandy & hope a <u>good use</u> may
be made of <u>every drop</u> of it, will endeavor to have most of it when you
return. Tomorrow morning I shall expect another letter, trust I may not
be disappointed, write me often every word is interesting to your truly
interested & affectionate wife*

*Susan and Adeline send love~ My love to N. York friends My Dear father
I long to see you and talk a great deal about you every day so come home
as soon as you can~ Your truly loving daughter Abby.*

*My <u>Dear Father</u> Mother wants me to be satisfied with writing one time but I
must write you again and tell you that I love you dearly your dear daughter
Abby.*[515]

Captain William Appleton, who drowned at sea in August of that year, was a ship's
captain for forty years. When he died he was a passenger on a packet en route between
Buenos Aires and Mountvideo. When a hurricane overturned the vessel, he was trapped in
the main cabin, unable to escape though he rapped on the walls for help. By then the water
was up to his chin, and he was unable to dive to safety, and others were unable to reach
him.[516]

Sarah's account of this incident seems to indicate that Captain Appleton had had a
premonition of his dreadful fate before he left for sea. Another letter written on November
14th is sent to New York.

Portsmouth Nov 14th 1830
*I find dear husband that you & I seem tacitly to agree on writing once a
week or <u>perhaps</u> <u>less</u> <u>often</u>. I need not say how much happiness it would
afford me if this mutual exchange of affectionate attention occurred more*

frequently, as it certainly tends in a great degree to ameliorate the pangs and anxieties of separation; for myself I would plead almost unintermitted domestic occupation & you I suppose the cares of business, which no doubt engross a very considerable share of your time. But it hardly seems right that the <u>Sabbath</u> should find us engaged in letter writing, when there are six days beside which apparently might afford us at least one or two hours for this purpose.

   But <u>I</u> am in rather peculiarly circumstances for really it is the only day I can get, as when my arms are relived from their burden of <u>Hope</u>. I am almost overwhelmed by claims for minding and making & today Abby was sent for to pass the day at her <u>gappy's</u> which has proved a very seasonable relief. Abby has been well since you left but Hope's health does not improve much, indeed not at all, I am up with her from one to three or four times every night, the variety is truly <u>delightful</u> it reminds me so much of <u>old times</u>.

   But I suppose I must not touch this string, I know in your ear the vibration cannot be sweet, it sounds too much of green apples, green plums & other good things. I say that Hope is not well, but no one would suspect it, as she certainly bears every mark of the most perfect health, She has grown amazingly I really believe she weights ten or eleven pounds.

   Abby goes in and kisses your picture everyday, not one feature is slighted, ears, nose, mouth, cheek & chin in turn receive their share of kisses. I think you have no reason to apprehend anything like forgetfulness, should you remain from home even longer than you expect.

   I have been out to walk once & did a little shopping & never in my life was I so tired. I suppose my excessive fatigue was owing to not having used any exercise for so long a time.

   Dr & Mrs Cheever have returned from their journey, and held a grand levee, dressed in considerable style and changed their pew to the other side of the meeting house. I think they have taken the most suitable means for putting down opposition & doing away present impressions & associations.

   There has been a splendid Military ball within a week, but I know nothing more particular, I believe the ladies were mostly daughters of mechanics & the gentlemen were what you might suppose. I understand there is to be a <u>mariner's</u> ball too, got up by <u>masters & mates,</u> what do you think of this?

   Pray let me know if you found Abby's writing legible~ I suppose you will say that it was a piece with her mother's dear little thing if she were here she would be delighted to write one or two more letters. I hear Miss Hope rustling in the cradle, so my dear husband I must bid you an affectionate but abrupt goodbye~ Sarah~
Give love to your Aunt G & whoever else may inquire~[517]

Portsmouth Nov 22, 1830

During the last week I have had the happiness to receive three letters from my dear husband, how great that happiness has been I will leave you to imagine. Shut up almost alone day after day & week after week with scarcely the least variety besides that which attendance on children gives, you may well suppose how delightful it is to me to receive that second best of pleasures the next to seeing you. Do not accuse me of flattery, for in the common acceptance of that word it is not so, and when you reflect on the satisfaction which your society has afforded me & the unfeigned pleasure with which I uniformly hailed your return, however short your absence might have been, you will not doubt it. Pa' comes to see me sometimes once and sometimes twice a week, he is as well as when you left, as are the rest of the family. Mr. Lord sent me your bank book together with some checks & a note, the same I presume which you requested me to burn I forget precisely what you told me about that & wish when you write me again you would let me know what note you had reference to & whether you still wish me to destroy it....

William is now ready for Fla, Emily I suppose under <u>present circumstances</u> will feel his absence more than ever, and she seems even <u>now</u> to be quite a <u>burden to herself.</u> I don't know how she will be able to wait her time.

You say you passed an evening with Mrs. Merrill & that she abounds in English airs, I can readily conceive of them; I long to see her that I may find a <u>model</u> of <u>true gentility</u> and <u>fashion</u> amidst the rusticity of Portsmouth to copy. When you see her please say I wish to be remembered.

I hear Hope crying & must quit and go to her~ hoping to hear from you again soon I subscribe myself with much sincerity your truly attached wife.
Sarah P. Goodwin
Our family all desire to be remembered~[518]

"*Gappy*" was Abby's name for her Grandfather Rice. William was Sarah 's older brother, and also a ship's captain working for his father. His wife Emily Pease was apparently pregnant with her first child, and in Sarah's estimation was not handling even the early stages of pregnancy well. She and William eventually had seven children.

Ichabod was still in New York two weeks later when a letter arrived with a message from Abby at the beginning.

Portsmouth Nov 30th 1830
Dear father I hope you won't think anything of my not writing you before, but the other day when Ma' wrote I was over to gappy's I have not much to say except that I love you dearly and am longing for you to come home~
Yrs affectionately
Abby

My Dear Husband

You will doubtless be surprised on opening this to find anything so sad as the writing which will first meet your eye, for if mine is not much handsomer, it is certainly more legible, but no sooner had I made my appearance with my writing materials than little Abby began to tease me to let her write a letter to her dear Pa' as she called you, and finding that it would be impossible for me to proceed a line unless I first complied with her wishes I did so accordingly. I am certain you need not give yourself any trouble about her forgetting you, for there is no one that she talks even so much of. Betsy has told her that you are going to bring her home a horse & chaise & a pair of shoes and she talks of them incessantly.

I went to meeting on Sunday both morning & afternoon & you may be sure it was a pleasant day to me in every sense of the word; it may readily be supposed that I enjoyed it after having stayed at home almost 6 months. I wish you could have been here you don't know how smart I looked (not to say how handsome) I had on my new pelisse which I know will suit you exactly it is as grave as you could possibly wish, a perfect ash color, believe me, I got it on purpose to please you for I know you hate anything dashing. And then my pink bonnet matches so nicely, you would be surprised to find out how smart it looks I have altered it myself into quite a plain one & have taken off the fringe & yellow trimmings, so you may be certain I look as much your mind this winter as if you were here to direct and advise,

I have been over to Pa's several times lately Pa' requested me to say to you that he is growing so fat that he can scarcely get out of his chair, that he would write you now if he had anything to say that would be worth as much to you as 18c & that he intends writing when you are at the south

Nancy and Sally are still with me & I like them if anything better than ever, for me particularly at the present time, there could not be better help. Nancy is always good natured and kind & makes out to get through before night & Sally is as attentive as I could possibly wish. Abby has got so that she can call Nancy very plain & she even opens the chamber door herself & without assistance seats herself in very appropriate style. Hope continues about the same I am sure you would never suspect who it is, if you were to see her. I think she looks very much as Abby did when a babe & am not certain that she will not be quite as pretty, but I believe no one else thinks so.

I received your last letter on Saturday & shall look forward with impatience to the reception of the next & feel grieved that any interruption should occur to the facility of our communication during your absence, yet there is something provoking too in being so near without the ability to meet; but absent or present far or near believe me ever to be your truly affectionate & deeply interested wife ~ S.P. Goodwin
Our family all send love[519]

Sarah's account of her first outing in six months marking the end of her period of confinement following Hope's birth is quite charming, and the length of her confinement confirms that she followed the custom of upper class ladies regarding the period of confinement.

The new pelisse she wore to meeting would have been a long loose cloak or robe, probably lined with fur, with slit openings on each front panel for her arms. Sarah's attempt to please her husband's conservative tastes in ladies' clothing implies that he often guided her in personal matters such as fashion. It also implies a paternalistic relationship. But that was the norm at this time in America, when the average marriage reflected this cultural bias. In addition he was eleven years her senior, and it is likely these tendencies were more pronounced in his nature when they first married than in later years.

The next letter was mailed in care of the *Sarah Parker* in Mobile, Alabama.

> *Portsmouth December 7th 1830*
>
> *This morning my dear husband I received the pleasing intelligence that you had sailed at last from New York....You say you have determined to go to Mobile. I should think by way of change it would be very pleasant to you that is if there is as good a prospect there as elsewhere & I presume there is or else you would not go there.*
>
> *Peter Parrott made me a much unexpected visit this morning. I did not know he was expected home, & I think him if anything <u>handsomer</u> than ever & he certainly appeared more interesting from the circumstances of bringing me intelligence of you. Frederick Toscan sailed about a week since...Wm Parrott had not been up when I called yesterday, so have not got my books.*
>
> *Mr. Ferguson has just called; he brought I. Goodwin's N.Y. dispatches, which consisted of your policy of insurance, a letter & doll from J. Elizabeth. Abby is delighted with the doll, which is really too pretty to be thrown among the other playthings, but Jane requested that she might have it now & I suppose I must comply.*
>
> *Charlotte Slater has lately been wholly deprived of her reason, I know nothing very particular of the case but believe it is ascribed to a cold, Henry's marriage has been delayed in consequence. Mr. Coues called to see me last Saturday,... Our girls laugh & joke a good deal about his bosom pin, which he has lately put in, they seem to think it is a sign of his being in the market.*
>
> *Hope is getting better I think She does not disturb me at night as much as she did, she laughs and coos very prettily.*
>
> *Trusting and earnestly desiring that this will find you long since arrived I subscribe myself with all affection Yours~*
> *S.P.R. Goodwin*
> *Pa' desires to be remember*[520]

Nancy and Sally were the girls who joked about Goodwin's business partner. Samuel Coues was a recent widower and wearing his bosom pin, which would have been in the shape of a heart indicating friendship or love, was taken as a subtle sign that he was either available and looking, or courting someone new at the time.

Portsmouth Dec 17ᵗʰ 1830

 I know my dear husband will excuse the tediousness of a scrawl dictated by one of the most stupid heads in the world, for really I don't know that a cold in the head with which I am afflicted at present, ever had so stupefying effect on me before & I thought if anything would draw me out of it, it would be scribbling a letter to you…

 I think Abby has it slightly too, she has appeared unwell two or three days and has a humour out on her face, but she is well enough to be over to her <u>Gappy's</u> whom by the way she can call Daffy & Danpa.

 Lucy Penhallow had a small party about a week ago, which I was at, it was quite pleasant & there were many inquiries for you. I don't know but you will be attempted to scold when I tell you I have attended the theatre lately knowing that you don't altogether like for me to go out or visit much when you are absent but as I have generally made it a point to communicate to you all my proceedings I will not omit this. Mr. & Mrs. Parsons' invited me twice, the first time I declined, the second I accepted, but was not pleased with the performance. Mr. Ferguson was there & we joked each other a good deal about telling tales out of school. I told him he might be sure of a scolding, but I felt privileged, as in my case it was only following the example which you set me while in N. York. Mr. Ferguson has called to see me but once, and that I believe I mentioned in my last.

 In the evening Mr. B. Toscan and Mr. Robert P_ and Mr. William P_ came and shortly after Susan & Adeline came also. They were all agreeable & seemed to pass a pleasant evening. B. Toscan, R. Hile & some others are about quitting the place for the neighborhood of Pensacola, where they intend purchasing a township & settling….

 I received the books yesterday, which you sent me by Wm Parrott, I feel quite pleased with this addition to our library…The Bible is a handsome one & the print is very excellent, I had a half a mind when I saw the blank sheets for records to begin with our own, but it seemed so premature I thought I would wait a little <u>until</u> perhaps <u>we might have more to add to the list</u>.

 Little Hope is I think is getting better, but she is yet very troublesome at night, last night I scarcely closed my eyes for independent of the trouble she gave I was not well. Sally is a remarkably good girl, she is so attentive & obliging I really feel quite attached to her. The moment she hears the babe stir or cry she gets up & wants to be doing something for her, in many instances she has got up in the night & set two or three hours with the babe when she has been worrysome, which you may suppose has been a great relief & assistance to me.

 I have been to meeting the last three Sabbaths all day & think it probable I shall be enabled to do so all winter…

 I believe I mentioned in a former letter something of Charlotte Slater's derangement. I am told she is no better, also that it was caused by religious excitement from a remark which Mr. Waterbury made at his lecture room,

*mainly that he had no doubt but many who had once filled those seats were
now suffering hell's torments. I will not positively assert that this is correct
but I have no doubt of its truth.*

*"Be but as happy as I wish & you'll be blest indeed" my dear, dear
husband, goodbye~*
Your affectionate wife ~
Sarah

*Lucy & I went yesterday to see Mr. Coues' little girl, she is a sickly,
miserable child & is troubled constantly with a humour similar to that
which caused her mother's death. She has an interesting countenance,
the expression of which is quite pensive. I do not think she will live many
months, but this is my opinion merely.*[521]

In the above letter Sarah alludes to her husband's displeasure because she attended
social functions in his absence. This is all the more interesting in light of the distinct
impression given by other correspondence that he continued to lead an active social life
while in New York and Liverpool. The reference to being privileged to follow his example
is puzzling. It may have been her way of pointing out that what was "good for the goose
was good for the gander," but it is more likely that the reference was to some private matter
known only to them.

The account of an impromptu gathering of a large number of friends, both male and
female, in the nursery one evening and the subsequent discussion about Pensacola, Florida
highlights the many possibilities for adventure and advancement that existed for young and
adventurous Americans during those years.

The next letter was written on Christmas day. At this time in New England Christmas
was not an official holiday. Banks, business, and schools were all open as it was a regular
business day, and there were no church services, with the possible exception of the
Episcopalian and Unitarian Churches. Both of these religions celebrated Christmas by this
time, but it was still considered a minor holiday.

Portsmouth Dec 25th 1830
*Somewhat longer than the usual time has elapsed since I wrote to my dear
husband & the only apology I have to offer (which by the way is a very
sufficient one) is the indisposition of both the children particularly Abby.
She took a violent cold which seem to affect her system generally but settled
more particularly in the side of her throat, we thought for a time that the
swelling & contraction in that part must be occasioned by viscose (in the
ear, but as there has been no discharge, from the ear and as she is very
materially we now think better, that such could not have been the case.
I was a good deal alarmed about her for a day or two as she lost all her
strength even so as to be unable to stand & accordingly sent for Dr Dwight
who paid her two or three visits & administered considerable medicine.
Hope's complaint is nothing out of the common course; I think she seems
to be growing better.*

Abby is crying beside me to get up a diddy & write letter to Dear Pa'! I tell her she shall directly & would now if I thought it would be the means of getting rid of her a little, for between her crying & Hope's screaming I am almost stunned.

Susan came over while Abby was sick & stayed several days. I was very glad to have her, as it served as a very great relief to Sally by night, independent of the pleasure found in her company.

Today is Christmas and I may safely say the oddest one I ever spent, for on that day I have usually seen a great many people, but today I have seen no one beside Nancy & Sally, for I have not even looked out of the window, ...I may safely say that of myself. It will be two months tomorrow since you left us, I almost wish sometimes that double that time might have passed and then I might be again expecting your return....

But Winter will soon be gone with its gloomy clouds and storms and Spring again bring its cheerfulness and its hopes.

I don't hear much in the way of amusements & believe there are no parties present either large or small at any rate I don't hear of them.

Mr. L. Lord called to see me last Sunday night, I was very much engaged in attendance on Abby it being just then the commencement of her sickness & I was very much alarmed, I regretted the circumstance and intend calling soon to explain, though to him I presume it was clear enough, that is if he can remember the cares which confined the mother of his children. But a second marriage is the tombstone of memory you know. On that odious subject you will say, how she harps upon it, so I say too I can't abide it & yet for all that I can't help a little fun now and then at the expense of the widowers, but enough of this I will now bid my dear husband goodnight & delightful dreams & subscribe myself once more with every assurance of affection & devotion yours S.P.R.G.[522]

At this point many would have celebrated Christmas much like New Year's Day, by calling on friends, and holding open house. That may have been the Rice family custom, and the reason Sarah was surprised at the lack of callers.

Portsmouth Jan #14 1831
I have been waiting a day or two to find some new ideas or incidents at least to communicate to my dear husband ....It is certainly no new idea that we all love you (I mean particularly Abby and me) and think as much of you as you can possibly wish, and beyond that I can think of little else
I suppose you have by this time obtained a <u>good freight</u> (for Mr. John Rice says you will get a good one) and you know, he knows a <u>great deal</u>) and that you are probably loading, so that I feel doubtful that this reaches you short of Europe. Be this as it may I think it best to write, as you may be detained longer than I suppose to be necessary.

Pa' does not seem to be willing to admit to any of us that business is improving, I presume he is fearful that we are disposed to increase our expenditures accordingly.

I was at a party at Mr. Jones last evening. Mrs. Jones observed that it was not convenient to give a general party at this time, but I suspect there were nearly or all her acquaintances invited. I thought the party a very agreeable one and everything appeared very handsome.

While talking with Mrs. Parker last night something was said about this tract society which I mentioned to you in my last, I found it rather a sore subject to her although she seemed disposed to converse upon it. I did not know until lately that Dr Parker was not engaged with the other clergy men in the selection of them. He, Mr. King & Mr. Howe being Unitarians and a universalist were left out upon the list of sinners for conversion. I found she did not like the idea of our parish receiving them & she observed that it would be a good thing for all to refuse them, about thirty having done so, as it was evidently paying our minister disrespect, I think so too, but don't know what to do about it, as they certainly so far are very improving & excellent.

Dr Cheever told me he expected I had got a chart engraved on my heart where I could follow you in your course and know just where to find you. I thought it was quite a pretty idea don't you? So now dear husband goodbye and believe me as ever your much attached wife ~ Sarah Goodwin[523]

The above letter was mailed to Mobile, Alabama. The continued references to the tract society started by the orthodox ministers in town, highlights Sarah's earlier references to a rift between the North and South Churches about the time she married Goodwin.

The final letter in the series was directed to Liverpool, England in care of the *Sarah Parker.*

Portsmouth Feb 10th 1831
I had the pleasure one hour since to receive another letter from my dear husband. Pa' is truly the harbinger of happiness. Whenever I hear his step in the entry I know another dear, valued letter is at hand and the pleasure of receiving it is if possible enhanced by the satisfaction which he evinces in being the bearer. It amuses me very much to see him in such a hurry to ascertain your prowlings, he always says "come let us know what he is doing, I have just left Mr. Coues & promised to tell him all about him;" Upon which I set myself to finding out all that relates to business and after reading it over to him two or three times I am at liberty to read the rest as much as I please

He [Coues] called to see me the day before yesterday, his stay was short and his conversation pretty much with Abby who seemed to claim a large share of his attention as a matter of course. He inquired as to what was going on in the fashionable world, observed there was much beauty and taste at Dr. P___'s church, but appeared to wish me to understand that he did not visit except very occasionally at Dr Parkers. He was dressed in a new Camlet trimmed very dashingly in frogs, braid &c. It is well for me to know that you are not here to hear me talk as I write, but I really mean no harm and should not think of commenting on what I have written if I did not know you so well.

I believe I wrote you in my last that I was going to Kittery with Alexander. Hannah, Susan, Adeline, Abby and my self with Alexander composed the party, we had a fine large sleigh & two horses. After we crossed the bridges Alexander proposed riding a little toward Elliott when he was about turning back one runner sank into the soft snow very deeply, and we were all very gently deposited in a snow bank. You may well suppose how badly I felt I had Abby in my arms under my cloak, which was tied up, and we were on the back seat among two or three buffalo skins, so that it would have been impossible even if I had foreseen the difficulty to have extricated myself. I went over on my back head down & poor little Abby (who I believe thought it was part of the ride) went over my head, I thought only of her & I leave you to judge how relieved & thankful I felt when I heard her screams which however were soon stopped by the merriment excited by our truly ludicrous condition. I had the least cause to laugh, although the greatest cause to be grateful which I reconcile to you, by stating the destruction of my beautiful India combs. However I made the best of it on account of Alexander's feelings which seemed to be much mortified & hurt, though entirely without cause, as it was purely accidental.

We called at Dr. Chase's and then proceeded to accomplish the principal object of our ride, which was to see Marcia. She came down stairs the first time to see us. She looks miserably though not so emaciated as I expected to see her. Her babe is a very pretty one, and so far very healthy she is not able to nurse it.

Peter Parrott goes to Philadelphia this week where I believe he has the prospect of a <u>situation</u>. Henry Salter is married and as you probably suppose lives in the Martin house. I have not yet called but intend soon to do so. Charlotte is much better I believe from what I can now gather that the circumstances of her situation were not so unhappy & hopeless, as the public would have it & am sincerely glad they were not.

Wishing you health happiness in short every thing you can desire I will bid you good night
Sarah Goodwin

Pa desires to be remembered, was much pleased at the reception of your letter also send love & Abby sends hers with a kiss.[524]

Sarah made gentle fun of his partner in this last letter in regard to his choice of clothing. A camlet is a rich cloth of oriental origin made of a combination of camel hair and silk. He probably wore a vest or jacket. Samuel Coues was apparently quite an eccentric man, and from the correspondence it would seem he was shy and not socially skilled around women.

During this voyage William Rice and Goodwin also corresponded, although not as frequently. There is one existing letter from Rice to Goodwin it indicates that William Rice, was very much in charge of a syndicate of shipping interests made up of close friends and families, which he oversaw and advised. The shipping trade was undergoing an economic slump, and Rice's future projections as to the effect a war in Europe is of interest.

Portsmouth Jany 1, 1831
Capt. Goodwin
My Dear Sir ___ It is so long since that I received your very kind favor of the
3 Nov. informing me of your progress with the Sarah Parker and sorry was
I to learn the dull Prospect before you~ But I do most devotedly pray that
your prospect has changed and that you have good business in hand Ere
this can reach you ~ Hope that you may be able to obtain <u>not less then 7/8</u>
<u>on a penny</u>~ But should you be obliged to take a low freight I hope it may be
a Coastwise one~ Then you may calculate on being on a chain of freighting
Ground when Ready to Return and by this means avoid a Winters Voyage to
Europe the Wari and Tari of which you are well acquainted with~
___ Wm in the Minerva sailed on the 24th Nov. for N .O., where I hope he has
safe arrived Long Ere this. And I have written him to this Purpose that I think
one ¾ freight will leave him more clear gain than two 5/8 freight will and that
our one freight will Leave More clear gain than two ¾ freights will gain and
that by retailing his Cargo may do better than taking a low freight anywhere~
In Short I am heartily tired of Working for nothing~ Wearing out our ships
without Thereby being Enabled to replace with New ones when gone~ I hope
there is or will be an end of this Dreary business Ere long~
The Late news from Europe has a warlike aspect and I think that Ere this
Rusia, Prusia, Austria & Holland are on one side and France, England, &
Belgium on the other have begun or will commence hostilities Early in the
Spring, and by which if we can keep out of the Scraps and keep out of the
Quarrel we shall have better times as the Premiums will be up on the vessels
of the hostile powers and thereby give us a chance to make up for lost time ~
Domestic affairs__ Sarah spent last evening at our home and dined with
us today with yours and our little Abbie~ She has been quite sick for a few
days but is now very well, as well as <u>Mys Hope</u>~
All other friends are well and join me in the compliments of the season~
Remaining with very great –Regards yours Wm. Rice

P.S. Three days since I assisted Mr. Coues with your name on a note for two
thousand dollars~[525]

In June of 1831 Ichabod Goodwin returned from Liverpool in the *Sarah Parker* with a load of salt. This was the last time he sailed in the ship that bore his wife's name, and it marked the end of his career at sea, perhaps because of the poor shipping prospects Rice wrote about. The *Sarah Parker* was retained by Goodwin and Coues and Ferguson and Jewett, and continued to sail under another captain primarily in the cotton trade until 1835 when she was sold, and while all the details are not known she was thought to have been used in the whaling trade. [526]

> *The Sarah Parker had to be sold because the cotton crop had so enormously increased & very large ships were found necessary to carry it to Europe~ The owner could not afford to keep her~*[527]

CHILDREARING

In 1832 the Goodwins purchased a large Federal style home on Islington Street in Portsmouth to accommodate their growing family. That year Sarah was expecting their third child.

> *When your aunt Hope was about a year & a half old we bought the house where you now live & as we have always been making additions & improvements & buying the land about us, where we could, we have made it a most agreeable & comfortable home~ I can truly say I have never desired another or a better~*[528]

This was the Goodwin family home for the next sixty years; and it was where their next five children were born. Sarah Parker Rice Jr., who was known as Sadie, was born there that first summer, followed two years later by her sister Georgette. Then three years after that in June of 1837 their fifth child, and first son, was born.

He was named Samuel Coues Goodwin in honor of Ichabod Goodwin's friend and business partner. The birth of the Goodwin's first son must have been a joyous occasion in the Goodwin household. But sadly their young son died fourteen months later, in September of 1838. The cause of

The Goodwin Mansion as it appears today at Srawbery Banke.

his death is not noted, nor is there an extant record of his death certificate. He may very well have died from a common childhood illness now eradicated or easily cured by the many advances made in medicine since then.

There is no mention of her son Samuel in Sarah's writings, other than the above reference to the fifth child, and the sad entry in the family Bible she had once been so eager to fill up. It does not appear to have been entered by Sarah.

> *Samuel Goodwin died Wednesday morning, September 12th 1838, aged 14 mo, 19 days*[529]

One can only surmise what a tragic time this was in the Goodwin home. Another son, and their sixth child, Frank, was born three years later in November of 1841. Then their last child, Susan Boardman Goodwin, named after Sarah's younger sister, Susan, the wife of Dr. John Boardman, was born on March 3rd of 1844. This completed the family.

Unfortunately, Sarah doesn't leave much of a record behind of those years when her children were young. It is known that she had household help throughout these years, but there is no indication she engaged a nanny other than the monthly nurses who attended her when the children were born. In addition to the monthly nurse Sarah employed a neighborhood girl who came to live with her during the early years when her first two children were born, and she herself was left alone a good deal of the time when her husband was at sea. Sally Cole is recalled in her journals and letters many years later.

> *Sally Cole came to live with me as a nurse to my first two babies~ She was fourteen when she came & I paid her the usual wages a quarter of a dollar a week~ She lived with me two or three years~*[530]

During this time period Americans were not quite as lenient with children as they had been during Sarah's youth, but European visitors still viewed American child rearing practices as much too permissive. The conventional Victorian adage that children were to be seen but not heard applied more to European children than American children. Americans were always less strident towards their children, who were not so rigidly disciplined as their European counterparts. It was true that in some upper class American homes the task of raising the children was assigned to a governess or nanny as was commonly done in Europe, but for the most part Americans raised their own children. [531]

During the nineteenth century motherhood took on new dimensions in both American and European societies. In fact during this time child rearing became somewhat of an art form viewed by many to be the primary responsibility in a woman's life. This was particularly true following Queen Victoria's ascension to the throne in the 1830s. As the mother of nine she was a role model for all women of this period. Motherhood became elevated in the eyes of society and was considered the highest calling in life for which a woman should strive.

Thanks to the proliferation of the many new ladies' magazines such as *Godey's Lady's Book*, which came into fashion about this time there were a growing number of women who earned their living by advising other women on how to run their lives and families. So there was no dearth of advice on how to dress, discipline, and guide children in every area of their lives.

Experts such as Catherine Beecher and her sister, Harriet Beecher Stowe, co-authors of *American Women's Home*, advised that a child's life should be scheduled and regimented in order to lend a sense of purpose and accomplishment to their daily activities. Obedience, submission, and benevolence were key traits to instill in a child, as they ultimately taught a child to "submit their will to the will of God." To achieve these lofty ideals parents were advised to set high moral standards for children through the example of their own actions, and to govern wisely, steadily, and kindly. The primary responsibility for overseeing that these children led exemplary lives, filled with high purpose and moral standards, of course fell upon the mother.[532]

It seems likely that Sarah's own experiences, as a motherless child would have impressed upon her the importance of a mother's continuing influence and presence. She once recalled how deeply the lack of a mother had impacted on her life.

> *I think children's troubles are as keenly felt as any in mature life~ Certainly my own experience bears me out in this assertion~ Losing my mother as I did at seven years of age & falling under the care of those who were unsympathising (always excepting my father who tenderly filled the place of both parents) I had many a bitter sorrow & crying spell all by myself~* [533]

The Beecher sisters also advised on the physical care of children, and though they conceded the necessity of exercise, they cautioned against walking or other aimless activities. Instead they urged mothers to have their children engage in activities that achieved some goal, such as sports, gardening, and domestic chores. Cleanliness was also considered important to the physical well being of the children. While the Beechers concurred that very young children needed to be fully bathed once a day to remove skin impurities, in their opinion scrubbing with a wet towel each morning was adequate for older children.[534]

Just as the image of motherhood was exalted during this time, so was the image of children. Victorians were especially enamored of babies, and viewed them as pure innocent creatures that needed to be sheltered from the harsher realities of the world. This innocence was emphasized in the literature of the day. Charming waifs and heroic children abounded in the novels of writers like Dickens and Alcott. [535]

Hair fashions and clothing styles also reflected this belief in the innocence of childhood. Boys and girls wore similar hairstyles. Loosely cropped hair or long curls differentiated them from adults, but created an asexual appearance amongst all children. This androgynous look extended to clothing. Stylish upper class families such as the Goodwins dressed their infants almost exclusively in long white gowns trimmed in lace. This accentuated their angelic look and gave babies an innocent asexual appearance [536]

As children grew more active, at about six months of age, matching white pantaloons, replete with lace trim, were added to the outfits. The boys' gowns were shortened about this time to give them increased mobility, but the girls remained in longer gowns for much longer. Starting in the 1830s the girls' gowns began to be shortened, as they grew older.

Within a decade their gowns reached just below the knees, nearly as short as the boys, creating once again an androgynous mode of dress distinctly different from that of adults. This fashion, which put girls in pantaloons for the first time, came from England and met with some initial resistance in America. But it soon became accepted as it eliminated gender differences, and maintained the image of innocence in childhood for a longer period of time.[537]

However, within a few years unexpected consequences arose from this new fashion. What the Victorians hadn't anticipated was that the addition of pantaloons to the wardrobes of young girls would change their activities in many ways. Their modesty protected and their mobility increased by the inclusion of pants into their wardrobe, girls started to became active in games that were formerly the preserve of young males like jumping rope, climbing trees, or trundling hoops.[538]

There remained, however, a subtle but sure guiding of children towards activities that reflected the cultural standards set for males and females. The girls were encouraged to play with smaller toys and to sew or knit, and in general emulate the activities of women. Toys and games for boys such as baseball, which came into fashion by mid-century, were larger or required more space and physical activity. The rocking horse Abby was promised was generally considered a toy for small boys rather than girls, as it encouraged active play. Dolls, especially ones too delicate and pretty to play with such as the doll Abby's father sent home to her, encouraged passive play or no play at all.[539]

Sarah did leave behind a list of rules on how to raise children, but it is not certain if these were her own rules, or if she copied them from an article. Either way the rules she wrote down are interesting, inasmuch as they give some insight into childcare concepts popular during the early or mid-nineteenth century.

Points in regard to a mother's duties

First~ a deep feeling of responsibility

Second~ maternal authority or the necessity of enforcing prompt & entire obedience even from infancy~

Thirdly~ To watch closely the different dispositions of children & adapt treatment accordingly~

Fourth~ control under all circumstances, not suffering herself to do anything which she would never have her children imitate~

Fifthly~ Never talk about children in their presence~

Sixth~ The mother should exert herself in every way to imbue her children with deep devotional feeling & strong religious principles~ She should not force the subject on them at all times, but should watch and seize on suitable moments for introducing such topics & for exciting devotional feelings~

Seventh~ The mother should be extremely careful, should her children show strong symptoms of piety, about speaking of it to others~ When a

thing of this kind gets publicity it soon, by some means or other, reaches the child &, unless their principles are more deeply rooted than they probably may be, they become vain, conceited, lose their spirituality & suspend their efforts~

Eighth~ If you wish your children to have a habit of teasing, indulge them one hour in what you forbid the next~ In this way, by occasionally conquering, they are not apt to despair of conquering always and seldom cease their importunities until they are compelled by some painful infliction to desist~ This course is nothing less than deliberate cruelty~[540]

Frank Goodwin, circa 1860.

It is safe to assume that the Goodwin children went on to receive a good education in Portsmouth, although it is not known if they attended public or private schools. During this time many upper class children in New England, both male and female, did attend private academies, as the old district schools were considered inadequate and substandard. There is some indication that Frank, who later graduated from Harvard, may have been educated at the Academy in Portsmouth, a private school for boys that specialized in maritime and navigational subjects. It was located at the corner of Middle and Islington now home to Portsmouth Library.

Starting in the 1840s a school reform movement led by the Massachusetts educator, Horace Mann, emerged in New England, and out of this came the model for today's graded and high schools.[541] In 1858, a new high school was built on the corner of Chapel and Daniel Streets, with one level for male scholars and one for females.[542] Susan Goodwin, and possibly some of the grandchildren, would have been the only ones in the Goodwin family who would have attended this school.

While there is no available record that the Goodwin daughters went on to institutions of higher learning, it is possible that they did, as by mid-century many of these same young ladies, who had invaded and to some degree taken over the male playgrounds of their youth, went on to explore other arenas of their world once thought to be strictly the domain of males.

Colleges for women, such as Colby Jr. College in New Hampshire and Mount Holyoke in nearby Massachusetts opened their doors around the time the Goodwin daughters would have completed their high school education. These all female colleges made it possible for many young women from upper class families such as the Goodwins to obtain the benefits of a higher education, much as Miss Willard's School for Young Ladies had in the 1820s. As the century progressed more and more young women began to claim their rights to not only a higher education, but also to positions and sometimes careers within the business and political spheres of life.

1830-1840
WHALING, WHIGGERY AND RAILROADS

When Ichabod Goodwin gave up the sea, he was named president of the Portsmouth Whaling Company. This was the very first whaling company ever to operate out of the Port of Portsmouth, but two other companies started up shortly after this one was organized in the spring of 1832. Like many of the businesses that began in Portsmouth around this time, the whaling company was a stock company formed by a group of investors willing to put up the capital necessary to finance the new venture.[543]

While each investor stood to gain as an individual as well as a group, the benefit to the community in the form of jobs, roads, bridges, and other enterprises was also great. At this time Portsmouth was still dependent on the shipping industries, but it was losing its stature as one of the major commercial seaports in New England. New sea related enterprises such as the Portsmouth Whaling Co. were needed to keep the Port of Portsmouth viable.

There was a great demand during the 1830s for whale oil. It was used as a machine lubricant and to make sperm candles, which were still in great demand at the time. But primarily it was needed to fuel the increasingly popular oil lamps used in homes and businesses. Because oil was more convenient than candles, many upper class families such as the Goodwins began to illuminate more rooms in their home during the evening hours. This extended the amount of productive time at their disposal, while it also created a warm and welcoming atmosphere in the home.

There were about five hundred different designs in oil lamps introduced around this time. One popular one was the astral lamp. This lamp's ring shaped font was pierced by holes, and it burned with a bright flame that fell from above into a star pattern. Also popular was the solar lamp, a tall round lamp, shaped like the sun. Although they were expensive, lamps such as these were considered very fashionable.

> *The Astral lamp followed by the Solar lamp came in just before gas was introduced*~[544]

The cost of oil was great, but so was the demand. The general economy was good about then, and the overall outlook for success in the whaling enterprise appeared promising to these men. However, many other whaling companies sprang up all along the northeast coast during this period, and it soon became clear that the New England seas were overly harvested. Because of this whaling ships were forced to travel longer and longer distances in search of their prey.

Ichabod Goodwin, who held one share in the enterprise, was chosen to be company's president and agent. Backed by a capital investment of $100,000 Goodwin purchased the whaler *Pocahontas* in Haverhill, Mass. He then traveled to Bedford and Nantucket in search of an experienced crew and captain. Local men were hired to fill less skilled positions.[545]

The local papers looked favorably upon this new venture, as did most of the community. Whaling was a novel new industry for Portsmouth requiring trips to far away lands, adventure, and when successful an exotic catch. The whole enterprise generated a great deal of excitement in the city, and at first when the whaling ships returned to port; they were greeted with gun salutes, and the ringing of church bells.

However, The *Pocahontas,* was never really successful. Her first voyage took forty-three months and the profits from that trip were not impressive. By the time she finished her second voyage in 1837, the country was in the throes of a financial crisis, and her investors deemed it wisest to sell her. All in all the company's investors took a net loss of $98.00 each when the company folded.[546]

Goodwin and Coues always spread out their investments, and they had other enterprises to which they could turn. Together with other investors including William Rice, Samuel Lord, George Cummings, William Parsons, and shipbuilders Raynes and Neal, they formed a syndicate to finance the construction of ships in Portsmouth. George Raynes was considered the premier shipbuilder of the area. A letter from George Cummings to Goodwin in 1835 contained a glowing appraisal of his skills.

> *Raynes will put himself at the top of his speed this time and I spake no flattery when I told him, that if his life is spared, his name will be enrolled first on the roll of naval architects in this country or the world, we shall therefore get the best ship he ever has, but not the best he probably will build.*[547]

This company benefited the general community as well as the investors, by employing ship joiners, rope makers, and sail makers. Many of these vessels such as the *Hindo* and the *India* were immediately sold for a good profit to firms in Boston or New York. [548] However, Goodwin & Coues retained a number of these vessels for use in their own shipping trade. In 1835 they were listed in the Portsmouth city directory as the owners of the *Marion,* the *Sarah Parker,* and the *Mary and Susan.* Goodwin was also involved in the insurance business, as was William Rice and Samuel Lord. Goodwin & Coues were listed as agents for the Piscataqua Insurance Agency and the Portsmouth Mutual Insurance Co in the city directory of 1839. They eventually became agents for two Massachusetts based insurance companies as well.[549]

There were many new innovations, inventions, and ideas that flourished in America and in Europe during these years. While on their wedding journey to Liverpool, England Sarah had observed the site of the construction of the Liverpool-Manchester Railroad. This was the first railroad in the world to carry both freight and passengers, and it is considered to be the forerunner of the public railroad system.[550]

> *I will mention here that I looked down from a high embankment, on to the unfinished railroad, between Manchester & Liverpool just where they were preparing to tunnel under Liverpool~ It was the first railroad in the world~ Now the world is covered with them~*[551]

This rail officially opened in January of 1830. Americans weren't far behind in developing this new form of transportation. Steamboats and canals had already opened up trade routes between the East and the rapidly expanding western territories, and the same year the Baltimore and Ohio's *Tom Thumb* thrilled Americans by steaming across thirteen miles of track.[552] With the advent of this new mode of transportation the possibilities for the expansion of trade between the old established cities in the East and the new developing states in the West seemed endless.

In New England Ichabod Goodwin was one of the early promoters of railroads. Like other enterprises started around this time these small, local railroads were funded by stock companies formed by groups of investors interested in making a profit and at the same time benefiting their community. Most of the railroads constructed in New Hampshire and Maine from the 1830s to the 1870s were small lines that paid little or nothing in dividends at first. In many cases the investors needed to develop businesses along the routes before a profit could be realized.

Goodwin was on the board of directors of the Massachusetts division of Eastern Railroad from its inception in the late 1830s, and he received a charter for the New Hampshire branch of Eastern Railroad in 1836. This was a small railroad consisting of a sixteen-mile continuance from the Massachusetts line that completed the connection between Boston and Portsmouth.[553]

The first steam railroad car arrived in Portsmouth on November 9th of that year. It ran near the Powder House on the corner of Essex and Islington Streets, and eventually the rail ran behind the Goodwin's back yard, as well as Uncle Flagg's house.

> *I did not then suppose that a railroad would ever run so near these premises~*[554]

Goodwin was president of the New Hampshire branch of the Eastern Railroad for twenty-five years. In 1847 he was elected president of the Portland, Saco & Portsmouth railroad that connected Portland, Maine to Boston, Massachusetts. Over the years he was also a director of the Eastern, Grand Junction, and Portsmouth, Great Falls, and Conway railroads.[555]

An undated letter of this period, from Captain Theodore Jewett of South Berwick, to Goodwin contains a proposal to start up a stock company to fund up a small railroad line between Great Falls and Portsmouth. The letter is quite persuasive and a good example of how such enterprises originated during these years.

> *I have thought much of the advantages Portsmouth & Great Falls would derive from the following plan to cause a Rail Road from Great Falls ....to Portsmouth... about 7 to 9 miles by land ... In my estimation (this) would be more advantageous to Ports than a Railroad to Boston or Portland....I think if you will make this known to a few friendly at Ports...they will not hesitate to take hold of it. ... If you should think well of the plan let us form a company ... this fall. Portsmouth is destined to be more than it is now.*[556]

However, as much as the railroads benefited other aspects of the economy, they were never really profitable for those first investors. By 1859 there were seven hundred miles of railroad in New Hampshire all owned by private investors. That same year the newly elected governor of the state, Ichabod Goodwin, spoke to this issue in his inaugural address. He conceded that since the profit from the railroads was less than the original investments, he and other early progenitors of the first railroads would have been wiser to wait for the state to develop the resources to help maintain the railroads. Still he added that he had no doubt that the railroads had greatly benefited the state by developing and augmenting its overall wealth and prosperity.[557]

Ichabod Goodwin became active in local and state politics around the same time he became involved in the railroads. While Goodwin was still at sea in 1828 Andrew Jackson, a Democrat from Tennessee known as "Old Hickory," wrested the presidency away from the Republican incumbent, John Quincy Adams. Unlike Adams, who had favored a strong federal government, Jackson and his followers were in favor of limited government. Promoting himself as a populist president, Jackson wanted to restore the power of the people and was against big business interests.[558] In reaction to Jackson's anti-business policies a new political party was formed around 1833-34. The members called themselves Whigs after a similarly named group of radical politicians who had challenged the power of the crown in England many years before.[559] Ichabod Goodwin and many other prominent businessmen in Portsmouth as well as other northeastern cities belonged to this party, which viewed itself as a party that incorporated moral issues and overall high societal values into their political beliefs.[560]

By 1836, when President Jackson did away with a central federal bank, many businesses and banks failed due to the unstable banking practices that followed. This led to the financial panic of 1837, which local historian Ray Brighton attributes to a quarrel between two Portsmouth men. Levi Woodbury, a local judge, was Secretary of the U.S. Treasury at the time, and Jeremiah Mason was the president of the Portsmouth branch of the Second United States Bank. It seems a disagreement over policy between the two led to the closing of the bank. According to Brighton this created a panic in Portsmouth that quickly spread throughout the country.[561]

The Whig party grew even stronger in reaction to this panic and other policies of President Andrew Jackson, whose populism was not appreciated by conservative northeastern businessmen such as Goodwin, nor by his wife.

> *I could tell terrible things of the days of Jackson & the* <u>*Loco Focos*</u>*~ In modern eyes Jackson is a truly great man & our grown children see him in a different light~*[562]

The Loco Foco referred to above was the nickname for an extreme radical wing of the Democratic Party. The name stemmed from an incident during an early political rally in which Jackson's loyal followers lit the hall with matchsticks after the gaslights were shut down. Loosely translated it means "crazy lights." In New England the Whigs soon became the dominant political party, particularly amongst wealthy businessmen. In 1838 Goodwin was elected to the state legislature, as a member of the Whig Party for the first of what would eventually be six different terms extending to 1856. He was also active in his community. He was a Portsmouth selectman in 1832 and chairman of the fire department in 1834.[563]

THE SERVANT PROBLEM

During the nineteenth century the roles assigned to males and females by the overall culture were distinctly separate. While Ichabod Goodwin established himself within the commercial and political world of Portsmouth, Sarah was expected to put her energies into the organization of the home. Within the domestic sphere assigned to women at that time, a well regulated and carefully run home was considered a reflection of her worth as a wife and mother.

Sarah's household duties were numerous. It was her responsibility to oversee the day-to-day management of the household. She was also responsible for the health and well being of all family members, as well as the overall character development of her children. To an extent a family's place and standing within the community depended on how well the home and family were maintained by the wife. With her husband's rising social position within the business and political community, Sarah was often called upon to be a gracious hostess to his business associates and friends.

At that time standards for cleanliness were changing. One of the primary reasons for this was the newly popular ladies' journals such as *Godey's Lady's' Book* or the Beecher sisters, who advised America's housewives on the proper way to manage almost every area of their lives and homes. In addition to these self appointed high disciples of household management, Sarah's old teacher, Lydia Maria Childs, wrote *The Frugal Housewife*, a popular book on household management, which covered almost every aspect of domestic economy. The result was that housewives set impossibly high standards for themselves, and their work seemed endless, even when they had domestic help.

> *Ladies who kept two or three servants had to be in their kitchen almost all the morning hours~ They had to make all the desserts, jellies, preserves, pickles and cake & iron all the ruffled shirts & other starched things~*[564]

Sarah wrote of the many daily or annual chores necessary to maintain a properly run home during the first half of the century. However, it is not always clear if she was recalling her early years as a wife or the household chores of her childhood. In many cases it seemed to be both. During her early married years there was probably not a great deal of difference in many of the housekeeping, or cooking customs and practices employed in her home compared to those common during her childhood. Yet modern technology and new methods of cleaning were already starting to change certain aspects of household management.

> *About the time I was married, it had become fashionable to varnish furniture but I had been brought up to see a great deal of waxing & rubbing with a stiff brush every day~ Brass abounded in every house & that had to be cleaned twice a week with rotten stone & lamp oil~ I need not say that no lady put her hand to that~*[565]

One chore which most modern housewives are never confronted with is the need to make the family's supply of soap for the year. Supervising this process was one of the duties, which Sarah had learned during her childhood, and continued to perform during the early years of her married life. Soap making was generally done in the spring of the year to take advantage of the winter supply of ashes for lye, and before the fat and tallow from butchering turned rancid. This was an annual chore in most New England homes until the mid-nineteenth century, at which time soap became available in stores.

> *Oh what fussy times there were over soap making, for soap for domestic purposes could not be bought then~ First a man accustomed to the business, must be engaged to put up the wash-tub that would hold twenty or thirty bushels of wood ashes (it must be remembered this was before the advent of hard coal) & fill in as much water as the ashes would absorb & every day a bucket or two added & in a couple of weeks the plug at the bottom was taken out, a tub was placed underneath to receive the lye, when that was full then another & another~*

> *When all the strong lye had run out a woman came & put the soap grease (which had been collecting a year & which had been boiled down & strained off from time to time) on to boil in the great brass kettle & then divided it hot, into barrels & there the lye was added & stirred until it came to soap~ I used to have made about four barrels~* [566]

Another annual chore was candle making. Although whale oil lamps were becoming increasingly popular by the 1830s, it was still necessary to have a good supply of candles to illuminate the home, and making them was another arduous but necessary chore in most New England homes. This was generally done in the fall of the year right after butchering, and several days had to be set side to make the annual supply of candles for the home.

> *Families saved their beef & mutton tallow & moulded candles~ Wax candles were used for Assemblies & large parties, but two wicked lamps & sperm candles were for ordinary use~* [567]

In both the spring and the fall of each year most housekeepers thoroughly cleaned every room in their home from top to bottom. Spring-cleaning was done in preparation for the hot summer months ahead. Even the fireplace was scoured and cleaned out in the spring, and all of the fire tools were scoured and polished, then put away for the summer

Closets were cleaned out and summer clothes replaced winter garments. Then these heavier woolen garments were washed and put away, generally protected from moths by camphor, black pepper and even tobacco. In some upper class homes woolen carpets were taken up and hung out in the back yards to have the dust and dirt of winter beaten out of them. In many homes they too were stored in the attic wrapped in a moth repellent mix, and in their place carpets made of straw matting or oilcloth were put on the floors.

Chairs upholstered in wool were covered with lightweight summer slipcovers to make the furniture more comfortable and cooler in appearance during the hot summer days. This process was repeated throughout the house. In the bedchambers winter bedding and curtains were washed and put in storage for the summer. Lighter curtains and bed coverings made of muslin, cotton, or dimity replaced these. This entire process was repeated again in the fall, but in the reverse.[568]

A plentiful supply of water was needed to keep up these standards of cleanliness in the homes. Fortunately the Goodwins were members of the Portsmouth Aqueduct Company, and had a ready supply of water. This water came in through the basement and was pumped into the home manually.

There were various devices sold at this time to move water about a home. However there was no indoor plumbing in the house as late as mid-century and therefore no water readily available on the second level. Chamber pots, portable tubs, and basins were carried up stairs to meet their basic needs.

Laundry, traditionally done at the start of each week in most New England homes, was an unpleasant, time consuming, but necessary job that took up the better part of a day. On washdays large tubs of water had to be boiled, emptied, and reheated. There were large cylindrical boilers that attached to the back of a stove range that kept a supply of hot water available, while keeping the stove top free for cooking. Most kitchens had them, but such boilers also overheated an already hot kitchen on summer days.

> *The great boiler on washing days...kept the kitchen black with smoke & made the cook cry~*[569]

Washing was still done by hand, scrubbing clothes against a rough washboard in a tub, with nearly boiling water and lye soap. However, washing machines had been around since Sarah's childhood, and they were getting more efficient by the time she was running a home. One model that was spring driven was quite popular in the 1830s, but these machines didn't hold a large number of articles, and still had to be manually filled and emptied.[570] With either method of washing, clothes had to be rinsed thoroughly several times, starched, wrung out, and hung to dry. In bad weather the clothes had to be hung indoor often in the attic or kitchen on wooden frames called clotheshorses. In good weather sheets and clothing were generally hung outside on clotheslines, spread out on the lawn, or draped over nearby bushes and shrubs. This method of drying often caused clothing to be stained. Since there were no commercial products to remove stains at this time, most women relied upon home remedies.

> *Fine laces are cleansed by rubbing them in the palms of the hands in box of magnesia~ Black laces are refreshed by dipping them in water in which a black kid glove has been dipped overnight~ They should be hung up till damp then pressed with a heavy weight between papers~*[571]

Ironing was done with a heavy cast iron flat iron that was heated upon the top of the stove. Washing and ironing were the least desirable of all household chores, and many women arranged to send their clothes to washerwomen. There is evidence that Sarah did this when she was older, but as a young woman she did her own ironing.

> *Ladies wore starched muslin ruffs, trimmed with thread lace & the lace must last a lifetime & of course had to be done up with great care~ I still treasure*

my first thread lace tucker~ In the first twenty years of my housekeeping, I always set apart one afternoon of the week for ironing~ Of course I had to say engaged if company called~[572]

Sarah did some of her own cooking during these years. In 1868 she listed some of her favorite recipes to cook, and they were all desserts she had perfected throughout the years. Amongst those listed were fifteen different types of puddings, four types of pie, and "Trifle," "Charlotte Russe," and "Apple Fool." She also recalled the cooking of her childhood.

The cooking of that day was of a superior kind~ no adulterations or makeshifts~ everything was the real thing & plenty of it~ Salaeratus, soda & ammonia & baking powders unknown only eggs & good yeast~[573]

The most excellent recipes for cooking were introduced here from England very early in our history~ Elegant gravies had a high place in the estimation of the old time people~ Venison merely browned on the outside & finished on spirit burners on the tables (each person having one) & swimming in rich brown gravy & current jelly was greatly enjoyed~

English plum pudding & stuffing for turkeys~ Turtle soup & mock turtle, when the turtle could not be had were common luxuries, & balmange, lemon creams, almond custard, jellies & preserves of every sort, were understood by every housekeeper~

The various pound cakes, almond cake & (sponge cake baked in a Dutch oven) were all made of the best materials~[574]

When Sarah set up housekeeping, much of the cooking was beginning to be done on cast iron stoves. These came into use as early as 1820 and along with other culinary inventions such as the Rumford stove that changed the cooking methodologies about this time. Many cooks found the transition from open hearth cooking to cooking on a stove quite difficult. Stove heat was more uniform and even, but it was hard to regulate and fingers were burned more often. A major objection to the stoves was the size of the ovens, which were not large enough for a weekly baking to feed an average family.

Air tight stoves, double sashes, stoves in houses about 1830 and furnaces still later~ The open Franklin stove, original patent was in almost every house~ We found one when we came to this house in a room that had been used as a nursery~ It is now in the attic~[575]

But oh it was cold~ The young people know nothing about the days when water froze all over the house & the rooms were cold & the warming pan was in great demand~ The fireplaces were all open & it took forever to get warm~[576]

These stoves presented other difficulties to the inexperienced cook and they were not too popular at first. During the 1830s when Sarah was first married, the baking of breads and pies in the brick oven was still a weekly ritual in most households, and there is evidence that the Goodwins relied upon their brick oven in the basement kitchen for a number of years. Although the hearth in the kitchen was eventually covered over to make room for a cast iron stove, the side ovens to bake bread were left exposed.

> *Sometimes in the palmy days of the crane & pot hooks things would get smoked in the pot or the kettle & I have even known the teakettle to suffer~*
>
> *The tin kitchen was in use & the roasts were very fine, though it must be confessed that a large turkey seldom got through without being devilled~*
>
> *For poultry I much prefer the range or cooking stove but for a fine roast of beef nothing can give the flavors like the open fire~*[577]

The tin oven Sarah wrote of was popular during her childhood. Tin ovens were large tin cylinders that sat upon legs in the center of the open hearth. The meat was roasted on a center spit, by the reflection of the hearth fire. As Sarah noted it was better for roasting beef than poultry, which often fell apart in the process and was more easily cooked in the conventional cast iron stoves of her day. [578]

Preserving the summer's bounty was another arduous chore that would have taken up several days of time each fall, and created much work along with hot and steamy kitchens.

> *Then there were pickles! And pickles could not be bought either~ Oh what times scalding peppers, cucumbers, walnuts, mangoes &c~ The latter I only saw at my Fathers~*[579]

All of these household chores mentioned by Sarah, in addition to basic chores such as everyday cleaning, laundry, ironing, mending, removing chamber pots, delivering and removing bath water from bed chambers, cleaning out privies etc. required a great deal of help. Without the modern conveniences made possible by such innovations as indoor plumbing and electricity, it was a necessity for Sarah, as well as the average housewife, to employ some domestic help. However, when Sarah first set up housekeeping, finding good help proved to be quite difficult.

> *Great complaint is made of servants in these days, but there is far more comfort now in New England households than there was half a century ago~ Only Americans could be obtained & for the most part they were worthless, often carrying vermin & disease into families~*[580]

There were several reasons for the dearth of good household help. Up until the 1820s the majority of American servants were native born. In many households during Sarah's youth the servants were local girls who apprenticed out to homes in the area to learn housekeeping skills. However, as more young women took advantage of the increased access to public education, as well as an increasing number of opportunities to further their education, jobs as servants became less desirable.

Many of these young women went on to school to prepare for positions as teachers in the expanding public school system, or sought travel and expanded opportunities working as governesses for wealthy city families. Other young women whose families were financially unable to provide an advanced education for them, sought employment in the factories and textile mills that had sprung up all over New England.

Even though working conditions and wages at the mills were inferior to those of most servants, many young women still refused to spend their lives waiting upon others. Something in the American spirit, perhaps an ingrained sense of equality that exists within republican societies, viewed a life based on servitude as undesirable and demeaning. From the country's beginning Americans complained of the lack of good household help just as Sarah did in the 1830s.

> *The servant girl subject was much discussed by ordinary housekeepers but*
> *there were a few who avoided the topic altogether~*[581]

Although finding good help was a difficult problem, nearly everyone who could possibly afford it kept at least one servant in their household as a "maid of all work." This position of general maid was the lowest position for domestic help. It was not only the most physically demanding, it paid less than positions in upper class households where two to three servants shared the burden. In Portsmouth thirty-eight percent of the homes had two or more servants by 1860. At the upper end of the echelon only the Goodwins and one other Portsmouth family, employed four or more domestics that year.[582]

> *The first Irish servant imported into this town was brought from Ireland for*
> *me, in one of my husband's ships~ I trained her thoroughly & she served me*
> *faithfully for years~ She is a widow now & has lost all her children~*[583]

It was probably sometime during the 1840s when Sarah came upon a solution for her "servant problem." The first official record of an Irish servant employed in the Goodwin home appears in the *1850 Portsmouth City Census*. The woman's name was Katherine Standish, and she was twenty-three at the time the census was taken. She might have come to the Goodwin home during the early or mid 1840s as Sarah claims she was the first Irish servant to arrive in Portsmouth. During the Irish famine, at the end of that decade, a large influx of Irish immigrants migrated to this city.

Unlike Americans or most other immigrants, the Irish seemed undisturbed by the stigma attached to servitude, and Irish women were quite willing to work in domestic service. By the time the 1860 census was taken all of the servants working in the Goodwin home were Irish. This was reflective of a greater trend throughout the country where the majority of the servants were of Irish birth.[584]

The same was true in 1870, with the exception of the English born coachman employed by the Goodwins. By 1880 their servants still had Irish surnames, but the census no longer listed place of origin. However, by this time the assimilation of the Irish into the culture was so successful, that many second generations Irish frowned on positions of servitude.[585]

Wages for servants were not high by today's standards. In 1870 general domestic help earned an average of $3.48 per week in many parts of New England, with the highest wage earners in the position of cook earning an average of $7.43 per week.[586] By the 1880s Sarah Goodwin noted that the cost of domestic help, along with everything else, had doubled.

> *A majority of the families who kept two or three servants lived at an expense*
> *of from a thousand to eighteen hundred dollars a year~ but a dollar then*
> *went as far as two would now~*[587]

Servant wages were higher than those of mill workers, and were second only to teacher's wages. They were further compensated by free room and board. This arrangement allowed the servants to save part of their pay, and many sent needed money home to support or send for family members still in Ireland. [588] In the Goodwin home large rooms on the third floor provided ample servant quarters for four or more servants.

The downside of living in the home, as the Goodwin servants did, was that most live-in domestics were "on call" from fifteen to eighteen hours per day. One study indicates that even on their days off, servants worked an average of seven hours. Before 1870 a full day off would have been unusual. One evening and one afternoon a week free was the norm for most servants.[589]

Of course there is no way to know what it was like to work as a servant in the Goodwin home during these early years. One can only make conjectures based on studies of immigrant servants in similar households. However there does exist an account of one young woman who was employed as a servant by Hope Goodwin during the early years of the twentieth century. She recalled that she was required to wear a uniform and that she was trained to curtsey and step aside in the presence of the family and guests.[590]

Length of service was a good indication of a satisfactory relationship between the servant and employer, as it was not uncommon for servants to leave for better positions. The census was taken every ten years, and therefore it is difficult to determine what the average length of service was. Notations in Sarah's journal during her later years indicate a fondness for the Irish.

> *The Irish are less materialistic than other races~ They recognize the*
> *spiritual & immortal~ They have more heart than head~ They allow their*
> *feelings to run away with them~ They do not leave their dead alone but feel*
> *their presence & the possibility that they may be more alive than ever & in*
> *need of sympathy & companionship~ They are becoming a dominant race*
> *& they will carry their religion with them~ Many great men have been born*
> *in Ireland~*[591]

By 1870 the Goodwin home was heated by a coal fired hot air furnace, illuminated by gaslights, and had indoor plumbing. These changes while making life easier brought with them new problems and concerns. Sarah also kept a Waste Book in which she entered information about household problems with the furnace or the plumbing. These entries are mostly in the form of advice and indicate that she was trying to master these new technologies.

> *When there is a bad smell in the Furnace have the smoke pipe cleared~*
> *Keep the hot air chamber of the furnace cleared out or there will be smoke*

& gas when the coal is put on...Put the damper quite up when the fire is made & open it when the fire is clear~

Take pains to secure valuable oil paintings from dust, gas light, the furnace heat~

Look well after drainage...to prevent buildup of sewer gas pipes leading away from "basin, sink or tub...In unused rooms water should be poured down each basin three times a week~[592]

THANKSGIVING HOLIDAYS

During the first half of the nineteenth century Thanksgiving was considered a much more important and therefore more widely celebrated holiday than Christmas. When Sarah was a child most families that belonged to the Congregational faith ignored Christmas altogether.

However, just about every family observed the uniquely American holiday of Thanksgiving, one that had its roots in early New England. It was a time of joy and abundance when families and individuals reviewed their accomplishments for the year, and gave thanks to God for their many blessings. It was traditional during this holiday to share baskets of food with those who were less fortunate, as well as to donate food and wood to the local clergy. Most importantly it was a time when families and friends were reunited with each other in an annual feast of thanksgiving and celebration.

> *My mother's family always observed Thanksgiving day by having the brothers & sisters with their children to dine & after I & my brothers & sisters were married my father made it a point to have us all, including babies & nurses, to spend the day with him~ Oh what immense preparations were made!*

> *Cousin Betsy the best cook in the world began a fortnight before to stone raisins & lay in stores for the great occasion~ Such heatings of the great brick oven! Such dozens of great mince pies & apple pies & pumpkin pies which had so much cream in them that you tasted but little of the pumpkin~*[593]

Thanksgiving called for an enormous amount of preparation, and cooks like Cousin Betsy worked for many weeks getting ready for the feast. Raisins and figs were needed in the mince pies and plum puddings, traditional fare for a New England Thanksgiving, and no meal was complete without them. However, cooks needed to remove stones and seeds from them both before putting them in these dishes.

> *It was the custom at my father's to spread out the pies (except the mince which were served hot) on the piano with the raisins, grapes, nuts, oranges &c & the little children gazed on these things before dinner with longing eyes & watering mouths~*

> *A long table was spread in the largest room with table cloth of finest damask, which hung in rich folds, & at every plate was a beautifully ironed napkin, a small roll & a tall glass of currant jelly~*

> *The silver & glass seemed to take on a higher polish & a large glass*

*pyramid crowned the center of the table covered with almond custards &
small glasses of strawberries & cream~ This pyramid had belonged to Gov
Benning Wentworth & was broken many years ago~*

*Such great big round & oval dishes of the richest plum puddings! These
latter were made so rich that when cold & cut in slices they were like
wedding cake, only better~ Enough of these were always baked to last until
Christmas~*[594]

Sarah's memories of the many dozens of pies cooked by her cousin for this feast
would have been quite accurate. It was not unusual for a household to cook thirty to fifty
pies in the great brick ovens for the holidays.[595] Of course not all of these pies were eaten
at Thanksgiving, many were put into baskets of food and given away to less fortunate
neighbors. The rest were put into cold storage to be brought out for the Christmas and New
Year holiday celebrations.

Thanksgiving was quite a feast in most New England homes, and the Goodwin
household as well as the Rice household would have an abundance of food, as Sarah
recalled. Turkey was traditional, but other cuts of meat, such as roast beef, ham, roasted
duck, and chicken pies would have complimented the meal. The fall harvest of vegetables
was well represented; squash, peas, carrots, onions, celery, turnip and potatoes with gravy all
complimented the meats.

*Cousin Betsy was renowned for her mock turtle soups but on Thanksgiving
day soup was dispensed with I suppose on account of the children~*

*The dinner began with a ham, handsomely decorated, at one end of the
table & a large roast turkey at the other~ Chickens & ducks followed, with
celery dressed & undressed~ Then Plum pudding with delicious sauce,
this was succeeded by pies & these by fruits of every sort that could be
procured~ after these coffee & tea~*[596]

Seating arrangements for so many people, both adults and children, would have
required a very large room and table. Even though the children in many Victorian homes
often took their everyday meals in the kitchen with the servants, on the holidays all but the
very youngest infants would have been seated with the rest of the family. The servants also
partook of the Thanksgiving feast, but they had their meal in the kitchen after serving the rest
of the family, as did the nurses who accompanied the families to her father's home.

General visiting amongst the family members often followed the meal. In large
gatherings family and friends might have gathered together in front of the hearth to share
stories of Thanksgivings past or around pianos to join together in song.

*Sixteen grandchildren & ten sons & daughters with Cousin Fanny & the
Major, who were always invited, these besides his immediate family, six or
eight servants & nurses made up a goodly household & there was enough
to spare & much to give away~*[597]

In good weather the children often enjoyed a few outdoor games, like skating or sleighing, but in cold weather, they either joined the adults in the formal parlor or gathered together on the second and third floors for indoor games such as Hide and Seek or Blind Man's Bluff.

> *It was a great day for the children & my father rejoiced in the thought that they would never forget it~ But oh the mischief & the spoiled dresses! On one occasion cashmere or rather thibet dresses were made for my eldest girls, designed to be best dresses for the coming winter ~*

> *The children had the range of the house & they were allowed the largest liberty~ They played Blind Man's buff & the pursued took refuge in a cold chimney upstairs ~ the condition of the dresses may be imagined~*[598]

Because the school year officially began on the day following Thanksgiving during the early years when children were needed for the harvest, it was traditional for children to get their best winter dresses and suits on this special holiday, much as the best spring clothes are first worn on Easter. Given the level of activity and the freedom the children enjoyed on this day, clothes spoilage was probably not that uncommon.

> *About seven o'clock a move was made about getting the children home & to their beds~ Generally the mothers returned to a ten o'clock supper, which was a repetition of the dinner except that the meats were cold & there were no vegetables~*

> *Oh what labor & patience it required on the part of the aunt to prepare & carry through all this~ My father wished it & his wishes were always obeyed~*[599]

During the greater part of Sarah's life Thanksgiving was not a national holiday. Although each state celebrated Thanksgiving, the exact date of the annual celebration was not known until the governor of each state issued a proclamation announcing when the day would be celebrated. Thanksgiving was officially announced the Sunday before the actual holiday, when the governor's proclamation was read from the church pulpits throughout the state.

However, Thanksgiving was always celebrated on a Thursday in late November or early December. Even when Sarah was young almost everyone knew approximately when the holiday would be, as it was necessary to prepare weeks ahead of time to have everything ready. Still there was always great excitement, especially amongst the younger parishioners, when the proclamation was actually read.

In 1859 and 1860 Ichabod Goodwin was the governor whose proclamation announced the coming of the annual holiday. During the first half of the nineteenth century most people observed Thanksgiving as a religious, as well as a secular holiday. Then Thanksgiving was very much like any Sunday. The schools, stores, and businesses closed, but the churches and meetinghouses remained open long enough for a morning service of thanksgiving.

For many years Sarah Josepha Hale, editor of *Godey's Lady's Book*, argued that

Thanksgiving should be a national holiday, with all of the states giving thanks on the same day. Then in 1863, in the midst of the Civil War, in an attempt to join the divided country together in a spirit of peace and reconciliation, President Lincoln issued a proclamation setting aside the last Thursday in November as an official day of thanksgiving.

A CANADIAN HOLIDAY

Sarah wrote a series of small vignettes, which are included as part of *Pleasant Memories*. One of them concerned a trip the family took to the mountains of Montreal with friends. This journey, which brought about a brush with British royalty, took place in the early 1840s.

Their traveling companions were Colonel John Winder, his wife and family. The Winders were from Baltimore, Maryland. Colonel Winder was the son of General William Winder, the man charged with failing to properly protect Washington, DC from British invaders during the War of 1812. The result being that the British plundered and burned the nation's capital. Despite this dubious distinction, the Winder family remained prominent in Baltimore and its environs.[600]

Colonel Winder was a career army soldier and an instructor at West Point for a number of years. Sometime during the 1840s he was appointed lieutenant governor of Veracruz, Mexico, and he eventually fought in the Mexican American wars.

Some years before this I went to the mountains & also to Montreal & Quebec with Col & Mrs Winder & their daughter Miss Eagles~ The Col. Had letters to officers of the army & to some in command~ This brought attention to the whole party~

At Montreal we were taken round a good deal by Sir James Alexander ...In Quebec we witnessed a good deal of military display & were twice invited to the Gov. General's~ We accepted the first invitation to an afternoon reception~ We were received by Lady Elgin on the Piazza & walked a good deal about the grounds, which commanded fine views of the river~

We were escorted by several gentlemen & I fell to the care of Col. Bruce a younger brother of Lord Elgin~ He was afterward governor to the Prince of Wales & was a most charming gentleman~

We were there a couple of hours & before we left went in to coffee &c & Lady Elgin urged very much that we would come to a Dejeune that was to come off in a day or two, but we declined on account of dress~

"Oh come as you are, your traveling dresses are all sufficient"~ We had scarcely got back to our Hotel where great cards were brought repeating the invitation~

Lord & Lady Elgin were said to be excellent specimens of the English nobility~ He died a few years after while Gov. Gen of India~ She looked exceedingly pretty & delicate & we were told was just getting over a confinement~

She had several children who were out with their little garden implements, playing in the grounds~ Your Aunt Hope lost this entertainment, greatly to my disappointment~ I could not persuade her to go~[601]

The Lord and Lady Elgin, who entertained the Goodwins in Montreal that year, were James Bruce, the 8th Earl of Elgin, and his wife. He was elected to the British House of Commons as a liberal Tory, but left the Commons in 1841 when he inherited his father's title.[602]

Lord Elgin implemented liberal policies during his reign as governor of Canada, against strong Tory opposition. As a result he was injured by a mob in 1849 and parliament buildings in Montreal were burned during that riot. After that he took government posts in both China and Japan, and was Postmaster General in England for one year before he went to India in 1860 where he died two years later.[603]

SARAH'S GARDEN

One of the pleasantest occupations I have had in life has been working among flowers & in the general cultivation of my garden~[604]

When the Goodwins bought their home on Islington Street in 1832 it was located in a fairly rural neighborhood. There were other homes on the street, but the Goodwin home was the last home on the right before open countryside. The house was bordered on the east by a side street, which sloped down to the North Mill Pond.

The garden area extended along the back of this house and eventually behind the yard of a neighboring home, allowing room for a spacious garden. The house overlooked a field across the street from the home that was part of the Goodwin property. It extended straight through to State Street. There were homes bordering both sides of this field and Sarah referred to it at times as the square across from the house. It was filled with apple, plum, and pear trees.

Oh, the comfort, the delight I have had in my garden~ I have loved my house & all my pleasant things in it, but the greatest most solid comfort I have ever had, has been in my garden~[605]

The garden, like the home, was her domain. When she first arrived she found some plants already in residence in the garden. The remainder were begged and borrowed from friends or purchased whenever possible.

In my first garden, after I was a housekeeper I had "Sweet Williams & canterbury bells & Foxgloves~"London Pride" made the garden very gay & roses of many kinds abounded~

A tiny little flower, pink in color, with feathery foliage I found in the garden, without a name & another little thing, called the "Azure blue gillia"~ To these were added Peonies of many kinds, white lilies, high & low, yellow lilies~ Purple lilies, lilies of the valley, in great profusion~

Snow drops~ a great tulip bed~ crocuses~ Pink spirea & white spireas of every sort~ Garden Heliotrope~ Dialetria~ Phloxes, of all sorts~ Cowslips~ Honeysuckles pink & sweet scented, yellow & red ~

Flowering almond, Double flowering white cherry & the double flowering pink cherry, Dentiass, Spirea, Primifolia, Scabius, Syringa, Mock Orange, Lilacs white & purple in clumps~ every where, Sophia Clematis, virgin's bower, Woodbine in profusion~ honeysuckles in great clumps, where the Catbirds love to build~ Gladiolas of every hue, verbenas, geraniums, double Asters & gay poppies everywhere~

In enumerating the flowers I would not forget the "Fleur de lis" or Flower de Luce as it was called~ The Purple is truly a royal flower~ I have to regret that I was never successful with pinks~[606]

From the country's beginning Americans have planted gardens. The first were simple in design and practical in content, relying mainly on vegetable and herb crops to meet nutritional and medicinal needs. By the end of the eighteenth and early part of the nineteenth centuries these crops were still a necessity, but amongst the well to do decorative floral gardens became fashionable.

These gardens were designed to subtly reflect the wealth and taste of their owners, as well as impress the onlooker. When Sarah was young, Portsmouth was a comparatively wealthy city with many impressive flower gardens within its environs, and these gardens reflected the prosperity of the city as well as that of their owners.

The gardens from her past were often practical as well as decorative, inasmuch as they provided families with a supply of fresh vegetables during the growing season, as well as a supply of vegetables or fruits to store through the colder months. Her own father had kept a garden filled with flowers and vegetables as did her next-door neighbors the Kennards.

Sarah's interest in plant life was probably further heightened by the study of botany, a required subject in the public schools of the time, and one that would have been considered an essential part of any good private education. Asa Gray, a medical doctor and professor of botany at Harvard when Sarah was young, wrote a text book geared to children that tied the worship of flowers and nature into one's duty to God.[607]

When I was a very little girl, my father gave me a little piece of ground, six feet by one, with what was called an alley board around it~ In that I had several small roots of very inferior value, that now would be thought scarcely worth cultivating~

Among them a bulb now rarely seen called a twelve o'clock~ It was a little white flower resembling the chicory in shape, which opened at twelve o'clock noon & closed in an hour or two after~[608]

When Sarah was first married most serious gardeners were male. But more and more upper class women in America began to emulate their English sisters, and took a more active role in the planning and actual planting of decorative flower gardens. Helping to fuel this trend were the leading botany writers of the period. The not so subtle implication behind many gardening missiles directed to women equated well cared for gardens and lawns to a duty to one's family, an ideal home life, and an innate high moral character.

Still many women were reluctant to garden, believing fresh air and sunshine along with strenuous exercise, somewhat detrimental to their health. By the 1840s there were even more botanical books geared towards American women. Enthusiastic authors stressed the health benefits of fresh air, and outdoor activity. They also appealed to a popular trend towards intellectual self-improvement that came from the mastery of new fields of knowledge. These books offered gardening advice on how to best care for various flowers, and tips on planting and designing attractive gardens. One popular ladies' book included a dictionary that listed popular plants replete with their botanical names.[609]

Sarah's notes on her garden look back over a span of sixty years, and they are records of how it evolved through the years. She began as a traditionalist gardener relying at first on the perennial plants of her childhood, which she called "old fashioned." At the Islington Street home Sarah found some flowers growing along with several rose bushes and purple lilacs. She brought with her some of her favorite flowers for the first garden.

> *I was very fond of the larkspur & the poppies, which were everywhere~ Mignonettes, forget me not & nasturtium too, for what garden is without them~*

> *I had for many years a large corner filled with elder bush, which I think is one of the most beautiful things in the world~ it blooms with the wild roses by the wayside in July~*[610]

Other favorites were borrowed from friends and neighbors, such as the Hart sisters, whose rose and carnation filled flowerbeds had impressed the young Sarah.

> *The spring after I went to housekeeping, as flower seeds & plants could not be bought here ~ with some timidity I went to these Ladies to beg a few ~ I shall never forget the solemnity of Miss Sally's manner when she impressed on me the importance of watching for the ripening seed & of gathering it at the proper time~*

> *She gave me a Rocket root, something new then, & the Rockets have never allowed her to die out of my memory, for if you once get them, you will never be without them~*[611]

> *Lucrecia Pearse gave me my daffies & snow groups~ Mrs S Lord gave me the lilies of the valley~Mrs Frank Miller gave me the fragrant violets~ Marcia...the white myrtle~ Clifford the Solomon's seal~ Mrs Parsons the climbing rose~ Mrs Eldridge the fleur de lis~ The starch plant sacred to Miss Hannah Cutter~ She gave it to me from her garden because I had such sweet memories of it when it found its way from Mrs Storer's garden into the school at the Academy~*

> *A small Boston from Mrs Albert Jone's garden & originally from Mt Vernon is in the garden~*[612]

Through the years Sarah tracked the progress of certain plants in her journals. Particular attention was paid to those started from cuttings or roots given to her by other amateur gardeners. Even when the name of the plant eluded her memory, the name of the donor remained.

I must not forget the myrtles, purple, white & golden the latter covering a mound & sometimes called nyoney~ Then there were the native plants~ Solomon's Seal & Jacob's Ladder both beautiful~

Dr Hill, late president of Harvard gave me a native vine the name of which I forget, but which at the moment is making a perfect tangle with the Roxbury wax work, sweet briar & globe flower~

Then there is the Snowberry, so pure & beautiful in the early Autumn & the strawberry tree which goes well with it, & the beautiful Elder, which has filled one great corner for forty years & the sweet currant and Pyrus Japonica which bloom together & grow very large because I do not have them disturbed~ [613]

The early 1800s were exciting times in the horticultural world. It was a time of great change and discovery. Many professional and amateur botanists financed by philanthropists, the government, or the relatively new seed stores and plant nurseries that sprang up on the East coast, searched for and discovered a large number of new plant specimens in remote areas of the world.

Starting with the Lewis and Clark expedition in 1803, led by Lewis who was trained in botany, many exciting botanical discoveries were made in the western half of the North American continent. The Azure Blue Gillia, which Sarah found in her first garden, was native to California. It would have been quite new to eastern gardeners at the time she found it in her garden.

The proliferation of seed stores, such as the one owned by Grant Thornburn or J.S. Beck of Boston, as well as nurseries like Parsons in Flushing, New York, along with improvements in the fields of refrigeration and transportation, made available plants not indigenous to the northeast. Improved or innovative techniques in transplanting or grafting plants, and the use of glass frames or greenhouses to gradually introduce southern plants to the chillier climes of New England made it possible to grow annual plants.

Many of these annuals were rare tropical plants from such exotic places as the Orient, Africa, Mexico, or Central and South America. They were known as half-hardy plants and they were quite popular by mid-century. They often failed to thrive for experimental gardeners like Sarah. However, she eventually embraced the newly popular annuals.

I had more or less disappointments in the half hardy things & had to learn almost everything from experience~ I almost always had great success with sweet peas & always planted them the first week in April~ One year when the ground was frozen too deep, I planted them on a mound & put three or four inches deep over them, & had a glorious show~

For many years I cultivated the Morning Glory & my husband was pleased to let me name a beautiful ship for that flower~ For many years I cultivated very successfully the sweet scented honeysuckle but in the last twenty years I have done little in cultivating but have contented myself with enjoying the perennials that the winter does not kill~

> *The fragrant honeysuckle is only a memory, but I used to cultivate it by laying down branches in the earth & transplanting in the spring~ The blossoms were always a delight, especially when the dew fell at early catching~*[614]

There isn't an extant plan of Sarah's first garden, but it was probably patterned after the gardens of her childhood with a long central path and symmetrically positioned geometric flowerbeds. In the late 1830s and 1840s she may have experimented with the latest fashion in garden landscaping known as naturalism. Naturalism had been popular in England for several decades before the well- known architect and landscape designer, Andrew Jackson Downing, introduced it in America in the 1840s.

Advocates of this style of gardening viewed the landscape as a work of art. Their aim was to emulate or improve upon nature. They extended the garden into the yard, and all of the land surrounding a home including the view became part of an overall design. Flowers came closer to the home in naturalism. Border and circular lawn gardens were planted in the yard, and plants placed in pots or ornamental urns were set out upon piazzas or alongside garden paths.

Yards were filled to capacity with fashionable wrought iron furniture, statuary, posts, and fences, along with vine covered trellises, decorative bridges, fountains, ponds of water, and bird or garden houses. They all combined to create an idyllic country image reminiscent of a scene from a Currier & Ives painting, even when the house was set in the midst of the city. A primary aim of naturalism was to insure a perfect view of the surrounding country from the prospect of the home.[615]

> *May 20, 1870~ Apple pear, cherry plum, lilacs purple & white cow slip, tree honeysuckle, pyrus Jacopnia, spice bush...all in bloom, cherry nearly gone~ day delightful~ I sit at the chamber windows I see lilacs of both colors, the tops of Norway spruces~*

> *May 3, 1878~ Like summer~ Leaves half out & cherry trees in bloom Red maple bloomed very full, but the maple rock back of the house did not bloom though last year it was loaded with yellow fringe before a leaf came out~*

> *Flowering quince, trout currant, cowslips in bloom, Lilacs, hawthorn, true honeysuckle all in full bloom, apple blooms gone~*[616]

Most people were somewhat influenced by naturalism, but only those with a great deal of money and property followed all of its precepts. Sarah, like many others, incorporated some aspects of naturalism into her garden landscape. She had wrought iron furniture and a pond in the garden, a garden trellis, and a large number of ornamental trees, bushes and shrubs throughout the property. The front of the home overlooked the field across the street and provided the family with the bucolic country prospect so important to naturalism.

> *The woodbine Sugar maple & apple trees full of bloom, the Hawthorn tree in the distance beyond the bit of water, green fields & glorious elms~ cows*

145

feeding & soft blue sky overhead~

The woodbine & Roxbury waxworth climb into the Hawthorne tree & add new grace after its own bloom has departed ~[617]

About the time Sarah began to plant many of the fashionable annuals in her garden, the newest fashion in gardening was referred to as "bedding out." It called for planting large masses of flowers of the same height, generally two to three inch high annuals in raised beds. Some ambitious gardeners incorporated designs into these beds of flowers. The design was often something simple such as a star or flag, but some were quite intricate. This practice was called "carpeting" or "carpet bedding," because the designed flowerbeds resembled oriental carpets. This type of gardening required a great deal of planning and work on the part of the gardener who designed the pattern by coordinating flowers with petals and foliage of complimentary hues.[618]

A new style in "bedding out" became fashionable after the Civil War. This was called "mixing" as opposed to "massing." It had followed closely the trend of "carpeting" in masses, but didn't really catch on until after the war, a time when scant attention was paid to garden designs. Mixing called for lines of same height, mixed annuals, planted side by side in contrasting colors to resemble long strands of brightly colored ribbons that lay side by side. The flowers were planted in rectangular garden beds.[619]

I like all the varieties of landscape gardening ~ I like bedding out & all the florists could do to beautify the earth but for my own comfort & delectation give me the garden where I can saunter & hide myself~[620]

The flowers that made up these patterns were often started in greenhouses, and transferred to the gardens during the summer after the perennials began to fade. Taller plants were sometimes placed in the center of the design in circular gardens. The overall aim of carpet bedding was as always to impress onlookers with spectacular floral shows. Sarah recalled several instances when mass plantings of large numbers of like flowers delighted and impressed her as well as others.

During several years I had great success with tulips~ The double lemon color & the double scarlet were my delight, though the knowing ones told me they were not as desirable as the single specimens~ I had fifteen hundred in bloom in one bed at one time~

One or two years I had a great bed of double asters verbenas & stocks & Mr. Slater who knew said it was the handsomest bed of flowers he ever saw~

Two years ago I had a splendid show of double hollyhocks in one great mass~ more than a hundred in perfection at one time~ I don't know why but last year they did not do as well~ They were of many colors & some of them of them variegated~ I planted them in masses four roots together~[621]

Writing in her journal in 1888, she recalled how fickle fashions could be in the garden world during these years.

> *In the early years I cultivated the marigolds, the African, the French & the velvet, but yellow flowers went out of fashion~ now they are preferred to any other~*
>
> *The dear peonies require very little care~ I have the white, pink & crimson & I like the latter best because they are associated with my earliest memories~*
>
> *All beautiful things come in their time~ After the blossoms & the bulbs come the peonies, buttercups, columbines & rockets~ The garden is a glow with them now~*
>
> *But of all things I like the season of the blossoms & the lilacs best~ I truly live then~ My apple & pear blossoms & the glorious purple & white lilacs what can be finer~ My white lilacs have grown into trees & have to be propped up~* [622]

In New England lilacs traditionally herald the end of long winter days, and Sarah, like many other natives, harbored a special fondness for these annual harbingers of spring.

> *My lilacs are trees, some of them twenty feet high~ There are weeping lilacs but they do not grow so high~*[623]
>
> *When I came here fifty years ago, I found several much trimmed purple lilacs back of the drawing room windows~ White lilacs were brought to Portsmouth after I came to this house~ I brought a small root of a lady long since dead & they have increased & grown into trees almost & have to be propped up all the time~*
>
> *The dear lilacs Oh I do love them all ~ emblems of sturdiness, vigor, constancy & perennial beauty~ They bring new life to me every year~ They bring me peace & content assurance & certainty of their returning sweetness & faithfulness~*
>
> *Other things I feel more or less uncertain about~ Will the winter be too much for them? Will the bugs or worms destroy them~ But never an anxiety about the dear lilacs, they are always true, full of vigor & ready to respond to the first thrill of spring & then can anything be handsomer? I think few things can compare with them~*
>
> *I sometimes wonder if I could have but one, which I would choose, & though I have loved both dearly I believe my heart would go with the purple I have loved it longer~*

I remember a beautiful face under a white chip hat with two plumes of purple lilacs on the side & a bow of white love ribbons with streamers of the same~ That hat did great execution~[624]

One flower found in most American gardens during every age is the rose, and Sarah's garden was no exception. Roses are revered for their beauty, their medicinal properties, and for rose water, a food flavoring as well as a beauty aid. When she first moved to her new home she wrote that "roses of many kinds abounded," and recalled "wild roses by the wayside" blooming in June.

These first roses were considered old-fashioned by the time Sarah wrote of them in her journals. They bloomed for just one week in the month of June. But by then botanists had developed hardy hybrid perpetuals and French Bourbons that bloomed throughout the summer months.[625] Though she loved her roses and cherished their history, she was not always successful with them in the early years.

The Curtis rose which I have had fifty years blooms after bugs have gone~ The dianthus so many years a bright ornament to the garden made a poor show last year~

Two years ago I removed several of my old fashioned damask roses from shady places & put them in the sun and this year they bear finally~ Roses must have the sun~

Oh I have had such joy in my roses this July~ Every morning for weeks one or another would come into my room with a handful of roses ~ I have thirteen kinds in all & they have all done well~

The mantle is decorated with the Curtis rose this morning~ The other morning the pink spirea & the white milifleur are brought in one given me by Elisha Hall and the other by Maria Decatur~ Both long since departed~

After forty years humiliation from visitations of bugs & worms, our roses have bloomed out gloriously~ Not an insect on any of them~ What has caused this change? I answer without fear of contradiction, it is the beneficent, alluring, attractiveness of the electric lights~ I have truly reaped the reward of my labors in planting & caring for the roses~ [626]

This delightful entry was written in July of 1890, just three years after electric lights were installed in Portsmouth homes. Sarah was eighty-five at the time. Since she attributes her first real success with roses to the addition of electric lights, the roses must have been in an illuminated area, possibly a streetlight.

Despite the advances made in the horticultural field during these years, no really efficient methods were developed to combat garden pests. Before pesticides became available, decorative birdhouses were often put in or near the garden area to attract songbirds to eat the insects.

Sarah wrote of the many birds that nested in the nearby trees, and she also wrote about the peacocks that roamed her garden for many years. The peacocks would have added to the beauty of the floral display with their majestic iridescent blue and green hued tail feathers, and also served a practical purpose by keeping down the population of pesky insects that plagued her roses and other plants.

It was quite some time after the end of the Civil War when plant diseases such as fungi or bacteria were discovered. Prior to that time, it was believed that blight and other such diseases were cause by some irregularity in the air such as a "morbid infection" or a "surcharge in the electrical field"[627] Everyday gardeners like Sarah contributed to the overall knowledge of horticulture by adding their own experiences and observations to the field. Sarah left behind a few tips on the care of her garden along with her observations of the effect of electricity, and even how to make a nostrum to relieve the pain of bee stings.

For twenty years the strawberry trees have been attacked by a small bug on the new growth~ I have been in the habit of snipping off the part wherever I could reach this year & they have almost entirely disappeared~ Perhaps they have accomplished a cycle and may come again~

The culture of clove enriches the soil~ Alcohol poured over very freshly gathered Plantain leaves & bottled after the leaves turn black~ a cure for bee stings~

John Elwin says the seeds of the sugar maple do not ripen in England~

It is said that the Lime of Linden is never struck by lightening as the elm & oak are likely to be~ The reason being there is no iron in its bark~ The Linden grows to an immense height & is a native of Germany~

I had magnificent success with the tall white lilacs~ I put them down in November in pure yellow sand & for two years they were very fine growing four & five feet in height~ They should be transplanted every three years~

When the rockets have done blooming they should be all pulled up; otherwise they will fill the garden to the exclusion of everything else~

Never plant evergreens near stone masonry~

A great many old fashioned flowers have lived their little lives in my garden but the winters were often too hard for them~ The Wisteria was among the first to cultivate & I took great pains to preserve it by dividing & transplanting, but it died out

There are two kinds of Gentian~ One is called the closed Gentian as it never opens~ The other requires the midday sun of a gorgeous October day to bring out all its true form~ fringed petals in the sunshine~[628]

Some technological inventions changed the field of gardening and landscaping around mid-century. The common use of cold frames and greenhouses by ordinary gardeners led to more experimentation, and hybrid plants. The development of the lawnmower, adapted in 1854 from a factory tool that sheared the pile on carpets to the first prototype of today's lawnmower, came about when someone added a handle to the rolling blades.[629]

Before this, rolling the grass flat with a steel roller, cutting it down with a scythe, or periodically pasturing cows and sheep on the lawn best controlled lawns. Sarah's father had kept a milk cow at their Deer Street home when she was young, and the 1870 Portsmouth census reports the Goodwins also had a cow, two horses, and a dog.

The cow was probably put out to pasture in the field across the street. The practice of keeping cows within the city limits became less and less common as the years passed. By the late 1880s, Sarah noted in her journal how few cows remained in the neighborhood.

> *I love to see the cows come from the pasture~*
> *It seems rural & lovely~ many families kept a cow in the olden time but now*
> *only two go by & I think they are owned by one man~ They have just gone*
> *by red & white ones with their udders full~*[630]

The horses listed in the census would have been carriage horses, as local travel was still by way of coach and carriage. They were kept in a stable near the garden. The Goodwins retained a coachman as a driver and caretaker for the horses, and he was probably expected to perform odd jobs around the home. There was also a carriage house on property. The dog was a beloved pet named Pip.

> *May 19, 1874 Little Pip died very suddenly in my room~ A dear loving*
> *obedient creature ~ buried in the garden~*[631]

Journal entries during the 1880s indicate Sarah wasn't very fond of lawnmowers. She seemed to think they destroyed the natural beauty of the grounds by cutting the grass too low. They also threatened two of her favorite wildflowers, dandelions and buttercups, which she always allowed to grow.

> *My garden is full of such mementos~ I am told that the grass has been cut &*
> *the path cleared from weeds & that Tanglewood looks beautiful~ I hope to*
> *walk there in a week or two~ I do not allow either buttercups or dandelions*
> *to be dug up~*[632]

Tanglewood was the name Sarah gave to a private grove of trees which she had had planted behind the home just thirty years after the Goodwins first arrived. It was not uncommon at the time for people of means to have their own arboretums, and Sarah had always desired to have her own woods. When the opportunity to expand her garden came about, she chose instead to plant Tanglewood.

> *In 1862, your grandpa' bought another garden, adjoining ours, with the*
> *house belonging to it & he then allowed me to take a large round, in which*

vegetables had been cultivated, for my own pleasure~

I had long desired to own a grove & I determined to appropriate this piece to that purpose~ That is thirteen years ago, and I have in it, Elms, Norway spruces, Hemlocks~ Fir balsam, Austrian pine~ Purple Beech~ White pines~ Some of these trees thirty feet high~ The Elms & one Norway Spruce very high –

In other parts of the garden, near the fences, I have an Oak, a white Ash, a Brown Ash, a Weeping Larch, English Linden, Red Cedar, Common Willow, Fountain Willow, & a Hawthorne tree more than twenty feet high~[633]

I have fourteen different kinds of forest trees & I superintended the planting of them~ I love them all, but especially the Oak, the Ash & the Linden~ I am more fond of the woods than the lawn~[634]

Adding to the beauty of the garden area, the yard, and the field across from the house, were a large variety of trees, including quite a few fruit trees. Sarah noted their cyclical progress in her journals throughout the years, and watched for their first blooms each spring.

April, 1871~ Our sugar maple in full bloom the last week of April~ cedar birds feed on thorn plums & pears~ Did you ever notice that the ash tree branches are crosses of double curvature?

May, 1871~ Horsechestnuts, mt ash, apple pear, tulips, lilies of the valley Japan quince, spice bush large snowdrops, cowslip tree honeysuckle, lilacs white ~ two purple…all in bloom~

May 23, 1875 Apple tree by the house in full bloom~

The rock maple near the house is a perennial delight~ The bugs come when it is in bloom & the autumn foliage is splendid~ The bugs come too, to the golden willow & the Linden when in bloom~ …The sweet currant & snowberry & the strawberry tree so handsome in the leafless autumn~

In my garden are the three trees most attractive to bees …the sugar maple, the linden & the golden willow~Yesterday the willow was full of bees enjoying the golden pollen & I don't know how much besides~[635]

Other trees that interested Sarah were those that grew in the forests of New England, the Evergreen trees.

Some day I will write of the evergreens of Portsmouth & its neighborhood~ We should hold them sacred, for after we leave Newbury port & all the way to New York on the Springfield & Worcester route & back again on the

Shore route, I saw no evergreens~

It was winter & I was always on the outlook for something beside the bare deciduous trees & snow~ Till then I had not learned to value the pines & hemlocks that are strew so beautifully within ten miles of us in every direction~ Oh trees! Trees! Big trees, bright trees, symmetrical trees! What would life be like without them?[636]

Sometime after Tanglewood was established the Goodwins hired Albert J. Hoyt, a local land surveyor and architect to design a new garden. He designed a garden with an arbor at one end, with a large circular garden surrounding some sort of statuary at the other end. Above the arbor were smaller paths and two more circular beds. Flowers and ornamental shrubs decorated a far border on one side and poles with climbing roses lined the other.

As the years passed bushes and trees continued to grow in well-ordered profusion around the entire property, and Sarah continued to tend to them all. Each long winter took her away from the garden and toward the end of the season she always longed for the coming of spring so she could once again return to her garden.

When Feb came, I began to count the weeks before the willows would blossom or the bulbs show themselves above ground, or the cherry tree bloom, or the crocus would peep through the snow & so on, always waiting & longing~

With old Ragan ...who did twice the amount of work when I was with him~ I would begin work suitably dressed directly after breakfast & many days did not return to the house until it was too dark to work longer~ Then & only then did I discover that my back was broken & leaving my dinner & tea which had been set up for me I made the best of my way to a bath & my bed~ Feb 1888[637]

Although Sarah did much of the work in her garden, she employed a gardener to assist her with the heavier chores. John Ragan, a native of Ireland, worked for Sarah for over forty years (although the memoirs below note that he had worked for her twenty-five years, a later notation in her journal credited him with forty years of working alongside her in her garden). During these years they became good friends. Unlike the household help, Ragan maintained his own residence in town.

Not withstanding my many cares, I always found time to work in my garden & I never allowed the gardener to medalle with my flowers unless I was with him~ Here I would embalm the name of John Ragan, who has cultivated my flowers under my direction about twenty-five years & in all that time offended me but once~

Three years ago when I was very ill & Father Welsh had prayers for me in the Catholic church, John Ragan mistook the case & rushed out of church thinking I was dead~[638]

As the years passed both she and Ragan grew older, and gradually became unable to perform the same arduous chores that they had when they were younger. Still the garden remained, not as well tended as before, but still beautiful and pleasing to its owner.

> *In the early years there were sweet Williams. Canterbury bell & Foxgloves in great quantities~ Every year I put down a few geraniums & verbenas, but now Ragan is too old to work & I don't allow myself to stoop & the things have to go without weeding & so they don't amount to much~ It is too much trouble to teach a new man~*[639]

> *Of late years I have worked little in my garden & have gradually given up annuals except such as sow themselves, as Petunias, poppies &c, but instead have increased the number of flowering shrubs & perennials which give no trouble~*[640]

> *For several years the clematis or virgin's bower was running over everything in my garden, but as pains were taken to partially exterminate it, it finally died out of itself, which I regretted~ It was very graceful~*

> *My garden in July is a tangle of buttercups, rockets, columbines & other things~ Then comes millfleur, phloxes, spireas & various grasses for I do not have the grass cut often enough to prevent its blooming~*

> *My garden is a wilderness the myrtle creeps everywhere~ The long branches toss & wave to their heart's content & I rejoice in their freedom~ Poor old Ragan who put out almost every tree & shrub has gone to Heaven~ We shall talk it over some day~*[641]

Sarah's garden sustained her through the years, and gave her a great deal of enjoyment even when she grew too old to tend it.

> *My garden has been a whole world to me~ It will be sixty years next May since we came here~ I brought Sweet Williams & canterbury Bells & other old fashioned flowers with me & found foxgloves & rose bushes already established~ I have had great success with white lilies, sweet peas, hollyhock & many other flowers~ Thanks to the electric light the roses once more flourish~*

> *The beautiful things are growing all over the world~ Go, bring them in, as many as possible for what is so delightful as a garden?*

> *Oh my garden! My dear garden! What a world of enjoyment I have had in it~ If only I can have a big delightful garden full of everything in the next world, I shall be happy~*[642]

MRS ABC

During this time Sarah's social life would have been quite busy. Ladies in her station generally set aside one or two afternoons a week for their designated calling hours. A calling card announcing the caller's intent to pay a visit would have generally preceded a visit to Sarah Goodwin. However, not all of Sarah's visitors paid attention to such formalities. Two of these less conventional callers were recalled with the most interest years later.

A lady with whom Sarah became quite friendly was identified in her notes only as Mrs. ABC. Sarah was apparently quite intrigued with this friend. Not much is known about Mrs. ABC other than Sarah's account of their relationship. She was not an old childhood friend, but a new arrival in town when they first met.

> *One of the most interesting & attractive persons I have ever known was Mrs A_ She came to P_ from a distant city about forty years ago bringing with her several boys & a little girl & took part of a house in our neighborhood~*
>
> *Her husband, who was under some cloud, had gone to the west & her means were apparently very small~ I had heard one of my girls talk of her youngest boy little Eddie but I had not become otherwise interested~*
>
> *One morning as I stood at the window I noticed a very interesting looking woman, with a little boy by the hand, coming up to our door~ I was moved to open it myself & at once Mrs. A__ introduced herself, with an apology for coming, by saying her little boy had hazed her to bring him in to see the Peacock in the yard~ Of course I asked her in & went with her to visit the peacock~*
>
> *Thus our acquaintance began & it continued most agreeably as long as she lived~ She was very graceful & had a great deal of presence~ Her face without being regularly beautiful was wonderfully interesting~ Her smile & tones of voice were captivating~ She looked as I think the Empress Josephine might have & I think I used to tell her so~*
>
> *She had the art of dressing to suit her peculiar style & her long ringlets shading the face & the cut of the dress in front, always revealing a snowy lace Kerchief were in perfect harmony with her beauty~*
>
> *She always addressed me as dear Mrs Goodwin & she was very tender & affectionate~*[643]

It was common during the nineteenth century, and the early part of the twentieth, for friends as well as husbands and wives to use the more formal Mr., Mrs., and Miss when addressing one another.

After her means were exhausted, she opened a boarding house but her tastes & habits unfitted her for so hard a life & she very soon relinquished it~

Troubles came thick & fast~ The husband & the boy one after another died & just when her sorrows had become unbearable she broke in upon me one morning, in the highest of spirits, with "Oh my dear Mrs Goodwin, the darkest hour was before day & I am going to be married"

Tell me about it I said~ "Well dear I was drinking tea at a friend's house & the moment Mr B_ entered the room, I knew he had come for me" "I had seen him two years before in P_ when his wife was living & dear Mrs Goodwin he was very much taken with me" so I was sure that was his errand"

"He accompanied me home, told me that he wished me to marry him & that he would come for me in a fortnight~ Of course I did not hesitate for I liked him very much & I knew that he was rich & influential and above all that he was a member of the orthodox church & so dear I want to consult with you about my dress & I want to ask the favor of you to order a suitable headdress for the wedding~"

I was delighted & congratulated her with all my heart & really felt as if some good thing had come to me~

A year or two after she came to P_ on a visit & while we were walking in the garden after tea "I said "now tell me about yourself" for I saw that she was not happy & then she opened her heart to me~

She said "I am miserable~ My husband is coarse & mean & curses & swears, (notwithstanding his religious profession~) He has neither taste nor sentiment & in fact he is so horrid that I have not been in to family prayers for months~

"Why my dear, where do you think he has put his Pig stye? Why up against the dining room window, now from that you may judge what he is!"~

*About two years after that she came one morning looking so happy that I ventured to ask for Mr B_*

"Oh my dear she exclaimed He is dead! Didn't you know it?"

"I'm glad of it I said but where is your mourning" for she was in bright

colors~ "Oh my dear he went all to pieces & didn't leave a cent & I couldn't have gone into mourning if I had wished it~[644]

During a period of mourning following the death of a spouse, a widow was expected to wear dark clothing for a prescribed period of time, which varied according to local custom and social station. In many cases a woman would remain in mourning for up to a year following her husband's demise. The new wardrobe would of course have to be made at a substantial cost to the widow.

Well about this time a brother in law a most estimable man had become a widower & having recollections of her attractiveness when he married her sister, many years before, took a very long journey from a western city to reconnoiter the situation and without hinting any preference, invited her to go home with him to visit her nieces & nephews for a year or two & he would pay all the expense~

He admired her so much that he was not satisfied to part with her & as the children liked her & she liked him, they were married in the course of a few months~

About a year after they were married they dawned on us one evening & a happier couple never was seen~ I was ill in my room & could not receive <u>him</u> which nearly broke her heart~ My dear Mrs Goodwin she said, he would rather see you than any other woman living" Why how can that be said I~ Why dear he says he never gets over laughing at what you said when I told you Mr B_was dead~[645]

The visit from her friend and her newest husband was apparently unannounced, and while Mrs. ABC would have been welcomed into Sarah's bedchamber to visit, it would have been off limits for an unrelated male to visit Sarah in her bedchamber when she was in bed recuperating from an illness.

One or two years passed when she came in alone, in the deepest & richest mourning, to talk of her great loss~ The dear Doctor the best man that ever lived, who had brought all the <u>real</u> happiness of her life, was dead~

Her hands & pockets were full of cuttings from newspapers to show what a noble, glorious man he was~ The next we heard was of her own death~[646]

THE WIDOW'S MIRACLE

Another widow, who came to Sarah's door unannounced one day, became the subject of another of Sarah's small vignettes. She titled this one "An Experience."

I had a curious experience many years ago which reminds me of the Miracle of the widows cruse~

A widow who had been unfortunate in losing her property in a distant city had come to P_ bringing with her two unmarried daughters, with the hope of earning subsistence by sewing ornamental or otherwise~

She asked me for work & introduced the subject of spiritualism at our first interview~ I gave her work which was done very nicely, but I think she did not meet with much patronage~

One day she came in great distress & asked me for a loan of sixty dollars She was in arrears for rent & her landlord had threatened to attach her furniture & pictures~

She had two very large pictures in raised embroidery, her own work, richly framed, which had cost her forty & sixty dollars & she wished me to hold the largest as security for the amount~

I told her I had not the money, but moved by her distress I set myself to think what could be done for her relief~ I suggested a raffle & advised her to put the largest picture in the window of Barton & Cobb (picture framers), & go around to every nice looking house & get people to take tickets at a dollar each for the raffle~

One morning early she came to me saying "You have drawn the picture, I was told in a vision last night that the tickets were taken & that the raffle came off the previous evening at nine o'clock~

"I went down to the shop early this morning & found it was true & you had better go down at once & take the picture away~"

I was incredulous & astonished & was afraid there must be some collusion~ I drove down to Messrs Barton & Cobb & asked for the particulars~

*They told me that as the right amount was all in, they concluded to raffle &
as two or three gentlemen happened to be in at nine o'clock they drew & the
picture fell to me~ I took the picture in the carriage & gave it to the happy
woman who had her picture back again & sixty dollars in money~*[647]

Sarah introduces the subject of spiritualism in this story. She, like many people in
America during the nineteenth century, was drawn to the spiritualist movement, and her
journal entries during the 1880s indicate that she was a believer in spiritualism.

OLD THINGS

Along the same mystical lines Sarah left behind a story about a piece of old furniture, which she acquired in the 1840s. A short genealogical sketch on the Gerrish family prefaces her story. Ichabod Goodwin's mother was a Gerrish, and the Goodwins had a family home on Gerrish Island.

   Sarah relates that Robert Eliot purchased the island from Captain Champernowne of Kittery. The original Champernowne Island was divided into two halves by a creek, and the western portion was first sold to a Nathanial Fryer in 1672. He sold about a thousand acres to Robert Eliot, who gave half to his son Robert and the rest to his son-in-law Timothy Gerrish and his wife Sarah. This side became known as Gerrish Island. The eastern side was deeded to Elizabeth Cutt and her husband Humphrey Eliot and was eventually sold to Richard Cutt. It became known as Cutt's Island.[648]

> *Timothy Gerrish the great, great grandfather of Beatrice, was grandson of the famous Major Waldron of the time of King Philip's war, in New England~*
>
> *Timothy Gerrish married Sarah Eliot, the daughter of Robert Eliot, who was one of the richest & most important men on the Piscataqua in the middle & latter part of the seventeenth century~*
>
> *Robert Eliot purchased the island now called Gerrish island of Capt Champernoun, sent to London for furniture & plate & presented the whole to his daughter Sarah on her wedding day~*
>
> *One piece of the silver remains in the possession of Mrs Sarah Eliot Hobbs, the grandmother of Beatrice & three pieces of furniture owned severally by Mr Wm Goodwin, Frank Goodwin & myself~*
>
> *In order to arrive at the point of my story it was necessary to wade through the foregoing that you may feel some interest in the old settee about which I am going to write~*
>
> *I have by heredity a love for old chairs, old china & all the other old things, if they are good~ An old chair had been given to me shortly after my marriage, by one of the Gerrish family & that chair I gave to Mr Wm Goodwin on his moving into the new house, built on the old site~ I thought the old folks might like to come back & see it & perhaps take a seat with the family~*
>
> *One day not quite fifty years ago I said to my husband "I wonder if the old*

folks at the island have a very old piece of furniture that they would give to me? What have they got down there?

To which he replied "They have nothing but old things down there~ When I was about eight years old uncle Joe sent me under the eaves of the house to pull out the pieces of an old settee, that fell apart when he was a boy~

I am going said he to tinker it together, & take my nap on it afternoons~ I pulled the pieces out & they were put together with hard wood pegs as was done in that day & Uncle Joe kept it so near the fire that one side of it I remember was charred~ We will go down this afternoon & if it is in being ask him to give it to you"~

So after dinner we started off & found uncle Joseph, aunt Sally, aunt Lucy, aunt Mary & the brother's widow all there & well & glad to see us~ By & by my husband reminded Uncle Joe of the old settee & asked him if it was in being~

Yes he said, but it has no seat now, only a board over it & the girls keep spare bedding on it in the spare chamber"

"My wife wants you to give it to her said Mr Goodwin~ Yes, I broke in, yes uncle Joseph if you will give it to me I will fix it up & put it in my best parlor~ I will send, it down to the latest prosperity with honor~

Uncle Joseph looked grave & shook his head I know he said you would fix it up & it would do the family credit but I could not bear to see it go out of the house where it has been one hundred & seventy five years by the family records~ I should feel as if we should all have to go out soon after it~

Don't say another word I said, I would not have it on any account if you feel so~ but while walking out with my husband on the farm, an hour later he became thoughtful & silent & then he said "Ichabod I think I am wrong to refuse your wife that settee~ It is of no use to us~ Nobody knows that we have it & if your wife has it she will fix it up & it will do the family some honor & tomorrow I want you to send down & get it"~

So the next day William Goodwin who was in his uncle's office at that time, took a wagon, with a big arm chair in it for uncle Joe, went to the island, brought up the settee & dumped it near the front door~

When my husband came home to tea & found what he took for a bier, used at that time for carrying the dead, at his door, his horror may be imagined but coming quickly to his senses, relieved himself by a little strong language~

Well now what was to be done~ Of course it must be taken on to the piazza

162

& have the dust of ages scrubbed off with soap & water, & what then? I will send it to Dockum & have it upholstered in the most approved style~

"Never~ said my husband "Dockham would knock it to pieces & think it only fit to be burned~ Do you get a young house carpenter in with you & do it yourself, that is the only way"~

So a young carpenter was brought in & he & I worked steadily two whole days & then carried it between us in triumph, to its place in what uncle Joe would call the best room~

Well now comes a thrilling story~ One day after dinner, when I was alone & the house quiet, I thought I would lie down on the settee & take a nap~ I don't know how long I had been lying there when to my great surprise I found myself holding a reception~

Six couples of very grand looking ladies & gentlemen dressed in the style of courtiers of two hundred years ago with coats & dresses of heavy silk & velvet knee breeches, buckles, wigs, laces, stomachers, hoops, mob caps & long mitts, entered the room in procession & all gazing in great love & admiration on me!

It is useless to say that I was not frightened~ I not only was scared but I made the most frantic struggles to escape, at last, with a convulsive effort I broke the bonds & landed in the middle of the street~

It was very funny to see how proud my husband was of the old Settee~ Everybody was taken in to see it & well they might be for it is the handsomest piece of furniture of its date (now two hundred and seventeen years old) in this part of the world~[649]

This vignette was written in the 1880s. The chaise is currently on display in Sarah's bedchamber in the Goodwin House at Strawbery Banke.

17th century chaise longue, or day bed, as it would have been known at the time of its construction, as well as when Sarah used it. Brought from England by Goodwin family ancestors.

The 1840s -1850s
FACTORIES, BANKS AND POLITICAL EVENTS

While Sarah was overseeing the home, her children, and the well being of her friends and family members, Ichabod Goodwin became involved in new areas of business and industry such as factories and the expansion of railroads, which were quickly changing the face of American communities. Textile factories, based on water powered spinning mills, had existed on a small scale in New England since 1790. But it wasn't until 1813 when Francis Cabot Lowell, a Boston businessman, had the first American loom erected in nearby Waltham, Massachusetts that these factories really began to proliferate throughout the area.[650]

By the 1820s and 1830s many of the larger New England cities such as Manchester, New Hampshire, and Lowell and Lawrence, Massachusetts were becoming mill towns supported primarily by factories where power was generated by the swift moving New England rivers. These factories manufactured mainly textiles and shoes. Yardage made in textile factories relieved many women from the chore of spinning and weaving their own cloth needed to outfit their families.

Industrialization was slower in coming to Portsmouth than to other parts of New England. However, by the1840s a steam engine was developed to power these mills, and manufacturers were no longer dependent on the rivers to generate power. Then mills could be built almost anywhere.

In 1845 there were ten steam factories of various sizes in Portsmouth. One of the largest was the Portsmouth Steam Factory on Islington Street, founded by William Rice and his cousin Robert Rice. It was originally located on Islington Creek Road. Then in 1845 a new brick structure, six stories high and two hundred and four feet long, was built on the corner of Pearl and Hanover Streets.

Ichabod Goodwin was named president of the company at this time. As in other enterprises the company's startup was funded by the sale of stock. This looked like a good business investment to most Portsmouth businessmen, and within the preliminary stages investors snapped up fifty thousand in stock within three days.[651] Eventually over half a million dollars in stock was invested in this new enterprise. [652]

This new factory was built with modern conveniences such as a gasometer that was installed in the chimney to allow for the eventual installation of gaslights. When gaslights were first installed it was one of just two such facilities in the whole country that were lit by gaslight.[653] Within a few years the corporation also built Sagamore Mills with 160 looms. This was located right near the steam factory alongside North Mill Pond.

The factory employed over five hundred workers, and as in most textile factories the majority of the employees were young females.[654] Many of these young women came to the city from the nearby countryside to seek employment in the mills. Others were Irish immigrants who came here seeking employment in any one of the factories in the city.

When the new factory officially opened on July 4th, of 1846, the town was invited to join in the grand opening celebration, which culminated with a spectacular display of rocketry shot from atop the facility's 150-foot chimney. This was a successful enterprise for many years despite a series of mishaps, which included a fire within the first week of operation that did a great deal of damage, most of which was covered by insurance. That incident was followed two years later by a tornado, an unusual occurrence in this part of the country, which lifted the roof off the building and thrust it into the barn of Robert Rice's Islington Street home, completely demolishing the barn's upper story.[655]

In May of 1846 another bad fire devastated Portsmouth. It started in a dye house on Hanover and Market Street. The fire destroyed a large number of homes and businesses on both Hanover and Market Street, including a grocery store operated by Samuel Rowe, which was located in a brick building on Market Street owned by William Rice.

One hero that emerged out this misfortune was the President of Eastern Railroad, Ichabod Goodwin, who quickly dispatched a locomotive to nearby Newburyport, Massachusetts. It returned within two hours with three fire engines and four hundred firefighters. His concern and his quick response helped to alter the outcome of the fire, and greatly reduced the amount of damage it wreaked upon the town.[656]

Banking was another enterprise in which Samuel Lord, William Rice and eventually Goodwin and Coues invested. For many years Goodwin's benefactor, Samuel Lord, was at the head of the banking enterprises started in Portsmouth. He was treasurer of Portsmouth Savings Bank for forty-six years and started the Piscataqua Savings Bank. By 1840, both Ichabod Goodwin and his partner Samuel Coues were listed as directors of the Piscataqua Savings, and the same year Goodwin was listed in the city directory as a trustee of the Portsmouth Savings.[657] Goodwin was also on the board of directors of the First National Bank from its inception years later, and was still President of this bank at the time of his death.[658]

During these years the Whig party continued to be the dominant political party in New England. As the Whig representative in the state legislature for six different terms, Ichabod Goodwin was one of the party's most prominent leaders. In 1844 he was chosen to be a delegate for Henry Clay at the presidential convention held in Baltimore. Sarah was probably there as well, as it was her habit to accompany him to these political gatherings.[659]

That year Clay failed to win his bid for the presidency. The people chose instead his Democratic opponent James Polk, an outspoken advocate of the policy of annexation, as their next president. Polk was a firm believer in America's "manifest destiny" to spread throughout the entire North American continent. With this mandate in hand Polk first tried to purchase Texas and California from the Mexican government, but when that failed he ordered General Zachary Taylor to move his troops into Mexican territory. The war between Mexico and America followed.

In 1846 Goodwin was the Whig candidate from New Hampshire for Congress. The local paper endorsed him as a fit choice for this office due to his mercantile experience as well as his high character. They took the position that he would impart to the U.S. House of Representatives a needed sense of "dignity and decency to its deliberations." Despite this strong endorsement the election went to a Democratic candidate.

In 1848 Goodwin was once again a Whig delegate from New Hampshire. This time the party bypassed their favorite son Henry Clay, to choose General Zachary Taylor, a hero of the Mexican American War to be their candidate. Many considered Taylor a strange choice as the Whigs were opposed to the war as well as Polk's expansionist policies. Taylor was one of the generals who led American forces during the war that took the areas of Texas and California from the Mexican government and made them American territories.

Further it was not certain if Taylor, who had never voted in a general election, was a Whig or a Democrat. A native of Kentucky, Taylor was a slave owner with over a hundred slaves on his plantation. However, though his political views were quite obscure in most areas, he took a firm stand against the westward extension of slavery. The Whigs believed that a military man had the best chance of winning the election that year, and they were proven right. Taylor, affectionately dubbed "Old Rough and Ready" by the journalists of his day, was a hero in the eyes of most Americans, and he was elected President of the United States under the Whig banner.[660]

Though he lacked previous political experience, President Taylor was proving to be a reasonably good president by the start of 1850. That July when visiting in nearby Vermont, Ichabod Goodwin headed a committee charged to invite the president to celebrate the 4th of July in Portsmouth. [661] Unfortunately, President Taylor chose to celebrate that Independence Day in Washington where he contracted cholera. He died within a few days on July 9th.

The next morning Goodwin announced the news of the President's demise to the New Hampshire State Legislature. In doing so he took advantage of this sad occasion to express his sincere hope that the country would now find a way to overcome the fractional feelings which were starting to divide the country. His remarks appeared in the *Portsmouth Journal* a few days later.

> Mr. Speaker - Upon coming out of my chamber this morning I was met by the startling intelligence, the President is dead! This event may well fill the nation with mourning.... May this sudden and deep affliction soften the bitter sectional feelings, which distract our union.... [662]

However, Goodwin's plea for unity was not heeded, and the issue of extending slavery to the West continued to create a division between the two sections of the country. President Taylor was succeeded in office by his vice president, Millard Fillmore, a cohort of Henry Clay, who was elected as a Congressman from western New York four times. Fillmore was not particularly qualified for the presidency, but he had risen through the ranks of the Whig party and was loyal to the party. He chose one of the true leaders of the party, Daniel Webster, to be his secretary of state.

During Taylor's first year in office gold had been discovered in California, and the resultant rush to settle California by large numbers of settlers seeking gold and other opportunities there hastened the move to officially admit California into the Union. However, before statehood could be bestowed upon this territory, it was necessary to come up with a solution to settle the slavery vs. free state question, while appeasing parties on both sides of the issue.

When President Taylor died this issue had not yet been resolved, and the task of finding a way to admit California into the Union as a free state, without alienating the southern states that threatened to secede from the Union, fell to Senator Henry Clay of Kentucky and Daniel Webster of Massachusetts, the true heads of the Whig party.

The Compromise of 1850, proposed by Clay, allowed California into the nation as a free state and permitted slavery in the District of Columbia, but not the sale of slaves. It also guaranteed tightened enforcement of the unpopular Fugitive Slave Act by federal agents. This law, which was enacted in 1850, mandated the return of all escaped slaves to their former masters, including those who had lived as freed slaves for many years. It was a very unpopular law in the northern states and almost impossible to enforce. Basically what it did do was fuel the fires of the abolitionist movement.[663]

All in all, Clay's compromise was not a good one, and despite Daniel Webster's eloquent plea to accept it in order to preserve the Union, along with President Fillmore's approval of the compromise, it failed when first presented for congressional approval. Later that year when Stephen Douglas, a Democratic Senator from Illinois with presidential aspirations, spoke out in favor of the bill it was passed. California entered the Union as a new state near the end of 1850.[664] However, Webster and Clay had fallen into disfavor with their party due to their pleas for the passage of this compromise and President Fillmore was not respected because of his close association with Webster and Clay.

During the election of 1852 Ichabod Goodwin was chosen to be the Whig delegate from New Hampshire for Daniel Webster. He and Sarah traveled to the convention in Baltimore that year. When Webster failed to get his party's nomination, President Fillmore agreed to turn his share of the votes over to Webster, but Webster still remained twelve votes short. His party's rejection of him was a dreadful humiliation for Webster, and after he lost the nomination to Scott, he reportedly turned to ask his most loyal lieutenant, Rufus Choate, "How will this look in history?"[665]

Choate, a one time Senator from Massachusetts, although not as well known as Webster was considered his equal as a public speaker. Like Webster he was a Dartmouth graduate, a Whig, and a lawyer with a legal practice in Massachusetts. Choate was said to be given to bursts of energy, followed by long periods of lethargy, and it was rumored he was an opium addict.

This rumor was bolstered by his exotic, somewhat oriental look. Dark, with a saturnine look, and prematurely wrinkled skin, he often wrapped his tall, thin, bent frame in several layers of long dark cloaks. He was reputed to be a bewitching speaker. His audiences were purportedly entranced by his eloquent speech, his power to persuade, as well as his overall dramatic presence.[666] Sarah was one of his admirers.

> *I twice enjoyed the privilege of hearing Rufus Choate speak~ the first time he argued a case in the parlor at the Tremont House in Boston before referees & my husband was one of them~ I was in the next room & did not see him but I had the opportunity to wonder at his great powers in argument~*
>
> *The second time Mr Goodwin was on his way to Baltimore as Whig delegate at large to nominate Daniel Webster for president & Rufus Choate was caught on the fey at the Astor House by a party of delegates who gave him a supper & he made them a speech...*
>
> *I invited the Decatars to sit in the next room with me & to listen to him & see him gesticulate & manfully throw his coat in the great excitement of the occasion~ He was rapaciously applauded~* [667]

This occurred at a time when it was not considered proper for women to take an active interest in politics, although some were starting to demand their place in the political arena. For the most part women were relegated to the sidelines as distant observers of the political proceedings. A reference in Sarah's journal, regarding another event that took place in 1850, left a small clue as to what she may have thought of this custom.

This happened when the Goodwins traveled to New York City that year to greet Louis Kossuth, America's latest international hero at the time. Kosuth was a Hungarian rebel, as well as a powerful orator, who led a revolt in his country that brought about the establishment of a Hungarian Republic for a while. Although Russian troops cut these new freedoms short, their leader Kossuth became an international hero.

President Fillmore arranged for his release from exile and subsequent journey to America in 1850. Upon arrival he was greeted as a conquering hero, much as Lafayette had been years before. He was cheered wherever he went, and treated like visiting royalty.[668] Sarah and Ichabod Goodwin were amongst the Americans who were there to welcome him to America. Years later she wrote in her journal.

> *Kossuth is still living~ He learned English in prison having only two books,*
> *the Bible & Shakespeare~ I heard him address the city government of New*
> *York at a dinner where I was permitted to be a <u>looker on</u> & I thought then*
> *& still think he was the most eloquent man I ever listened to~[669]*

The fact that the phrase "looker on" in the above entry was underlined twice seems to indicate some resentment on Sarah's part that she was not allowed to fully participate in such an event. As the wife of a powerful man, Sarah was quite fortunate that she had the opportunity to meet and mingle with some of the movers and shakers of her day, and to be present at many of the crucial political events that helped to shape the country during this transitional time in America's history. However, because of the social stigma against women participating in politics during this period of America's history, she often had to observe these proceedings from a discreet distance.

Within a few months of the Whig convention in Baltimore, Daniel Webster, the famous orator and politician who was Sarah's North End neighbor during her childhood, died. New Hampshire as well as the rest of the nation mourned the loss of this great statesman. In death America forgave him.[670]

The Whig nomination finally went to General Winfield Scott, the same General Scott whose wife the Goodwins had met at Mrs. Storer's boarding house in New York many years before. He too had been a key player in the Mexican War and was a military hero. However, the press was not as fond of Scott as they had been of Taylor and they dubbed him with the unflattering moniker "Old Fuss and Feathers," because he was considered to be somewhat of a dandy in his manner of dress. Although a southerner, Scott remained with the Union during the Civil War, and Lincoln appointed him as the army chief of staff during this conflict.

That year General Scott lost the election to Franklin Pierce, who was elected as the country's fourteenth president. Pierce's ascendancy to the presidency was totally unexpected by political observers of his day. There had been three front-runners in the Democratic Party that year vying for the party's nomination, but none could raise the necessary two-thirds vote to win. This opened up the way for a compromise candidacy. The nomination was to have gone to Levi Woodbury, a respected and prominent lawyer from Portsmouth. However, Woodbury died before the election took place, and the party chose instead Franklin Pierce, his former law clerk and another New Hampshire native.[671]

Franklin Pierce

FRANKLIN PIERCE

Franklin Pierce was a native of Hillsboro, New Hampshire, but he had spent a year in Portsmouth as a young man studying law under Judge Woodbury. That was in 1825, the year following his graduation from Bowdoin College in nearby Maine. He was twenty-one years old that year and Sarah was twenty.

> *In my young girlhood there sat in a pew at the North church, next to my Father's & against the wall on a line with myself, the partition only between, a very young man with almost red hair, cut very short, & who could hardly look up for shyness~ This young man, was Franklin Peirce, son of the then reigning Gov. of New Hampshire~ He was reading law with Judge Woodbury & had hired a seat in the pew referred to~ I was not acquainted with him until many years after when he had become a well known politician~*[672]

According to the biographical reminiscences of his former classmates and teachers at Bowdoin, Franklin Pierce was by most accounts a good looking, and not particularly shy young man during his college years. However, he may well have felt somewhat intimidated in the presence of the fashionably attractive young ladies in Portsmouth such as Sarah and her sisters. A letter from Pierce to his sister written during this time indicates he made few acquaintances in the city during his short stay there, and spent most of his time concentrating on his law studies. In November of that year Judge Woodbury was elected to the United States Senate, so in May of 1826 Franklin Pierce left Portsmouth to attend law school in Northampton. Massachusetts.[673]

His father General Benjamin Pierce, a Revolutionary War hero, was not yet governor in 1825, but he was one of the most politically powerful men in New Hampshire at the time. He served on the Governor's Council for two years, and was also the unsuccessful Democratic candidate for the governorship in both 1825 and 1826. The following year in 1827, when he ran uncontested he was chosen for the office of Governor of New Hampshire. He lost his bid for reelection the following year, but was again elected governor in 1829.[674]

Franklin Pierce and Sarah met again in 1850. That year New Hampshire held a constitutional convention for the first time in fifty-eight years. Franklin Pierce headed the convention and Ichabod Goodwin was one of the participants. Sarah accompanied her husband to the state capital in Concord, New Hampshire. While at the convention, the Goodwins stayed at the Phoenix House. This was a small hotel located on the Main Street of Concord where most out of town members of the Whig Party stayed, while the nearby Eagle Hotel was the stomping ground for the state's visiting Democrats.

> *I went to Concord with your grandpa' when the Constitution of the State of N.H. was to be amended & Frank Peirce was made President of the Convention, although Mr. Woodbury & many other distinguished men,*

were present~

There had been a great deal of wire pulling among the Democrats to bring this about but other people did not understand it~[675]

By this time Pierce, a Democrat and a devoted Jackson adherent, had served in the U.S. House of Representatives as well as the Senate. He had left the Senate and declined the position of U.S. Attorney General offered by President Polk, because of his wife's frail health. He had also served in the United States Army during the war with Mexico and received an army commission as a brigadier general. At the time of the convention he was practicing law in Concord, and was a federal district attorney.[676]

The day after the Convention was organized, Gen. Peirce knocked at my bedroom door (the Phoenix Hotel there, very simple in its arrangements, having no Ladies' Parlor) with a little riding whip which he carried & asked me to go up to the State House with his wife, at eleven o'clock & that they would call me~[677]

Almost a decade after he left Portsmouth, Franklin Pierce married Jane Means Appleton. She was the daughter of Jesse Appleton, the late president of Bowdoin College, who had died in 1819.

They did so, & he placed Mrs Peirce & myself in the gallery, where we could conveniently see & hear all the doings of the Convention~ After one hour or so we both became tired & Mrs Peirce proposed leaving~ We moved out very quietly but before we were down stairs the Gen. Had requested Col. Ichabod Bartlett take his place & insisted on walking home with us~[678]

They seemed to have been a mismatched couple. She was frail, tubercular, and suffered from ill health all of her life. In addition she is remembered as quite shy, retiring, and prone to severe bouts of melancholy, made worse by 1850 due to the loss of two of her three sons. Pierce was just the opposite. Often buoyant, social, and somewhat vain, he loved the political arena and to socialize in taverns. He often drank too much during his early years, a habit that displeased his wife, but one he had renounced by 1850.

We both protested again & again, until Mrs Peirce made some errand at a store we were passing & the Gen then took leave, making me promise to take very good care of her~

Many people thought he made a great show of affection but I believe he was tenderly attached to her~ The best thing I ever heard of him, was in answer to Clem March who in a coarse lisp asked him how he came to marry such an invalid? "Because I thought I could take better care of her than anyone else was the reply."[679]

His affection for his wife was apparently very sincere, and he is remembered for being excessively fond of her. One biographer wrote that he was always fawning over her, and trying desperately to please her at all times. But she, while appreciative, remained for the most part unresponsive to most of his affectionate ministrations.[680]

Many of the constitutional amendments proposed at the convention reflected changing social mores. Amongst these proposals was an amendment to change the gubernatorial elections from annual to biennial, another sought to do away with religious and property qualifications, which prevented people of the Catholic faith and non-property owners from holding public office in New Hampshire.

This convention went on for several months, although it adjourned for a short time. None of the proposed amendments passed during this convention. Pierce, branded as anti-Catholic by his opponents, was credited with carrying the religious and property qualification amendment in the convention. However, the voters defeated this at the polls.[681]

Two years later, in June of 1852, Franklin Pierce, a dark horse candidate, received the Democratic Party's nomination for president. It is said that when she received the news of his nomination Mrs. Pierce, who hated politics, fainted.[682] During his campaign for the presidency against General Winfield Scott, his organizers dubbed him as the "Young Hickory of the Granite Hills." Pierce did not enjoy widespread national recognition, but he was helped by a campaign biography written for him by his Bowdoin classmate and lifelong friend, author Nathaniel Hawthorne. He in turn rewarded Hawthorne after he was elected with an appointment as the United States Consul to Liverpool.[683]

Shortly after the election Franklin Pierce's remaining son was killed in a tragic train accident. This occurred while the family was traveling home to prepare for a subsequent journey to Washington, DC and his inauguration. The loss of her last son was felt so deeply by Mrs. Pierce that she became a recluse and never participated in social functions during or after his administration.[684]

During his tenure as President, Pierce became somewhat of a pariah in New England, when he attempted to placate southern voices calling for secession by rigidly enforcing the unpopular Fugitive Slave Act. However, he had misjudged the extent of support abolitionists enjoyed in the North by this time.

Pierce was basically a genial man, who tried to please all, but he was not very successful in holding the country together during his term in office. His stand against freeing the slaves, along with his inability to deal with the struggle in Kansas over the Kansas-Nebraska Act, which divided the Nebraska territory into two states leaving the decision of free versus slave states to "popular sovereignty," and his leanings towards imperialistic expansion policies in regard to Cuba, made him an unpopular candidate with northern liberals and Whigs.[685]

Pierce sought his party's nomination for the election of 1856, but James Buchanan, a member of his cabinet, and Stephen Douglas vied for the position. This three-way split for the prize once again made it so none of the contenders held the necessary two-thirds needed for nomination. Eventually Buchanan won out, and went on to win the presidency over General Charles Fremont, the former Whig and military man who ran on the new Republican Party ticket that year.

That October, after Pierce lost the Democratic nomination, but before his term in office expired he returned to New Hampshire. On October 6th and 7th of that year Portsmouth held a celebration to honor the centennial of printing in New Hampshire. Pierce was invited but was unable to visit in time for the celebration. However, he decided to visit Portsmouth two days later. He gave such short notice that there was not as large a crowd to greet the President as would have been expected. Still the mayor and other dignitaries arranged to meet him, and he was accorded a twenty-one-gun salute upon his arrival. Then, after a short round of speeches, the Buchanan Guards escorted the President to the Rockingham House where he dined. A reception followed the dinner

Later that evening a ball was given in his honor at the Navy Yard. It was well attended by the naval officers and their wives, along with other prominent members of the community. Pierce was scheduled to leave Portsmouth the following day, but before his departure he paid one last visit to old friends.

> *But I should have mentioned the most interesting visit we ever had from him & that was when he was President of the United States~ He came north on a visit & spent a day or two in Portsmouth, attended by a suite of military & other gentlemen~*

> *The morning after his arrival, while we were at breakfast, to our utter consternation, the <u>President</u> was announced! We had a young lady visitor in the house who looked aghast~*

> *What was to be done? Should we change our dresses? No was the inspiration of the moment & we all rushed in & gave him the heartiest of greetings~*

> *He saw that we were delighted & we had a merry time~ As he was leaving the Hotel, several of his suite offered to attend him but he preferred the walk by himself~*

> *Although he was not very popular with "our party" yet we were much gratified at receiving a visit from a "live President"~ He had come North by rail & the Frigate Wabash took him from our navy yard to Washington~*[686]

From the Goodwin home the president proceeded to the Navy Yard landing and boarded the USS *Wabash*. As the frigate passed the Naval Yard, a salute was fired in honor of the President, and that afternoon the captain of the *Wabash* gave a collation in honor of his visit. When they set sail for Washington that evening, a large contingent of people gathered at Fort Constitution cheered when the presidential party passed by, and an exchange of gun salutes took place between the fort and the frigate.[687]

Pierce and his wife returned to Portsmouth in August of 1857 for three months.

> *The summer after they left the White House, was passed at the Rockingham House in Portsmouth, & it was his habit to drive her out in a chaise daily~ He told me that he believed they had not left a nook unexplored, on either side of the river, within miles~ I used to send her flowers from my garden sometimes, & I never did so that he did not come in the evening to thank me for them~*

> *During that summer a son of the famous Alex. Hamilton, was at the Hotel*

some days & both he & the Gen attended an evening party at our house~ The last time I saw Gen Peirce was on his last visit to Portsmouth~ I was in the garden, just after sunset, one evening with my daughters, Frank, Capt Bradford & perhaps others, when who should come rushing toward me but the Gen~ I presented him to the party & he then put my arm within his, turned without even saying "by your leave" & made for the Piazza, where he seated me & himself~

Your grandpa' was in the parlor & he might have addressed himself to him, but he chose otherwise~ He then began to tell me how much he valued & had always valued the leaders of the whig party in N.H. that they had always been his most cherished friends & he wished my husband to know it & that I must tell him so & then he took leave~

I always thought him a most genial graceful & agreeable man & he was very kind & civil to me~[688]

Five years later Mrs. Pierce died, and the former President was barely out of mourning the following year when his friend Nathaniel Hawthorne died. It is said that for a while the bereaved Pierce began to drink again, and he became quite ill. Then in 1865 he purportedly underwent a religious conversion that restored his health and peace of mind. Pierce returned to the seashore near Portsmouth to spend the last four summers of his life at the idyllic eighty-four acre retreat he had purchased at Little Boar's Head in Rye. During the summer of 1869, he suddenly became ill and died. To this day Franklin Pierce holds the distinction of being the only New Hampshire native ever elected to the office of President of the United States.[689]

THE FAMILY IN THE 1850S

Sarah was forty-five at the start of the 1850s, and her husband was in his prime, active and successful in the world of business and politics. Their family was changing and growing, with the oldest daughters starting to marry and raise their own families. Abby, who turned twenty-one in 1850, was the first to marry. By this time Abby had grown into quite a handsome woman, and according to all accounts she was as charming as she was beautiful.

The groom was twenty-five year old Lieutenant William Winder of Baltimore, Maryland, the oldest son of the Goodwins' long time friends, Colonel John Winder and his wife, who had accompanied their family on a trip to Canada during the early 1840s. The Winders were married on Christmas Eve of 1850, with the Unitarian minister, Rev. Peabody officiating. It is likely the wedding took place at home as this was still the prevailing custom at the time. It was also quite traditional in New England to wed on or near the holidays as they chose to do. When Abby and William married he was stationed at nearby Fort Constitution in New Castle, and the young couple lived there during their first year of marriage.

William was an army career man, carrying on his family tradition of military service, as his father and his father before him had done. Although Col. John Winder had taught at West Point, William was not a graduate of this prestigious institution. He had, however, been active in the war with Mexico, as had his father, who served with distinction during that war under the command of General Scott.[690]

This happy family occasion was followed by a very sad one for Sarah when her beloved father died the following May. William Rice was eighty-four years old at the time of his death. The loss of her father deeply affected Sarah. Rice left all of his children well provided for in a generous trust fund worth close to ninety thousand dollars, an amount that would today compute into the millions.[691]

> *He left us twenty thousand dollars a piece well invested & so that we could not spend the Principle~ It is still a great comfort to us all~*[692]

He also provided well for his niece, Elizabeth Rice, the "Cousin Betsy," of Sarah's childhood memories. She had remained with him and cared for him until the end of his life.

> *My father left to her by his will, his house & furniture & seven hundred dollars a year during her life, so that her last years were undisturbed by anxieties or cares~ She survived him seven years & died at eighty~four years of age, which was also the length of his life~ She was the eldest child of his eldest brother~18 Oct 1882*[693]

The summer following her father's death Sarah took a needed holiday in the White Mountains.

*In the summer of 1851, the year of my father's death, when family cares &
troubles had thickened around me, I determined to go to Gorham in Maine
the then Terminus of what is now called the Grand Trunk R.R. with which
Mr. Goodwin had much to do & get a few weeks of rest & recreation at the
Hotel~[694]*

Although Sarah is generally quite accurate in her recollections the above statement is
in error. She would have visited Gorham, New Hampshire rather than the town of the same
name in Maine, as the railroad in question was the Atlantic and St. Lawrence. It opened in
1851 and during its earliest years of operation ran from Portland, Maine to its terminus in
Gorham, New Hampshire.[695] By 1853 the line extended from Portland, Maine to Island Pond,
Vermont, and was then leased to the Canadian Grand Trunk Railroad for a period of nine
hundred and ninety-nine years.[696]

*That road seemed then like a wonderful enterprise, for few had then had
dreamed of a railroad through the mountains~[697]*

Building a railroad through the mountain was quite a feat and required a lot of ingenuity,
engineering skill, foresight, and daring. Track beds had to be cut into the hillsides of the steep
mountain ledges, and in places bridges, some as high as eighty feet, were built on spindly
trestles that spanned the mountains. Riding these mountain trains must have also taken a bit
of daring as well. But from its inception this train, which carried freight, bound for Europe
and serviced the pulp mills in Berlin, had a large summer patronage eager to experience the
splendor of nature in the White Mountains. [698]

*I took with me Sadie who had been quite an invalid & Susie who was seven
years old~ Frank two years older came up with his father every Saturday,
and remained until Monday~*

*My daughters came in turn except Abby who was living at Ft. Constitution
and was not well enough to be with us~[699]*

Sadie, her third daughter, was nineteen. By this time she was probably already been
stricken with the illness that eventually took her life. It was common at the time for upper
class men to leave their families for extended periods at nearby mountain, lake or ocean
resorts, where they could join them on weekends, while tending to business during the week.
Abby would have been in the latter stages of pregnancy by the summer of 1851 and unable
to travel.

*What wonderful times we had! The freshness & gaiety, the novelty &
delight of people at everything around them! The freedom from reserve &
conventionalism! The sociability & kindness! The readiness to be amused
made that simple Hotel the most delightful of places~[700]*

The Gorham House was one of the first mountain resorts that sprang up in the White
Mountains during the 1850s to accommodate the large influx of wealthy guests who traveled

by rail from the city to stay at the mountains. Before long many other much grander hotels were built.

> *It was roughly built, in fact put up in a hurry~ The rooms only plastered & without paint except the great Parlor, though the bedrooms were comfortable & the table excellent~*
>
> *Trouting parties were out all day & at supper we ladies had the benefit of their sport~ One night after such a supper, the spotted creatures attacked me in the shape of leopards, and my cries, brought people from their room~*
>
> *The people came from everywhere~ All Portland, the whole state of Maine & the rest of the world generally~ The Portland people put their hearts & their purses into the enterprise & were proud of it to the last degree~*[701]

Like many of the business ventures started in Portsmouth about this time the railroad lines and the hotels that sprung up around them were probably financed by business enterprises formed by investors such as Goodwin who were eager to capitalize on the burgeoning tourism trade in New England. Goodwin was apparently involved in this one, at least the portion of it that oversaw the construction of the railroad line.

> *Every evening hundreds of people were in motion at the invitation of the band & the great parlor was a scene of the liveliest excitement~ Things had not settled into distinctions & every body danced with everybody else while the elderly people, & the flirts walked the broad piazzas & looked through the open windows at the dancers~*[702]

The broad piazza was likely a large wrap around porch, designed to accommodate the many guests who chose to view the beautiful mountain prospects from a safe and comfortable perch. Here, according to Sarah, flirtatious young ladies promenaded while the elderly sat about in wicker or wrought iron chairs to socialize and take in the fresh mountain air, thought to have restorative powers even then.

> *Ellen Pearson, Almena Bates, Mrs Glentworth~ Maria & Hattie Neal~ Maria & Susan Decatur & their brother John & many pleasant people composed our party~*
>
> *Wm. Goodwin of Portland, an engineer on the road & his sister Nelly, now Mrs. Starr, gave us delightful music at the piano, assisted by rich voices & the violin~ Oh how they were inspired! They sang because they could not help it & when another party gathered around the piano, we would all adjourn to some room upstairs & have our concert there~ Mr Goodwin brought Col Bartlett one Saturday & he assisted at one of these Chamber concerts~*[703]

The parlor music of that day was quite lively and consisted of gay polkas and little ditties that called for group sing a-longs.

> *Every day parties were made up for Berlin Falls or the Glen House (then a small shanty) or to go on foot over Mt Washington or to Bethel the town below~*[704]

The Glen House, located at the entrance of the carriage road that led to the summit of Mt. Washington, began as a public house about this time. By 1873 it had become one of the grandest hotels in the White Mountains offering fine dining, and many other amenities. Entertainment such as dancing, billiards, bowling, and baseball games, along with hiking or wagon excursions to the nearby mountain attractions kept the wealthy clientele amused. Many returned annually and remained for the summer.[705]

> *I matronized a party to go over Cherry Mountain to the Notch & we filled an immense wagon with four horses ~ Mrs Glentworth ~ two of my daughters besides Susie, Isa Little & some other girls, and Frank Peabody & his brother Willie composed the party~*
>
> *We had a good time except that Mrs Glentworth & Frank Peabody were upset in the notch & somewhat scratched and bruised but no other harm done~ Mrs Glentworth was very gay but worried me by breaking her hand glass, which she said, was a bad sign in her family~*[706]

Although there are several notches in the White Mountains, Crawford Notch at the time was referred to as the White Mountain Notch, and was where Sarah and her party traveled.[707] From her account Sarah and her friends were quite adventuresome and enthusiastic about the mountains. Like many they were determined to enjoy every aspect of this new rustic playground for the well to do. Interest in the White Mountains, with its magnificent natural sites, had peaked as early as the 1830s thanks in part to authors such as Hawthorne and Thoreau, as well as famous painters such as Thomas Cole, or Winslow Homer who immortalized this area in their writings and canvases.[708]

> *Oh those were rare times & I forgot all my troubles~ Mr & Mrs Little, Mrs Chamberlain, Dannie Paine, Mr Edward Upham, Gen Tower, Judge Preble, Julia Furbish the delicious singer & many many others come up to my memory as I write~*
>
> *Sometimes I found the care of so many young people rather too much for me~ One evening in particular, Mr Upham & one or two other mischievous gentlemen got all the ladies of my charge into the great parlor, about ten o'clock and invited me to join them, which I declined on account of the lateness of the hour*
>
> *There was no objection raised by the young ladies, & I could do nothing with them~ I finally became imperious as they were very gay & I was afraid*

they would disturb the Clapp family who had rooms overhead~

I was about to leave like Mrs Varden in a huff, when I found the doors locked & the keys missing~ The next day I had the Clapp's down on me for not controlling my party~

That Hotel was burnt & many larger & grander have been built all about the mountains, but I do not think there have been such good times since, any where~1879[709]

Sarah's story of her failure as a chaperone for the young ladies is amusing, and indicates not all of the mountain resort adventures took place during their daytime excursions. Sarah's reference to Mrs.Varden is apparently a literary reference to a fictional character from a popular story of the time.

Sarah also wrote briefly of a trip she and Sadie took to the Catskill's during the 1850s.

I don't remember whether I have written of a beautiful journey, that I took with Sadie to Catskill in the month of June~

The mountain was all aglow with laurel & the flowers were of every shade from the deepest pink to the purest white~

We gathered an armful of them and put them in water in our room, but it was a great mistake for the next morning, we woke with eyes swollen & headache & so we found that the Laurel was poisonous to sleep with~[710]

The Goodwins became grandparents for the first time on September 18th of 1851, when Abby gave birth to William Winder. Named after his own father, as well as two great-grandfathers on both sides of his family, he was called "Willie" by his family and close friends.

During the latter part of the 1850s two more Goodwin daughters wed. Georgette Goodwin, who was known as Georgie, married Naval Lieutenant Joseph Bradford, on July 11, 1857. The Reverend Peabody officiated. Georgie was twenty-three at the time of her wedding, and her husband was thirty-three. Bradford was assigned to a receiving ship in Boston from 1857 to 1859, and it is assumed that the newlyweds lived in Boston during the first years of their marriage.

Bradford, a native of Tennessee and the son of Morgan Bradford, was raised in Huntsville, Alabama. He enlisted in the navy in 1840, was assigned to the Naval Academy in 1846, and was promoted to the rank of Passed Midshipman in July of that same year. Prior to his marriage, Bradford was attached to the African Squadron on the sloop the *Jamestown*, stationed off the African Coast to intercept illegal slave traders.[711] Sarah was apparently quite fond of him.

Your Uncle Bradford loved dearly to go about anywhere with us, and he was always most kind and courteous to me~[712]

Georgie gave birth to their first son, Henry Morgan, the following July. This was the Goodwin's second grandchild. Unfortunately he died within two months. The cause of his death is not known.

When Sadie was twenty-seven she became engaged to Samuel Storer, a thirty-nine year old lawyer from Portsmouth. He was a member of one of Portsmouth's most distinguished families, and both sides of his family traced their connections to a personal relationship with the country's first president.

Samuel practiced law in Portsmouth during the 1850s, but extant letters indicate he had some difficulty in establishing a lucrative practice in Portsmouth. Some months before they married Samuel traveled to Peotone, Illinois to set up a law practice, and build a home for his future bride. A letter to his father, Admiral George Washington Storer, written a month before their marriage indicates that up until then their engagement was a secret.

> *... When I left Portsmouth in March it was with the understanding that should things look at all favorable, I should return the later part of this month, be married about the middle of June, and bring Sadie to Illinois with me~ This determination, however we thought better should be kept to ourselves as far as possible till just before I should leave here, consequently but few have any suspicion of the matter & now that I find that I can probably leave here in the middle or latter part of next week, I think it is but proper to inform you of it~ ... I have been very much delayed in my work this season, but now the painters are putting on the last coat & the joiner has nearly completed his job~ The house when they leave has been sufficiently comfortable for a summer residence in the country~... The man who came out here a year ago has left as his wife said the work was too hard for her~ So I have an Irishman in his place of whom I know nothing about~ I feel a great deal disturbed at being obliged to leave him here in my absence, but I could not wait for any other person~*[713]

Reverend Daniel Austin married the Storers on June 1st of 1859. Shortly after their wedding they traveled by rail to their new home on the prairie. Excerpts from a second letter to Admiral Storer from Samuel tells a little about their journey.

> *We arrived here at the Richmond House on Thursday evening last, after a very pleasant journey from Portsmouth, stopping on the way at Springfield, Albany, & Detroit overnight, as well as one day & two nights at Niagara Falls~ On Saturday we went to the farm & found everything in excellent order...Sadie's health is very much better than it was when we left~ her cold has entirely disappeared. She is able to walk for a couple of hours without feeling fatigue~*[714]

In Peotone Samuel set up a law practice, and oversaw the cultivation of a 600 acre wheat farm, while Sadie, set up housekeeping on the prairie.

1850-1860
CLIPPERS, GASLIGHTS, ELECTIONS

In June of 1850 Portsmouth Gaslight Company was incorporated with a capital stock of $60,300. When the company was started Goodwin was serving in the New Hampshire House of Representatives, and was a member of the House Committee for Incorporations, which ‑oversaw passage of legislation favoring this incorporation. He was also president of the company for several decades.[715]

Gas lighting had been available in larger cities such as Boston and Baltimore since the 1820s, but this service was slow in coming to Portsmouth. Many people were wary of this new technology. They feared that poisonous gas leaks could endanger large portions of the community or cause major explosions and fires. Despite these fears there was a growing demand for this type of lighting in the large textile factories and the municipalities throughout the region.

The Portsmouth Gas Light Company opened in December of 1851 on Islington Street, not too far from the Goodwin home. The local papers reported that when the first lamps were lit in downtown Portsmouth in mid December of 1851, the stores shone with " a lively and brilliant aspect." In addition the papers bragged the streets were so brilliantly lit that even on a dark night a pin could be spotted on the ground.[716]

The Goodwins along with other affluent families would have been the first to enjoy this new technology in their homes. However, an 1872 entry in Sarah's waste book indicates that even two decades later she was still somewhat leery about this new technology.

> *Never allow a gas leak for a day~never sit or sleep in foul air~ Gas flames give off Carbonic Oxide...Charcoal gas is Carbonic oxide...Gas flames give off Carbonic acid which is not so poisonous~*[717]

In the 1850s shipbuilding in Portsmouth reached an all time high. At the start of this decade there were three major shipbuilders in the area. Due to the increased demand for ships during these years, several other firms came into existence. Ichabod Goodwin was involved in many aspects of this trade financing new companies, buying ships, and as an agent for other ships.

There were several reasons for this shipbuilding boom, which brought a large influx of money into the area. First there was a flourishing cotton trade between America and Europe, and fast ships were needed to expedite these international journeys. In addition, when gold was discovered in California there was a demand for a large number of Baltimore Clippers to carry miners and other speculators to the West Coast. Clipper ships were designed with such sleek and lean lines that they were able to shear through waves faster than the average ship, shortening a trip around the Horn of South America and up the Pacific Coast from an average of six to four months.

Many of the privateers that operated out of Portsmouth during the War of 1812 such as the *Fox*, were clippers. Local historian, Ray Brighton, in his informative book *The Clippers of the Port of Portsmouth* speculated that George Raynes, who was hailed as a genius ship-builder during his day, as well as Samuel Badger, another skilled shipbuilder and a relation of Sarah's, might have recalled the design of the *Fox* from their younger days.[718]

During the 1850s fifty-nine three mast, square-rigged ships were built in Portsmouth, and twenty-eight of them were clippers.[719] The *Red Rover*, the *Nightingale*, the *Water Witch*, and *Dashing Wave* were just a few of the clippers for which Goodwin was an agent. The sale of one of these vessels was generally an occasion for celebration, and Goodwin hosted a number of collations at the Market House in Market Square to celebrate the launching of a ship.[720] These ships were quite ornate in design, with no expense spared in their construction. In Portsmouth, as in the larger cities such as New York and Boston, the price of a thousand or more ton clipper ship was approximately sixty-two dollars a ton. Although twenty-eight out of two hundred clippers built in the United States during these years came from this region, not one returned to the Piscataqua after they were launched.

One of the most memorable ships ever built in Portsmouth was the *Witch of the Wave*, built by George Raynes in 1851. It was considered the most beautiful clipper ship ever built in Portsmouth up until then. Not only was the design and craftsmanship superior to other clippers, the cabins and stateroom were luxuriously furnished and a library on board boasted of over one hundred volumes of books. It was sold to a firm from Salem, Massachusetts for $80,000.

When it was launched on April 5th of that year hundreds of notables were on hand. Morning trains carried from two to three hundred ladies and gentlemen from Boston and Salem to attend the festivities. The new owners hosted a banquet, complete with entertainment on board the ship, and evening festivities at the mansion of George Raynes near North Mill Pond followed this celebration. The Goodwins attended this affair, and local legend still `tells of how the usually staid Ichabod Goodwin danced through the night in his stocking feet.[721]

Shipbuilder Samuel Hansom was not so fortunate with the *Nightingale*, a similar clipper built soon after, although it was said to be the grandest and most expensive clipper ever built on the Piscataqua. The bow was graced with a figurehead of Jenny Lind, P.T. Barnum's "Swedish Nightingale." It was intended to transport wealthy travelers to the World's Fair in London where it was to be on exhibition. There was not enough interest in its maiden voyage, and Hansom was facing financial ruin until he appointed Goodwin as agent for the ship. Goodwin managed to save him by auctioning off the ship in Boston for forty-three thousand dollars. That buyer eventually sold it for seventy-five thousand dollars.[722]

The *Morning Glory* was a clipper ship owned by Ichabod Goodwin, Jacob Wendell, and William L. Dwight, the husband of Sarah's youngest sister. It was launched without ceremony on October 30, 1854. Unlike many of the clippers, the *Morning Glory* was engaged in the transatlantic trade until the Civil War began. Then it was sold.[723]

> *At the time we all had a passion for "Morning Glories" & they were running every where~ they sowed themselves & were of many colors~ Your grandpa asked me to name a beautiful ship & without hesitation I called her the "Morning Glory"~*

The name pleased everywhere & one time when a law suit grew out of some difficulty in Bordeaux in France connected with this vessel, the case was decided in favor of her owners & uncle Dwight thought the name had something to do with the decision~

I quote your Uncle Dwight because he went out to France to protect the interest of the owners~[724]

Other vessels listed in the 1851 city directory as owned by Goodwin and associates were the *Mary Hale*, the schooners the *Alice Parker,* the *Banner*, and the *Frank*. Two others built for the still flourishing cotton trade were the *Hope Goodwin*, named for Goodwin's second daughter, and the *Anna Decatur* in honor of William Parson's wife. Parson, a ship's captain, invested in ships with Goodwin. In addition he and his wife were close friends of the Goodwins. Unfortunately, on her second voyage out a rebellious crew in Mobile Bay, Alabama burned the *Hope Goodwin*. The reason for this rebellion is not known.[725]

The Hope Goodwin, built for Ichabod Goodwin and associates in 1851, named in honor of Goodwin's second daughter, Hope.

Also in 1851 Ichabod Goodwin was named president of the Portsmouth Bridge Company. This was the same company William Rice and a group of other investors had first incorporated in 1819, when they built the first bridge between Portsmouth and Kittery. It was still a toll bridge that generated revenue for the company and their investors. Goodwin retained this position for at least two more decades.

During these busy years Ichabod Goodwin remained active in his community as well as his nation. In the 1856-7 city directory he is listed as a trustee of the Mercantile Library Association, an organization dedicated to the intellectual improvement of the community through their provision of "selected volumes of books," as well as lectures at the Lyceum.

Goodwin was in the state legislature as a member of the Whig party in 1850, 1854, and 1856, and by this time was the acknowledged head of the Whig party in New Hampshire. However, the national party was in disarray by the late 1850s. It had divided into two factions over the issue of extending slavery westward. Before the party entirely disbanded the southern members became known as the "Cotton Whigs," and the northern members the "Conscience Whigs."

In New Hampshire Goodwin was the unanimous choice of the Whig party for Congress for several years running. However, by this time the Democrats were the dominant political party in the state, and the nomination was honorary.[726] Eventually most of the southern members of the Whig party became assimilated into the Democratic Party, while the northern Whigs along with some Independent Democrats joined with smaller parties such as the Free Soilers, and the American Party (also known as the Know Nothings). These parties were united in their opposition to slavery and they eventually grouped together to form a new political party in 1856.

For a while Goodwin stubbornly clung to his former allegiances, and remained loyal to his old political party. He was the last Whig candidate to run for governor in the state of New Hampshire in 1856. During that election he received less than 2,000 votes scattered throughout the state. Shortly afterward he joined the new party.

The following year Goodwin was a candidate for the gubernatorial nomination of the American Party. The party chose William Haile as the party's nominee. Haile went on to win the election for governor, and was reelected the following year.[727]

One well deserved honor which Goodwin, the recipient of two years of formal education, received that year was an honorary Masters of Arts degree from Dartmouth College. This was given in recognition of his interest in legislation to benefit the educational system.[728]

THE GOVERNORSHIP

Two years later, in 1859, Ichabod Goodwin was the gubernatorial candidate of the new political party, by then officially called the Republican Party. During these years the governor was elected on an annual basis, and elections for state office were held in March. His opponent was Democrat Asa P. Cate. Goodwin beat out his opponent by over 4,500 votes to become the state's twenty-ninth governor.[729] Interestingly, while Goodwin carried the state, he failed to carry the city of Portsmouth in that election. Still there was a great celebration in Portsmouth on the day he was elected. Local Republicans assembled in Market Square at sunset to celebrate his victory by firing one hundred guns, and after this official salute to the new governor they marched to the Goodwin home on

Inaugural portrait of Governor Ichabod Goodwin, circa 1859-60.

Islington Street. The Coronet Band led the way past a large number of well-lit homes, as well as large crowds of townspeople, who were gathered along the route cheering loudly.

From the Goodwin home the new governor and his family were escorted to the Masonic Temple for a round of congratulatory speeches. By then the crowd had grown so large there was an overflow of celebrants, and not all of them fit inside. After the speeches the evening activities were topped by a social collation held in the new governor's honor at Jefferson Hall.[730]

> *But Oh! What a time we had when your grandpa' was nominated Governor! He had been previously nominated by the Whig party & he was their last nominee~ But this time he was nominated by the Republican party, which was in the ascendant & Oh such times! With Bands & speeches & excitement of all sorts~*[731]

In Governor Goodwin's first message to the state legislature he spoke to the growing division between the North and South. He promised that New Hampshire would always be a part of the Union, and that the state would never encroach upon the rights of the southern states. However, Goodwin affirmed that New Hampshire was bound to prevent the expansion of the "curse of slavery" over free territories.[732]

His strong statement against the expansion of slavery was followed by a joint resolution from the legislature. They went on record stating that the state had officially adopted the position that slavery was anti-Republican, as well as an "element of national weakness."[733] This was New Hampshire's strongest official stance against slavery up until that point in time.

There was no governor's mansion in the state, so Goodwin continued to live in Portsmouth and to maintain his positions on the boards of various companies and other institutions. He would have commuted by rail between Portsmouth and Concord, and probably stayed at the Phoenix House in Concord when it was necessary for him to be there for any length of time. There is some evidence Goodwin conducted much of the state's business from a make-do office in his home, and his office on Market Street.

The years in which Goodwin served as governor must have been busy ones in the Goodwin household. However, Sarah left behind very little in the way of personal recollections of this time, other than two vignettes about these years. One told of a visit from a sculptor commissioned to do a bust of Goodwin during his second term; the second recalled a visit the Goodwins made to Canada to attend a royal ball.

During Goodwin's first term tensions between the northern abolitionists and southern secessionists grew greater. When he ran for reelection in March of 1860, he won by an even larger margin than before.[734] This boded well for the Republican candidate, Abraham Lincoln, who was making his bid for the presidency that coming fall.

In June of 1860 Goodwin was escorted to his second inauguration at the State House in Concord by three ceremonial militias. One was a local group known as "Goodwin's Guards." It was led by William Sides of Portsmouth and was composed of a group of seventy local men. Another was named "Goodwin's Rifles" a group of about one hundred skilled marksmen from Concord. The third was the "Governor's Horse Guards," a contingent of cavalry formed in 1860 by Brigadier General George Stark of Nashua, primarily to escort Governor Goodwin to his second inauguration, which took place in Concord, the state capital.

> *The second year of his Governorship, a squadron of cavalry was organized by gentlemen of military tastes & called the "Governor's Horse Guards"~ It was the most elegant military display that had ever been seen in this state & was greatly admired~*[735]

The Governor's Horse Guards were quite grand outfitted in navy blue fitted uniforms, decorated with gold braid criss-cross. They wore matching navy blue helmets also trimmed in gold. A swatch of bright red velvet at the front of each helmet, along with ostrich plumes, added a dramatic flair to the overall impression. A Boston military tailor designed these uniforms especially for this auspicious occasion.

After the display at the state capital the Governor's Horse Guards came to Portsmouth to honor the governor in his own community.

> *They came to Portsmouth for a day, in compliment to the Gov. & manoeuvered in the square, before the house & then paraded on the streets~ Our house*

was thrown open, during the whole day & all were liberally entertained~

Then we had an encampment at Nashua, and Gen Stark had us all to stay at his house & a grand reception in the evening & Gen Butler sent his elegant barouche & horses & coachman for our use & came himself with his staff, which made a most elegant display with gold lace & chapeaux with great feathers of the bird of paradise color~

The whole thing was a great success in fact it was like a "tournament"~[736]

Brigadier General George Stark, of Nashua was their host for the military reception. In less than a year after the encampment, he was assigned to Ft. Constitution in Portsmouth's neighboring community, New Castle, to organize the second regiment of New Hampshire Troops.[737]

The General Butler to which Sarah refers was General Benjamin Butler. A native of Deerfield, New Hampshire, for many years he was a criminal lawyer and politician in Massachusetts. During the war Butler held the position of Major General of Volunteers. He was also the general who oversaw the military occupation of New Orleans.

At the start of Goodwin's second term as governor Henry Dexter, a sculptor from Boston who received a commission by President Buchanan in 1859 to create marble busts of the governors of each state during 1860, contacted Governor Goodwin with this proposal. Goodwin was at first reluctant to take the time necessary for sittings. However, it was arranged for these to take place in the Goodwin home and the bust was completed.

In 1859 Mr Buchanan, or his cabinet, commissioned Mr Dexter the sculptor, to obtain marble Portrait Busts of all the Governors of 1860 & promised him a permanent place for them in a wing of the Capitol~

Mr Goodwin was governor that year & the request was made that he would give sittings for a likeness at the Rockingham House~ He was very busy & at first thought it impossible to give the time, but it was soon decided that Mr Dexter could have a room in our house with all his apparatus & he was glad to fall in with the arrangement~

It was very interesting & pleasant to watch a sculptor at work~ The process was all new to me & I considered it a great opportunity~

A kind of sink was placed on a table & on that the clay model was formed~ A box on the floor held the clay~

One morning he said to me "Now Mrs Goodwin I should like to be undisturbed today~ Please do not call me to dining, or let any one come to my door~ If I want anything I will come down & ask for it~

About six that evening he appeared looking very weary & said he believed it was all right, & asked Mr Goodwin if he would bring in some friends the next day to inspect it~

His friends came & pronounced the likeness perfect & then Mr Dexter invited me to witness a part of the process preparatory to cutting the marble~

He first oiled the model thoroughly to prevent sticking then he poured liquid Plaster over it, layer over layer~ Leaving time for it to <u>set</u>, until the Plaster, was some inches thick~

Then he turned it over & Oh the desecration!

Took his trowel & dug out the clay as if it had never been consecrated by the approval of friends & threw it back into the box~

Then he washed out the cavity with soap & hot water & wiped it dry~ Then he oiled it again & filled it full of liquid plaster~ That made the block from which the portrait was to be cut~ He did not peel off the outside while here~ but he described to me the careful process of picking it off so as not to injure the Block~

He had taken likenesses of several of the Governors before he came to Portsmouth & they had gone to his studio for their sittings, but he was so much pleased with our arrangement that he took care to mention it in other states & the fashion was adopted by all the others~

I believe every Governor ordered one likeness in marble for himself, but the original Block in plaster we think is even more valuable as a likeness than the marble~[738]

given

The Goodwin family retained the original block for themselves, as well as the marble one. A duplicate bust was given to the National Museum in Washington, DC. and there is a marble copy in the Portsmouth Library.

A visit to Montreal to meet the Prince of Wales was the subject of a second vignette that Sarah recalled happening during Goodwin's second term as governor. In the summer of 1860 H.R.H. Albert Edward, Prince of Wales and the eldest son of Queen Victoria, was sent off on a grand tour to visit the Royal Canadian provinces. Upon his arrival an invitation was extended to all of the New England governors to attend a royal

Bust of Governor Ichabod Goodwin displayed in Goodwin House, circa 1860 by Henry Dexter.

ball to be given in his honor in Montreal.

> *Well then the "Prince of Wales" was coming to the British Provinces & all the New England Governors were invited to share in the festivities of the occasion~ We went to Montreal, where of course the preparations were on a very grand scale & where your grandpa' was presented, (that honor being accorded only to gentlemen) & where we attended a grand Ball & I stood very near the Prince & his suite & enjoyed all he did~*[739]

Frank was born on November 1, 1841. At the time of the visit both he and Prince Edward were looking forward to celebrating their nineteenth birthdays that fall. In the nineteenth century British royalty set the social standards and fashions for many upper class Americans. When Frank was young, the English Prince was somewhat of a role model for young America boys, who were subtly urged to emulate his clothing, manners, and interests. As a very young child Frank Goodwin may have admired him or even envied his position.

> *I liked the looks of him very much & thought of my Frank who was said to cry because the Prince was born two days before him~*[740]

An invitation to a royal ball given in honor of the young Prince was considered quite an honor, and one many other Americans would have coveted. This became clear that fall when following his trip to Canada the Prince arrived in the United States for a tour of parts of the country. Although his original plans just called for a visit to Canada, President Buchanan, former Minister to the Court of St. James, sent an invitation to Queen Victoria for the prince to visit America.

The Queen graciously accepted the invitation, but requested that while in the United States the prince not travel as royalty, but under the name Baron Renfrew. Of course the American public ignored this injunction of the Queen, and gave the Prince a royal welcome. Wherever the young prince traveled in America crowds of admirers turned out to greet him. Journalists reported his every move to an adoring audience, which never seemed to tire of hearing about him, and many young American ladies vied for the Prince's attention, which he willingly gave.[741]

While in Canada the Goodwins joined with governors from nearby states, and visited some of their more prominent Canadian neighbors.

> *Gov Buckingham of Conn was in Montreal at that time, & the two Governors & their suites & myself were almost constantly together~ We took two carriages & went to call on Lady Franklin, the widow of the unfortunate Arctic navigator, & she seemed much pleased with the attention~*[742]

Lady Jane Franklin was the widow of Sir John Franklin, a noted Canadian explorer and rear admiral in the British navy. He is credited for having discovered the Northwest Passage, the Canadian Arctic waterway that connects the Atlantic and the Pacific Oceans. After two successful voyages into the Arctic region, which he memorialized in two books, Sir Franklin set out with two ships and one hundred and thirty-eight men in 1845 to search for this passage.

However, by 1847 when no word was received from the expedition, the first of forty search parties was sent to find him. These searches discovered his ships crushed by the ice at Victoria Strait. They also discovered the passage Franklin had sought. His second wife, Sir Lady Jane, arranged the last expedition in 1859, just a year before the Goodwins met her in Canada. This final search party found the skeletons of the crew, and learned from an elderly Eskimo woman that the survivors had starved while attempting to walk across the North American mainland. They also found a written account of the expedition up to April of 1848.[743]

> *She was staying by particular invitation with a Mr. Stephens who was living in the finest house in Montreal~ He was a poor Vermont boy who went penniless to M__ & by industry & shrewdness acquired a great fortune~*
>
> *I had noticed the day previous, in driving, that he had in his grounds the finest & largest trees in the city, I remarked upon them & he asked me how many years I thought it had taken to build the house & produce all the other pleasant things, the trees among them~*
>
> *"Oh I said I could not guess~ the trees looked older than himself & yet evidently planted with a purpose"~*
>
> *This house said he & these trees have all been placed here within two years!*
>
> *He invited us to walk in the grounds which were full of beauty, with one exception~ A row of sunflowers in full bloom were all ranged along the back of his house! I tried not to let him see me look at them~*
>
> *But he was not ashamed of them, on the contrary, he was proud of them and to him they were fuller of sentiment than any thing else that he had~ "My mother he said, "loved sunflowers & always had them at her door & to me they are more beautiful than anything else"~ Didn't he deserve to be rich?*
>
> *About the trees, he said that in the fall he had the holes dug & around the trees (which were brought from the mountain) trenches cut at a distance from the trunk & then with tackle & oxen, after the ground froze pulled them out, drew them into town & placed them in the holes prepared for them~ He said he did not lose one~*[744]

Sarah's offhand remark that this man deserved wealth because of his good character, or at least his sentimental nature, is characteristic of the Victorian outlook, which took the stance that those that did well in life were somehow morally superior. This attitude legitimized the nineteenth century interest in the then new theory of social Darwinism that grew out of Darwin's theory of heredity published a few years prior to this time.

There were not many gardens of note in most of the Canadian provinces during this time with the exception of Montreal. The editor of *The Horticulturist* visited there in 1858 and found a flourishing horticultural society in this city along with twenty large estates with admirable gardens.[745] He also noted that the Canadian government was probably the only one that gave financial support to horticulturists. It is not known if the garden belonging to Sarah's host was one of the twenty mentioned, but it is likely.

The visit to Canada occurred just weeks before America's pivotal presidential elections of 1860. One reason the prince may have dropped his royal title while visiting America was a fear that was felt even in Europe that war between the North and the South might erupt if the election went to the North. When war did begin British sympathies seemed to favor the southern cause.[746]

Abraham Lincoln, a former Whig from Illinois and a prominent member of the nascent Republicans, came to New Hampshire earlier that year seeking his party's nomination for the presidential race, but many in the state even in his own party failed to recognize him as a viable presidential candidate. Lincoln, who had recently come to national prominence because of his highly publicized debates with Stephen Douglas, visited Concord, Manchester, Dover, and Exeter during his stay in the state.

However, he never visited Portsmouth. The only Goodwin he met according to one biographer was William Goodwin, a lawyer, journalist, and Democrat, who questioned his reasoned argument against the extension of slavery in America. It is reported that Lincoln's reply satisfied this gentleman. Lincoln later graciously honored William Goodwin's written request for a rare inscribed copy of the Lincoln Douglas debates.[747]

Lincoln apparently impressed enough of the Republican leaders in the state. At the Republican National Convention in Chicago that year, New Hampshire supported Lincoln overwhelmingly, with state delegates casting all ten votes for him on the second ballot. This support was even more impressive because Salmon Chase, a native son and well-known abolitionist, as well as a friend of Goodwin's was also on the ballot.[748]

After Lincoln was elected President, Salmon Chase was named Secretary of the Treasury in his first cabinet. Amongst some political observers in the state there was serious speculation for a while that Ichabod Goodwin would be Lincoln's Secretary of the Navy. The *Nashua Gazette*, a prestigious paper in New Hampshire endorsed Goodwin for this position. The *Concord Standard* agreed he would be a good candidate for this post, noting that Governor Goodwin was a "sound and solid man…of good judgment, probably more acceptable to the people at large than any other man." The *Salem Gazette* of Massachusetts concurred with these lofty sentiments. However, they noted with tongue in cheek that if he was nominated for this position, "We shall think the end of the world is coming…if an appointment so obviously fit and proper as this should be made." [749].

Lincoln passed over Goodwin, the faithful leader of the Whig party with his years of experience on the sea and in shipping, to choose instead Gideon Wells, a former Democrat and a journalist. Even though it must have seemed shortly thereafter that the end of the world, or at least the nation was coming, Ichabod Goodwin remained as Governor of the State of New Hampshire until June of 1861.

CIVIL WAR BEGINS

After Lincoln was elected tensions between the northern and southern states grew even stronger. The burdens of office must have weighted heavily on Goodwin at this time, but he still sought a third term as governor in January of that year. However, he was defeated at the Republican State Convention that January, and in March Nathaniel Berry, a fellow Republican, was elected governor.

By then a conflict between the two sections of the country seemed inevitable. Goodwin's term didn't expire until June of that year. So in March in an effort to calm this climate of increasing animosity, he issued a proclamation setting aside April 11th as a day of fast and prayer in New Hampshire. In his proclamation he asked the people of New Hampshire to assemble at their various houses of worship that day to pray for a "spirit of reconciliation, justice and patriotic consideration" for themselves (the North), and "a spirit of candor and of consideration for our erring brethren." (The South)[750]

In Portsmouth the day was observed with the closing of the Naval Yard. Meeting for worship was held in the North and Middle Street Churches. The weather was so nice that large numbers of people took advantage of it and engaged each other in cricket matches and baseball games.

Ironically the following day the rebels fired upon Fort Sumter. The regular federal army consisted of just seventeen thousand men when the war began. To build up temporary forces President Lincoln issued a call for seventy-five thousand volunteer militiamen to fight for the Union for a period of just ninety days.[751] No one thought the war would last any longer.

In Portsmouth the local press was supportive of their new president. For the next week the local papers were filled with the story of the surrender of Ft. Sumter. The headlines of the *Portsmouth Journal*, proclaimed in large bold print 'WAR-CIVIL WAR!!!" The editorial of the day dramatically exhorted all to support the Union. "This evil is really upon us. The die is cast-the blow is struck…and shoulder to shoulder the lovers of the Union come forward to pledge their sacred honor, their fortunes, and lives in defense of constitutional liberty."[752]

Come forward they did! Within days of Lincoln's declaration of war, Governor Goodwin set up recruiting offices all over the state in all the major cities including Portsmouth. Between April 17th and April 30th over two thousand men came from every region to enlist in the Union Army. There were so many volunteers that these first men made up the First and Second Regiments of New Hampshire.

At the start of the war Portsmouth was filled with patriotic fervor, as were many communities in the North as well as the South. Throughout the state there was a show of great support for the cause. Union flags decorated the streets of the cities and towns, and porches of private homes. The flag was also found draped over the pulpits of many churches, where the sermons generally were given over to patriotic discourse urging support of the Union cause. Women in the state rallied to sew for the men who volunteered to fight. In nearby Dover over a hundred women sewed four hundred shirts in a few weeks time.[753]

The average age of the volunteers was thirty, and there were no class distinctions at first. Farmers, mechanics, and merchants signed up to fight alongside doctors, lawyers, and bankers. However, as the units formed those with higher degrees were given officer's commissions, while the rest were assigned to the regular rank and file of enlisted men.[754]

The Governor's Horse Guards, formed to escort Goodwin to his inauguration, made up the nucleus for the First New Hampshire Regiment.[755] They trained at Camp Union in Concord, and merchants in that city provided the government with wagons, horses, an ambulance, and other necessary equipment or supplies.[756] An article in the Portsmouth paper gave a run down of the troop's supplies and uniforms for the first two New Hampshire regiments.

> The troops are all to be uniformed and dressed as follows: Grey coats and pants, Grey overcoat, grey fatigue cap, two flannel shirts. One pair flannel drawers, one extra pair socks, one pair shoes, and one large camp blanket.[757]

It was up to each state to outfit, train, and pay the regiments from their state coffers. In New Hampshire no state money had been put aside for that purpose, and the legislature was not in session at the time. Governor Goodwin realizing that there would be an unacceptable delay if he called the state legislature together, went out on his own and raised $680,000 from private citizens and banks in a matter of a few days. This amount was more than sufficient. In fact only $100,000 was needed to outfit the first two New Hampshire regiments.[758]

The local papers praised Goodwin for his quick action, saving the state both time and money, and showing that New Hampshire was as prompt as any other state in answering their country's call to duty.[759] However, when the state legislature convened again in June of that year, ninety-one Democrats signed an official protest stating that the governor and his council had assumed despotic power when they acted without legislative approval.[760]

Democratic disapproval aside, the consensus was that Governor Goodwin had responded quickly and wisely in a time of great emergency. The state legislature then passed the "Enabling Act." This act ratified Goodwin's actions, and assigned responsibility for the debt to the state.[761]

The local papers reported on a ceremony honoring Goodwin's Guards, attended by a contingent of prominent citizens from the city. On this occasion, held at the North Church in May of 1861, they were presented with an "elegant silk flag on which thirty-four golden stars," had been embroidered. The Sons of Portsmouth presented this flag to the regiment, and Governor Goodwin spoke to the men and urged them to "do all in their power to bear the glorious flag in triumph."[762]

The First New Hampshire Regiment left Concord dressed in new gray uniforms on May 25th. They were cheered along the way at cotillions given in their honor by the "Sons of New Hampshire," contingents of New Hampshire natives residing in Boston and New York. They were presented with an elegant silk flag in New York, but left too soon to receive another silk flag intended for them. New Hampshire natives living in California had sent this second flag. It was embroidered with the head of a grizzly bear and the coat of arms of California. It was given to the Second Regiment, after a group of New Hampshire ladies changed the one on the flag to a two.[763]

When the First Regiment arrived in Baltimore they marched through the streets with the Manchester Cornet Band playing "Yankee Doodle Dandy." This constituted a brave and defiant act, as Baltimore was the scene of a riot that erupted when the Massachusetts Sixth passed through that city earlier in the month. From there they took the train to Washington. Upon arrival they marched down Pennsylvania Avenue for a presidential review, and President Lincoln sent a message to their commander noting that they were the "best appointed regiment" he had viewed thus far.[764]

During the month of May of 1861 over one thousand men came to Portsmouth. There were three full companies in the small city that month, and the facilities were badly crowded. About two hundred men were sent to Fort Constitution, and the other eight hundred were put up at the ropewalk in Portsmouth. Their training grounds were the fields by South Mill Pond and the streets were filled with these men marching in military order to the tune of the fife and drum.

They had all signed up for ninety days, but it soon became clear the war would last longer than three months. Then orders arrived from Washington to send no more ninety-day troops. The majority of the Second Regiment then signed up for three years. The nucleus of this regiment was made up of the local militia known as "Goodwin's Guards" led by William Sides. Although he resigned in July of that year four of his family members remained as members of Company K of the Second Regiment. [765]

"Goodwin Rifles," the ceremonial sharpshooters from Concord led by Captain Simon Griffin, formed Company B of the Second Regiment. Other Portsmouth natives served in other companies throughout the war. However, more than any other, the Second seemed to be Portsmouth's own.[766]

The Second New Hampshire Regiment left Portsmouth on June 20th. The Sons residing in both Boston and New York City cheered them along the way, and honored them at cotillions, replete with patriotic speeches. This regiment arrived in time to open the first battle of Bull Run. It was not a happy introduction to war. During this battle their leader, Col. Marston of Exeter, was badly wounded, and the toll of this battle was seven killed, thirty-six wounded, and forty-six missing.[767]

The First New Hampshire Regiment never engaged in any battles. They were mustered out in August of that year. Only thirty-five casualties were listed, and this list included four deaths, five captured, and seven deserters. Most of these men reenlisted in other regiments following their discharge. However, a number of them, disillusioned by the failure to win a quick Union victory, rested on their laurels and remained at home throughout the rest of the war.[768]

The community of Portsmouth was somewhat paranoid and fearful that the city might be the target of Confederate aggression because of the proximity of the Naval Yard. One rumor making the local papers stated that a reliable source confirmed that Jefferson Davis visited the Portsmouth Naval Yard less than a year before. Although he had not identified himself, others who saw him taking notes at the facility recognized him.[769]

Despite the legitimacy this rumor gained by its insertion into the local paper, it was never proven that Jefferson Davis had actually visited the Naval Yard. If he had he no doubt would be hard pressed to recognize it four years later. As with all the changes the war brought to Portsmouth, the change at the Naval Yard was the greatest. The second greatest change was the negative impact it had on the merchant marine trade.[770]

At the war's start Goodwin also worked alongside Commander Pearson, head of the Portsmouth Naval Yard. One of the first things they did was arrange to protect nearby Fort Constitution with twenty-five enlisted men and one hundred and fifty volunteers from the

Portsmouth Volunteer Corps. Goodwin was also responsible for overseeing the purchase of needed munitions, and he helped to equip the Naval Yard with equipment needed for their defense.[771]

Because he was the one responsible for purchasing equipment, Goodwin received many offers to supply the New Hampshire troops from munitions manufacturers. One popular firearm at the time was the Parrott rifle manufactured in Cold Springs, New York. It had been designed and manufactured by Portsmouth native, Robert Parker Parrott, Sarah Goodwin's cousin.

While the Parrott gun was never as popular as the Colt or the Winchester rifle, some experts such as Admiral Goldsborough, the Commander of the North Atlantic Squadron claimed they were the best naval guns ever made.[772] Others such as Admiral George Dewey disagreed. A lieutenant during the war, Dewey stated in his autobiography that they posed more danger to the crew than the enemy because of their tendency to explode.[773] There is no evidence Goodwin favored his family member with a large order of these guns.

Ichabod Goodwin's term as governor expired on June 5th of 1861, but his legacy as New Hampshire's Civil War Governor remained untarnished throughout his lifetime. Goodwin's place in history was assured by his prompt if somewhat illegal action in answering his country's call for troops, and his quick actions in preparing the state and his community for war. These acts earned him the nickname "Fighting Governor Goodwin."

On a more personal level in the Goodwin family, two of their daughters were married to Union officers. Although both of these young men were natives of the South they remained true to the Union throughout the war. However, their loyalties must have been severely tested, as each had family members on the other side.

> *Capt Bradford had a cousin that he was very close to & they went into the*
> *US Navy as soon as they were old enough~ When the War of the Rebellion*
> *broke out, one staid & the other went into the Confederate Navy~*[774]

William Winder's father, Colonel John Winder, his brother, and his namesake cousin all resigned their army commissions with the federal government, and defected to the Confederate side when the war started. In the South, Colonel Winder was promoted to Brigadier General in the Confederate Army. He was made Provost Marshall in charge of the secret police squad, and eventually was put in charge of all the Confederate prisons in Alabama and Georgia. With the help of his son and nephew he oversaw both the infamous Andersonville and Libby Prisons.[775]

William, who fought in the Mexican War alongside his father, opted to remain with the Union army. This decision apparently was the subject of much attention in both the North and the South at the time. Northern authorities at first ordered him to Washington, DC and eventually assigned him to a post in San Francisco, where he was away from most of the action throughout the war.[776] It is not certain if Abby and Willie went with William at this time, but they eventually did join him out West.

At the outbreak of war the California State Legislature immediately declared their allegiance to the federal government, and during the war more than sixteen thousand men joined the Union forces. These men trained at Fort Drum, close to the present city of Los Angeles. Some of these troops did see action in the East, and those that remained in the West were needed to engage in smaller battles with those Texans and other settlers in southern

California who were loyal to the Confederate cause.

Early on in the conflict the Confederate forces in the West overtook New Mexico and parts of Arizona. It was believed that if the Confederates could control California, with her gold mines and harbors, the European powers would be more likely to come to the South's aid. This fact made it even more important to keep California within the Union.[777]

Captain Bradford, Georgette's husband, served the Union cause admirably, and was promoted to the position of Fleet Captain of the South Atlantic Squadron throughout the war. She remained at the Goodwin home during these war years. Frank, the Goodwin's son who turned twenty the year the war started, was attending Harvard. He continued his schooling and remained out of the conflict for the entire war. Susie, their youngest daughter was eighteen at the start of the war, and before it was over she became engaged to a young naval lieutenant assigned to the Naval Yard in 1864.

Characteristically avoiding less than pleasant memories, Sarah's only references to the war were indirect, with the exception of a brief entry in her journal.

> *The war of the rebellion was brought about by Southern women & Presbyterian ministers & encouraged by northern democrats for their own advantage & aggrandizement~*[778]

Although it is not certain just why she affixed the blame on these groups, it was probably because Sarah believed, as many others did at the time, that women constituted the morally superior sex. Therefore it followed that southern women should have taken the moral high ground and led the movement to rid the South of dependence upon the institution of slavery. The blame she affixed to the Presbyterian ministers was due to the fact that many southern ministers of the Presbyterian or similarly inclined faiths found ways to justify the institution of slavery through the manipulation of key Biblical passages.

At the start of the war many politicians, of varying political persuasions on both sides, encouraged the war between the two sections of the country. It was also true, as Sarah so wisely noted, that their less than admirable motive was to promote their own advantage and personal aggrandizement, as well as to increase their monetary profits.

A TRIP TO THE PRAIRIE

The summer after the war began both Frank and Susie traveled by rail to the area of the country then known as "The Grand Prairie." Their destination was Peotone, Illinois where their sister Sadie and her husband Samuel Storer had settled shortly after their wedding in 1859. The Storers were amongst the first white settlers of the village of Peotone, which was settled in 1856 although it was not officially incorporated until 1869.

Many years before the area became Peotone there was an Indian Village nearby that was known as Nabenekanong, which meant "Twelve miles from any other place." Today it is known as Twelve-Mile Grove, and is now a part of neighboring Wilton. A treaty set this land aside for an Indian reservation for the Sounouchewome Indian tribe. The locals called it "Se-Natch-E-Wine." However, in 1833 the tribe of the Pottawatomie Indians signed a treaty agreeing to sell all Indian rights to lands in Illinois to the federal government.[779] This apparently was inclusive of the Sounouchewome tribe.

There wasn't much to attract new settlers to the area at this time. The land was fertile, but it was isolated. There was no timber nearby to build homes, and just one small stream of water, a branch of Forked Creek, ran across the area. By 1850 there was no railroad line that reached Peotone, and there wasn't even a line to Chicago at the start of that decade. Therefore there was no easy way to grow or to market their produce.

The first two white men to settle in Peotone came from Massachusetts in 1849. They were followed a year later by New Hampshire native, J.C. Cowing. The first two settlers didn't remain too long, but Cowing did and others followed.[780]

By 1859 the Illinois Central Railroad Company had connected Peotone to Chicago and the rest of the country. The railroads soon took away the business from the Mississippi River barges, and dominated the shipping market in Chicago. Before long they controlled the distribution of all prairie produce shipped to the northeastern cities.[781]

This turnabout came during the early 1850s when both the Democrat and the Whig parties joined forces to push for legislation favoring land grant aid to the railroads in order to encourage the railroads to develop this part of the country. This legislation gave the railroads alternate sections of free land that were six miles wide on each side of the road. In return for this government largess, the Illinois Central agreed to donate seven percent of its profits back to the state to build schools for the children of all the new settlers the railroads were bound to attract.[782]

The railroad bill was passed in 1851, and by 1855 the Illinois Central was the terminus for over 22,000 miles of track. Then in order to stimulate agricultural production in this region the railroads sold off the remaining land with liberal payment terms and very low down payments. This offer of bargain price land attracted many to the region.[783]

When the railroad was completed in 1856 the village of Peotone was built on land bought from the railroad. A store, a school, post office, and a grain warehouse were the first to be built. By 1858 when Samuel Storer arrived speculators had purchased all of the land not owned by the railroads. The population had reached one hundred and twenty-five. Of these twenty-five were eligible voters.[784]

The majority of these first settlers of Peotone came from Germany, Ireland, England, New York State, and New England. When Samuel Storer purchased his six hundred acres of prairie land, farm acreage, in this incredibly fertile section of the country that came to be known as "America's Bread Basket," could be purchased very cheaply from both the government and the railroad.

At that time many eastern businessmen and speculators took advantage of these bargain prices, by establishing ownership of land in these mid-western states, even if they had no immediate plans to develop it. It appears from Samuel's letters that his own father, Rear Admiral George Washington Storer, owned undeveloped land in Iowa.[785] Also, it is known that his father-in-law, Ichabod Goodwin, owned 160 acres of farmland in Kansas City.[786] A few years after the Goodwins were there the government passed the Homestead Act, which gave anyone who agreed to work the land one hundred and sixty acres free.

Around the same time that the railroads came to the prairie, new advancements in farm equipment such as the development of the McCormick reaper, and the John Deere plow, both of which could be purchased on credit and paid for by crops, changed the face of farming. Also the development of barbed wire and the windmill combined with these new farming equipment and shipping methods to drastically increase the output and profits for farmers, and thus created a revolution in American agriculture.[787]

Samuel, like many others who went into farming about this time, was a professional man and looked at farming as a potentially profitable business enterprise. In a letter to his father just before his wedding to Sadie he remarked on the favorable outlook for sales of grain.

> *The European war news has caused a great rise in the flour & grain market~ In Chicago common flour having advanced a dollar a barrel in a few days~ I was in the city on Tuesday & saw decided evidences of increased business's prosperity~*[788]

In addition to overseeing the farm, there is evidence that Samuel opened a law practice in Peotone. He was also a member of the Illinois House of Representatives during the Twenty-second General Assembly in 1861-1862 representing the County of Will.[789] That fall Frank returned to the East to resume his studies at Harvard, but Susie stayed behind to be with her sister who was expecting her first child. Then in the latter part of September their parents, Ichabod and Sarah Goodwin, joined them.

> *In the Autumn of 1861 about the middle of Sept, your grandpa' & I started for Peotone Illinois, where my Sadie had been living two or three years~ Frank & Susie had gone out in the previous summer & Frank had returned leaving Susie with Sadie~ We were all rejoiced to meet & found Sadie well & in excellent spirits~*

> *Mr Storer had a section of six hundred acres of land, a portion of which was under cultivation~ The house was about one mile from the station & the village of Monee~ A broad avenue curving around a flower garden as it approached the house, gave the place quite an elegant effect~*

The house was of two stories, with a front piazza & contained a parlor, dining room & kitchen besides an addition back, where the Farmer a Scotchman & his wife, boarded the men~ Sadie had a first class servant, whom she had trained & the house keeping was perfect~ Jane was an excellent cook & I particularly enjoyed the game which Henry often shot almost at the door~[790]

The Illinois Central set up railroad stations about every ten miles, and small villages grew up around these stations. It was the station and village of Monee where Sarah first arrived on the train. The details of Sadie's house, and Sarah's interest in the housekeeping arrangements indicate Sarah may have worried about Sadie's living quarters. To Sarah, as to many people in the East, this area of the country represented the western frontier during these years. However, in Peotone there are still many examples of homes that were built around this time, and their design is reminiscent of stylish New England area homes of that vintage.

The wildest imagination could not have dreamed of provisions from California or Chicago~ indeed Chicago was not~[791]

Peotone was not too far from Chicago, and the Goodwins must have stopped there en route to Peotone. Chicago was founded in 1803, but was not incorporated as a city until 1837. By the time the Goodwins visited Illinois Chicago bragged of a population that reached over one hundred and fifty thousand. It was still growing, and ten years later the number of residents would double to reach over three hundred thousand. Even by 1861 Chicago boasted a booming economy, with new industries, new parks, first class hotels, and theatres. All in all it was becoming quite a cosmopolitan and wealthy city.[792]

Sarah indicated that she found the living conditions on the prairie quite adequate, and her pleasure with the garden was evident.

The flower garden in front of the house was laid out under Sadie's special inspection & it was the most beautiful flower garden I ever saw~ The soil was as rich as virgin soil could be & every thing flourished –

The vegetable garden was very large & I have never seen such large rich products from any place, particularly the eggplant which were of enormous size & as rich as possible~

Every morning Mr Storer would bring in one ~ Sadie would sit down at her dining room table & slice the plant & pile it on a dish, with salt between all ready to be fried in butter for dinner~[793]

The farms were large and Samuel's 600-acre spread was not unusual. Some of these early prairie farms were built over Indian burial grounds, and it was not uncommon for farmer's plows to uncover the remains and artifacts of these first inhabitants. The primary crop at the time was hay, both timothy and native and the first staple crops were wheat and rye.[794]

We had been there but a day when Mr George & Mr John Smith, & others came over to call on us & staid to tea~ In the evening Sadie put candles on the piano & played until ten o'clock~ Susie & the gentlemen all sang~

The next morning, Sadie was taken sick~ Mr Storer went for Dr Verneck six miles distant & at four in the afternoon Mabel was born~...

Dr Verneck, Sadie's physician was the handsomest man I ever saw~ He was an excellent doctor & very scholarly & elegant but like most Germans, he did not cultivate social relations with the Americans~ Their modes of living are very different from ours~ Carl Schurtz lived near Monee also~ [795]

Sarah's approval of the handsome German physician was in keeping with the trend of the time, when most Americans had a favorable image of German immigrants, especially when compared to Irish immigrants. This is because Germans were perceived to be more intelligent and industrious than the Irish.[796]

Many of the women who settled in isolated areas on the western frontier continued to depend upon midwives for assistance during childbirth. However, an increasing number of male physicians began to set up practices in these mid-western towns, and they often found their first clients amongst the ranks of middle to upper class women such as Sadie. The custom amongst the upper class that relegated the care of newborns to a special nurse engaged just for this purpose was still followed.

Sadie's ... nurse was engaged in proper time but she lived off on a distant railroad & Sadie's home was on the Illinois Central about two hours from Chicago~

As soon as Sadie was taken sick a telegram was dispatched to her, but she did not get there, until two days after~ When she came we were all sorry, for Mrs O'Neal the farmer's wife knew just what to do & Susie & I were very efficient & she really seemed like an intruder~

She was a Scotchwoman & had been brought up on the estate of Lord Fife & she talked very much of "My Lady"~ But she loved flowers as the Scotch do & knew a good deal about them~[797]

It is not known if Ichabod Goodwin stayed out on the prairie after Mabel was born. But it is unlikely that he did, as the war and business matters would have been pressing on such a busy and involved man. He must have taken some interest in the war efforts that took place in Illinois at this time.

The state of Illinois did not have a militia at the start of the war. However, the people responded promptly to President Abraham Lincoln's call for volunteers. The men from Illinois fought valiantly in most of the major battles of the war, and they eventually sent more men to war than every other state with the exception of New York, Pennsylvania, and Ohio. In addition President Lincoln and General Ulysses S. Grant, two of the most prominent leaders of the war were from Illinois.

Of course the war impacted the people of Illinois throughout its four-year duration. However, on the surface it almost seemed that business went on as usual, and the state prospered during this time. There was a number of new war related industries that sprang up overnight, to provide munitions and other supplies for the Union Army. In addition other industries unrelated to war such as the railroad continued to flourish and grow during these war years.[798]

Sarah and Susie remained until November when winter was well on its way and Sadie's period of confinement was nearing an end. Then Sarah and Susie returned home.

> *Sadie had a very good getting up, in fact she was so well, that we made a sort of sun room of her chamber~ Susie & I staid with her until the last of Nov & then we had to come home~*

> *Prairie scenery & life were very interesting to me~ We could look many miles in any direction & houses which were four or five miles away looked quite near & sociable~*

> *The prairie fires were often terribly magnificent~ One night they were burning in almost every direction & one came near enough to burn up all our coarse prairie hay, that was stacked not far from the house~*[799]

Prairie fires were often started when lightening ignited the dry hay in the fall months. One narrative left behind by an earlier settler attributed the prairie fires to the Indian tribes who set fire to the prairie grasses each fall as part of their "grand hunt." Once the dry grasses were lit the fire spread rapidly all over the prairie. Then the arrows of the hunters felled the wild game, which fled from safe retreats in an attempt to escape the fires. These annual fires were a primary reason that large sections of the prairie were completely devoid of timber.[800] These fires drove many of the white settlers away from their prairie homes as well. In an effort to keep the prairie fires away from their property, many homesteaders burned backfires. The smaller fires eventually joined together to form fire streaks, often as wide as five miles across. They were carried across the sky by alternating wind flows. During the daytime these fires blotted out the sun creating a hazy red sky filled with ashes that dusted the prairie land below. At night the fires burned a bright red and yellow that lit up the sky, creating quite a grand spectacle over the entire prairie. At times the reflection of large plumes of smoke could be seen at distances of more than forty miles.[801]

> *The sand hill cranes, as they were called interested me very much~ They assembled in a flock one day, very near the house & screamed & danced for hours~ There were more than a hundred of them & they would spread their great wings & rise in a stately way from the earth up & down without any cessation~*[802]

Sand Hill cranes are large birds that stand two to three feet tall and have a broad wingspan. In late fall when Sarah watched them they were migrating to a warmer climate, in order to escape the harsh prairie winters. In extant letters from Samuel to his father there is some indication that Samuel and Sadie also left the prairie the following winter. In their absence they left the farm in the charge of hired caretakers. A letter from Samuel to his father, the following November refers to their preparations prior to leaving.

> *We hope to be in P_ with you on Thanksgiving day ~ Peotone, Nov 16 1862,*
>
> *My dear Father*
> *It is now our intention to leave here on Thursday next if it be possible~ The only impediment to doing so will be a storm which would prevent some threshing being done that must be attended to before we leave~ It was quite unpleasant this morning & I fear we may have rain before night~ We shall go by the way of New York & expect to reach there by next Tuesday, remain there until Monday evening & be in Portsmouth on Tuesday morning that is if Sadie finds it possible to go through to New York without stopping~*
> *As the time approaches for us to leave, we find innumerable things to attend to ~ all our clothing must be packed up, & carpets taken up, as we are to have new people in the house this winter~ I shall leave but one man on the place & he has a family of a wife & two children~*
> *Thus far the fall has been quite pleasant, we have had snow but once & not many cold days, but the weather at this season cannot be calculated on & I only hope that our journey can be accomplished without much cold or stormy weather~*
> *I think the West takes McClellan's removal as a matter of course, after reading Halleck's letter of the report of the military commission~ Burnside is a great favorite here & people feel some confidence in him, but are prepared to see any General put on the shelf who does not act with vigor~*
> *Mabel is beginning to stand up a good deal & tries to walk a little ~ She is very well but quite a care as she is not willing to have her mother away from her for a moment~*
> *Sadie sends her love to you all & we hope to find you all well on our arrival~*
>
> *Your affectionate son*
> *Samuel Storer*[803]

The Storers did not return to the prairie to stay. The following year Samuel's name was listed in the *Boston City Registry* as a resident of the U.S. Hotel in Boston. His occupation was a representative of Henry A. Breed and Company, manufacturers of stone flour. Extant letters indicate that his wife and their two-year old daughter were also residing in Boston.[804] In 1864, Samuel was listed in the *Boston City Registry* as the treasurer of the Boston Milling and Manufacturing Co. By this time the family was settled into a residence at 19 Beacon Street in Brookline.[805] The next year they moved to nearby Roxbury, at that time one of Boston's most fashionable suburbs. They remained there for several years, but by October of 1867 Sadie and Mabel were residing at the Goodwin home in Portsmouth and Samuel was in Sitka, Alaska.

My dear Sadie had the loveliest taste in arranging flowers and when she was with us I always brought the basket to her~ The garden is more associated with her, than with either of my children~ One of my last pleasantest recollections of her, is of her sitting in the iron chair under the lilacs, while Mabel played with the gravel around~ Every morning after breakfast, she used, when the weather permitted to walk in the garden~[806]

THE WAR YEARS

The Portsmouth Naval Yard expanded rapidly throughout the first year of the war. At the start of 1860 only two hundred were employed at the Yard. By the following November the working population had increased to twenty-two hundred, and continued to expand to the end of the war. Ship builders and related workers flocked to Portsmouth from other parts of New Hampshire and southern Maine to fill these jobs. Their very presence changed the face and pace of the city, and also caused a severe housing shortage.[807] The Declaration of Paris made the privateering enterprise, which had made Sarah's grandfather and father wealthy, illegal in 1856. The United States did not sign this document; however, when the Civil War began the North did honor it. Jefferson Davis signed a proclamation declaring privateering a legitimate activity in the South. In response President Lincoln vowed to treat any ship engaged in privateering as a pirate ship. There was considerable concern in the North over the specter of southern privateers making trade and travel even more difficult.

At the very start of the war while Goodwin was still in office, Sarah's cousin, Commander Enoch G. Parrott, seized the southern privateer *Savannah* just sixty miles north of Charleston. As a reward he was made commander of the newly purchased steamer USS *August*. He was later raised to rear admiral.[808]

By the end of the first summer most privateering had ceased, with the exception of the CSS *Alabama*, a British built ship manned by Confederates who acted as pirates. It attacked northern merchant and naval ships throughout most of the war. This was of great concern to Portsmouth merchants as well as other northern merchants.[809]

In the first year of the war the USS *Kearsarge* was built at the Naval Yard. The Yard was also involved in testing new ammunition and camouflage for ships. They eventually began to refit and ironclad old ships, as well as build new iron clad ships.

The year of 1862 began with a strike at the Yard. About nine hundred workers demanded higher wages. For a time tensions ran high, but this matter was quickly resolved to the benefit of the workers. This same year Seavey's Island was acquired, but not in its entirety until 1866. A reservoir was dug there and construction on a new hospital began.[810]

The Goodwin's son-in-law Joseph Bradford was stationed at the Naval Yard in 1862 and that summer Georgette gave birth to their second son, Fielding. A month later Bradford was promoted to the rank of lieutenant commander, and given the command of the steamer USS *Nipse* in the South Atlantic Squadron.[811]

One can only speculate on specific war related activity within the Goodwin home. Most of the family probably became involved at some level in the various groups which sprang up in the North to bring aid and comfort to those fighting and wounded, by preparing needed knitted goods, medical supplies, and newsletters from home.

The Goodwins were active members of the Unitarian Church, a local leader in the abolitionist movement. In the fall of 1862 a group of black sailors, former slaves, arrived in Portsmouth on the USS *Minnesota*. The ship had docked for repairs, and during their stay the crew was granted ten days of leave time. Ichabod Goodwin was the one who found boarding houses in Portsmouth where they could stay.

The black sailors were given a cordial reception in Portsmouth according to the local papers. One night about twenty-five of them appeared at the Temple to sing spirituals on the same stage where Frederick Douglas, the well-known black abolitionist, had appeared earlier that year. They related their personal experiences with slavery, and expressed their feelings about the secessionist movement in the South.

There was some prejudice directed towards them, but for the most part the city of Portsmouth welcomed these former slaves and helped them to a new start in life. A number of local ladies took it upon themselves to instruct them in reading and writing. These ladies rowed, or were rowed out to Seavey's Island on a daily basis to teach them to read and write. All in all Portsmouth had a favorable impression of these former slaves, and the *Chronicle* reported that they had never seen "more civilized, well-behaved men" visit the town. [812]

In 1863 the former paranoia about Confederate spies and ships in northern waters was legitimized by several Confederate raids off the coast of Maine, resulting in the destruction of two northern vessels. A short while later two Confederate prisoners, escapees from Fort Warren in Boston Harbor, were spotted on Rye beach.[813]

The same year the garrison around the Navy Yard was strengthened. Forts Constitution and McClary were enlarged. Fort Sullivan was built on Seavey's Island; the Yard was designated as a transport station where gun power was stored before being sent to the front lines by rail.[814]

By this time much of the patriotic fervor had cooled considerably, and it wasn't as easy to find volunteers to fight the war as it had been at the beginning. Many questioned the morality and wisdom of this war. Portsmouth became divided on this issue, and those that were southern sympathizers were labeled "copperheads," a derisive term.

One such man was Joshua Foster. He moved to Portsmouth from Dover at the start of the war to set up a newspaper called *The States and Union*. Foster was a southern sympathizer, as well as a racist. His newspaper was used as a vehicle to express his viewpoint on issues pertaining to the war. [815]

When President Lincoln signed the Conscription Act in 1863 initiating a draft, many in the North were angered by the inclusion of a provision, which allowed those that could afford three hundred dollars to hire substitutes to replace them. In the minds of many this loophole in the law verified the belief that the poor were fighting the war for the wealthy.

Because of this riots erupted in New York City, Boston and Portsmouth. The riots in Portsmouth were much milder than elsewhere and might have been averted but the city officials had unwisely forbidden a public meeting to discuss the issue. Many ignored this official edict and met at the South Church on July 11, 1863. The majority of them were Democrats.

Foster put out an anonymous handbill urging all citizens to protest the Conscription Act that was to go into effect on July 14th. He announced that there would be a second meeting at the Temple. This attracted such a large crowd that the people flowed out into the streets. The mood of the city was so explosive that the town officials thought it best to delay the draft for one day.

On the night of July 14th a mob of approximately two hundred men marched on Fort Constitution. It is not clear what their aim was, but it was symbolic of the march to Fort William and Mary made by their forefathers during the American Revolution. They all dispersed when guards flashing bayonets confronted them. Because of this the draft was officially delayed in Portsmouth for an indefinite period of time.

However, the mob regrouped at Market Square the following day and many protesters milled about the streets in anger. The local police confiscated a pistol, and this angered the crowd so that eventually several pistols were discharged. It was only after Mayor Jonathan Dearborn called in the Marines from the Naval Yard that the crowds dispersed many of them to the saloon on Water Street (now Marcy Street), This section of town in particular was known as the "Copperhead Ward." At the time it was the rough section of town, populated with houses of prostitution, saloons, and warehouses. There were only four arrests that night, and all were residents of Water Street.[816]

At the same time the draft riots were taking place, the USS *Bermuda* brought in over one hundred Confederate prisoners, and one hundred former slaves to Seavey's Island. The former slaves filled a need for manpower, but first they had to be trained at Fort Sullivan. Many of the women of Portsmouth were rowed over to Seavey's to teach them to read and write, as they had with the first group. Not all of the citizens were so tolerant by then and there were several racial incidents. In August during a target practice session with the black sailors, a shot went astray and accidentally killed a twelve-year-old boy. Foster and others jumped on this incident to further exacerbate racial tensions.[817]

In 1864 Commandant Pearson recommended to Secretary of the Navy Gideon Wells, that the black sailors at Fort Sullivan be given promotions. One former slave was made ship's corporal and another was rated as a nurse. Pearson also complained to local authorities when an assault was made on a crew of black sailors, on leave in Portsmouth. On a more positive level it was reported by the local paper that almost all of the former slaves had mastered basic reading and writing skills, and that many were also able to master simple math problems.[818]

1864 was also the year that the USS *Kearsarge* finally sank the CSS *Alabama*, shortly after the latter captured and burned the *Rockingham*, a Portsmouth vessel sailing under the American flag while carrying a shipment to one of the neutral countries. This news was welcome to all supporters of the North as this one ship had burned at least fifty-five Union merchant ships in twenty months and captured ten more. The victory cheered not only those in Portsmouth, but the entire North. Her captain, John Winslow, came home to a hero's welcome. In 1869-70 he was the commandant of the Portsmouth Naval Yard.[819]

That same summer the USS *DeSoto* arrived at the Yard from Key West with a sick crew. They were infected with Yellow Fever. The ship's captain was unaware of the city's quarantine regulations, and Pearson and the naval surgeon allowed them to dock. Eventually there were fourteen deaths from this and many others were infected.[820]

This created a real panic in Portsmouth and as a result the Naval Yard and all the civilian shipyards were closed for several weeks. The Portsmouth Sanitary Committee unaware that the real culprit was a mosquito, tried in vain to contain the fever. They issued orders for a cleanup of public sewers, privies and rotten vegetables. Lobster was even banned for a while. The fever eventually disappeared and the cost to the city for the clean up and caring for some indigent patients was $2,000.[821]

In July a fire broke out in a paint shop on Penhallow Street. By the time it was extinguished fifteen buildings were destroyed in downtown Portsmouth and the Portsmouth Bridge had even caught fire. Joshua Foster's newspaper office was also damaged, as was the building that housed the *Portsmouth Chronicle*. The Naval Yard came to the rescue with a steam pumper and Newburyport sent their hand tub "Button" to the city. The steam engine was so much more efficient at fighting the fires that in December of that year Portsmouth's fire department purchased their first steam driven pumper.[822]

For many Portsmouth families the war years provided a large number of occasions for elegant gatherings in some of the finest homes. Throughout the war prominent families such as the Goodwins entertained official dignitaries and naval officers visiting or assigned to the Naval Yard. Many threw balls or collations to celebrate the launching of Union war vessels built at the Naval Yard during these years.

It was at such an occasion that Susie Goodwin first met her future husband, Lieutenant George Dewey. Although it is clear Sarah loved all of her children, her youngest daughter Susie held a special place in her memories.

> *I write only of pleasant memories and many more could I record of good times with Susie in Boston & Newport & at other times~*[823]

Dewey, a graduate of the Naval Academy at Annapolis was assigned to the steamer USS *Agawam*, when he first arrived in Portsmouth at the start of 1864. Local legend tells that her father and thirty-three year old Naval Commander Alexander Rhind accompanied Susie. Rhind's pursuit of the lovely Susie Goodwin, who celebrated her twenty-first birthday that March, was at the time a major topic of conversation in Portsmouth's social circles.

Commander Rhind was also Dewey's commanding officer. The twenty-seven year old lieutenant was as taken by Susie's charm and beauty as was his commander, and he was brash enough not to let the rank of the older man intimidate him. It was noted by the local wags that Dewey managed to dance with Susan three times that evening. A few days later they took a carriage ride together, and by the following week he, along with Commander Rhind, was invited to a party at the Goodwin home.[824]

An extant letter from Dewey to Susie, dated February 26th of 1864, written during a week long visit to his family home in Montpelier, Vermont, confirms she had totally captured his heart in a short amount of time.

> *Montpelier, Vt.*
> *Friday*
> *My little Darling,*
> *I don't know the day of the month and am too tired to find out ~ I only know that it is Friday and that it seems a week since I left Portsmouth.*
> *I was eleven hours on the road and completely tired out. Everybody seems delighted to see me, and the consciousness of having done my duty makes me less unhappy than I had expected; still I almost count the hours until Tuesday.*
> *But enough of <u>self</u>~ I turn to a dearer sweeter subject. How is it with you? Are you very unhappy? Gov must not be, it will do no good and only make my darling ill and then what will I do? I am not fully satisfied that I have done right in leaving you at such a time. If I was the least consolation to you in your affliction I should have staid and still I acted for the best as I thought.*
> *I thought of you a thousand times yesterday and always as I last saw you smiling through your tears. God only knows how dear you are to me. Without your love I don't care to live, I could not and would not. Everything here seems to be uninteresting and insipid. Dear knows how I shall kill the*

time till Monday.

I shall be at Parkers in Boston on Monday night. May I not expect a little note from my darling? God bless and keep your dreams and make you love one, as much as I do you is the prayer of yours ever, Geo Dewey [825]

When Dewey left Susan she was grieving over the loss of her sister Georgie, who had died of consumption just two days earlier on February 24th. Georgie was only twenty-nine when she died and her son Fielding was less than two years old. It is not known if her husband was away at war at the time of her death. Nor is it known how long she had suffered from this terrible disease now called tuberculosis. It was such a common disease during the nineteenth century, it is now known as the "Victorian disease."

At the time of Georgie's death it wasn't known what caused consumption, which seemed to consume the affected areas of its victims and gave the impression they were wasting away. It most commonly affected the lungs, and in the final stages the disease caused a terrible hemorrhaging of the lungs. At the time consumption was believed to be an inherited disease, as it seemed to run in families. In 1864 after Georgie died, it was discovered that it was a contagious disease spread by close contact. [826] Georgie's son Fielding lived with the Goodwin family, and Joseph Bradford remained in the navy, in the position of fleet captain of the Atlantic Squadron until the end of the war.

The romance between Dewey and Susie continued, as history and other extant letters will attest. An incident occurred at Portsmouth Naval Yard shortly after Dewey's arrival there, which could have resulted in a court marshal and ended his career. In a fit of anger he had collared a Naval Yard worker, for not performing quickly enough when the USS *Agawam* was towed into the Yard. However, he had no right to touch a civilian, and the civilian in question made a formal complaint against him to civil authorities. This incident is a matter of record. A short letter written in April of 1864 to Susie gives his side of the story.

Sunday April 10 1864

Agawam

My own little darling, I am again in trouble~

Did ever one have so much happiness and so much trouble all at once? Mr. Rand the gentleman I choked "until his eyes and tongue came out etc" has lodged a complaint against me at the office of Mr. Webster in Portsmouth, who has written me a most polite note to the effect that I can "call and settle" and hereby save a frustration~ I have placed the matter in the hands of Mr. Hackett who I have no doubt can arrange matters without making an item for the "Chronicle."

And even now perhaps if everything is quiet and orderly towards evening, I may be able to get out for a short time till 10:30 or so. You can't imagine how cheerless and miserable it is on board today. The men are troublesome, the ship cold and for me nothing to look forward to but a lawsuit tomorrow. If only I could see somebody and take her hand in mine for only a minute I should be all right, "alls well that ends well" If I could only have one of those torches, it would seem to do me some good. But even that slight consideration is deprived me by my little Tyrant.

The more I try to convince myself that it is my duty to stay on board tonight the more I can't and I think it is more likely that I shall completely break down before tonight. Goodbye little sweet heart for a little while and believe me Yours ever~ Geo Dewey.[827]

Mr. Hackett was the name of a local lawyer. Dewey ended up paying a small fine, and the incident was quickly forgotten. He left Portsmouth shortly after this matter was resolved. The two young people became secretly engaged, and continued their romantic relationship by mail with daily letters in which Dewey continued to profess his deep love for Susie.

> *U.S. Steamer Agawam*
> *James River, Pa*
> *Sunday Evening 17 July*
> *I wrote my dearest little girl last evening but from some misunderstanding the mail was not sent so you will be one day without a letter from your gossey. Will you care? We send our letters every day, but only receive a mail time once a week everything seems to be completely upset since the* <u>invasion</u>. *Today has been as quiet and peaceful as every Sunday should be, and I have spent the greater part of it in thinking of a very dear little girl far away. Tell how has she passed the day, I wonder? That she has been happy and good and has "prayed" for somebody I believe… . But all will be well in the end; did I not firmly believe it I should indeed be an unhappy man. Gov love cured me from some bad habits, and without using a good deal of firmness, but in the matter of spelling I fear there are doubts. I think I can safely say now I do not swear it has been so long since I have, that I believe I am cured.*
>
> *I am not good, no indeed far from it but I do not do or say anything <u>bad</u> now-a-days so I have no confessions to make to my little girl~ I surely am becoming better for everything seems to go as smoothly as possible, and to think I owe all my happiness, indeed, whatever good is in me to the one who is so dear to me indeed makes me twice as happy. I know you as you are better than anyone else~ For indeed I flatter myself with the belief that no one knows you as I do. I <u>know</u> no one, not even my father, understands me as my darling does and I would not have it different for the world. Gov ought to know me better than anyone else and I should you as well.*
>
> *I have no secrets from you and should be very unhappy if I thought you had from me. Goodnight darling pray for me every day and love me very very much as your own Geo* [828]

In the spring of 1863 the Goodwins' only son Frank graduated from Harvard with a degree in English literature. For the next year he studied law under George Sanger, a Boston lawyer. Then he entered Harvard Law School in the fall of 1864.[829]

That fall Lincoln was reelected for a second term. Running against General George McClelland, a popular peace candidate, Lincoln prevailed in all the Union states except Delaware, Kentucky and New Jersey, and won by fifty-four percent of the popular vote.[830] During his campaign for reelection that previous summer, his chances looked slim. Salmon Chase, Secretary of the Treasury, was mentioned as an alternative Republican nominee.

There was no love lost between the two men. After Lincoln received his party's nomination, Chase tendered his resignation. Lincoln accepted this to the relief of many in the financial world, who believed Chase's "soft or paper money" policies were inflationary. Shortly after this Chief Justice Roger Taney died. Then at the insistence of the Massachusetts Senator Charles Sumner, a noted abolitionist like Chase, Lincoln offered this position to Chase. However, It went so against Lincoln's grain to do this, that he is said to have told one friend that he would rather "swallow his buckhorn chair," than make Chase the new Chief Justice.[831]

Very soon after Mr Lincoln raised Mr Chase (who had been Sec of the Treasury) to the Chief Justiceship of the U.S., he came to Boston, on a visit of a few days.

Two or three great war ships, then exciting much attention were about coming round to P__ & the Chief Justice who had been promising us a visit for some time telegraphed your grandpa that if convenient to receive them, he & Mr Sam Hooper, with whom he was staying would visit us next day~

Not much prepared for such visitors~ Yet the proposition was accepted & they arrived about six in the evening to tea~ All the officers of the Dictator, Miantinonea & the other ship, whose name I have forgotten, & all the gentlemen stationed at the yard beside a large number of residents of the town, were invited to call on the Chief Justice & at ten a supper of ices, champagne &c was served~

The evening was very hot & the Judge who seemed to like to talk with me asked me to sit down in the door with him as the lights made the house so hot~

He talked with much feeling of the war troubles he had passed through & when I asked him what he would go through it all again for~ he replied with emphasis "not for the world"~

They remained until the next evening & truly the visit was a great treat~[832]

One historian recalls Chase as a " humorless & vain, but able man." He was widowed a number of times, and another biographer recalled that he fancied himself as a ladies man. He was a native of New Hampshire and for years he was a prominent player in the Whig and Republican parties in Ohio, just as Ichabod Goodwin was in New Hampshire. Their association went back many years, and Chase apparently valued their friendship.[833]

I had met Judge Chase some years before at a great political mass meeting, whereupon grandpa' presided, at Wolfborough & came very near getting into an embarrassment with him~

He was sitting between Mrs John P Hale & myself in the Hotel parlor, when

*I began talking to him about his first baby that I used to tend at Boars head
& was just going to ask for his wife when Mrs Hale suddenly interrupted
me by calling his attention to something else~*

*Just then a messenger called him out & Mrs Hale exclaimed Oh! Mrs
Goodwin I have saved you from a precipice, that wife is dead & a second &
third & he is about being engaged again~*

*After that I felt as sheepish as if I had done something wrong & avoided him
all the rest of the evening~ The next morning he sought me & asked me if he
should see me to the boat~ He talked of Dickens novels & said he thought
Dickens genius culminated in David Copperfield~*[834]

Mrs. Hale was the wife of Senator John P. Hale of New Hampshire, an avid abolitionist
whose oratory skills brought him to national prominence when he debated the slavery issue
with Franklin Pierce.[835]

THE END OF THE WAR

Throughout the early spring of 1865 news that traveled to Portsmouth from the South was encouraging. Clearly the war was nearing an end with a Union victory in sight. The Goodwin family, along with the rest of the country, must have felt a sense of relief.

Sarah, who turned sixty that May, had lived through a period of great changes in her nation, community, and family. She was still leading an active life, and her husband remained a power in the business and political world. It would be ten years before she began recording her life story.

On March 3rd of 1865, Susie's twenty-second birthday, George Dewey was promoted to lieutenant commander. He had been waiting for this promotion to ask Susie's father for her hand. When he did family legend recalls that Ex-Governor Goodwin, already the father-in-law of two military officers, replied in jest, "What another officer to support?"[836]

Then came the month of April. And just as things had turned upside down in the country during the month of April four long years before, the events that followed tossed much of the country into a whirlwind of emotions. It began with great celebration and ended in deep tragedy. On April 4th the news was received in Portsmouth that Richmond had been taken by the Union forces. At the Portsmouth Naval Yard, a twenty-one-gun salute was fired at noon to celebrate this significant victory.[837] Then on April 10th the news was received that Lee had surrendered.

Work was suspended at the Naval Yard that day. The workman and officers gathered beneath the flagpole and gave a rousing cheer in honor of the American flag flying above. The entire day was devoted to the celebration of the Union victory. Church bells rang all day long into the evening. The Cornet Band marched the streets of Portsmouth, and people spontaneously gathered downtown to cheer, congratulate, and embrace one another. Throughout the city it was an occasion of great joy.[838]

At night there were bonfires along with brilliant fireworks that lit up the sky. Just about every home was illuminated as well, welcoming friends and neighbors inside to join together in celebrating the great victory. At the Unitarian Church a Union prayer meeting was held, and this was repeated in other congregations throughout the city.[839] However, two unpleasant incidents marred the day in Portsmouth.

The first incident occurred when a group of men marched to the offices of the *States and Union* and called out to Joshua Foster to display the Union flag. When he failed to comply they became more agitated. The local press reported that after a short while the angry crowd, which had grown to nearly two thousand, stormed the newspaper office. The rioters flung the presses to the street below, and threatened to do the same with Foster. He escaped harm; however, one of his workers was badly injured, and the mayor ordered the sheriff to shut down all the saloons for the remainder of the day.[840]

A tragic accident occurred later that day in Market Square. Naval Yard workers celebrated the victory by firing off one hundred cannon shots. Unfortunately the cannon fired prematurely and blew off both hands of John McGraw, a leather worker.[841] A collection was taken up to help the man and his family, but of course nothing could undo this tragedy.

Five days later the citizens of Portsmouth, as well as the rest of the nation, were stunned and thrown into deep mourning upon receiving the news of the assassination of President Lincoln. In Portsmouth church bells tolled all day long, flags were flown at half-mast, and most establishments were closed. The local papers reported that the community as a whole exhibited in "proper ways great sorrow and gloom" at the news of the President's death.[842]

The same scenario was repeated at the Naval Yard. Work was suspended and flags dropped to half-mast. The USS *Vandalia* fired a one-gun salute every half-hour from sunrise to sunset in honor of the fallen President.[843]

The following day most of the businesses and private homes in Portsmouth were draped in black mourning crape. A memorial service and procession in honor of President Lincoln was led by the Governor's Horse Guards, with the Cornet Band playing "mournful music" they marched through the streets of Portsmouth. The local press estimated that between 1,200 and 1,500 citizens and dignitaries joined the military funeral parade in Lincoln's honor.

The procession was composed of prominent local and state dignitaries, as well as naval officers and a company of marines from the Naval Yard. One contingent consisted of a number of maimed war veterans from Portsmouth. Funeral services were held in Market Square. Reverend Patterson delivered the eulogy. It was over an hour long according to the local paper, which noted that the assembled crowd was silent," as if in a church," as they paid their last respects to the fallen President.[844]

While Sarah neglected to mention any of this in her writings, it can be assumed that the joy and the sorrow, which affected the rest of the country that April, were keenly felt in the Goodwin home. They all must have been grateful as a family to see an end to the war that had begun during Goodwin's last term as governor, as well as saddened by the death of the President who had successfully brought the county together again.

By July of 1865 many of the men returned home to a hero's welcome. Portsmouth celebrated the Fourth of July that year in a grand way to honor the newly reunited country, and those who fought to preserve it. At a reception held in honor of the veterans' ex-Governor Goodwin, the same man who had sent them off to war welcomed them home. The papers reported that Goodwin addressed the men with a "felicitous speech", expressing his appreciation of the perils they had undergone, the debt of gratitude due them, and his joy on meeting them again- "Victors, and Peace perching on banners."[845]

The Second New Hampshire Regiment was mustered out in December of that year in Concord, New Hampshire. There they were honored with a grand feast and many notable dignitaries were there to honor them. They had been in service longer than any other regiment in New Hampshire, and had distinguished themselves by their bravery in battle. Throughout the war there were over three thousand names on the roll of this regiment, which fought in more than twenty battles and lost almost a thousand men.[846]

The Goodwins too welcomed home their men from the war. Lieutenant Commander Dewey had been assigned to USS *Kearsarge*, shortly after his promotion, and it had pulled into Boston Harbor on the 27th of March for repairs. By then Lieutenant Commander George Dewey was the Executive officer for the USS *Kearsarge,* and he recalled in his memoirs that they dressed the ship the honor of the "happy day," Lee surrendered to Grant.[847] Susie was also in the Boston area visiting her sister Sadie in Roxbury at that time. Susie and George Dewey may have celebrated the end of the war with the Storers in Boston.[848]

Lieutenant Commander Joseph Bradford was relieved of his command of the South

Atlantic Squadron at the end of June 1865. By the following year he was commissioned as a full commander. He also received an assignment to the Portsmouth Naval Yard.[849]

It is not known if the Winders visited the East immediately following the war's end, but there is evidence that they resided in California until 1867. William's father, General John Winder, had died towards the end of the war in 1864, but not before he had become a pariah in the eyes of the nation for his inhumane treatment of Union prisoners at Andersonville.

By the summer of 1864 General Winder was in command of the entire post at Andersonville. With as many as thirty-three thousand prisoners in an enclosure meant to hold ten thousand, Winder worried more about security than his charges, and refused to let local women supply the starving prisoners with vegetables.[850] He also ordered his guards to shoot on sight any prisoners that attempted to escape. By the end of the war there were thirteen thousand graves, silent witness to the atrocities that had occurred in Andersonville during these war years.[851]

Winder's predecessor, General Wirtz, who had been in charge of the prison interior during most of the war, was the only Confederate to be tried before a war tribunal and executed for his inhumane treatment of prisoners.[852] It's likely William suffered some feelings of personal shame because of his family's ties to this infamous Confederate prison.

The effects of the end of the war were felt most strongly at the Naval Yard. By early May of 1865 there were more than twenty-five hundred workers employed there.[853] As the year progressed there were further changes both at the Yard and in the city. That May about seven hundred and fifty workers were laid off. This resulted in a high rate of unemployment in the city, which in turn pushed down the rental rates.[854]

In December of that year the local paper noted that while only five hundred men were discharged from the Yard up until that point, it was believed many more would be let go after the holidays.[855] Their prediction proved accurate. By the end of the following year there were only eight hundred and seventy-six men employed there, and by 1871 a skeleton crew of seventy-one remained.[856]

During the preceding four years twenty-five ships had been built at the Naval Yard. In addition many ships deemed unfit for services at the start of the war were refurbished, iron clad, or repaired at this facility. By then it was considered to be a first rate naval facility.

Throughout the war the Portsmouth Steam Factory continued to operate. It is not known where the factory bought their cotton, nor if they manufactured any of the shoddy, a fiber made from shredded wool, that was used to make many of the Union uniforms. But by July of 1865 the local papers reported that the company was in dire financial straits due to the drastic drop in cotton prices. Following the end of the war the price dropped from a dollar and eighty cents a bale to twenty cents. The article made it clear that the company's president, Ichabod Goodwin, was not to blame in the minds of the stockbrokers, who voted to hold on to the company at that time.[857]

However, by November of 1865 the company was forced to sell to a Massachusetts firm.[858] The fate of the steam factory was repeated within various industries throughout the North. This was especially true in war related industries. Once fueled by the war, they were subsequently snuffed out by the cessation of the fighting.

Along with his many other interests Goodwin had always remained active in the shipping trade. However, during the war he and his partners sold the clipper *Morning Glory*, as well as other ships which had been involved in transatlantic and European trade prior to the war.[859] Portsmouth's merchant marine industry and ship building trade suffered during the war and never rebounded. One reason for this was that Portsmouth ship owners, like many other shippers in the North, sold their vessels to foreign countries during the war, as travel and shipping by sea became too dangerous. One estimate holds that about 1,613 Northern vessels were sold, lost at sea, captured, or condemned during the war.[860]

Many of these losses were due to illegal attacks by Confederate raiders and also because the British and other Europeans were sympathetic to the southern cause throughout most of the war. This bias on the part of the Europeans made travel dangerous for northern traders.

In November of 1865, the national elections guaranteed the ratification of the Emancipation Proclamation. Locally the *Portsmouth Journal* announced the results of the overwhelming Republican victory with a tongue in cheek article, which ran as an obituary for the Democratic Party. Under the title "Deceased" the article announced that "after a lingering sickness of five years, the Democratic Party died on the evening of November 6th.[861]

Toward the end of the year the *Portsmouth Journal*, reflected on the "Progress over the Past Five Years." The paper noted with pride that the evils of slavery had been abolished, and that in New Hampshire there was no longer a feeling that it was necessary to compromise one's moral stance, out of a concern for the legal rights of the South.[862] A change in public opinion on the moral and legal rights of Afro-Americans, and their right to the protections given to all citizens under the United States Constitution, was one of the most significant and enduring legacies of the Civil War in Portsmouth.[863]

THE FAMILY IN THE 1860S

In 1866 Captain William Winder resigned his army commission, and went into the mining business in San Francisco where he had been stationed during the war. The following year Willie turned sixteen, and his parents accompanied him East to arrange for his enrollment in the Naval Academy at Annapolis. They probably traveled via a combination of stage and railroad connections, as the transcontinental railroad would not be completed for two more years.

In July of 1862 a race began between the Central Railroad on the East Coast and the Union Pacific Railroad of the West Coast to connect the two lines. When the railroads finally did meet at Promontory Point in Utah in May of 1869, the news of that momentous occasion was relayed to the entire nation via the Western Union Telegraph Company. All across the continent crowds of people gathered at these stations to listen for the signal that the final spike to connect the railroads was in place. Within a few years it was possible to travel non-stop from New York to San Francisco in seven days.[864]

> *In those days there was no communication from Cal & no steamers running the Isthmus~ San Francisco had to be reached by way of Cape horn ~ which took months & friends had to wait a long time for news~ Now there are four railroads across the continent besides one at the Isthmus~*[865]

There was increasing competition amongst the railroads after this first continental line was started, and before very long several other lines also connected the Atlantic and Pacific. At the same time the Western Union service was expanded throughout the country. This came about because most of the railroads allowed the telegraph company to string their wires along the same roads in exchange for free telegraph service.[866]

Although plans were already underway by the 1870s to open a transoceanic canal to expedite shipping between the East and West coasts, it wasn't until 1913 that the Panama Canal was built. It is likely that the isthmus to which Sarah referred was the Erie Canal. It was built in 1825 and it was populated with steamships from the beginning. However, by the 1870s the steamships were much larger liners, and they transported both merchandise and passengers to and from New York. These ships also linked up with the transcontinental line of the Erie Railroad.[867]

Abby remained at the family home in Portsmouth, while her husband returned to the West to pursue his interests in prospecting and scouting. Although San Francisco had grown rapidly since the discovery of gold nearly two decades before, it was still a rough, uncivilized town in the 1860s. It is likely that the lifestyle in the West attracted more men than women during this time. Like many men who settled in the western part of the country during those years, William might have wanted to get a fresh start in life and distance himself from unpleasant past associations such as the disgrace attached to his family name because of his families connection to the Confederate prisons.

By 1866 Frank, the Goodwin's only son, finished his studies at Harvard Law and was admitted to the bar in Massachusetts. Then he joined two other attorneys from Charlestown, Massachusetts, and together they founded the law firm of Dehon, Bryant & Goodwin. It was located in the old Sears' Building in Boston.[868]

During his years in Cambridge Frank met his future wife, Mary Buttrick. Friends and family called her Molly. She was the youngest daughter of Ephrim Buttrick, a prominent attorney and former town alderman from Cambridge. He was a Harvard graduate and a native of Concord, Massachusetts. Ephrim had achieved a modicum of fame a few years earlier when his name appeared on a list of the state's most prosperous men in a publication by Forbes and Green entitled *The Rich Men of Massachusetts*.[869] This exclusive group consisted of men with a minimum personal net worth of fifty thousand dollars or more.

In Concord the Buttrick family was numbered amongst that community's leading families. During the American Revolution, the family name became part of the legend of the Minutemen when an ancestor of Molly's, Major John Buttrick later named Colonel, became the first commander to order his troops to fire upon the British. A monument in his honor stills stands at the North Bridge in Concord.

Molly grew up in an imposing home at 2 Divinity Street in Cambridge overlooking Harvard Yard. She was a member of the first class to graduate from Berkley Street School, a prestigious private school for young ladies in Cambridge.[870] Memoirs left behind by a classmate recall the great fun these young ladies had playing the popular new game of baseball, which had caught on in popularity all over the East Coast by the time of the Civil War.[871]

During the war Molly was an active member of the "Banks Brigade," an organization of young women in their late teens and early twenties that met each week to sew for the men who were fighting for the Union cause. When the war ended they changed their name to the "Bees" and continued to meet socially. Molly was the first in the group to marry.

> *Some time while Frank was engaged to be married, your grandpa,' Capt Bradford & I took rooms at the Revere House & capt B_ & I made two most agreeable excursions~*
>
> *We took a day for Wellesley, to visit the grounds of Mr Hunnewell~ The most tasteful private grounds I have ever seen~ The land had been in possession of the Wells family (one of whom, Mr Hunnewell married) for generations~*[872]

The gentleman who escorted Sarah and Captain Bradford around his summer estate was Horatio Hollis Hunnewell, a well-known Boston philanthropist who earned his fortune in banking and railroads. In the 1830s he was married to his cousin, Isabella Welles.[873]

The Hunnewells built a home in the Back Bay section of Boston, and by 1843 the Hunnewells and their nine children began to spend their summers on a family farm in nearby Natick. This land had been in his wife's family for generations, and was part of her inheritance. Hunnewell liked the country and one of the first things he did was to turn an old pasture on the property into a garden. Through the years he transformed over forty acres out of several hundred into a magnificent ornamental garden overlooking Lake Waban. Then in 1851 he had a mansion of his own design built there, along with a conservatory.[874]

In its midst was a gem of a lake surrounded by grassy & wooded hills about one or two hundred feet high~ They sloped gently to the pure water which had a bottom of white sand & gravel~[875]

He named this summer estate "Wellesley" in honor of his wife and her family. It was from this name that nearby Wellesley College, founded by Henry F. Durant, a neighboring cousin, took its name. Then in 1881 the community surrounding this estate voted to change the name of the town to Wellesley in honor of their chief benefactors, the Hunnewells.[876] This estate eventually included a nine-acre pinetum, an arboretum devoted to a rare collection of evergreens. At the time privately owned pinetums were popular on large English estates and they acted as showcases for the many new species discovered in the field of dendrology. This was the first one in America for a number of years, and it remained the most comprehensive collection of evergreens found anywhere for years.[877]

Prevailing European fashions in landscape gardening heavily influenced Hunnewell's landscaping design. In England the fashion was a more sculpted formal look with carefully clipped hedges and formal fountains. There was also a revival in classical styles, and Italian gardens became fashionable in England[878]

Hunnewell was the first to bring this classical revival style in garden landscaping to America. In 1854 he designed a three-acre, six tiered, terraced Italian topiary garden on the banks of Lake Wabash. The terraces were planted with several hundred evergreens shaped in tightly clipped geometric shapes. Topiary, designing trees in animal or geometric shapes, had been out of favor in England for about a hundred years, but around this period it underwent a popular revival there. Hunnewell was one of the first to practice this art in America, and this unusual style drew many admiring visitors like Sarah and Captain Bradford to his gardens.[879]

Nature had done everything to make this place beautiful & to this Mr Hunnewell had added all the attractions of art~ He had been several times in Italy & was able to carry out some ideas derived from the landscape gardening of that country~

The lake was a beautiful oval & his house & conservatories were at one end, which was terraced & balustraded with occasional flights of steps quite to the water~[880]

Although Sarah failed to make note of it, one of the most unusual attractions Hunnewell had imported from Italy was a gondola complete with gondolier who rowed visitors leisurely around the lake.[881]

On the balustrades at short intervals, were Italian vases and the terraces were adorned with small evergreens & flowers embedded in the emerald grass~ The only thing that distracted from our pleasure, was the material used in building~ It was all of wood & the feeling that it ought to be of something more durable, was continually thrust upon us~[882]

Hunnewell loved to experiment with various types of plants. He had a number of glass houses throughout his estate where he grew out of season grapes, peaches, and oranges. All of these items were costly out of season, and one paid as much as two or three dollars for one orange or pear before the railroads began to transport them from California and the southern states.[883]

> *In these days of fresh fruit all the year round, few remember the olden times when bananas were not, when oranges could not always be had & when gentlemen had to content themselves with almonds, figs, raisins, & nuts of various kinds, to give zest to their sherry & Madeira~*[884]

He also had the largest collection of rhododendrons and azaleas in New England. It was due to his promotion of and experimentation with these broad-leafed evergreens that many varieties of rhododendrons were introduced and adapted to the northern states.[885]

> *The original forest, beautiful lawns, everything that could delight the eye was there~ I noticed that all the underbrush usual in a forest had been cleared away & in its place was the Rhododendron by thousands, some of the plants very large~ These had been imported from Holland~*[886]

Hollis Hunnewell opened his garden estate at Wellesley to the public every spring when the rhododendrons and azaleas were at the height of their bloom. Sarah and her party may have been amongst the public visitors, or she may have received a private tour.

> *The next day with the addition of Molly & Frank to our party, we visited Concord Mass.~ We took a large carriage & driver and after visiting the Monument, the Ripley House, where Hawthorne had lived, taking a look at Concord river, stopping a moment before the house where Hawthorne then lived, another before the Alcott home & more than a minute before that of Mr Emerson, we drove on to the goal of our wishes & the chief object of our visit to Concord "Walden Pond", which Thoreau had made classic~*
>
> *We looked reverently into the cellar which he had dug, wandered among the Pines & by the water & should have been too late for the train, if the hack man had not taken care of us~ We arrived at Mr Buttrick's about eight o' clock where we passed the night~*[887]

This visit to Concord, Massachusetts must have held special meaning for Sarah, a lover of history and literature, as well as an admirer of the transcendentalist philosophy that grew out of the Unitarian church. This movement found its strongest adherents amongst the large number of talented authors who lived in this small community in western Massachusetts during the 1840s and 1850s. One of the town's most prominent members was Ralph Waldo Emerson, a Unitarian minister. He was a well know lecturer and writer and one of the foremost promoters of transcendentalism during these years.

The monument the party from Portsmouth visited was one honoring the Concord Minutemen led by Molly's ancestor. The Ripley House wasn't one of the Concord homes where Nathaniel Hawthorne had lived, but it may have been the home of George Ripley, the founder of Brook Farm, an agricultural commune based on transcendentalist tenets.

Hawthorne, the author of *The Scarlet Letter* and *House of the Seven Gables,* was not a convert to this philosophy, but he was nonetheless a shareholder at this early experiment in communal living, and lived at Brook Farm for a short while alongside many of the intellectual leaders of his day. When he married Sophia Peabody they rented the Emerson family home overlooking the North Bridge, and he immortalized it in his works as "*The Old Manse.*" Later he purchased the old Alcott family home known as "Hillside," and changed the name to "Wayside."[888]

Hawthorne died four years before the Goodwins visited Concord in 1866. A handsome man all of his life, he suddenly began to age overnight in his late fifties. His deterioration was both physical and mental, and his illness progressed rapidly. He died in 1862 in Plymouth, New Hampshire, on his way to the White Mountains in search of a health cure. His old friend and classmate Franklin Pierce was with him.[889]

Bronson and Louisa May Alcott were living in the family home known as "Orchard House," at the time the Goodwins visited Concord. Louisa May Alcott published *Little Women*, her most famous book two years after the Goodwin party stopped in front of her home.[890]

Henry David Thoreau, was just twenty-seven and an aspiring philosopher and nature lover in 1845 when he built a timber framed cabin in Walden Woods near Concord on land owned by his friend and mentor Ralph Waldo Emerson. He lived there alone for twenty-six months. Later he wrote *Walden Pond*, the story of his search for enlightenment in the solitude of the woods. The book was already a classic by the time the Goodwin party visited the pond twelve years later.

Thoreau had died in 1862 of consumption, and the cabin he had built at Walden Pond had been moved to a neighboring farm by1866. However, the rocks that marked the cabin's foundation remained, and throughout the years visitors, who wanted to mark the spot where Thoreau once sought to blend his spirit with nature, added to this cairn.[891]

It would seem Captain Bradford was an enjoyable and adventurous traveling companion whose own enthusiasm for sightseeing matched that of his mother-in-law. Her husband she explained cared very little about such things, and he remained in Boston tending to business.

> *You wonder perhaps where your grandpa' was all this time~ I can only say that he was busy with his ships & cared very little about the matter~ your Uncle Bradford loved dearly to go about, anywhere with us & he was always most kind & courteous to me~*[892]

This visit to meet Molly and her family probably occurred in the spring of the year when the flowers were in full bloom at the Hunnewell estate. That September Frank and Molly were wed in Cambridge. He was almost twenty-five years old and she was twenty-two. They moved into her father's home on Divinity Street, and lived with her parents for a few years while Frank pursued his promising future as a Boston lawyer.

> *Frank too has gratified me by graduating respectably at Harvard & by his success in his profession~ for all which I am very grateful~*[893]

In addition Frank became active in Cambridge civic activities, and served on the school committee in that city. Their first child Mary was born two years later on February 18, 1868. She was the Goodwin's second granddaughter.

The family continued to grow, and in 1867 Susie married her military officer Lieutenant Commander George Dewey. Dewey had been assigned to duty in Europe with the North Atlantic Blocking Squadron for nearly two years following the end of the war. He was a native of Montpelier, Vermont and the third son of Dr. Julius Yemans Dewey. His father, a rural doctor for many years, was the president of National Life Insurance of Vermont by the time of the wedding, and the family was quite prosperous.

Dewey had entered Norwich Military Academy in Vermont when he was just fourteen. Upon graduation he received an appointment to the Naval Academy at Annapolis. At the time the Academy had been in existence just nine years. Of the sixty candidates who entered the Academy with him in 1854 only fifteen graduated. Out of that number Dewey, who by his own admission had racked up an impressive number of demerits during his years there and done poorly in both history and geography, ranked fifth out of the fifteen who remained in the prestigious military academy's class of 1858.[894]

The Rev. James DeNormandie of Portsmouth married Susie and George Dewey in Portsmouth on October 24th of 1867. Dewey was thirty at the time of their wedding, and his bride twenty-four. One Dewey biographer described their wedding as a large military affair, followed by a "gay" reception at the Goodwin home. Dewey wrote in his autobiography that for the next "three happy years," they lived at Annapolis, where he was in charge of the Fourth Class Midshipmen. He recalled that under the benevolent watch of Vice-Admiral David Porter, there was such an active social life for the young couples living there at the time that the school was known as "Porter's Dancing Academy."[895]

Two letters written to Susie from her sister Sadie who was living at home at the time of Susie's wedding give some insight into the family dynamics and events during the years following the war.

Portsmouth Oct 31ˢᵗ (1867)
Thursday morning

It hardly seems possible my dear Susie that it is a week today since you were married~ To you though I dare say it seems quite that long, as there have been so many events crowded into your week. With us it has been the priority itself, as you can imagine after the excitement of the preceding week. However, we were glad to rest. Abby & I got your boxes all off yesterday & hope you will find everything alright.

We were delighted to hear from you night before last and know that you were well and enjoying yourself & we think of you today on your way to New York and congratulate you on having such lovely weather for the trip~ How pleasant it was in Mr. Dewey's family to meet you in the last & their presents too were lovely. I am mad Mr. D. did not give you the buttons & studs before you left Portsmouth as I should like to have feasted my eyes upon them.

We have seen but few persons since the wedding but everyone says they hear the bride was perfectly lovely. Mother wrote you I believe all that the family, have said for the occasion~ This has been not only our opinion that is that throughout it was an entire success. The Boardman's (Jack & Sadie) have been enthusiastic over your appearance & indeed over the whole thing~ Fanny T. too had expressed herself warmly on the entirety & she is especially enthusiastic over Mr. Henley, thinks he is perfectly splendid.... Annie Pillow came over yesterday afternoon on an errand & remained to tea. She asked me to give a great deal of love to you~

This afternoon we are expecting Mrs. Buttrick to stay a few days & mother thinks of going back to Cambridge with her for a day or two and then pass a night with the Bartletts, before returning to Portsmouth....

Hope is getting much better though still quite miserable~ She is up this morning & dressed for the first time in the morning since you went away. She has passed two or three very quiet evenings in her room this past week, from which you will conclude that we have not been brilliant.

...I think the cake was all right, in every particular. There was a slice sent to everybody who ought to have had it, & to most places a slice of bride cake as well. There is about a loaf left for you, as you will perceive, I wish I had a big slice of it now though I should hardly feel the better for it, as I have a charming headache this morning! Father is in Boston today. Mother flying around generally preparing for her visitor. Abby gone down to Mys's Lane's to have her new dress altered, which must partially be finished. Hope "clothed and in her right mind" sitting in my room. The children, as usual bothering our livery out playing with water. A charming family picture!

I hope you will write to us & tell us everything about yourself~generally how you arrange your pretty things &c &c. Everybody sends you both oceans of love. We can hardly realize that we are not to see you this winter.

Give my devoted love to my dear brother "George" & tell him to be a good little boy~ With oceans of love dear Susie from your aft. Sister. [896]

It is possible that Hope, the only one of the Goodwin children who remained single and at home throughout her life, suffered from periodic bouts of depression, as the above letter seems to imply. However, this may be a misreading of the facts. Another letter from Sadie to Susie, written ten days later gives another look at the family in the 1860s.

Portsmouth Nov 10th (1867)
Sunday morning

I was delighted my dear Susie to get your letter from Annapolis yesterday & we are all charmed that you find your new quarters so attractive I think I am able from your description to form a very clear idea of your surroundings, but I do wish I could look in upon you & see for myself... .

Mother, Father & I went to the Lyceum several evenings since. There are reserved seats this winter & we have them with the Boardmans which is quite pleasant... We hear nothing yet from Mr. Bradford & of course I have heard nothing from Sam I am getting very impatient for some news of him, but I fear I will have to wait a long while yet~

Mabel & Fieldie begin with their school tomorrow & they are anticipating a great deal of pleasure. They are now bothering poor Pip's life out of him & I have threatened to write to you to send for him... A threat which has had the desired effect I heard Fieldie talking to Mabel lately that he thought Pip had improved very much since the wedding!

I am happy to report to you that I am getting along very comfortably in our domestic concerns~ We have a cook who was Pastry cook and head baker at the Farragut last summer and so far she does splendidly. Bell has gone and we have Joanna Immins~ Little Margaret who is very smart ...in short "peace reigns once more within our borders" I only pray that it may last. Irene must be disgusted to find we could get so good a person in her place, the day after her departure and it was a remarkable stroke of luck~

Fanny Treadwell passed by day before yesterday afternoon & mentioned that Mrs. Dwight is circulating the most fabulous stories about your trousseau! Tells for one thing that your bill at Hoovey's for dresses <u>alone</u> was two thousand. Isn't that disgusting? She has been here but once since the wedding and then she attacked your <u>cake</u> soundly. Fortunately nobody heeds her talk...Mother took her shopping last Wednesday & as I had some shopping to do in Boston I took Mabel for company Mr. Buttrick & Frank met me at the station and then I took leave of them...Mabel was as good as company as I should desire... .

Well dear Susy I must say goodbye as I have to dress to make a call before tea. Abby & Hope send you both oceans of love. Hope says she will try to write soon. So take good care of yourself your Sister Sadie~

<u>Should</u> you write Sam direct to "Sitka Alaska"[897]

The Mrs. Dwight spreading the gossip was Sarah's youngest sister Adeline. The Boardmans would have been Sarah's sister Susan, and her husband Dr. John Boardman. Family records indicate that the Boardman's two unmarried sons George, 25 and Robert, 27 were killed at sea near Havana, Cuba in 1865. It is assumed that their ship went down in a hurricane, but that is not certain.[898]

Fielding and Mabel were Georgie's son and Sadie's daughter. Pip was the family dog. All the servant problems were apparently not solved, but at least they were temporarily resolved at this point in time.

Sadie's husband, Samuel Storer had left for Sitka, Alaska in the fall of 1867. This was the year that the United States, under the direction of Secretary of State William Seward, purchased Alaska from Russia for seven million and two hundred thousand dollars. The treaty between Russia and America was first signed in March of 1867, but the transfer was not officially completed until that October, when a United States army troop transport ship arrived in Sitka. When the Americans arrived in Alaska, the Russian flag was removed, and the American flag was raised over the country's latest and most controversial acquisition. At the time of purchase Alaska was not brought into the Union as a state, instead it was merely a customs district of the United States.[899]

There were neither railroads nor roads on which to travel in Alaska in 1867, so the

Army Corps traveled there by ship navigating through a large number of waterways. Sitka is part of the area of Alaska known as the mainland, which extends to some outlying islands. The military post in Sitka was one of five that the army oversaw.[900] Along with the army came a few settlers and other government officials, and it is likely that Samuel came on that first ship. It is not certain what Samuel Storer's official capacity was, but there is some family correspondence that refers to him as the United State Consul General to Alaska.[901]

However, this may not be the case as there was no civil government or form of representative government at that time in Alaska. Even the commanding general of the troops stationed there had no legal authority. Any illegal acts had to be prosecuted in the courts of Washington, Oregon or California. For the first two years the treasury department was the only real authority, and they were primarily concerned with the custom revenue.[902]

It is not known how long Sam remained in Alaska, but less than two months after Sadie wrote the above letter she succumbed to consumption, the same illness that had killed her sister Georgie. She died just five days before the Christmas of 1867. The death notice in the local paper is brief noting only that she was a "beautiful and lovely young woman," whose early death would sadden a "large circle of friends." Mabel was six years old at the time she lost her mother, and she remained with the Goodwins until she was an adult.

It is not known if Susie returned home when Sadie died, but she and Dewey were in Portsmouth on her twenty-fifth birthday the following March. A note from her husband indicates she was having a difficult time accepting her sister's death, and Dewey apparently was unable or unwilling to help her cope with her grief.

> *Wednesday Noon*
> *My darling Susy,*
>
> *I have heard all. Be brave and think "what is is right"~ Perhaps I shall not see you today ~ I don't know what to do. I want to be with you to tell you that though you have lost a dear sister, you have not lost all. I think I had better take a few days now and visit at home. I ought to go and perhaps now is the best time. I shall go over to town this evening so as to take the early train in the morning. I shall not be gone long, certainly not longer than Monday or Tuesday next.*
> *I am miserable and don't know what is right. I ought to go and still feel that I cannot. I will see you a moment tonight unless I hear from you at the Rockingham to the contrary. Be brave my darling and time will heal this terrible wound.*
> *Ever yours, Geo Dewey*[903]

Susie and Dewey remained at Annapolis until 1870. During those years her nephew Willie was also at Annapolis. Sarah recalled some years later meeting two of Susie's admirers from this period while she was visiting Mount Desert, a resort in the Bar Harbor area of Maine.

> *I have some very pleasant memories of a visit to Mount Desert~ On the steamer we fell in with Mr & Mrs Upton & daughter of Boston & saw a good deal of them while we were there~ Mr Upton was one of the most genial &*

delightful men I ever saw, just the man for a picnic or an excursion~ Boston owes much to him & appreciates his memory for he is gone~

Gen & Mrs Fremont had a cottage across the fields from our hotel & when they found we were there, they called on us~ This attention was owing to their fondness for Susie, who had been very kind to their son at Annapolis~

I have a beautiful locket which Mrs Fremont sent from Paris to Susie~ Mrs Fremont was only one of <u>very many</u> who loved & admired Susie~[904]

General John C. Fremont was a hero of the Mexican War, as well as the Republican candidate for president in 1856. He won the vote in the North, but the votes from the South for the Democratic candidate James Buchanan were greater. An explorer as well as a soldier also known as "the Pathfinder," Lincoln put him in command of all Union troops in the west.[905]

History recalls Fremont as a striking, charismastic man.[906] His wife, Jessie, was also a handsome woman, and as a couple, many considered them the perfect pair to preside over the White House. [907] Early on in the Civil War Fremont angered President Lincoln by pronouncing the slaves of secessionists automatically freed. Lincoln responded by relieving Fremont of his command and Fremont became the darling of the abolitionist movement.[908] In 1864 he was the presidential nominee of the anti-Lincoln wing of the Republican Party.

ADMIRAL FARRAGUT

During the Civil War the North's greatest naval hero was sixty-one year old David Farragut. He was originally from Tennessee, and was the adopted son of David Porter of Norfolk, Virginia, a naval hero during the War of 1812. Farragut's own service with the United States Navy reached back to that same war with Britain, when Farragut was made a midshipman at age eleven. The following year, at age twelve, he was given command of a prize British ship that Porter had captured.[909]

When the Civil War began Farragut moved his family North to Brooklyn, New York where he awaited orders. He was a captain in the navy at the time and he remained loyal to the Union. A year later he was put in command of a fleet of twenty-four ships. One of these was the USS *Mississippi.* a steam frigate

Admiral David G. Farragut, circa 1860s, hero of the Civil War.

Susie Goodwin hadn't met her future husband at this time, but twenty-five year old George Dewey was the executive officer aboard this ship. Farragut took note of Dewey early on when an older more experienced man complained that he was passed over for a younger man. The Admiral conferred with the ship's captain who said he was satisfied with Dewey's performance, and Dewey kept his position.[910]

Farragut's fleet joined General Benjamin Butler's troops in 1862 at a point approximately thirty miles north of the Confederate Forts Jackson and Phillip. These forts were critical to the Confederacy, as they guarded the river approach to New Orleans. Farragut intended to destroy them.

The forts seemed to be impassable; as they were guarded by a line of old hulks that stretched between them, and just beyond the forts sat a small fleet of Confederate ships. Farragut's first plan of attack was to destroy the forts, and the Union fleet shelled them night and day with a barrage of heavy artillery. However, when the forts remained standing after six days, Farragut decided on a more audiacous tactic. He ordered two gunboats to go ahead of the fleet. Then in the middle of the night, undetected by the enemy, their crews cut the mooring chains.

A few evenings later Farragut's fleet bypassed the forts at two o'clock in the morning. When the Confederates saw the fleet attempting to pass by the light of the moon, they opened fire upon them. Farragut's flagship was hit innumerable times and finally caught fire. Fortunately, the crew managed to douse the flames and save the ship. In a little under two hours all but four ships made it past the forts, and attacked the fleet of eight Confederate ships on the other side, destroying all but two.

This battle constituted a stunning defeat for the South, and a crucial victory for the

North, which gained control of the upper Mississippi and of New Orleans in one fell swoop.[911] When Farragut returned to Washington he received a hero's welcome, and was made America's first rear admiral. One of his staunchest admirers was the youngest officer in his fleet, George Dewey. Years later he also won a great naval victory.

During the battle Dewey's ship was damaged by heavy artillery fire. So when the rest of the fleet went on ahead, his ship remained in New Orleans for needed repairs. While there the crew was ordered to help maintain order for General Butler who was in charge of the Union occupation of New Orleans.[912]

General Butler, the same man who had been so genteel to the Goodwins during their visit to the military encampment in Nashua, was very unpopular with the populace of New Orleans. An overweight, unattractive man in his mid forties, with a droopy eye, and officious manner, Butler earned an unfavorable reputation throughout the South. Those who accused him of raiding the homes of wealthy southerners, and taking their silver and other valuables for his personal use called him "spoons." He was also given the derisive moniker "Beast Butler," for his harsh rules and treatment of the populace of New Orleans during the Union occupation.[913]

They had good reason to dislike him. One of the first things he did there was to order the execution of a local man who cut down the Union flag. Also, Butler's stated policy was to treat southern women who expressed contempt for the Union soldiers, as though they were prostitutes.[914] This outraged the southern sense of chivalry. Dewey recalled in his autobiography that Butler was often found seated at his desk, in full uniform with a sword and two guns at his side ready to thwart any assassination attempts made upon his life.[915]

Dewey remained in New Orleans in charge of the USS *Mississippi* until the spring of 1863. By then Grant and Sherman's troops were marching towards Vicksburg, shutting off southern supplies by land. It was Farragut's mission to shut them off by water. To do this he had to take Port Hudson on the Mississippi. This was not as successful a mission as the one in New Orleans had been. Farragut was successful in getting past the fort, but he lost three ships. One of them was the USS *Mississippi*. It caught fire when hit by friendly fire from one of the ships in the fleet. The ship went down in flames, but before it did, Lieutenant Dewey saw to it that all the men were off, and the ammunition either saved or destroyed to prevent any from falling into Confederate hands.[916]

> *Capt Dewey's order at the frigate Mississippi, when this took fire from another ship that came drifting down the river against him was much applauded~*[917]

In July of 1864, the North was blockading all ports. However the Port of Mobile, Alabama, remained open to southern shipping, and Admiral Farragut wanted to see this port closed off as well. Leading a fleet of eighteen Union ships past three Confederate forts to do this, he forced the surrender of a Confederate fleet positioned there.

The 63-year-old Farragut suffered from vertigo so severe that he ordered his men to lash him to his ship's rigging for the attack on Mobile. At the start of the run, a mine (called torpedos at time time) sank his lead ship, causing the captains of the remaining ships to fear passing through the heavily-mined waters surrounding the city. However, Admiral Farragut chose to disregard the sodden mines, the majority of which careened harmlessly off the ships. Tied to his flagship's mast, Farragut went on to lead his fleet past the forts all the while shouting out the rallying cry for which he is remembered to this day, "Damn the torpedoes, full speed ahead!"[918]

By December of that year all but two major forts on the Mississippi were under Union control. Those remaining under Confederate control were in Charleston, South Carolina, and Wilmington, North Carolina. The Union Navy was able to blockade the fort at Charleston, but Fort Fisher in Wilmington located at the mouth of the Cape Fear River, with two inlets was much more difficult to blockade. Since the control of Fort Fisher was of strategic importance, plans were made to take Fort Fisher.

Originally this was to be accomplished under the command of Admiral Farragut, but his health was compromised during the battle of Mobile, so this command was given to Rear Admiral David K. Porter, his foster brother. The plan was for the naval fleet to bombard the fort with fire, to be followed up by a direct assault by troops brought in by transport under the command of General Butler.

George Dewey was the executive officer aboard the USS *Colorado,* which was part of the largest fleet of assorted ships ever assembled during the war. The first day of the battle Porter's fleet fired upon the forts with great effect, but Butler's troops did not arrive until late that night; so a cease-fire was called until morning. That next morning the USS *Colorado, Wabash,* and *Minnesota,* all heavy ships, were positioned directly in front of Fort Fisher giving them an effective range of fire, but after waiting in vain throughout the day for the land troops to launch their assault on the fort, orders were given to withdraw leaving behind only the *Colorado* and *Minnesota,* who were ordered to cease fire but to remain in position.

The Confederates assumed that these remaining ships were disabled, and opened fire on them. The assault was heavy. Commodore Thatcher was unable to respond due to orders, but unable to withdraw for the same reason. Seeing that this was to be a slaughter he was about to disobey orders and withdraw. However, the ship's newly assigned executive officer, counseled him to return the fire since he believed a retreat might be misunderstood as an act of cowardice.

Thatcher took Dewey's advice and as the senior officer present at the time commanded the *Minnesota* to follow his lead. The renewed attack silenced the Confederate fire and the two remaining ships were ordered to return to their base in Beaufort, South Carolina, as General Butler had decided to withdraw his troops from the action before they had a chance to launch an assault on the fort.[919]

Three weeks later a successful attack on Fort Fisher was launched and as a result of his actions during the first assault Commodore Thatcher was made an admiral. Major General A.H. Terry replaced General Butler during this assault, and Butler's decision to retreat ended his military career. It was sometime after the war that Sarah learned of Dewey's role at the battle of Fort Fisher.

> *I met Mr Albert Jones up the street one day & he said to me "Admiral Thatcher took tea with us last evening & I never heard one man praised so as he praised your son in law Capt Dewey"~ He is coming to tea with us tonight I said I will bring him out on it~*
>
> *He came & after tea, my husband, Capt Jsph Bradford & captain Dewey being present I took a seat by the Admiral~ "Did Capt Dewey behave pretty at Ft Fisher?" I said~ Capt Dewey sprang up & ran to the corner with his back to us~*

The Admiral turning his whole body toward me (as his manner was) replied, "Mrs Goodwin Capt Dewey behaved so pretty at Fort Fisher that if I had the power of Congress I would make him not a Rear Admiral, nor a Vice Admiral, an Admiral"~

After he was gone I asked Dewey (who was never one to blow his own trumpet) what it all meant~ "It meant said he that I made him an Admiral, when we were before Fort Fisher, Admiral Porter who was there with a squadron ordered the Colorado to take a certain Fort~

Com Thatcher who was in command had never been in battle & was disposed to rely a good deal on the judgment of his officers~ They all in a body except Dewey, advised him to turn from the fight ~ as he was about to yield, Dewey said to him "Com do you know what the world will say if you withdraw?

"What will they say said the Com. They will say sir that we are cowards"~

Dewey was execution officer & the Com said go ahead sir & order the attack~ Dewey flew from one deck to another & ordered the men to stand to their guns & take that Fort in five minutes & in five minutes the Fort was silenced~[920]

After the war Dewey was on duty in Europe for over two years. Just before he sailed for home in 1867 he again met Farragut in Cherbourg, France. Farragut was sixty-six years old by then, and a four star admiral. Dewey recalled that he seemed quite fit at the time of his European tour. However, when he returned to the states his health was failing, and he had grown quite frail.[921]

His last voyage was from Norfolk, Virginia to Portsmouth, New Hampshire in 1870. He stayed at the home of his brother-in-law Commander Pennock at Commanders Quarter's, Company A, at Portsmouth Naval Yard. The local newspapers noted the presence of this distinguished man in Portsmouth, and reported he was there to recuperate from heart disease.

When Admiral Farragut came to Portsmouth after the war your grandpa' visited him & he very soon returned the visit in company with other gentleman~

I thought him very gentlemanly & agreeable & afterward when he was very sick at his relative's Com. Pennock's at the navy yard, we called on him & both he & Mrs Farragut made a special effort to see us & that was the last day he was down stairs & the last day he saw company~

We, that is your grandpa', aunt Abby & myself enjoyed the visit very much as the Pennocks & Farraguts seemed very glad to see us~[922]

George Dewey accompanied his father in-law, Ichabod Goodwin, on his first visit to Admiral Farragut at Company A Headquarters. There is no record of who else may have accompanied the Admiral when he in turn called at the Goodwin home. Perhaps Commander Pennock was also there, as Sarah reported the Pennocks and Farraguts were quite welcoming when they returned the visit.

Admiral Farragut died in Portsmouth on August 14, 1870. His funeral was held three days later at St. John's Church on August 17[th.] All work was suspended at the Naval Yard that day.[923]

> *On the day the Admiral was buried, many very distinguished gentlemen came to Portsmouth to pay due respect to so great a Captain~ Among them were Gov. Sterns of New Hampshire Ex Gov. Clifford of Mass. Mr Samuel Hooper & Mr Robert C Winthrop~*

> *My husband said to me on the morning of that day, "Don't wait for me at dinner, as I may dine at the Rockingham House"~ So we had our dinner at two o'clock & then as was my habit, I went upstairs, partially undressed & lay down for a nap~*

> *At three o'clock Abby rushed into my room & said, "Do get up for Father has brought home a party of gentlemen & wants lunch & the family at once"~*

> *Just then he appeared & said he had brought home ex~Governor Clifford of New Bedford, Gov. Sterns of New Hampshire, Congressman Samuel Hooper of Boston & Robert C. Winthrop~ I was aghast!!!*

> *But Abby said "Mother dress yourself at once & I will make it all right"~ In fifteen minutes lunch was announced~ Abby came in, the lunch was perfect, champagne & all, & we had a good time~*[924]

The list of dignitaries included Onslow Sterns, the Governor of New Hampshire that year, Congressman Hooper of Massachusetts, who had called before with Salmon Chase, and Robert C. Winthrop, a former member of Congress from Massachusetts, and speaker of the house between 1848 and 1852. He was a direct descendent of Massachusetts's first governor, John Winthrop. In addition he was a lawyer, a constitutional scholar, and a well-known orator and writer.

> *I had Mr Winthrop on my right~ Abby sat between two & was very bright & pleasant~ Talk was kept up for more than an hour & the gentlemen were very complimentary –*[925]

> *I talked a great deal with Mr Winthrop & he asked me if I had read his books, saying also that he should have great pleasure in sending them to me, which he did very soon after~ Of course they are among my most*

treasured possessions~ [926]

The majority of Mr. Winthrop's published works are copies of speeches that he delivered on such auspicious occasions as college commencements, political conventions, eulogies, and dedications. He also wrote a biography on the life of his venerable ancestor, Governor John Winthrop.

A Harvard law school graduate, Winthrop was admitted to Harvard at age fourteen. While there he formed a close friendship with Charles Chauncy, a younger but short- lived brother of Ralph Waldo Emerson. [927] After graduation he clerked for Daniel Webster, and eventually became a prominent member of the Whig party. He was elected as the Whig representative in Congress seven times.

When Winthrop was speaker of the house he failed to push the Whig anti-slavery party line despite pleas from such eminent abolitionists as Ralph Waldo Emerson, and John Greenleaf Whittier. These men believed his opinion would carry great weight.[928] However, Winthrop was very conservative and although he considered himself an abolitionist, he refused to consider any changes to the Constitution or interference with the rights of southern states in order to affect the cause of freedom for the slaves. Although he had been a Whig for many years, after the party disbanded he refused to join the Republican Party, and was considered to be a Democrat by the time of the Civil War.[929]

Through the years Sarah became known as a gracious hostess and it would seem that both she and Abby rose to the occasion on the day of Admiral Farragut's funeral. One Portsmouth man, of that time in recording his memories of Portsmouth many years later, recalled Sarah and her daughter Abby about this time. Of Sarah he wrote she was "a woman of such intellectual and social gifts, that if her lot had been cast in less obscure regions she would have without effort proved herself one of the most memorable American hostesses of this century."[930]

Abigail Goodwin Winder, 1870, the Goodwin's oldest daughter.

He also recalled Abby as, a "mite" of a woman, so "pretty and sparkling" while in her early forties he could hardly believe she was the age of his own mother. As the above vignette attests, Abby had indeed inherited her mother's social skills and graces. Sarah believed that all of her daughters were blessed with a special charm, and once wrote of them:

> *I will say here all my daughters had &*
> *those who are left have remarkable*
> *power to attract~*[931]

After the funeral services for Admiral Farragut in Portsmouth, three US Naval vessels escorted his body to Washington, DC. There he was buried with full honors, following a national funeral ceremony. Years later a plaque in his honor was erected in front of the Commander's Quarters Company A at the Portsmouth Naval Yard. Dewey the same man who was once the youngest executive officer in Farragut's fleet gave the dedication.[932]

FAMILY IN THE 1870S

In 1870 Dewey and his new bride left Annapolis. He received orders to report to the USS *Narragansett*, as the ship's commander. This was his first regular command. The ship was stationed in New York Harbor, and for three months that fall it sat in the harbor awaiting orders that never came. At the start of 1871 he was transferred to the USS *Supply*. It was one of three American ships chosen to transport supplies contributed by the American public for the relief of Parisians, whose city was under siege by the Prussian Navy.[933]

While Dewey and his crew prepared to embark for Europe on their humanitarian mission, Sarah traveled to New York to escort her daughter Susie home to Portsmouth.

> *In the Feb & March of 1871 I went to New York to be with Susie whenever her husband might sail for France, whither he was ordered to take supplies to the suffering French during the war with Prussia.*

> *Mr Dewey was busily engaged about his ship from eight in the morning until six in the evening and during those hours Susie & I improved our leisure in exploring New York & in seeing every thing worth seeing~*[934]

By 1871 New York had undergone great change since Sarah visited there for the first time. For one thing it was much larger and still growing. The wealth that once clustered on the Battery had moved "uptown," near Fifth Avenue. By mid-century the city was moving northward and the wealthy were building their homes between Fifth Avenue and Madison Square.

Sarah indicates that this was where she and her family always stayed. They may have stayed at a hotel near Fifth and Broadway, such as the Fifth Avenue Hotel or the St. Nicholas. These were both luxury hotels that provided their guests with planned socials, as well as all necessary accommodations such as meals, housekeepers, and a parlor in which to mingle and meet the other guests.[935]

Broadway remained the main thoroughfare, but magnificent stores, grand hotels, and restaurants had replaced the stately old homes that once lined it. Well-dressed pedestrians, horse drawn cars, and omnibuses, filled with fashionable passengers, traveled up and down the wide boulevard at all hours of the night and day. It now extended far beyond the Bowery, but Harlem was still a country town, and the Bronx didn't yet exist.

Above all this ran the elevated transit system. This was an overhead rail system where steam driven trains clattered along at speeds as high as thirty miles an hour. Known as the EL, the rail began at the Battery and ended at Harlem River. Construction on the Brooklyn Bridge had begun in 1871, but would not be completed for at least a decade.[936]

New York was still America's cultural center. In 1871 the Metropolitan Museum of Art was in the works, but wouldn't open until the following February. However, there were a large number of nationally famous theatres in the city. Magnificent hotels, bars, and theatres lined the mile long stretch of Broadway between Madison Square and Forty-second Street known as the Rialto.[937]

> *We went with Mr Dewey to the Theatres in the evenings & once after coming from the burlesque of Booth in Richlieu, by Fox, we had a supper of oysters at Fulton Market ~ and such oysters! I had heard of them but had never seen such~ Shrewsbury oysters, as large as a small saucer! Oh how happy & full of fun we all were that night!*
>
> *We saw Booth in Richeleu at his own magnificent Theatre & we saw Lester Wallack in comedy at Wallack's Theatre~*[938]

Edwin Booth, for many years America's most famous stage star, was born into a family of actors. Booth is credited for introducing realism to the New York stage. When his brother, John Wilkes Booth, assassinated President Lincoln, Edwin left the stage for a year. When he returned in 1866 he was warmly welcomed back by a cheering New York audience. Three years later he built his own theatre on Twenty-third and Sixth Streets. It was quite large and elegant and boasted of the latest technology in staging. It was also the first theatre in New York to offer its audiences the luxury of cooled air in the summer and warm air in the winter, which was blown into the theatre via a huge fan located in the basement.[939]

Wallack's, the home of high comedy, had been an institution in New York for many years, and was very popular with the fashionable crowd. Many sophisticates considered it superior to the Comedie Francaise. Lester Wallack was an innovative comedic actor who managed and acted in his own theatre of comedy. About the time Sarah visited there he had just opened a new theatre on Broadway and Thirteenth. This was a handsomely designed and elegantly appointed theatre that ranked amongst the city's largest and finest establishments. It came to be known as the place to see and be seen by the elite and famous members of both New York's theatrical and aristocratic societies. [940]

Stewart's was the same store Sarah had visited in 1827, but it had grown to be the largest department store in the world. The new Stewart's was a six-story Italianate building made of cast iron that was painted white to resemble marble. It covered an entire city block on Broadway from Ninth to Tenth Streets. It had fifteen plate glass windows, and was the first store to use display windows and mannequins to promote its merchandise.

Stewart's was considered a must place to visit by the upper class ladies who shopped in New York. There was always a line of expensive carriages outside of Stewart's. The store employed over two hundred clerks, and its daily sales reached upwards of ten thousand dollars. The large line of fine merchandise featured luxury items from all over the world such as Belgian carpets, Parisian dresses, Irish linens, English woolens, and cashmere shawls from Tibet, some of which sold for several thousand dollars.[941]

The store's owner, Alexander Stewart, was a self made man and one of New York's wealthiest men. He lived in a marble mansion on Fifth and Fifty-second Streets that outdid the home of his neighbor William Vanderbilt, and he owned one of America's most prestigious private art collections.[942]

There certainly was no lack of fashionable shops or dining establishments for Susie and Sarah to explore during their daily journeys to New York's shopping district. After the Civil War many other fashionable clothing emporiums sprang up along Broadway between Eighth and Twenty-third Streets. This area was known as "Ladies' Mile," and eventually Brooks

Brothers, Bonwit Teller, and Lord & Taylor were all located along this stretch. [943]

> *We spent hours at Fouper rooms~ we climbed to the highest rooms at*
> *Stewarts, we visited all the best stores on Broadway again & again~ We*
> *bought delicious little plum cakes every day at Purcell's & other good*
> *things & one day we patronized Delmonico's & tried to look calmly at the*
> *bill but we did not go there again~*[944]

Delmonico's where they stopped for lunch one day was the city's premiere restaurant. It was owned and operated by the Delmonico brothers, Charles and Lorenzo. They had opened their first establishment years before on South Williams Street right off of lower Broadway. From the start its discerning proprietors admitted only the socially elite into Delmonico's. They were so successful that by the 1850s they opened a larger place on Fifth and Fourteenth Streets with a grand ballroom.

One source indicates the price of one meal there would have fed an average family of four for a month. There is an account of a wealthy patron, trying to break into the right circles about this time, who paid ten thousand dollars to entertain seventy-two guests at Delmonico's. What the cost of the lunch Sarah and Susie ordered was is open to speculation, but apparently it was high enough to shock them[945]

> *The weather was so mild that we went out to Central Park & spent most*
> *of the day accomplishing that enterprise~ We took tea at the Rice's, in*
> *Madison Avenue & declined several invitations to dine from other friends~*
> *We felt that we could not afford time to visit when there was so much to be*
> *seen~ One dinner at Mrs Putnum's was the exception~*[946]

It was the Charles B. Rice family with whom they had tea. They were relatives of Sarah's, as well as former Portsmouth residents. Their home was located at 316 Madison Avenue in New York City.[947]

Central Park, only ten years in the making by 1871, was still expanding. Wealthy New Yorkers who wished to show European critics that Americans had a sense of civic duty and cultural refinement had founded it. It was the world's first urban landscaped park. The park, which was designed by the landscape architects Frederick Law Olmstead and Calvert Vaux, stretched out over eight hundred and forty acres right in the center of Manhattan. It was two and one-half miles long and extended from Fifty-ninth to One hundred and tenth Streets.[948]

From its inception the convention was established that this was a place where New Yorkers of all classes met and mingled on common grounds. It was also one of the few places where proper ladies and gentlemen could meet without a chaperone. Over ten thousand people could be found ice-skating on Central Park's numerous ponds on a typical winter day. Fashionable ladies, who once would have graced the Battery, now promenaded each day on the park's esplanade to the tune of some of the city's top bands. Daily the city's elite strove to outdo one another in equestrian fashions during their carriage parades or trotting races, and many of the common folk evidenced interest in equestrian activities by betting on the trotting races, which were held daily on Harlem Lane during the 1870s.[949]

It is not certain how long Sarah's visit to New York lasted, but it was probably less than a fortnight, since she and her daughter felt constrained to limit the number of social engagements they accepted in order to see the best of the city. After Dewey sailed to France, Susie and her mother took the train to Portsmouth. Sarah, with her keen eye for nature, noted that the train route was devoid of the evergreens so common to her native state.

> *A day or two after Mr Dewey sailed Susie & I took the Shore line train for home~ I went to New York by the New Haven route & I was much impressed on both routes with the absence of evergreens~ There are twice as many of those between Portsmouth & Newburyport, as I saw elsewhere on the whole trip~*[950]

When Dewey's ship arrived in France he was unable to deliver his cargo as the ports were already laden with neglected supplies. He went from there to London, and turned his ship's bounty over to a committee of American financiers who sold the cargo and used the money to aid the French.[951] Dewey spent a month in London visiting friends. He was then assigned to the Boston Naval Yard. For a while he and Susie set up housekeeping in the Back Bay section of Boston on Beacon Street.[952]

In nearby Cambridge Frank Goodwin and his wife Molly were now the parents of two young girls. Their second daughter Sarah Storer had been born the previous summer on August 1, 1870. She was named in honor of Frank's sister Sadie.

Captain Joseph Bradford was also at the Boston Naval Yard in 1871. He retired from active duty in the navy that year after he was diagnosed with heart disease. The following spring, while on a trip to South Carolina, he became quite ill and was admitted to the Naval Hospital in Norfolk, Virginia. He died there on April 14, 1872. He was forty-six years old at the time of his death.

Two weeks later a large military funeral for Captain Bradford was held at St. John's Church in Portsmouth. The local newspaper reported that his remains were escorted by a platoon of Marines who were accompanied by the Marine Corp Band. In addition a contingent of sailors from his ship, along with many relatives and friends attended the funeral. He was buried alongside his wife, Georgette, in the Goodwin family plot at Proprietor's Cemetery in Portsmouth.[953] The Goodwins raised his son Fielding, who turned ten that June.

Just days before Captain Bradford died George Dewey received a promotion to full commander.[954] He and Susie had been living at the Torpedo base in Newport, Rhode Island since the beginning of 1872. She was expecting their first child. Then at some point that fall Susan received the news that her mother was sick, and she traveled by train all by herself to Portsmouth.

> *I could write of her coming from Newport without the least preparation on learning that I was sick~ She took the train just ready to start & was with me Friday till Monday when she was obliged to go home to her husband~*
>
> *She sat on the bed with me much of the time & combed my hair, washed me & changed my clothes~ She never looked more beautiful than when she left my chamber for the last time~*[955]

Sarah may have had the flu during that last visit. She often wrote that she suffered from recurring bouts of the grippe. However, she was well enough that Christmas to travel with her husband to Newport so they could be with Susie and her husband for the holidays, as well as the birth of their first child.

George Goodwin Dewey was born on December 23, of 1872, just two days before Christmas and three days before his father's thirty-fifth birthday. Then inexplicably five days later on December 28th Susan died. It is not know if she died of complications of childbirth or typhoid fever, which was epidemic, killing several hundred people a week in Massachusetts and Rhode Island during this time.[956]

Puerperal fever was the most common cause of death during childbirth up until the twentieth century. Even though the cause of this infectious fever had been discovered in 1848, as late as the 1870s many physicians in America still refused to believe that they transmitted the germs from patient to patient. Therefore these doctors steadfastly refused to wash their hands and instruments with an antiseptic solution prior to delivery, and the deaths continued.[957]

Susan's body was returned home and buried in the Goodwin family burial grounds in Proprietor's Cemetery. One Portsmouth paper in an article titled "Sudden Death of An Estimable Lady," lamented the loss of the "beautiful and accomplished" Susan Dewey, and lauded her as "a young woman of rare beauty and grace, endowed with an amiable disposition and cheerful temperament...loved by all who knew her."

The shock to her mother was great, as it was for the rest of her family and friends. In a letter to her longtime friend, Mrs. Anna Decatur Parsons of New York written shortly afterwards, Sarah expressed her deep sorrow at the loss of her youngest daughter.

> *I would have thankfully given my life to save her. She was young, and beautiful, a power among her friends, an idol with her husband, and having everything to make life desirable The expectation of this baby completed everything. Millions of money could not have added one iota to her happiness*
>
> *I think I never knew anything like the general lamentation over her. Wherever she had lived, wherever she was known, regret and sorrow are expressed. Frank says he never heard anything like it in Boston and Cambridge except in the case of a public character.*
>
> *Oh my dear Anna what a good time we had in New York when you saw us together, and in Boston and Newport and wherever we were together she was always the leader and took charge of me and told me what I must have and do and it was my pleasure to obey. She always called me Sarah and I liked all she said and did.[958]*

George Dewey was purportedly undemonstrative in his grief. He never talked about Susan for the rest of his life, nor would he allow anyone else to talk about her in his presence. However, he had two identical ivory medallions painted with her miniature on them, and always carried one with him.[959] After Susan died Dewey concentrated all of his energies on his career. Sarah spoke of his plans for the future in the letter to her friend.

> *His friends in Washington have been very kind and considerate and*

Admiral George Dewey, hero of the Spanish American War, circa 1900.

have given him the command of the Narragansett... .

There will be a corps of scientific men which will give him pleasant companionship... It is a fine command and we are glad of anything that takes him out of his loneliness... But, oh he is so crushed...[960]

From this point in 1872 to 1875 he served on the Pacific Survey, and was appointed Lighthouse Inspector in 1876. After that he was Secretary to the Lighthouse Board of the Navy for five years, while commanding the USS *Juanita* in the Asiatic Squadron.[961]

The Goodwins raised young George Goodwin Dewey along with his two cousins, Mabel Storer and Fielding Bradford. From the start Sarah felt a special love for Susie's only child.

> *The dear baby is a fine strong child and has become the light of the house. His father is tending him by the light of the fire in my room and feels about him as you can imagine. I have a little bed in my room and on that he takes his naps by day. Mrs Munroe our precious Susie's nurse takes care of him and she is a superior person.*[962]

What little is known about his childhood was gleaned from various entries in his grandmother's common daybooks. In July of 1873 an entry noted the arrival of his first tooth, a later entry marveled at the ingenuity and entrepreneurial proclivities of this child who staged shows or circuses for the neighborhood children, charging them up to eight pins for each performance.

Sarah started writing *Pleasant Memories* in 1875 when she was seventy years old. The Goodwin household was as busy and active then, as it had been when Sarah was a much younger woman. With three year old toddler Georgie holding reign, along with Fielding and his cousin Mabel respectively thirteen and fourteen that year, Sarah needed a great deal of help.

There were four live-in servants, three females of Irish extraction and one male coachman from England in the house at that time.[963] In addition Hope and Abby lived at home. Neither worked outside of the home, and both were actively involved in raising the children of their younger sisters. The two ladies also devoted much of their time to charitable causes.

Hope had belonged to the Ladies' Charitable Society in Portsmouth for many years. This was an organization formed to aid indigent women with an aim towards the "suppression of street begging."[964] She was also involved in the Mount Vernon Society, as was her mother. In New Hampshire the regent of this organization, which was dedicated to the preservation of the home of the nation's first president, was her sister Abby Winder. [965]

Abby traveled to Washington, D.C. and New York City on many occasions according to various journal entries. Her son Willie, who graduated from Annapolis in 1873, often accompanied his mother on these trips. Not a great deal is known about Willie during his young adulthood. He graduated from Annapolis in 1873, and was a naval career officer, eventually attaining the rank of captain.[966]

It is not known if the Goodwins attended the nation's centennial celebration held in Philadelphia in 1876. Sarah made note only of attending what must have been the bi-centennial celebration of New York City in 1853.

I saw the first sewing machine made by Elias Howe at the centennial celebration in New York more than forty years ago~[967]

Elias Howe, a machinist who had worked at the Lowell Mills during the 1840s, invented this foot treadle powered machine and obtained a patent on it in 1846. Despite the exposure that was provided at this bi-centennial exhibition he did not make a lot of profit on this invention. Within a decade sewing machines were a common household item in America, and they eventually transformed the garment business. Sarah marveled at this machine and recalled the past.

Housewives did not rejoice in the sewing machine until they were safely in Heaven where they can still be glad for those who have come after them~[968]

Visitors to the nation's centennial celebration in 1876 witnessed the first demonstration of the telephone, which had been developed that year by Alexander Graham Bell. Within a year telephones were adapted for commercial usage, and by the end of the decade phone service was available in most communities across the country. But not everyone subscribed to the new service in the beginning.

Three years later in 1879 Thomas Edison succeeded in developing an incandescent light that soon replaced gaslights as the primary method of illuminating American homes and businesses. Electrical service was not available in Portsmouth until 1886.[969] Although not every home was wired for electricity at first, the Goodwin home was by 1890. Well to do families such as the Goodwins were generally the first to enjoy the benefits of these new inventions that so drastically altered American life styles.

Throughout the decade of the 1870s Ichabod Goodwin continued to be a leader in business and community affairs. Twice during this decade he was one of the town leaders who extended a hand of welcome when President Grant visited the city of Portsmouth. During his 1871 visit Grant just passed through the city on his way to a European and North American Railroad convention in Maine. His wife, daughter, and various government, military, and railroad officials accompanied him. Ichabod Goodwin was amongst the invited guests from New England who joined the party in Portsmouth. During this brief stop the President spoke to the crowd gathered at the railroad depot from the platform of the presidential train. It is likely that Sarah would have accompanied her husband on this trip, as it was her habit to attend political as well social events with him. Sarah once wrote a short treatise comparing General Grant, to that of Odysseus, the hero of the *Odyssey,* the second epic of Homer, the Greek poet.

Yesterday I was reading an account of Gen Grant's travel's around the world ~ a big book & almost more wonderful than the Arabian Night's~ Then I looked at his likeness~ Nothing remarkable perhaps & yet it is strong throughout not one fibre of weakness~ And then I noted his name Ulysses~ How strange that such a name should have been given to an infant whose manhood was to be so remarkable~

Strangely enough the man who seemed so ridiculously named away in the far west of America, who hated war & a military life, who was by nature domestic & fond of quiet was constrained by his Father's will & choice to receive a military education & after a fall, to rise to more success & honor than has fallen to the lot of any other man~...

Although war is & has been necessary yet God loves the peace maker ...Perhaps it would not be amiss here to note the blessing which follows obedience to Parents~ That good old fashioned trait so insisted on by the staunch puritans of New England was in force in the family of Jessy Grant~ Did the father regret his course when his son had saved his country~ Does the son regret it when all that the world can give of splendor & honor due him & his?[970]

Then in 1873 President Grant once again passed through the city on his way to Maine, and greeted an assembled crowd at the depot from the platform of the train. The local paper noted that during this stop ex-Governor Goodwin acted as the "medium of communication" between the President and the assemblage gathered at the station.[971]

In 1878, the year of his eighty-fourth birthday, Goodwin assumed the presidency of the First National Bank in Portsmouth. At the time he was the president of the Piscataqua Bank, as well as the Portsmouth Gas Company, and the Portsmouth Bridge Company, of which William Rice had been a founder in 1819. He held all of these positions for the remainder of his life.[972]

In addition Goodwin continued to work to benefit his community, and his family. He was instrumental in setting up the Rice Library in Kittery funded by Sarah's cousin Arabella Rice in honor of her father Robert who had died some years before. He remained as president of the Howard Benevolent Society, and in 1873 he headed a committee to organize the second Return of the Sons of Portsmouth reunion scheduled for that year's Fourth of July celebration. He had been involved in the first successful town reunion in 1853. [973] This time his son Frank, who was in charge of the Massachusetts contingent of "Portsmouth Sons," joined him. At 10 o'clock on the morning of the celebration a special thirteen-car train from Boston pulled into the railroad depot in Portsmouth, packed with festive native sons of Portsmouth headed by Frank Goodwin.[974]

Just the year before, in 1872, Frank had left the law firm of Dehon, Bryant & Goodwin to strike out on his own. He set up a practice at 30 Court Street in Boston, where he specialized in maritime and real estate law. [975] Frank and Molly continued to live with her father and mother until her father's death in 1874. Then they purchased a large Italianate style house at 20 Lowell Street, a small side street in the prestigious Brattle Street neighborhood of

Cambridge.[976]

Frank and Molly's small family continued to grow, and in June of 1877 their third daughter Eleanor was born. In the fall of the following year their son Robert was born. It can be assumed he was quite a welcome addition to this family.

FAMILY IN THE 1880s

In May of 1880, a biographical article by Frank Goodwin entitled "Hon. Ichabod Goodwin" appeared in the *Granite Monthly*. He wrote of his father's prestigious ancestral background, and his impressive rise in the world of business and politics starting with his early apprenticeship for his cousin Samuel Lord. He also recounted the story of how his father so nobly rose to the occasion at the start of the Civil War to answer his President's call for volunteers by personally raising the money needed to outfit the First and Second New Hampshire regiments. [977]

The decade of the 1880s had barely begun when two more tragic events marred the happiness of the Goodwin family. At the start of 1881 Frank and Molly's oldest daughter, Mary, was stricken with catarrhal pneumonia around the time of her thirteenth birthday on February 18th and she died eight days after her birthday. There were no antibiotics to fight this infectious disease then, and it was often fatal. She was buried in Mt. Auburn Cemetery in Cambridge, Massachusetts.[978]

The following year Ichabod Goodwin died after suffering for several weeks with an abscessed liver. He was eighty-eight years old when he died on July 4th at his Islington Street home. The local paper noted that although his death had been expected it still came as a terrible shock to his community and his family.[979]

He was active in the affairs of his adopted community right up to the end. That Memorial Day, just two months before his death, he had appeared in public for the last time at the Portsmouth Music Hall to pay homage to those New Hampshire men who died in the Civil War. When he died the local paper noted that it was somehow fitting that a man who devoted his life to the prosperity and well being of his country should die on the nation's birthday.[980]

The local newspapers lauded him for his many successful achievements in business and politics, and above all for his highly developed sense of honor and impeccable character. *The Portsmouth Chronicle* wrote:

> Notwithstanding his many public positions and posts of honor…it is in the recollections of his private life that his memory will be dearly cherished…. He was always honorable in his dealings, as he was unselfish and patriotic in his public duties…. With opinions upon political, religious, and business concerns…certain firm and decided, he respected the views of others.[981]

The Daily Evening Times wrote:

> He has been all through life, a ready friend, helper and advisor to all who have seen fit to ask his aid, full of sympathy for all in need of assistance. By the death of Ex-Gov. Goodwin the city loses one of its most respected citizens. It is a loss, which will be keenly felt by the community.[982]

The Portsmouth Journal wrote:

Gov. Goodwin had a personal magnetism, a kind of popularity, which while it gave him a strong hold upon the people of the state, was a quality frequently in demand by his political friends… His urbanity of manner, kindly disposition, generous traits, charitable acts, and the encouragement he so readily extended to the young, the inexperienced, or the unfortunate, was the trait in his character which called forth the admiration of everyone… His life for the past century identified as it has been with the best interests of Portsmouth, is the best index of his character and his departure is a loss…to our whole community.[983]

His funeral was held at the Unitarian Church that following Saturday. The Reverend James DeNormandie officiated and delivered an "eloquent eulogy," according to the local paper, and mourners filled the church to capacity. There was a large contingent of city officials, naval officers, business associates, and bank and railroad officials.

In addition three ex-governors, two ex-congressmen, the United States District Attorney from Massachusetts, and his many friends and family members were present. Business was suspended throughout the city of Portsmouth during this time, and flags were lowered to half-mast. A governor's salute of minute guns was fired in his honor from the Naval Yard that day at noon. Ichabod Goodwin was interred at the family tomb in Proprietor's Cemetery.[984]

Looking back from the perspective of more than a hundred years, one can only speculate on the devastating effect these two deaths had on the Goodwin families in both Cambridge and Portsmouth. Sarah, true to form, doesn't mention them in her journals or memoirs. She was seventy-seven years old when her husband of fifty-five years died. Her home was still a busy place filled with servants, grown children, and grandchildren.

Of her seven children only three remained. Hope and Abby were respectively fifty-two and fifty-three years old. Frank was forty-one. Most of the grandchildren living in the home were adults. Fielding was twenty, and probably finishing his education. There is no record available of where he went to school. Notations in Sarah's journals during the late 1880s indicate he was serving in some branch of the service in Montana.

His cousin Willie was thirty-one. He remained close to his mother. He may have been married by this time, but there is no extant record available of when he married or his wife's name, nor is it recorded in the family Bible. That fall Mabel celebrated the twenty-first anniversary of her birth out on the prairie. Two years later she married Stephen Decatur 1V of Boston on the 30th of December 1884. Mr. Gooding, the Pastor of the Unitarian Church performed the ceremony. It is not known if it was a church or home wedding. Also it is not known if her father, listed on the marriage certificate as a "stock raiser," was present at the ceremony. [985]

Mabel was twenty-three and her husband was twenty-nine at the time of their marriage. He had entered the Naval Academy at Annapolis in 1870, but resigned as a midshipman in 1872. Afterward he attended the Massachusetts Institute of Technology graduating from there in 1877.[986] His parents Commodore Stephen Decatur III and his wife, Anna Philbrick, of Boston were friends of the Goodwins.

Stephen came from a long line of naval heroes. The most famous one was his great uncle, Commander Stephen Decatur II of Maryland, who gained fame at the turn of the century while protecting American merchant ships from the Barbary pirates. He again gained recognition at Tripoli when he successfully led an expedition into enemy territory to burn the frigate USS *Philadelphia*, after it was captured.[987]

Decatur fought with distinction during the War of 1812, and was immortalized for his famous words spoken in response to a toast while celebrating a successful battle in 1815, "Our country! May she always be right; but our country right or wrong."[988] This famous ancestor was killed in a duel in 1820. He left no heirs, but his name was passed down through successive generations of his brother's descendents. Mabel's husband, a second son, was originally named William Beverly, but this was changed to Stephen after his only two brothers died as children.[989]

Stephen and Mabel settled into a home on Middle Street in Portsmouth not far from the Goodwin home. Within the first four years of their marriage Mabel gave birth to two sons. Stephen Decatur V was born on April 10, 1886, and his brother Storer two years later on April 9th.

George Goodwin Dewey was ten when his grandfather died. His own father seldom visited the Goodwin home when he was young. He did provide a generous allowance of $1,500 a year to pay for a "gentleman's education" for young George at the prestigious St. Paul's School in Concord, New Hampshire, once he was in high school. One Dewey biographer wrote that his son once claimed that if he ever saw his father on the street then, he was sure he wouldn't have recognized him.[990]

Records in both the Cambridge and Boston directories indicate that Frank left his family soon after his oldest daughter died. He first moved to a room in a tall gray granite and marble building at 11 Beacon Street. It was near the top of Boston Common directly across from the

George Goodwin Dewey, circa 1890s. Son of Admiral George Dewey and his first wife Susan Goodwin Dewey.

prestigious Boston Athenaeum. On one side of his boarding house was Charles Bullfinch's gold domed State House Capitol, and right down the street was the historic King's Chapel and Parker's Hotel. The city registry indicates he remained at this location for ten years, and then moved two blocks away to 103 Beacon nearer Boston Gardens, for the next ten years.

Frank was in good company in the Beacon Hill neighborhood, as some of Boston's most elite citizens lived nearby during these years. Dr. Oliver Wendell Holmes, John Greenleaf Whittier and Louisa May Alcott were all his neighbors. He also moved his law practice to a one-room office, within easy walking distance of his boarding room. This new office was located in a large office building next to Boston's Old State Capitol.

Molly and children remained in Cambridge for several more years. Then in 1886

Molly moved the children to Concord, Massachusetts soon after her own mother died. She remained there the rest of her life.

That same year Frank began working part time at the Boston University School of Law. Over the years Frank became well known in Boston as a lecturer, and writer noted for his expertise in the fields of maritime and real estate law. He was eventually made a full professor of real estate law at the university.[991] However, he retained his small private practice on State Street for many years.

Sarah and Molly corresponded through the years. The children saw their father when arrangements could be made for visits.

> *Saturday Nov...I want to see Eleanor~ Can't she come for a week~ Dear love to her & Robert & yourself from us all~ Ever yours Sarah PR Goodwin*[992]

> *June 1889~ On Monday we expect Molly & her children to spend a fortnight with us~*

> *May 22 1895~...I learn from Mary Goodwin that dear Sadie has a cold~ She must make haste & get well~ Her father & we are very impatient to see her~*[993]

The first of these notations is undated. Eleanor, the youngest of Frank's daughters, would have been living at home at the time of this notation, as she was just nineteen when her Grandmother died a year later. By 1889 her older sister Sadie was attending Smith College in Boston. She graduated from there in 1892, and by 1895 she was teaching at the Gilman School in Cambridge.[994]

Sarah continued to write in her journal throughout her life. It is not known just when she finished her memoirs. The last family event she recorded in the original *Pleasant Memories* was the story of her trip to New York with Susie.

GOODWIN PARK

One important event in the life of the whole family easily traced in Sarah's journals, town records, and newspapers was the founding of Goodwin Park in the field across the street from the Goodwin home. This park, along with the war memorial in its center, was established to honor the memory of the New Hampshire men who lost their lives in the Civil War, as well as the governor that first readied them for battle. It was dedicated on July 4, 1888 six years to the day after Ichabod Goodwin died.

This project from conception to completion generated a good deal of excitement in the town, as well as in the family. Preparations for the park and memorial began in the spring of 1886, two years before it became a reality. During this time, and even two decades prior to it, there was a movement underway in America to beautify cities by setting aside portions of land for public parks.

England had long been famous for her many beautiful public parks, and by the 1860s Americans, led by such men as Frederick Law Olmstead, began to emulate the civic pride, refinement, and taste demonstrated by their English cousins by establishing their own public parks in the midst of most large American cities. This beautification movement was the major impetus behind the development of Central Park in New York City.[995]

In Portsmouth, as well as other small cities throughout the country, the drive to establish public parks for the benefit of all took a little longer to catch on, and when it did it was in a much smaller way. By the fourth quarter of the century several public parks opened in Portsmouth. The five-acre Langdon Park near South Mill Pond was first established in 1876, a number of years after a civic-minded citizen left it to the community for that purpose. When it was dedicated, Ichabod Goodwin was one of many prominent men who spoke at the official dedication.[996]

There was also a movement about this time to honor the men who fought in the Civil War. More than twenty years after it had ended, many looked back nostalgically upon the war years. Others gratefully recognized the many sacrifices made by their fellow countrymen who fought to preserve the Union for all Americans. In both the North and the South, citizens began to erect statues and dedicate parks to honor these men.

Portsmouth was no exception. It was April of 1886, when Mayor Marcellus Eldredge, owner of the Eldredge Brewing of Portsmouth, first approached the members of the Storer Post Grand Army of the Republic with a proposal for a Civil War memorial and park. He asked them to raise $2,000 of the sum needed for a memorial, and gave his personal pledge to provide the remainder.

Within a short time a public meeting was called, and twenty-five men in the community responded to help raise funds for this project. Some of these men had fought in the war; others had paid for substitutes or were too young to have fought. At least one had fought for the Confederacy, but all were in agreement that a memorial was needed. Workers from Eldredge Brewery started the fund rolling with a total contribution of eighty-one dollars.[997]

By September the fund was high enough to warrant the formation of a search committee to look for a park site. That following February Mayor Eldredge announced that his family would donate the Goodwin field for the memorial once the monument fund reached five thousand dollars. He stipulated this arrangement was pending upon the city's agreement to maintain the site as a park forever.

He had approached Sarah earlier and presented his proposal for a memorial park in her field. She had liked the idea, and arranged for him to meet with the executors of her husband's estate to negotiate the terms of the sale. This was contingent on the city's agreement to honor her stipulations concerning the care and future use of the field. By April of 1877 everything was in place.

> *Sale of the field to Mr Eldridge on Saturday May 14, 1887~ We hope that Mr Eldridge will present it to the city on Memorial Day~ The field is sold to Mr Eldridge on the condition that he gives it to the city as a possession forever~*
>
> *By the terms of occupation of the Park by the City no building or studio of any kind what ever can be erected on it, or ever impinge on its border~*
>
> *May 17th The field resplendent in green & gold~ No longer mine but mine always to enjoy~ We came here in 1832 ~ fifty~six years ago~ Trees planted in 1834~ We bought & planted in faith & hope~*[998]

Sarah loved the field across the street from her home. Most of all she loved the trees and flowers she viewed from her chamber window each day. Many of her journal entries from this time indicate she was concerned about the fate of these trees.

> *May 21, 1887 The apple & pear trees are in bloom & pyrus Japonica in all its glory~ I have never seen it handsomer~ The daffys are gone but the snow drops are abundant & the forget me nots are very bright~ The stout currant in bloom~ The lilacs not fully out yet~ Dandelions glorious in the field~ I wonder if the city will tolerate them~* [999]

In June of that year the finance committee was still short of their goal, and it was determined to solicit former residents in nearby Boston for help. However, plans for the memorial were all in place by then.

> *June 29, 1887~ Mr Eldridge came in last evening to tell us about the decisions of the Committee on the Soldiers & Sailors monument~ It is to be of white bronze, 42 feet high, base 12 1/2 feet square~ Two figures a sailor & soldier, each six feet high~ At the top a figure of the Goddess of Liberty, eight feet high ~ also a medallion~*
>
> *Mr Eldrich is as kind & courteous as possible & is disposed to spare the trees & especially the apple tree~ I suggested a Norway spruce hedge against the Adams fence & also between the trees near the Haliburton place~ He seemed to be pleased~*[1000]

By July of 1887 the goal had been met and surpassed by five hundred dollars. Small contributions along with a very generous donation of one thousand dollars from Frank Jones, former mayor and owner of Frank Jones Brewery, as well as many other businesses in town put them over the top. From her journal entries about this time it is clear Sarah was pleased by the plans for the park and memorial, but felt nostalgic about the field.

An apple tree from the Old Assembly House on Raitt Street stands near the entrance to the field~

July 1887~ I have been recalling the years past as associated with the field~ We had croquet there after dear Georgie died, when Mr Bartlett of Concord, Mass came so opportunely & taught Hope & the others to play the game~

We had tennis there when Fielding & Mabel & their friends played with poor L___ now so ruined~ Another year will probably bring the monument & the field will be a park "Goodwin Park"~

Could my husband be more pleased than by the arrangement made in this thing? It is just about what my heart craved~ A good neighbor has done it with the cooperation of executors, for which I am profoundly grateful ~ 1889[1001]

In October of 1887 the field was graded and by the following spring work was fully underway. The dedication was planned for the coming July Fourth. Sarah tracked the progression of the Park from her window, and recorded her daily thoughts on its development in her journal.

I have no end of amusement in looking out the windows at the works in the park~ Hundreds & hundreds of loads of stone & earth brought in in carts~ It is to be graded on every side from the foundation of the monument to a level with the street~[1002]

The historic apple tree was one that had once stood in the yard of the Assembly House during her youth. Mr. Raitt presented it to the Goodwins when the hall was cut in half in 1838, and they in turn had planted it at the edge of the field. Although Sarah was pleased about the park her agony over the fate of the plants and trees continued.

I rejoice in the park & its name, but I am anxious about the trees~ I hope that those that remain will be spared many, many years~ The larch so much in advance of other trees in the early spring, I am afraid it is doomed~

Oh my historic apple tree! The neighbors too mourn its loss~ No more blossoms~

There are some men so ignorant & destitute of all sentiment or good taste that nothing pleases them better than to hack a fine tree to pieces or cut it down altogether~

I am so thankful Mr Eldridge is putting rock maples into the park~[1003]

There was a great deal of activity in town prior to the dedication. To encourage a large attendance, deals were cut with the railroads to lower their prices to as little as a penny a mile. Forty bands and drum corps were engaged for a parade, and plans were made to provide a full day of activities and entertainments.[1004]

This is the 18th of June a perfect day & indeed the whole month so far has been perfectly beautiful~ The blossoms & flowers have not been spoiled by wind or rain & their beauty has lasted wonderfully~ The filling up is steadily going on in the park & I trust all the monument & all the doings on the fourth will be a success~[1005]

The morning of July 4, 1888, finally arrived. Everything was in place. The weather was bright and fair that morning offering the prospect of a nearly cloudless day. Homes and businesses throughout the city were festooned with red, white, and blue bunting, banners, and flags. The city was in a festive mood that day.

According to the local newspaper crowds began to assemble near the railroad station early in the morning, and before it was over, an estimated five thousand visitors joined in with the townspeople to view the scheduled parade. At nine o'clock memorial and parade organizers, accompanied by contingents of marines, met at the railroad station to await the arrival of several out of town trains bringing more visitors and dignitaries to Portsmouth for the celebration. Unfortunately, many of the railroads ran behind schedule on that national holiday, some more than an hour. Because of this delay Governor Sawyer and his staff were unable to wait for the dedication, and they left Portsmouth before it began to attend an Independence Day ceremony at Amesbury, Massachusetts.[1006]Finally at noon the last scheduled train arrived. According to the local paper an "immense throng," of marchers was assembled and the "splendid procession" got underway shortly after this. The reporter noted that a large number of "battle-scarred" veterans marched with the Grand Army Corps. Several one armed veterans, and at least one veteran with a wooden leg marched the whole of the route, as did a man who was totally blind. He was guided by two of his comrades, who marched alongside him, their fingers interlocked with his. The reporter, impressed by the sublime heroism showed by these men, cited them as fine representatives of all the men who fought for their country during the Civil War.

Three companies of naval men and a battalion of marines followed the veterans. The fire department was there as well. It is reported that they were smartly dressed, and brought along their fire fighting machines, which were decorated for the occasion. The local police, and many other civic, charitable, and business organizations were also prominent in their finest dress.[1007]

At two that afternoon the parade arrived at the field across from Sarah's home to dedicate it in perpetuity as Goodwin Park, in honor of her husband and the many sailors and soldiers of New Hampshire who lost their lives in the nation's war between the North and the South. From all accounts it was a very patriotic ceremony.

The Misses Fei-Fi Sinclair and Sadie Eldrich unveiled the monument. At first the covering became snagged on one of the figures, but a retired seaman who climbed up to unhook the cloth quickly corrected this. The crowd cheered his gallantry, and then cheered again at the sight of the imposing monument. The entire monument reached a height of forty-two and a half feet. Top and center was "Lady Liberty," nearly nine feet high. She gazed benevolently down from her pedestal upon the crowd assembled beneath her with her right arm extended outward bestowing a laurel wreath in a gesture of reconciliation, while her left hand remained firmly clasped to a sheathed sword and shield by her side.

The Goodwin Park Civil War Memorial as it looks today.

On each side of this imposing figure were two life-sized figures, one of a soldier and one of a sailor. There were many other patriotic symbols on the monument, which was inscribed with the names of the battles in which New Hampshire men fought. On one side of the lower die a bas-relief of the USS *Kearsarge*, with a mounted Parrott gun aimed directly at the rebel ship *Alabama,* recalled one of the Portsmouth's finest moments of the war. On the front of the upper die, facing in the direction of the Goodwin house was a medallion, embossed with the image of ex-Governor Goodwin. Behind this was a similar medallion of President Lincoln.[1008]

> *July 11, 1888~ The monument is finished & it is finer than I had dared hope~ Mr Goodwin's likeness is good but looks older than he looked when he raised the regiment for the war~ It was copied from a photograph taken after he was eighty years old~*[1009]

Former Mayor Marcellus Eldredge officially presented the monument to Mayor George Hodgdon. Many speeches followed, the dedicatory ones being by the heads of the Grand Army and the guard of honor from Storer post.[1010] A chorus made up of eight hundred school children from all over the state singing the "Star Spangled Banner followed the presentation. Then the children's chorus sang "America" following an address by Judge Charles Levi Woodbury. The First Regiment of Manchester accompanied them.

After the benediction was given and the official dedication was complete, the procession left Islington Street and marched down state to Court Street where a collation was set up under a tent. There was also a band concert at this site. Both events were successful, and a "sympathetic" rendition of "Home Sweet Home," by the Highland Band of Lake Village created a perfect ending to the day's activities. [1011]

There was also great excitement over the opening of the park across the street at the Goodwin home. Many friends and family members were there to celebrate the dedication of the park, and memorial.

> *The hubbub is over~ The monument was dedicated on the 4th of July~ Charles Levi Woodbury gave an ovation in the park~ Thousands of people came from abroad~ Military companies, bands of music & children singing*

the "Star Spangled banner~"

Here in the house a large number of friends came to view the show from the windows & many remained to lunch with us~ We had lemonade & ice cream on the piazza & more solid refreshments in the dining room~

The whole thing was a success & everybody seems delighted with the monument~ Between it & my window there is a draping of larch & apple, it suggests to me "tears for the brave"~

Only Fielding & dear little Eleanor were absent~ All the other children & grandchildren were with us~ Dear Fielding was a long way off in Montana ~ he stayed away at the call of duty~ Fielding is all right & has all the fine traits & qualities that go to make up a man~[1012]

There is no mention of family members speaking at the ceremony in the newspaper account of the day. Nor do Sarah's journal entries indicate that they were present at the dedication. Rather it seems the family remained in the background, discreetly viewing the proceedings from the piazza across the street. However, it is likely Frank Goodwin attended the ceremony to represent his family. The grandchildren may have also been at the dedication or joined in the town activities that followed.

That evening there were fireworks in Langdon Park, with ten set pieces of pyrotechnic displays. The paper reported that in between the lighting of these pieces, there were "liberal & handsome" displays of owl lights, rockets, mines, shells, mountains, fountains, and water-serpents. The paper noted the water-serpents got the biggest share of the laughter and applause.[1013]

An illuminated boat race on South Mill Pond was hampered somewhat by high winds that extinguished some of the boat lanterns. The addition of three musicians from the Highland Band to the front boat lent a festive touch to the overall effect, and compensated for the problems with illumination.[1014] Finally the day came to an end, and it was agreed by all that it had been a success.

The paper reported there was less drunkenness than usual, and this must have pleased Sarah, as she disapproved of drinking to excess. In the months following the dedication, Sarah continued to oversee Goodwin Park from the prospect of her chamber window. A part of her still looked out over the field of the past, where she had planted trees and flowers more than fifty years before. They were gone, but she found comfort in their memory, and viewed the park as a triumph to her husband's memory.

The splendid dandelions are gone forever & the buttercups & the daisies & the scythes & the mowers & the swath & the haystacks & the load of hay on its way to the stable~ All gone ~ thank heaven we have the Memory left & a few big trees to brighten the Autumn~

But it is well~ It is best I am thankful~ The monument is beautiful & appropriate & I am thankful for that too~[1015]

It was fortunate that the day of the dedication had been bright and fair, because Sarah described an unusual amount of rain that summer and fall, which created havoc in the new park turning the grounds into mud.

I have been waiting for a chance to visit the park & enjoy the glorious trees but the mud has been so forbidding that I had to give it up for the present~ If I had not obeyed an impulse & gone over to see the monument the day it was finished~ I could not have gone since for I have had three months of whooping cough & now the mud~

Well I have enjoyed it all from my windows~ The crowning figure of the monument & the likeness of my husband are always looking this way~ Next year if I live I shall see the park beautifully green~[1016]

Throughout the winter and early spring she enjoyed watching children play in the park. However, she despaired of less desirable visitors who failed to respect the park and the trees Sarah so loved.

Jan 29 1889~ How pleasant it is to see the children with their sleds & double runners having such a good time in the Park~ I hope those elevations in the Southern corners will be allowed to remain, they diversify the scene & take off the flatness & for the children's sake also~

May 1889~ the dear larch is dead~ It took a brilliant leave last March~ such a show of the brightest green I have rarely seen except in the horse chestnut, and it was the only green thing to be seen anywhere~

When the clods were piled on John barleycorn, & sun & showers had access to it, it came up in spite of them, but too many clods were too much for the larch~

Well if they will only not kill the great elm & the beech, which stands in such full relief against the church, I will be most thankful~[1017]

John Barleycorn being a nineteenth century euphemism for alcohol indicates she blamed the death of the larch tree on people drinking in the park. Unfortunately even then public parks, designed to benefit all of the people, often attracted an element of people whose lack of respect for the park took away much of its beauty and enjoyment from others.

It has been my great desire that I should live to see the park green & great trees in their glory~ I took advantage of the beautiful summer evening twilight & walked all around, but best of all is the view from my own house~[1018]

Sarah also had a beautiful view from her back window that overlooked her beloved Tanglewood and she derived great pleasure in the contrast the two views provided.

July 30th 1890~ Went into the garden today leaning on Willie's arms~ The Hollyhocks looked lovely~ Tanglewood is as great a contrast to the park as could possibly be found~ On one the grass is scraped away to the bare ground, in the other nature has it's own sweet way & trees & grass & shrub indulge in the wildest luxuriance~ I look out into a forest from my back window & my grove is like the deep wood~ Thank God for Tanglewood~[1019]

For the rest of her life Sarah derived much pleasure from overseeing the park from the widened prospect of her chamber window. She also derived a certain amount of satisfaction in knowing that Goodwin Park would always exist as a quiet reminder of the nation's Civil War heroes and her husband.

The departure of three apple trees has caused me many a heartache but a wider prospect is opened to me & I wouldn't have them back~

It is a great comfort to feel that the field will always be kept open~ It will depend on what kind of city government we have in the future, whether the trees will be protected & the grounds kept in order~[1020]

19ᵗʰ CENTURY
SOCIAL AND RELIGIOUS REFORM

A lot is now known about the family and important events in Sarah's life, but it isn't always clear what she thought about important issues of her day. However, there are entries in her journals that make note of a number of social and religious movements, which began in the nineteenth century and helped to shape the way many Americans viewed their world.

As early as the 1830s there was a strong temperance movement in the country. Groups, which called themselves the Sons or Daughters of Temperance, were formed all over the country. They held rallies and conventions where the speakers railed against the evils of drink. Both male and female temperance activists believed that most of the problems in society including poverty, crime, and wife and child abuse were caused by the consumption of alcohol.

At about the same period of time many were starting to speak out particularly in the northern states against the evils of slavery. These people became known as abolitionists. By 1834 there was an anti-slavery movement in New Hampshire, but even when so eminent a personage as the Quaker poet John Greenleaf Whittier spoke out against slavery on the steps of the State House in Concord, he was assaulted by an angry mob. New Hampshire did not actually come together as an abolitionist state until 1846.[1021]

The women's rights movement arose about mid-century, and to many women and men it seemed to be the most outrageous and unlikely movement of all. A woman's place within the sphere of the home was considered to be a somewhat sacred haven, where privileged women of the upper classes were put on a pedestal far removed from the everyday happenings in society. However, from its inception the movement attracted a good sized following of these same upper class women, as well as a handful of liberal men who sought to lead them.

About mid-century transcendentalism, a new school of thought that blended religious thought with a reverence for nature into a new uniquely poetic world-view developed quite a following. Spiritualism and the Theosophical movement both came into fashion in the latter half of the century, as did an animal rights movement, pacifist beliefs, and a new temperance movement that resurged in the last half of the century under the banner of the Women's Christian Temperance Union. In addition there were many other movements during the nineteenth century dedicated to social reform in the home, school, health, religious, political, and work arenas throughout the country.

There is no documentation that Sarah was an active disciple of any of these popular movements. However, some speculation can be made about her beliefs on the basis of the friendships, which she and her husband formed, as well as their involvement in various social, political, or religious groups. Most of these assumptions are based on pure conjecture, but some sense of her interest in, or support of, certain schools of thought can be gleaned from journal notes written during the latter part of her life.

One subject in which Sarah clearly expressed a strong interest was women suffrage. The nineteenth century women's movement officially started in the summer of 1848 in Seneca Falls, New York. At that time a handful of concerned women decided to hold a convention to protest the country's inequitable laws pertaining to women's civil and social rights. Up until then any property or inheritance left to a woman was legally under the full jurisdiction of her husband, and he could sell or dispose of it as he saw fit. Married women could not sign legal documents, or buy or sell their own property, and it was almost impossible for the average woman to obtain a proper education or employment outside of the home. In addition women were kept from participation in the democratic process, because they were denied the right to vote and to run for political office.

In an attempt to address this myriad of complaints, Elizabeth Cady Stanton, the wife of Henry Stanton a well-known abolitionist, and Lucretia Mott, a Quaker minister, along with three other women drew up a platform for their convention based on the Declaration of Independence. They named this a Declaration of Sentiments, and closely followed the wording of the original document inserting the word "women" in key places, and listing a series of resolutions that addressed women's needs. The ninth resolution called for women to work towards the legal right to vote.

Although the convention was pulled together within less than a week's time, it attracted three hundred women along with forty men, who traveled to New York by horse drawn carriages and wagons to participate in a day long rally of speeches and debates. In the end they voted for and passed all of the resolutions. Yet if it hadn't been for an impassioned speech in its favor by Frederick Douglas, a former slave and prominent abolitionist leader, the ninth resolution probably wouldn't have been passed. Even at the women's rights convention the issue of women's suffrage was considered almost too bold and shocking to consider.[1022]

The movement continued to grow, as many more women became aware of the need for legal and social reform. Susan B Anthony, a Quaker activist who had worked for the abolition and temperance movements, joined these women a few years later, and soon became one of the movement's primary leaders. She worked alongside Elizabeth Cady Stanton, and together these two women devoted the remainder of their lives to this cause. However, there were then, as there always are, a certain percentage of women, who were content with the status quo. They shunned these women and viewed their policies as dangerously radical. Sarah was not one of them. She apparently agreed with the need for reform. By the time she recorded her personal sentiments on this issue in her journals, women had achieved significant victories since their first meeting in Seneca Falls. One woman had declared herself a candidate for the office of the President of the United States, and a few western territories had granted women suffrage as early as 1869.

There were two petitions put before the New Hampshire legislature that same year to extend voting rights to their female constituents, and another petition to abolish all marriage laws in New Hampshire.[1023] All of these petitions failed. Women had come a long way by this time, but not as far as they needed to go. Sarah noted these changes in her journal, and expressed her anger at prevailing laws that kept women from achieving nationwide suffrage.

> *In three territories Washington, Wyoming, Utah Women's suffrage is an accomplishment~*

> *The judiciary committee in New Hampshire House July 13, 1887 reported favorably a bill conferring municipal suffrage on women & permitting them to hold municipal offices!!!~*

Women's service in private matters is invaluable~ What are public matters but private matters in the wholesale?

The... symbol of moral power... the Declaration of Independence was intended to cover the whole human race~

The constitution of the United States was not intended for men only, but for the whole people~ A man's right to vote is not measured by his muscle~

Women are in the majority in Massachusetts & yet a single man with a ballot in his hand outweighs them all politically~

Taxation without representation was the cause of the Revolution~ Women have as much interest in the organization of the government under which their children are to live as men~

I think it is the mission of women to lift man (in the great future) out of the bestial condition in which he mostly lives~[1024]

Sarah's station in life had provided her with many more comforts and privileges than the majority of women enjoyed. She was aware of this, and felt a sympathetic tie to the plight of the average woman who worked long and hard to benefit her family, yet had no real control over her own life or of her children's. At the time it was practically impossible for a woman to obtain a divorce or be granted custody of her own children no matter how cruel or unjust the husband. In fact it was not unusual for men, especially upper class men, to institutionalize uppity wives in mental institutions if they threatened to leave the marriage or expose their husband's questionable activities in other areas.

A woman in the "Forum" writes of the condition of married women in relation to money~ She thinks that the withholding of money on the part of the husband is owing to a supposed irresponsibleness on the part of the wife~ I do not think so~

The average man will secure in one person all that he needs for his comfort~ A woman ~ a wife ~ a mother for his children ~ a nurse ~ a maker & mender ~ a housekeeper ~ a filler of breaches & all this for some shelter & some clothing~

He pays his cook three or four dollars a week & he pays other servants because they are free & can at anytime leave, but the wife is a slave & a pensioner & must take what she can get~

Men fall in love & are ready to promise all but wait a few years~[1025]

This diatribe against the state of married women was followed by an explanation that Sarah's beliefs applied mainly to working class women. Many of the founders of the

Women's Suffrage Movement, including Mrs. Stanton and Susan Anthony, became involved in the temperance movement popular during the first half of the century, as well as the abolitionist movement that came to full force in the North sometime during the 1850s. It continued until former slaves were guaranteed freedom, citizenship, and the right to suffrage under the 13th, 14th, and 15th amendments in the 1860s and 1870s. [1026]

Sarah made little mention of temperance. There was a newspaper article amongst her papers that featured Miss Frances Willard, leader of the Women's Christian Temperance Union, which she apparently clipped out and tucked inside her journal. It is quite possible Frances Willard was a relation to her former teacher Mary Willard, and therefore the reason Sarah had saved the article. Sarah wrote of serving champagne at social gatherings as late as the 1870s, indicating she was not against drinking in moderation in the earlier years. However, a few journal notes written in her later years give the impression that she grew decidedly anti-alcohol in her outlook as she got older.

> *One of the greatest accomplishments a man can have is the power to say no! It will save him from extravagance, from degradation, of every kind & from drink~ When the rum is in the man is out~*
>
> *From fermented & distilled cereal & fruits & perhaps from other things we get alcohol~ From alcohol come evils~ What a world we should have if there was no alcohol~*[1027]

A certain amount of speculation can be made that Sarah was in favor of both temperance and abolition, at least when she was older, based on both family friendships and her associations as well as those of her husband. For the most part the Goodwins presented as one mind in political thought, and it is likely that they also agreed on social issues. Like most people during this time their outlook on these issues probably evolved through the years as the need for social reform became more pronounced.

There are indications that Ichabod Goodwin was at some point a temperance man, as was his political associate and friend, Salmon Chase, and his close friend and business partner Samuel Coues. In general members of the Whig party were interested in progressive and moral reform. Chase was also a prominent leader in the abolitionist movement. Coues' viewpoints on abolition are not known, but he was of a liberal mindset, and was once president of the American Peace Society.

An early letter written to Ichabod Goodwin in 1832, by his brother Daniel, a schoolteacher from Hallowell, Maine was not supportive of the viewpoint of William Lloyd Garrison, one of the first and most radical leaders of the abolitionist movements. Daniel's thinking on abolition during the 1830s was not uncommon in the North.

> *That wild enthusiast of a Garrison from Boston has been about here for the last week ~ scattering firebrands, arrows & death. It is inexplicable such a headstrong fanatic should make so much impression upon the minds of sober men. He pours forth all the vials of his wrath against the Colonization Society calling its members a set of kidnapers & purveyors of human blood ~ he denominates it as a compact between honest men & thieves and denounces it in the most unmeasured terms. He thinks a*

> *slaveholder, under any circumstances whatever even of apparent necessity,*
> *to be nothing better than a murderer ~ a daily murderer. He denounced the*
> *constitution of the U.S. as a standing disgrace to N.E. as it is a compact*
> *with slaveholders. He would have all 2,000,000 slaves of the south cut*
> *loose at once without further ceremony and if not set free ~ stirred up to*
> *insurrection and yet with all these doctrines he carries a majority of the*
> *people here with him~*[1028]

It isn't known if Ichabod Goodwin concurred with his brother's sentiments, but it is known that he favored the emancipation of the slaves by the time he was elected governor. He was the first governor in New Hampshire to address the underlying immorality inherent in slavery. Sarah never directly expressed her opinion about slavery other than to note that Dinah and Boston, her grandmother's slaves, were both wonderful people whom she considered members of the Rice family.

Although Sarah was raised as a Congregationalist, she joined the Unitarian Church when she married in 1827, and was a faithful member of the congregation for the remainder of her life. Her journal notes indicate she was a spiritual seeker throughout her life intent on learning as much as she could about all religions.

> *Cabala that which is received by tradition~ An ancient Jewish system of*
> *philosophy of Theosophy~ The Cabala attempted to explain the return of*
> *God & the Universe~*
>
> *His Holiness Pope Leo 13th~ The Pope's life is very quiet & frugal &*
> *simple~ He is mostly alone~ His breakfast is coffee & a biscuit about*
> *eleven he has a light broth~*
>
> *There are three modes of faith in Japan~ Buddhism ~ Confucianism &*
> *Shintoism~ The latter recognizes spirits in human shape in earth & air~ It*
> *is somewhat akin to Spiritualism~*
>
> *Buddhism teaches reincarnation not annihilation~ Pantheism elimination*
> *from nature~*[1029]

Transcendentalism was a philosophical school of thought more than a religion that was started by a group of New England writers during the 1830s, and it was quite popular amongst liberal thinkers for a number of years. Although these writers were loosely formed with no real organization, their leader was Ralph Waldo Emerson, a Unitarian Minister from Concord, Massachusetts, and other prominent Unitarian Ministers such as Theodore Parker in Boston were also advocates.

The transcendentalists taught that all individuals, women as well as men, were equally worthy. They believed in an over-soul of creative energy that existed along side the material world, and that this was in reach of everyone who called upon their intuitive powers to transcend the material world. Emerson once compared this state of transcendence to being born into a "living poem."

Sarah never specifically referred to transcendentalism in her notes. Yet she listed many of the books written by transcendentalists amongst her favorites. She also admired the works of an earlier poet, whose philosophies on the spirit world of nature mirrored her own and those of the group of New England writers that lived many years later.

> *Wordsworth first among the poets of the day aimed not only to describe but interpret nature~ By constant communication with her forms & varying aspects he came at last to see that She was spiritually alive, and that his own soul was not only touched & inspired by intently viewing her eternal shows & appearance, but that the soul animating nature was akin to his own, and that if "the discerning intellect of man were wedded to this goodly universe in live & holy passion the Fantastic dreams of the old mythological poets would be more than realized, would indeed be a simple produce of the common day"~*[1030]

Sarah once entertained one of Emerson's friends and a fellow transcendentalist in her home. He was Father Edward Taylor, an Irish sailor and self-educated poet/philosopher, who served as pastor at the seamen's bethel in Boston for over forty years. Emerson once described him as a "Beautiful philanthropist! Godly poet! The Shakespeare of the sailor and the poor." Father Taylor was also the model for Melville's Father Maple, in his classic novel *Moby Dick.*[1031]

> *A notice of Father Taylor in an old "Century" reminds me so forcibly of a visit we had from him & the impression he made on me I feel constrained to make a note of it~*
>
> *He had been lecturing me in favor of establishing a ministry for the poor & staid with us~ He had had no supper & ours had been waiting for him from seven to ten~ He & my husband & I sat over the table until two in the morning & he was to leave in the seven o'clock train~*
>
> *Oh what a talk we had! He asked me why I did not speak in meeting & raised his eyes in contempt when I told him I had not been brought up to do so~*
>
> *We had finished breakfast & the carriage was at the door when Father Taylor said "I cannot leave without praying for you" & he fell upon his knees in prayer & such a prayer! I have never heard the equal of it! Then he & my husband drove to the station, but the train had just started~*
>
> *As soon as he returned he said "Now Sister Goodwin sit right down here with me & let us have a talk~ So we sat down by the fire & talked until eleven when he left for Boston~ That visit was one of the most remarkable events of my life~*[1032]

Sarah read up on various religions, and often copied down interesting facts pertaining to her readings. Her journals contain quite a few comments on the lives and habits of holy men living in Tibetan monasteries, as well as Buddhist monks and Quakers. These religious groups were similar to each other inasmuch as they were grounded upon a belief in pacifism. She was also intrigued by the pacifist philosophy of the famous Russia novelist Count Leo Tolstoy. She had read his book *My Religion,* which along with its companion volume *The Kingdom of God is Within*, promulgated his belief that the societal rule that demands an "eye for an eye," by which the majority of the world has lived for centuries, was futile and ultimately led only to an endless round of killing, war, and death. In his writings he called for Christians and all people of faith to practice a policy of non-resistance citing Christ's command at the Sermon on the Mount to not resist evil.

> *The corner stone of Tolstoi's religious & social philosophy is non~resistance to evil ~ cease from anger & forsake wrath ~ fret not thyself in any wise to do evil~*

> *Bible ~ retaliation is a germ from which springs broad coils, never ending still beginning~*

> *Oh people are so fragmented what a Herculean task to make a Christian out of anybody~*

> *These Christian ministers, divines they call themselves, like to be made a DD & LLD, very unlike their master~*

> *Christ came to us as an ideal & illustrated it in his person~ When will this wicked world reach that idea "The end of all things is a moral end~ "*[1033]

Two other philosophical movements in which Sarah expressed an interest were spiritualism and Theosophy. Both of these were quite popular during the latter part of the nineteenth century. The two movements shared certain commonalties. For one thing each school of thought challenged prevailing male dominated theological teachings. A large percentage of the leaders in both of these movements were female.

This came about because women were traditionally the caretakers of society, and were therefore thought to be innately more sensitive, compassionate, and spiritual than men. Thus they were considered inherently superior in spiritual matters. Many of these women conducted séances in the privacy of their homes, a place that was considered sacred during Victorian times.

> *Only the privacy of the home or the retirement to ones own room is certain to ensure a genuine* [spiritualist] *communication with some exceptions~*[1034]

However, some women spiritualists conducted séances at larger gatherings. Although women were not accustomed to speaking out in public, as spiritualists they were able to speak in public, because they thought of themselves as instruments of God through which authentic communications from the spiritual realm were channeled. This validated and empowered them. The messages they received were generally filled with loving and seemingly authentic advice purportedly from departed souls, and brought comfort to the relatives and friends.

Spiritualism~

I cannot reconcile consistent lying with consistent beneficence~ spirits come to us to say I am your father, your mother, or some other dear departed friend, whom we mourn, & tell us they are happy & say loving words to us~ Why should we doubt them? If they lie what is their motive? This is a difficult question to answer~[1035]

Many of these spirit messages did seem to be quite authentic. They contained information known only to the deceased and their loved ones, and in the minds of many followers they offered incontrovertible proof of the existence of an afterlife. There were many frauds and charlatans attracted to this movement, both male and female, who profited monetarily from these readings. However, many spiritualists seemed to be genuinely sincere in their beliefs, and a good many of them never charged.

One thing is certain~ The moment a transaction in spiritualism becomes commercial it cannot be depended on~[1036]

The movement was never rigidly organized, but it attracted many prominent people, including at one point the President of the United States. Abraham Lincoln and his wife Mary Todd Lincoln held séances in the White House during his administration in an attempt to communicate with their deceased son. Horace Greeley, William Jennings Bryant, William Lloyd Garrison, and the members of the well-known Beecher family were all followers of this movement at one point. In fact it was estimated that by 1890 eleven million out of a total population of twenty-five million people believed in the authenticity of these messages.[1037]

Sarah's former teacher Lydia Maria Childs wrote that nothing had undermined the authority of the Bible as much as Spiritualism. Many people viewed it as an extension or outgrowth of transcendentalist beliefs; Emerson and Thoreau, two of the primary transcendentalist leaders were not complimented by the comparison. However, Sarah apparently believed that spiritualism was an authentic phenomenon.

Victorians were quite interested in the mystery surrounding death. It was widely believed that in the moments just prior to death people stood on the threshold of the spiritual and material worlds. Therefore a great deal of attention was paid to last minute utterances made by the dying. Sarah like many others was intrigued by anecdotal accounts that seemed to confirm this theory.

My Uncle Badger exclaimed in his last moment "My mother," and John Parrot exclaimed, "Open the window & let them come in mother! grandmother! all!

Anne Rice exclaimed, "It is beautiful! Oh why did you not tell me of this before?"

My cousin Robert Rice exclaimed "Oh what a beautiful spark" & then "My mother" and was gone~

Hannah Moore exclaimed, "Here is Patty"~ Patty was her favorite sister~

Mrs. E.B. Browning was a spiritualist~ Mrs. Browning's last words were "All is beautiful"~[1038]

During the last half of the nineteenth century Madame Helen Blavatsky, a member of the Russian nobility, came to America and started a new philosophical movement. A religious seeker, and an unhappily married woman, Madame Blavatsky, as she was known, had spent many years in foreign lands studying various religious beliefs, particularly the beliefs of mystical eastern religions in Asia and Egypt. She also studied occult knowledge of the supernatural forces and the magical traditions of several east European countries. She once likened her studies to a search for the fabled " philosopher's stone."[1039]

Out of her varied studies there eventually emerged a new theology, which she called Theosophy. Madame Blavatsky also authored several philosophy books. Her most well known The *Secret Doctrine*, is a compendium of all of her findings. Theosophy was basically an eclectic blending of Christianity, eastern religious beliefs, magic, existentialism, quantum physics, astrology, women's rights, animal rights, dream prophecy, reincarnation, and spiritualism. [1040]

Theosophy is the science of the human soul~ It teaches of the eternity of the present & the future... We must go on until we are perfect~ Theosophy is an extension of Christianity~[1041]

Madame Blavatsky attracted a huge following in America during the last half of the century. She had an equally large number of detractors. People seemed to either love or hate her. Sarah never mentioned her by name, but expressed a positive interest in and acceptance of Theosophy.

One might say there is no God because we cannot understand his mode of governing the material universe, or say there is no God because we can not understand the mode of governing the spiritual universe ~

Can it be that by the exertion of the Great Creator's 'will' we seem to be ~ to see ~ to suffer ~ to enjoy & that it is all seeming? And if so how long will it continue?

My late reading in the Theosophical doctrine of cycles makes it clear to me some things heretofore inexplicable~ I am led to think I did not begin life in 1805 & that sometime I may come again~ I don't want to but I must~ I hope I shall be a better woman then~[1042]

Sarah also expressed an interest in mesmerism, another popular movement of the time. Mesmerism was the early name given to the phenomenon of hypnotism as first demonstrated by Franz Mesmer, an Australian physician in the nineteenth century. He claimed that subjects placed in a hypnotic state were able to tap into an unseen universal fluid, which he named animal magnetism. While in a mesmeric trance the subjects were purportedly able to diagnosis and heal people who suffered from a variety of illnesses. There were also many spiritualist healers who claimed to possess the ability to diagnosis and heal the sick, and it was believed that these spiritualists tapped the same energy forces as the mesmerists. [1043]

> *Mesmerism consists in drawing off the connective link between spirit & body~ The spirit is left free & the operator controls the brain for his own purpose~ I saw a dozen boys put into that state by Professor Carpenter~*[1044]

The popularity of these new schools of thought can be attributed to the fact that religion had lost much of its traditional authority due to the great advancements made in the field of science during the span of Sarah's life. The surge of interest in spiritualism, Theosophy, and mesmerism was in part due to the fact that these practices seemed to offer scientific proof of an afterlife.

Darwin's theory of evolution changed the way many people viewed the world, as did the discovery of the magnetic force fields, electricity, and gravity. These discoveries of unseen forces seemed as mystical to the average mind as the esoteric tenets of Theosophy, or the spiritual and magnetic animal forces inherent in the practice of mesmerism and spiritualism. Most people including the scientists didn't see a real conflict between religion and science; rather they viewed them as two different paths to uncovering the mystery surrounding the true nature of reality. [1045]

> *No one could count the number of waves of sounds that go to make up a musical note~ The siren does it~ With such tones as those to make love with & never have a response? ~ Ye Gods!*

> *I don't know anything of the science of music but I am all alive to the essence of it~ That is I have a great feeling for it & a great enjoyment~*

> *On returning home from the shoals by moon & starlight Mr Moore drew my attention to the phosphoresce in the water produced by the jelly fish~ He says they are of every size from pin head to a great size~ I remember twice when the river & sea seemed molten gold~*

> *I was looking out the window the other night & I noticed a ball of fire projected from the window glass apparently in mid air~ Then I turned & looked at the gas burning in the chandelier~*

> *Then remembered I did not see this flame at all as it was only a picture on the retina & I should know nothing about it at all if the optic nerve & the retina did not tell me~*

> *But the picture was upside down & if I am to believe the scientists I had to learn to see this picture by experience~ How amazing~ Do the animals learn by experiences? But it is all wonderful~*

Sometime the grand drama of life looks like a dream~ What's more real than a nightmare? But I suppose the better we behave the happier we are~

1890 From August 1827 when the first great arch in the heavens appeared there were great shows of brilliant aurora & many comets until 1865~ The last great comet in 1882~ No great displays in the last twenty years~

Photos ~ phones ~ graphs ~ phonos~ All beautiful things come in their time~

Dr Brown Leguards (?) "Elixir of Life" consists of some of the living tissues of rabbits or guinea pigs triturated in distilled water until it is dissolved~

I think grip came over from Europe in a fog~ Ships that arrived at the same time have reported a dense fog all the way over~

A writer in Science Monthly says colds come from too much food~ When the system is clogged with matter the action of the viscera is impeded & there is no power to resist the chill~ I believe it is true~ Jan 25th 1888~[1046]

SARAH
The 1890s

S arah lived to celebrate both her ninetieth and ninety-first birthdays. Although there were no more entries in her common daybooks after 1892, extant letters from the period survive, two to her daughter-in-law, Molly Goodwin, and another to her friend the Reverend Alfred Putnum. The first was written in November of 1894.

> *Saturday Nov 94*
> *My dear Molly I enjoyed your letter highly but it put me into a strange mood~ your fiftieth birthday!!! Good Heavens where have I been all this time? & then the awakening & then the desire to bury it all~*
>
> *And now I can thank our Heavenly Father that it is no worse~ In the great future we shall see clearly~ we talk glibly of heredity but how few realize what a terrible power it may prove & what a burden to carry but when one fights manfully & comes out grandly, what cause for rejoicing! Dear Molly I feel that you & I have been directed by a wise Providence~*
>
> *Our dear Sadie is filling a great place in the Emerson family~ She will be everything to them all~ This disaster to the mother is terrible~ Sadie will see that trouble comes to all, even under the most promising conditions~*
>
> *I sent Mrs Emerson's letter to Frank~ On the lovely first day of Nov. Annie & I & a trowel went into the garden & planted some daffy bulbs which the Pillows sent to me in full bloom last March~ I want to see Eleanor can't she come a week? Dear love to her & Robert & yourself from us all~ Ever yours*
>
> *Sarah PR Goodwin*
>
> *Thank you <u>very</u> <u>very</u> much for sending Mrs Emerson's letter~I shall write to dear Sadie very soon~*[1047]

Molly's fiftieth birthday would have been on October 16th 1894. That year her daughter Sadie, who had graduated from Smith College in 1892, and taken a position at the Gilman School in Cambridge, where she was picked to tutor Helen Keller in preparation for entrance into Radcliff College, took a leave of absence to travel to Europe with Dr. and Mrs. Edward Emerson. Dr. Emerson was the grandson of Ralph Waldo Emerson who had died the year that twelve-year-old Sadie and her family moved to Concord.

It is not known what was wrong with Mrs. Emerson, but it can be assumed she was ill or incapacitated in some way. Sadie may have traveled with them in the capacity of a tutor/

governess/friend of the family. While in Cambridge, England she attended Girton College, at Cambridge University. Upon her return she was made principal of the Gilman Elementary School. [1048]

Sarah planned on marking her ninetieth birthday quietly with little or no fanfare. However, her family and friends believed it was an important occasion, one that deserved to be noted with some celebration. The day was filled with congratulatory messages and gifts from her family as well as her many friends and admirers. Special guests for dinner that evening included her grandniece, Susie Yates, and her granddaughter Mabel, with her five-year-old daughter Anna, Sarah's great granddaughter.

> *May 22/95*
>
> *My Dear Molly it seems late to thank you for your kind & sympathetic letter on my ninetieth but I <u>tell</u> you that <u>that</u> birthday has kept me busy ever since~ I had begged my family not to speak of it & they had promised or rather seemed surprised that I should think it of any consequence~*
>
> *I felt that I deserved no special credit or praise for living so long but I didn't see why I should be snubbed~ Well I said nothing to neighbors or relations & felt sure the day would pass without observation~*
>
> *When Lo & behold! At seven o'clock on the morning of the 15th the boxes began to arrive & boxes & letters & other beautiful things & friends & continued until the late Express brought flowers from Mrs Emery~ By the way I had three letters from the Emery family~*
>
> *Susie Yates & Mabel & Anna came to dinner~ Mrs. Baxter brought a poem which lifted me into the third heaven~ My old friend the Rev Alfred Putnam sent me the most wonderful letter I ever received~ It has been read to everybody & some day I shall try to <u>revise</u> myself & acknowledge it~*
>
> *I hear…that Dear Sadie has a cold~ She must make haste & get well~ Her father & <u>we</u> are very impatient to see her~*
>
> *Abby's in Washington~well & happy~ Love to all*
>
> *Ever Lovingly*
> *SPR Goodwin* [1049]

Sarah responded to Mr. Putnum's letter the following day. In this letter dated May 23, 1895, Sarah recollected different periods of her life under several presidential administrations. The main focus of her reminiscences was the time of the War of 1812, when she was a small girl of seven who had recently lost her mother. The contents of this have been presented elsewhere as part of her childhood memories, with the exception of a final tribute to the memory of her father.

> *We had the best father in the world & he used to say to us " You have all*

of you good abilities & it will be your own fault if you do not succeed in life~ "[1050]

Sarah lived another year and a half. She died in her Islington Street home on October 12th of 1896. She was ninety-one. Her death certificate listed "old age" and consumption of the stomach," as cause of death. However Sarah really never did grow old in mind or spirit.

The Portsmouth papers duly noted the passing of one of the community's oldest and most respected members.

> In the death of Mrs. Sarah Parker Rice Goodwin, the widow of Hon. Ichabod Goodwin there has passed from out this community one of its life long & most beloved members. She came from a set of families, some of which had been identified with this locality from the time of the early settlement of America...the dignity and queenliness of her demeanor were supported by a strength, which marked the vigorous people from whom she was descended.
>
> Her father was an eminent merchant of Portsmouth...forty years ago he left a fortune the amount of which was more rare at that time than the possession of several millions is now.
>
> Her home for fifty or sixty years was a favorite resort for many friends who sought an agreeable evening's entertainment, and who were braced by the strength of her vigorous mind and soothed by the grace and charm of her brilliant and instructive conversation.
>
> She was indeed a remarkable conversationalist; for she possessed what was no less than real eloquence in parlor talk; and this was constantly enlivened by the sportiveness of her mind and elevated by the dignity of thoughts which were born to her in her hours of serious meditation.
>
> She always read many years before this had become common among women; and a very tenacious memory, enabled her to retain with clearness whatever she had once added to her mental acquisitions.
>
> Her character and her spiritual nature were in harmony with all the rest of her. They were vigorous. They both possessed fiber. There was nothing flimsy about them. To do what is right and because it is right to do it, was of her character; and to have a real childlike faith and trust in God was ... the nature of her spirit.
>
> There was nothing flippant about her. She did not think the latest discovery of science had drawn the limit of present human knowledge but rather that the scientific mind in its mighty march through the period of her ninety-one years has been advancing toward that line where Christ began; and that he was all in all. [1051]

The above memorial from the October 17th 1896 edition of the *Portsmouth Journal* is presented here almost in its entirety. Its sentiments seem to verify the picture that emerges of Sarah from her personal writings of a warm, charming, generous, and playful woman whose intellectual curiosity and capacities knew few boundaries. It was unusual for such an in-depth obituary about a woman to be in the newspapers of that time. But Sarah was clearly an unusual woman, loved and admired by many in the community in which she had lived for most all of the nineteenth century. In that same paper another memorial to Sarah was published under the heading, "The Tribute of a Friend."

> Mrs. Goodwin…was long the center of a wide family and social circle, attracted by her intellectual accomplishments and generous appreciation, by the popularity of her husband and the cordial hospitalities of their elegant home. Both husband and wife were distinguished by that fine courtesy which took time for expressions of friendliness and respect toward everyone, rich or poor, high or low, making people better and happier for having met them.
>
> Always a keen observer of people and things even from childhood, a wide and constant reader taking lively and thoughtful interest in all public affairs She kept everything in mind. This gave to her conversation a dramatic vividness, which made her a delightful companion…She delighted in books, in pictures, in flowers in her garden, in everything which made her home bright and attractive. It was indeed a spot that warmed and cheered….Mrs. Goodwin long survived the friends of her youth and three beautiful daughters who died in their early-married life, yet she never grew old…She read and thought and wrote to the last… On the great foundation that God is love she rested her faith…How we shall miss her![1052]

Sarah was buried alongside her husband in the family tomb at Proprietors Cemetery. In her will she stipulated that her personal papers, journals, and *Pleasant Memories* be left in the care of Abby, who was charged with seeing that her story was passed down to her grandchildren.

EPILOGUE

P resident Grover Cleveland was just completing his second term in office when Sarah died, and within a few weeks the country elected Republican William McKinley as their new president. The following year America's relationship with Spain became strained over the issue of Spanish versus nationalist rule in nearby Cuba. Eventually the suspicious explosion of the USS *Maine* that killed 230 Americans in waters right outside of Havana led to the Spanish-American War, and out of this war emerged a new American hero by the name of George Dewey.[1053]

After Susie died in 1872, Dewey devoted himself solely to his naval career. Through the years he rose through the ranks somewhat slowly. A stickler for details and military rules and somewhat of a loner, Dewey was not too popular with his fellow officers. Some of them tagged him with the derisive nickname of "Dandy Dewey," because he was so meticulous in his dress, and always adhered to the latest fashions in clothing.[1054]

However, Dewey had impressed the then Assistant Secretary of the Navy, Theodore Roosevelt, who in turn prevailed upon President McKinley to appoint Dewey as Commander of the Asiatic Squadron in the Philippine Islands in 1897.[1055] When the Spanish American War broke out the following year, Dewey was in position to move immediately against the Spanish base at Manila Bay.

At the break of dawn on the first of May in 1898 Dewey led the American attack against the unsuspecting Spanish fleet stationed at Manila Bay, and destroyed all ten of the enemy ships. The American fleet remained intact, with no deaths and only eight wounded. This victory was so impressive that the United States Navy was transformed overnight into a major power in the Pacific, and its stature rose in world opinion.

The press loved Dewey and wrote admiringly about his attention to detail, as well as his confident demeanor. He had mapped out every particular of his strategy months ahead of time, right down to painting the ships a winter gray to camouflage them from the enemy. His cool detachment under fire, as well as his command at the start of the battle to Capt. Charles Vernon Gridley of the USS *Olympia*, "You may fire when ready Gridley," became legendary.[1056]

Dewey was immediately promoted to Rear Admiral. Americans adored this sixty-two year old naval hero, and he returned home to a grand welcome. Endless rounds of ticker tape parades, ceremonies, and parties were given in his honor. During a tour of New England, Boston named a square after him, and presented him with a jeweled sword and the keys to the city. The University of Vermont gave him an honorary degree of law.

In Washington, D.C. President McKinley gave a dinner in his honor and presented him with a congressional sword of honor. The American public donated over fifty thousand dollars to purchase a home for him in Washington, D.C. There was even a serious movement underway to make him the next president of the United States.[1057]

In 1899 Dewey was promoted to the rank of Admiral of the Navy for Life, the highest honor the navy ever bestowed on any one, including his mentor Admiral David Farragut, who like Dewey had achieved fame after age sixty. That same year Dewey, widowed for twenty-seven years, married his second wife Mildred McLean Hazen. She was the widow of

General William Hazen.

Dewey's son and namesake, George Goodwin Dewey, turned twenty-five the year his father became a household name in America. As he grew older Dewey made some attempts to become acquainted with his son, but for the most part they remained distant from one another. When George Goodwin Dewey graduated from Princeton his father was not present.

In September of 1898, when the national and local papers were still filled with accounts of George Dewey's meteoric rise to fame, the local papers recalled another Goodwin son in-law. Samuel Storer died of the grippe in San Diego in September of 1898, thirty years after his wife Sadie had succumbed to consumption. Samuel was seventy-nine years old at the time of his death. His remains were brought to Portsmouth for interment in the Goodwin family grounds at Proprietor's Cemetery. Although Samuel had lived far from his place of birth for many years, he was remembered fondly in the local papers.

> [A] Son and old resident of Portsmouth who took a deep interest in this town. He belonged to an ancient and distinguished family, which for generations was associated with all that was best in this locality...Mr. Storer possessed his culture with marked taste and facility for "historical and belle lettre learning, and was possessed of a very genial humor.[1058]

His only child Mabel remained in Portsmouth throughout the years. By this time she and her husband, Stephen Decatur had three children, ranging in ages from eight to thirteen. When the Spanish-American War began in 1898, Stephen Decatur, a graduate of Annapolis, who had resigned his commission many years before, enrolled in the navy as a lieutenant junior grade. He served at the blockade of Santiago and at Puerto Rico, and was honorably discharged in 1899.[1059]

Five years later, in March of 1903 the remains of another son in law were shipped home from the West. Abby's husband, William Winder, died of cancer of the tongue in Omaha, Nebraska at age seventy-nine. Although a continent, and very dissimilar life styles had separated the Winders for over thirty years, his wife Abby arranged for his body to be buried in the Goodwin family burial grounds in Proprietors' Cemetery.

His obituary gave some details of Winder's life in the West, noting that he had been "remarkably successful" in the mining business. He may have been connected with J. Pierpoint Morgan's Western Mining operations as his nephew, John Winder, is listed as the manager of this operation at the time of William's death.

The paper also noted that William was given a government appointment as Indian agent in the late 1870s to oversee the apportionment of land amongst the Indian tribes, a position he still held at the time of his death. In addition his obituary stated that through the years Winder had achieved "great renown as a pathfinder and prospector."[1060]

At the time of his father's death, Willie, who had graduated from Annapolis in 1873, was captain in command of the steamer USS *Michigan* stationed in the Great Lakes in 1903.[1061] Abby continued to live at the family home on Islington Street with her sister Hope.

That same year Frank, the only other remaining sibling, was forced to retire from his teaching position at Boston University citing the pressures of private business and failing eyesight. When he retired the university bestowed on him the title of Emeritus Professor of Law.[1062] Frank moved to Portsmouth in 1904 where he set up residence at the Rockingham

House, just a short distance away from the family home where his oldest sisters lived.[1063] In 1905 his lectures were incorporated into a book entitled *The Law of Real Property*, published by Little Brown & Company.

Three years later, in May of 1906, Abby Winder died at the family home on Islington Street. Her son Willie was by her side. She was seventy-seven years old. Abby was buried in Proprietor's Cemetery alongside her husband of fifty-eight years. The local newspapers noted her passing and credited Abby, as well as her sister Hope, with rearing the three Goodwin grandchildren left motherless many years before.

> Mrs. Winder was a lady of fine presence and distinguished talent. Her kindness of heart and generous impulses were proverbial…. She was a beloved and beautiful woman in the center of a large circle of loving friends…She endeared herself to young and old, and while her wit and brilliancy delighted society her sympathy and thoughtfulness made her a real friend to the friendless and a helper of the helpless.[1064]

Hope was the only one of the Goodwin children still living at the Islington Street home in 1908 when George Dewey and his new wife were received there as honored guests. At that time Admiral Dewey returned to Portsmouth to preside over a dedication ceremony honoring the memory of his former mentor, Admiral David Farragut. An iron plaque, which bears an inscription by Dewey hangs in front of Commander Quarters A where Admiral Farragut died in 1870.

The following year, on July 3rd of 1909, seventy-nine year old Hope died at the family home she had lived in for most of her life. The local papers remembered her only as a woman of "a quiet, shy, and retiring disposition…highly esteemed by all her acquaintances."[1065] Frank, the sole remaining child of Sarah and Ichabod Goodwin, continued to reside at the Rockingham House until his own death from pneumonia on June 7, 1912. Upon his death, the faculty of Boston University Law School formally expressed their sorrow and their appreciation for his fine character and scholarly habits. On a more personal touch they noted that his "untiring interest in the students under his charge…won for him the lasting esteem and grateful affection of his former students"[1066]

Then in 1917 Admiral Dewey died. He was eighty years old. Dewey who never retired from the navy served as President of General Board of the Navy until his death. He was buried with full military honors in Arlington Cemetery. However, his wife then requested that his remains be removed to the Washington Cathedral of Saints. Though she later reversed her decision this is where his remains are interred today.[1067]

By 1919 all of the Goodwin children and their spouses, with the exception of Molly Buttrick Goodwin, had died, and only the grandchildren remained. The first grandchild to die after Sarah's death was Frank and Molly's youngest daughter, Eleanor, who was married to Howard Snelling and living in Asheville, North Carolina at the time of her death in 1919. The Goodwin family Bible contains little information about Eleanor and her family, but a brief genealogical sketch found at Thayer Cummings Library indicates that she had at least three children. These children have been generous donors of many family heirlooms now on display at the Goodwin Home in Strawbery Banke.

Willie Winder retired from the navy as a captain in June of 1907. He had been married, but was separated from his wife at some point. He continued to remain in close contact with his cousins and the Portsmouth-Kittery area. Following his retirement from the navy, his summers were spent at the Champernowne Hotel in Kittery and winters in his apartment at Brookline, Massachusetts.

Then on the evening of October 3, 1922 Willie shot and killed himself. His body was found lying on the path to the house known as the old Hawthorne House on Harvard Street in Brookline, a .32 caliber pistol by his side. Letters to his family and friends were found in his pocket. He was seventy-seven years old at the time of his death. He had been ill, and afflicted with "melancholy for sometime," according to the papers. His wife was abroad with her sister.[1068]

Willie's will stipulated that his share of the Goodwin farm in Berwick was to be shared amongst his cousins. Also, that since he had provided generously for his wife previously, all that remained of his "worldly goods" was to be shared by his cousins, his Aunt Molly, and a friend who cared for him while ill. He left Abby's guitar to his cousin Mabel. Many of the personal items listed in his will were Indian artifacts and pictures perhaps given to him by his father, or collected by him as a younger man. His last request was that his ashes be buried between his long separated parents now joined in death at Proprietor's Cemetery.[1069]

When Mabel died at her Kittery Point home in 1927 she was sixty-four years old. The *Portsmouth Herald* reported that she was quite ill for some months prior to her death, but noted that her illness had been "borne with great courage and even cheerfulness." Her husband and three children survived her.

The paper noted her impressive family connections both maternal and paternal, and recalled both Mabel and her family of the past.

> Many Portsmouth people will recall that remarkable family of brilliant and interesting persons who figured so prominently in the [past] life of the town. Mrs. Decatur possessed the family characteristics…cheerfulness and humor and a wonderful gift of entertaining conversation with unusual qualities of mind and disposition…which made her a delightful companion to her many friends.[1070]

In 1913, the year following his father's death, Robert, by then a thirty-five year old attorney, purchased a large Queen Anne style home for his mother and his sister Sarah on River Street in Concord, Massachusetts. Molly Buttrick Goodwin continued to live there until her death in October of 1929.

Not a great deal is known about the adulthood of Georgette's son, Fielding Bradford. Sarah's journal indicates that during the 1880s he was serving his country in Montana. When his grandfather Goodwin died, he left several parcels of real estate to be divided amongst his heirs. One of these parcels was 160 acres of land in Kansas, and also debentures in the Kansas City Investment Company. The other heirs signed these along with other stocks that could not be divided over to Fielding in December of 1899.[1071] Fielding was thirty-nine years old at the time of this transaction. Fielding may have settled in that part of the country or he may just have handled certain financial transactions for himself and his cousins.

In January of 1911 when he was forty-nine years of age, Fielding married Elsie Thayer the daughter of Edward Thayer from Brookline, Massachusetts. This was apparently a first marriage. The bride was ten years his junior and they had no children. Fielding and his wife were living in Portland, Maine at the time of his death. He was seventy. The local papers noted that he was retired from Maine Central Railroad where he had worked for several years as paymaster.[1072]

After George Goodwin Dewey graduated from Princeton he became a member of the New York Stock Exchange. He lived in Chicago for many years. According to the obituary notice in the *Portsmouth Herald*, he had accumulated over a million dollars in stock by the time he died in 1963.[1073]

Before Admiral Dewey died he had expressed a desire to leave the home purchased for him by the public's generous donations to his son. However, due to the terms of the gift it first had to be deeded to his wife Mildred, and she in turn was to give it to his son. But, after the Admiral died, the home remained in his second wife's name.

After Dewey died Mildred became a strange and reclusive figure in Washington, DC. She remained in mourning the rest of her life, and always wore old-fashioned long black dresses. She set up her home as a shrine to Dewey. By the time she died in 1931 she had changed her will a total of five times. Originally she left every thing to young George Dewey, but her final will gave her entire estate to a nephew. [1074]

George Goodwin Dewey fought the will in an effort to claim his father's war mementos, including the jeweled sword given to his father by Congress, and a flag given to his father by Admiral Farragut. He eventually won, and in 1933 one-third of his stepmother's estate, the portion that came from Admiral Dewey, was awarded to him. He in turn placed many of his father's papers and his Manila Bay diary with the Library of Congress.[1075] George Goodwin Dewey never married. He was in his ninetieth year when he died, and had been confined to a wheelchair with a broken hip for the last three years of his life.

Sarah Storer Goodwin, Frank and Molly's second daughter helped to establish, and was the first headmistress of Milton Upper Academy for Girls in Milton, Massachusetts. Tributes from former students indicate that she was quite loved and respected by all of her students. Unfortunately she was plagued with poor health and was forced to retire in the early 1920s. Although it is not stated what the health problems were, it is possible that she too had developed a form of tuberculosis. However, Sadie did live for many more years either at her Concord home on River Street or at times at the Emerson home on Lowell Road, which was closer to the country. She spent her summers at a cottage in Jaffrey, New Hampshire. At all of her retreats her former students came to visit frequently. During her later years she enjoyed the devoted companionship of her niece Roddy Snelling, Eleanor's daughter.

Sarah Storer Goodwin was widely recognized as an outstanding teacher and an expert in her field who tried to balance tradition with progressive ideas. She was one of the early proponents of eliminating standard grading, as she believed it was too competitive a way to denote progress. As she grew older she became so distressed at the turn of world and national affairs during the tumultuous 1960s, that she was advised by her physician to stop reading the papers. She followed this advice and lived to be ninety-five. When she died in May of 1965, a memorial service at the Concord Episcopalian Church was filled to capacity with former students and other friends and family. Goodwin Hall at Milton Academy is named in her honor.[1076]

Frank's son, Robert, was the last of the Goodwin grandchildren to die. Like his father and maternal grandfather before him Robert attended Harvard. There he was noted for his academic achievements, and his impressive record as a coxswain on the Harvard Rowing Team. He was a member of the Hasty Pudding, and of the Harvard and Somerset Clubs.[1077]

After his graduation from Harvard in 1901, he went on to attend Boston University

Law School, where his own father was a professor. There he was a member of William E. Russell Club, the Law School Quiz Club, and during his final year was elected president of his law class. He graduated from there in 1903 at the top his class the same year his father gave up teaching.[1078] In 1914, two years after his father died, Robert, along with two of his Harvard classmates, founded the law firm of Goodwin, Proctor and Ballantine at 84 State Street in Boston.[1079] When World War 1 began Robert volunteered, and was enlisted as a major and promoted to colonel when he was made Commander of 101st Field Artillery of the 26th Yankee Division. He served in France with the 101st and was awarded the Distinguished Service Medal for his service to his country.[1080]

After Robert's mother died in 1927 he married Elsie Nause of Michigan. She died in 1948. Then he married Mrs. Marguerite Summer. When he died in July of 1971 at his home at Longwood Towers in Brookline, Massachusetts, he was ninety-two, and the last survivor of the original Goodwin grandchildren. Robert was buried at the Auburn Cemetery in Cambridge along with other family members. By then the law firm he had founded more than a half-century earlier was called Goodwin, Proctor, and Hoar. Today it is known as Goodwin, Proctor and is one of Boston's oldest and most prestigious law firms, with offices in New York, New Jersey, and Washington, DC.[1081]

Both of Mabel's sons served their country during World War 1. Following family tradition Stephen Decatur V had entered the Naval Academy when he was young. However, just about the time his Aunt Abby died in May of 1906, Stephen was involved in a hazing incident at Annapolis, and was suspended from the school just sixteen days before he was due to graduate at the top of his class.

Local newspapers at that time carried an account of the incident, indicating his fate was hanging in the balance with two state senators working towards his reinstatement, while President Theodore Roosevelt stated that he was against such an action.[1082] The president's wishes prevailed, and in the end Stephen, who was nineteen years old at the time of the incident, was not reinstated.

Eleven years later in May of 1917 Stephen offered his services to the navy in Washington, DC and was made an ensign. From there he went to Newport, and served aboard the USS *Henley* during World War 1.[1083] According to the Goodwin family genealogy Stephen married Winifred Rogers, daughter of Rear Admiral Charles and Alice (Walker) Rogers in April of 1919.

Storer graduated from the University of Pennsylvania, and went into business in New York. In 1917 he gave up this business to volunteer in the US Naval Reserve, and during World War 1 was a Chief Boatswains Mate at Newport, Rhode Island. [1084] His widow Mrs. Mary Decatur still lives in the seacoast area. [1085]

Anna, who was six when her grandmother died, married Capt. Meirs Fisher Wright from Philadelphia in June of 1914.[1086] She was either widowed or divorced within the next fifteen years, as the Goodwin family Bible notes that on the 2nd of August in 1929 she was married at Kittery Point to Ralph May.

Descendents of the Decatur and May family still live at Kittery Point and many of the donations given to Strawbery Banke, including Sarah's papers, have come from Mabel's descendents, as well as Eleanor Goodwin Snelling's family.

The Goodwin heirs sold the home on Islington Street after Hope died. For a while it was used as a colonial tearoom. Then in the early 1960s it was sold to the owners of Atherton Furniture Company. They purchased the house with the intent of demolishing it in order to erect a furniture store on this prime corner lot along one of Portsmouth's busiest commercial thoroughfares.

Some citizens protested the destruction of this historic home, and attempts were made to move the home to the lot directly across the street, once Sarah's field and by then a memorial park. However, the terms of the original deed forbade the placement of any permanent structures upon this area, and the house was slated for demolition.

Then, thanks in large part to what must have seemed like divine intervention by one of the former Goodwin servants, whose own son was the Governor of New Hampshire at the time, the house was saved. Her name was Mary Gosse Powell, and her son was Wesley Powell, who was elected Governor of the State of New Hampshire in 1960, just one hundred years after the former owner of the house held the same office.

Mary Gosse was twenty in 1904 when she first arrived in Portsmouth from her native Newfoundland. She had come there to work alongside her sister Rose in the Governor Goodwin mansion on Islington Street. At the time both Abby and Hope Goodwin were there, and Frank was nearby at the Rockingham House. During those years Mary recalled a visit from the famous Admiral Dewey and his wife, as well as other dignitaries.

Heeding the cry to save the historic old manse where his mother once worked, Wes Powell went before his executive council to present his case for saving the home. A legislative act was then put before the state legislature and it was agreed that the State of New Hampshire would purchase the house and arrange to move it to Strawbery Banke Museum less than a mile away from its original Islington Street location.

Strawbery Banke is a ten-acre historical museum located in the south end of Portsmouth between Prescott Park and Washington Street in what was once a working class waterfront. A neighborhood that grew up around a tidal inlet, it was given the name "Strawbery Banke" by the Mason settlers who arrived there in the 1630s. The surrounding neighborhood became known as the Puddle Dock area. Following the Civil War this area of the city deteriorated rapidly, and over the years it became a haven for immigrants and others such as naval yard workers who came seeking low-income housing.

By the 1950s the federal government designated the Puddle Dock neighborhood a site of urban blight and took it by eminent domain. The homes were destined for demolition and were to be replaced by low-income housing. However, concerned citizens led at first by Dorothy Vaughan, the town librarian at the time, protested the removal of these homes. Amongst them are some of the oldest homes in the country. The story is told that she asked the local Rotary members for help and when one member asked who cared about the old homes, she passionately replied, "I do!"

This lit a fire under others who came to aid the cause of saving the old homes, and out of their intervention Strawbery Banke was formed in 1957. Its original mission was to preserve the historic homes of the city, and to use them to interpret the social history of Portsmouth. Originally the museum contained only buildings located on their original sites. However, there have been several important homes saved and moved there since the museum was founded. These include the law office and home of Daniel Webster, Stoodley's Tavern, the Joshua Wentworth home and the Goodwin Mansion.

In order to remove the Goodwin house to its new site, it was cut into three pieces then moved by truck. The Goodwin house exhibit was officially dedicated at Strawbery Banke in 1963. Present at the official dedication ceremonies was Wesley Powell, with his proud eighty-year-old mother by his side. During the ceremonies, Councilor Harold Weeks unveiled a portrait of Mary Gosse as a young woman. This portrait still hangs in the hall of the Goodwin home today in tribute to the young servant girl who came there to work for the Goodwins many years before, and eventually helped to save the grand old home from destruction.

Today visitors to Strawbery Banke can visit the Goodwin home, restored to the decade of the 1870s, and learn the story of New Hampshire's first Civil War governor and his family. The house is a white, green shuttered, three-story Federal house, circa 1811. Greek Revival touches added about the time the Goodwins purchased the home are reflected in the imposing Ionic podium at the front of the house with laurel wreaths engraved in the portico above, along with a side porch that is surrounded by stately Doric columns.

The grounds outside the Goodwin house were restored by the museum's horticultural department to reflect that period. Within the available space they have attempted to duplicate the garden designs drawn up for Sarah in 1869 by local architect Albert Hoyte. Although there is no evidence that Sarah had a greenhouse, a period greenhouse has been constructed there. In addition there is a facsimile of "Tanglewood," the grove of trees of which Sarah was so proud.

Sarah's childhood home in the North End was also in danger of the demolition teams of urban renewal during the 1960s. Citing the need for economic expansion, The Portsmouth Housing Authority decided to level four hundred homes within the Vaughan and Deer Streets neighborhood to make way for improved shopping and parking areas. However, Portsmouth Preservation Inc., a for-profit group, and Nelson Aldrich, a Boston based architect, intervened and saved thirteen of these buildings. As a result of their joint efforts these "saved" buildings were moved to an area of Portsmouth in the North End known as the Hill. These homes were renovated and used as commercial buildings.[1087]

The home, which belonged to Sarah's "Uncle Kennard," was once again moved across the road on Deer Street and was used as a senior citizen center for a few years. Built in 1725 by Captain Hopley Yeaton, it was sold it to Captain Kennard who lived in it during Sarah's childhood. It is now remembered as the Sherburn House.[1088] The Sheraton Portsmouth Hotel presently dominates the area Sarah's family home once overlooked. But her childhood home, now known as the Hart-Rice home, continues to oversee this area of the North End from the safe prospect of the Hill. The Rice home and all others in this enclave are listed on the National Register, and in 2000 were purchased by a new owner for resale.[1089]

Sometime during the late 1830s Goodwin and Coues sold the *Sarah Parker*. It is not certain what happened to this ship, but there was some speculation that she was first involved in the East India trade, and then in the whaling trade off Nantucket. In 1849, during the gold rush, the ship was sold and taken to the West Coast where she worked for a while hauling lumber out of the Puget Sound. After that her fate is not known.[1090]

All of the railroads in New Hampshire during these years were short lines of railroad and none were too profitable. During the same time that Eastern Railroad was expanding from Massachusetts to New Hampshire and Maine, the Boston and Maine Railroad developed lines that ran through the same areas as Eastern. The Boston and Maine did lease the Portland Saco & Portsmouth railroad but the contract was broken in 1871, at which time the Boston and Maine built their own line to Portland. The competing line caused a financial depression for Eastern and finally, two years after Ichabod Goodwin's death, the Boston and Maine Railroad leased the entire Eastern Railroad system. [1091]

The Mountain House remained one of the most popular resorts in the Catskills for over one hundred and fifty years. In the 1960s it was burned to the ground. This was a "planned burn,' and before it was done there was an auction to sell the rich furnishings and glassware, silver, china and linens. Many local residents have some memento of this hotel that was for many years the jewel of the Catskills.

The Hotel Pulaski was demolished in 1956 to make way for a nine-story modern office building. When it was the former, dungeon-like slave quarters were uncovered, and it was noted that in one of these underground chambers there was a massive fireplace. Even more curious were several bricked-up passageways that led from the basement to the hotel northwards indicating that they may have led to a tunnel passage that ran all the way to the river. No one knew who built this nor for what purpose. But it is probable that smugglers who were trying to avoid paying a duty on their ship's cargo dug these tunnels.[1092]

The Glen House in the White Mountains was destroyed by fire in 1893, less than ten years after it had been rebuilt. It was not rebuilt again.[1093] Most of the grand hotels built in the White Mountain region during this time period were either razed or victims of fire. However, in recent years some have been restored to their former splendor, and other grand hotels have been built to reflect the elegance of this time.

The Revere House in Bowdoin Square where Sarah's paternal grandmother was born is further distinguished by being the oldest house within Boston's city limits.

The copy of the Lincoln Douglas debates given by Lincoln to William Goodwin are on file at the Tuck Memorial Library archives in Concord, operated by the New Hampshire Historical Society.

The Governor's Horse Guards are still active and through the years they have continued to escort New Hampshire Governors to their inauguration ceremonies. In addition there is a reenactment group, which portrays the original ceremonial militia formed in 1860 to escort Ichabod Goodwin to his second inaugural as governor of New Hampshire. Photographs of the original uniforms can be found on New Hampshire Historical Society's web site.

Joshua Foster, the editor who stirred up agitators against the war and fought against equality for the former slaves, left Portsmouth a few years after the war ended. He started a newspaper in his old hometown of Dover named *Foster's Daily Democrat,* which is still published.

The South Church is a still a Unitarian-Universalist Church with a large and socially active membership, and the congregation still meets in the1830s circa, Greek revival, stone, church. The North Church, with its rich history, remains a more traditional Congregational parish and continues to be one of the most prominent churches in the area. The building built in 1855 remains as the home for the parish. Throughout the years, both the North and South Churches along with St. John's Chapel, built in 1813, have catered to the religious and social needs of the city's most influential members. The story of each parish enriches and embellishes the overall history of the city.

The Hunnewell family continues to maintain the Wellesley estate, as it was when Sarah visited. The pinetum, the topiary, and the Italian gardens remained open to public groups several times a year. There have been four generations of Hunnewell men that have acted as conservators of their Horatio Hunnewell legacy. The last conservator of the estate was Walter Hunnewell, a great grandson of Horatio Hollis Hunnewell. He was president of the Massachusetts Horticultural Society until his death at age 82 on December 30, 1999.[1094]

The Rice Tavern was demolished in 1940. The last Rice family member to occupy this home was Miss Elizabeth Rice. A frequent visitor was her cousin, Sarah Orne Jewett, the well-known writer from Berwick, Maine. The connection between the Rice and Jewetts began when Captain Thomas Jewett married into the Rice family and Sarah Orne Jewett was one of their descendents.[1095] The one-story Rice family home on Government Street in Kittery has also been demolished.

Sarah's cousin Robert Rice built an Italianate home that covered an entire block on Islington Street, between Parker and Pearl Streets. This was once considered to be the grandest home in town. It was demolished to make way for a car repair garage. The Rice Library dedicated to Robert Rice by his daughter Arabella Rice, still serves the town of Kittery. Portraits of both William Rice and Ichabod Goodwin, who helped to establish the Library, are on display in the library.

The city of Portsmouth has kept up its agreement to maintain Goodwin Park on Islington Street. Although the park underwent a period of neglect and was, much like the city a victim of urban blight, it recently has undergone a facelift and is now a credit to the city, the Goodwin name, and the memory of the men who valiantly fought for their country during the Civil War. In addition the Civil War statue has recently been restored to its original splendor. Sarah would certainly approve.

The small coastal city of Portsmouth, which Sarah so loved, has also undergone many changes, both good and bad, through the years. It is currently considered New Hampshire's premier city, recommended by several national magazines as one the most desirable cities in America. A 2002 edition of *Fodor's Travel Guide* listed Portsmouth as one of the top ten hidden treasures in the country.

The city boasts, as always, of citizens with a passionate interest in its history. With its downtown area, comprised mainly of tall, narrow, nineteenth century brick buildings, and its working seaport harbor, Portsmouth retains much of the charm of Sarah's time. It is easy to understand why she might have felt "constrained" to leave behind her pleasant memories of this *"grand old town unlike any other."*

ENDNOTES

PREFACE
[1] John Hayes Goodwin, *The Goodwins of Ancient Kittery, Maine* (Berwick, ME: self-published, 1985).
[2] Ibid.
[3] Ibid.
[4] Ibid., 2-3.
[5] Ibid., 14, 29a.
[6] Frank Goodwin, "Hon. Ichabod Goodwin." (NH: *The Granite Monthly,* 111 No. 8, May 1880), 293-297.
[7] Ibid.

INTRODUCTION
[8] S.Goodwin, *Pleasant Memories.* Unpublished memoirs, MS4, Box 9, Folders 1-8. On file, Thayer Cummings Library, Portsmouth, NH, circa 1870-90, (History), F 1.
[9] S. Goodwin, *Journal Notes.* On file, Thayer Cummmings Library, Portsmouth, NH, circa 1880-90.
[10] Ibid.
[11] Ibid.
[12] Wendell Barrett, *Recollections of Jacob Wendell Barrett.* Unpublished typescript, Portsmouth Athenaeum, 100.
[13] S. Goodwin, *JN.*
[14] Ibid.
[15] Ibid.
[16] Ibid.

TRANSITIONS DURING THE 19TH CENTURY
[17] S. Goodwin, *PM,* (Servants), F 8.
[18] S. Goodwin, *JN.*
[19] S. Goodwin, *PM,* (Servants). F. 8.
[20] S. Goodwin, *JN.*
[21] Ibid.
[22] S. Goodwin, *PM, (*Servants), F 8.
[23] S. Goodwin, *JN.*
[24] S. Goodwin *PM,* (Servants), F 8.
[25] Ibid.
[26] Ibid.
[27] Ibid.
[28] Ibid.
[29] S. Goodwin letter to Molly Goodwin, Nov 1894.

[30] S. Goodwin, *PM,* (Servants), F8.
[31] Ibid.
[32] S. Goodwin, *JN.*
[33] Ibid.

TOWN HISTORY
[34] S. Goodwin, *PM,* (History), F1.
[35] Stackpole, *OK&HF,* 12-13
[36] Stackpole, *OK&HF,* 20. This includes portions of present day South Berwick, Eliot and Kittery, ME.
[37] Brighton, *TCTF,* I, 13.
[38] Stackpole, *OK&HF,* 14. Neither Mason nor Gorges ever came to America. However, both men spent a great deal of money and time towards their dream of colonizing New Hampshire and Maine. When Gorges died in 1647 his grant, which comprised about one-sixth of the present state of Maine, was left to his heirs.
[39] *Piscataqua Pioneers,* 54. Sir Gorges died in 1647.
[40] Brighton, *TCTF,* I, 5. These mergers were agreed upon only after it was clearly stipulated that the residents of both states would be admitted as free men, retaining their right of suffrage regardless of their church affiliation and status within the Puritan Church. This right was not granted to Massachusetts's residents who were not members of the church.
[41] Stackpole, *OFKM,* 15. Massachusetts paid 150 pounds for Maine.
[42] Hobart Pillsbury, *New Hampshire: A History* (New York: Lewis Historical Pub., 1927), I ,67.
[43] *Piscataqua Pioneers, 55.* This date also includes portions of King Williams War.
[44] S. Goodwin, *PM,* (History), F 1.
[45] Brighton, *TCTF,* I, 23.
[46] Ibid., I, 24. Before marrying Martha, Benning first courted courted Molly Pitman, a young lady in her twenties. When she scorned his love and married a younger man, Benning had him impressed into the British Navy.
[47] Brewster, 1, 101-106.
[48] S. Goodwin, *PM,* (Dressmaker), F 5. After Benning died Martha married another Wentworth and when George Washington came to Portsmouth in 1797 their Little Harbor home was honored by a visit from the country's first president.
[49] Brighton, *TCTF* II, 25.

[50] S. Goodwin, *PM*, (History*)*, F 1.

[51] Brewster, I, 106. It was under John Wentworth's watch that New Hampshire's road system, first begun during the reign of his uncle Benning, was finally laid out and constructed. He also started the first summer resort in the state. Once a highway was built to connect the town of Wolfeboro to the central part of the state, he built his personal summer residence in that remote area. Dartmouth College was also founded during his reign. Later Wentworth was Royal Governor of Nova Scotia.

[52] Everett Stackpole, *History of New Hampshire* (NY: The American Historical Society, 1919), 2. After the Revolution Portsmouth was once again the meeting place of the official state legislative meetings until the early eighteen hundreds when legislative meetings began to be held primarily in Concord, at that time the center of the trade route. After a state house was built there in 1816, Concord became the official capital of the state.

[53] L.H. Butterfield, *The Adam's Papers* (Cambridge, MA: The Harvard Press, 1961), I, 355.

[54] Brewster, 1, 143.

[55] S. Goodwin, *PM, (*History), F 1.

[56] Brighton, *TCTF,* I, 47-48. The liberty pole still stands on Marcy Street overlooking Prescott Park and Strawbery Banke. Recently Ron Raiselis, the cooper at Strawbery Banke, carved a replica of the original eagle's head that adorned the flagpole.

[57] Saltonstall, 89.

[58] Ibid., 100-101. Local legend tells that the flag flown on the *Ranger* was sewn for Captain Jones by a group of young ladies from Portsmouth who sacrificed pieces of their best gowns, including one bride's wedding gown.

[59] S. Goodwin, *PM, (*History), F 1.

[60] Ibid.

[61] *Strawbery Banke Guide Book* (Portsmouth, NH: Strawbery Banke, Inc., 1971), 12.

[62] S. Goodwin, *PM,* (History), F 1.

[63] Ibid.

FAMILY HISTORY

[64] Saltonstall, 105-107.

[65] Ibid., 5. In Portsmouth Judge Joshua Brackett presided over these trials, and seldom found reason not to condemn the prizes, since he was also a privateer investor.

[66] S. Goodwin, *PM,* (Childhood), F 2.

[67] Charles W. Brewster, *Rambles* (Portsmouth, NH: Charles W. Lewis, 1869), Vol. II, 44-46. Henry II owned the first brick house in town, a two-story structure built in the vicinity of his grandfather's tavern. It was later converted into a hotel that operated for many years as the Portsmouth Hotel.

[68] Sherburne family genealogy. Archives, Tucker Memorial Library, Concord, NH.

[69] S. Goodwin, *JN*.

[70] Brewster, I, 29. John Cutt was New Hampshire's first royal president when the Puritan takeover ended, and quite a successful merchant. Richard was a fisherman. Between them they owned the land that composed the major portions of present day Portsmouth.

[71] Stackpole, *OK&HF*, 617.

[72] S. Goodwin, *PM*, (Grandfather Parker), F. 2.

[73] Richard Winslow, *"Wealth and Honor": Portsmouth During the Golden Age of Privateering* (Portsmouth, NH: Portsmouth Marine Society, 1988), 35.

[74] Pillsbury, II, 45.

[75] Brighton, *TCTF*, II, 102.

[76] Saltonstall, 94.

[77] Ibid., 113-116. The *General Sullivan's* top prize came in 1780 when she brought in the *Charlotte,* a British ship and cargo valued at 350,000 pounds.

[78] *Piscataqua Pioneers*, 328. Many privateers were disfigured, killed or imprisoned for long periods of time in gloomy, dank English prisons

[79] Winslow, *W&H.*

[80] Everett Stackpole, Lucien Thompson, Winthrop Meserve, *History of the Town of Durham* (Somersworth, NH: New Hampshire Publishing Company, 1923; reprint. 1973.), I, 123. This was expected of all patriots at this time, as a test of loyalty to the cause.

[81] S. Goodwin, *JN.*

[82] S. Goodwin, *PM,* (Grandfather Parker), F 2.

[83] Mrs. Marston Fenwick, "William Rice's Give-Away Program," *Portsmouth Herald*, 24 Jan. 1959.

[84] S. Goodwin, *PM,* (Grandfather Parker), F 2.

[85] S. Goodwin, *JN.*

[86] Brighton, *TCTF,* II, 27.

[87] S. Goodwin, *PM,* (Grandfather Parker.), F 2.

[88] Stackpole, Thompson, Meserve, II, 64.

[89] Ibid., II, 301.

[90] S. Goodwin, *PM,* (Grandfather Parker), F 2.

[91] *Piscataqua Pioneers*, 328.

[92] S. Goodwin, *PM,* (Grandfather Parker), F.2.

[93] Ibid. Possibly this was a Masonic ritual. Parker, like many of the men in the area, would probably have been a member.

[94] Ibid.

[95] Stackpole, *OK&HF,* 33.

[96] S. Goodwin, *JN.*

[97] Stackpole, *OK&HR,* 64-65. It was not uncommon to divide marshland lots amongst the early settlers, as the marsh hay provided needed fodder for farm animals.

[98] Ibid., 66-67.

[99] Ibid., 33. Because Withers was so prominent in the affairs of the town of Kittery, and such large grants of land were given or sold to him, this indicates he was highly respected. His family may have been members of the English nobility. At the time English inheritance laws were based on the rule of primogeniture, and he may have been a younger son seeking his fortune in a new land.

[100] Ibid., 71.

[101] *Piscataqua Pioneers*, 470.

[102] Stackpole, *OK&HF, 64-69.*

[103] Ibid., 33, 69.

[104] Ibid., 86.

[105] Ibid.

[106] S. Goodwin, *JN.*

[107] Stackpole, *OK&HF,* 86-87.

[108] S. Goodwin, *PM,* (Childhood), F 2.

[109] Ibid. The Revere House is one of the oldest structures in Boston. Other neighbors beside Governor Bowdoin included the family of Charles Bullfinch, America's most prominent architect during the first half of the nineteenth century.

[110] Bruce Ingmire, "Rice Family Owned Ferry, Tavern," *Kittery Press,* 2, 27, 92.

[111] S. Goodwin, *PM,* (Childhood), F2.

[112] Stackpole, *OK&HF,* 185-186. There were three meetinghouses in Kittery by this time, as the township then included the outlying communities that now make up the towns of Eliot and Berwick as well as present day Kittery.

[113] Ibid., 189-192. Newmarche also taught school in the area for many years.

[114] S. Goodwin, *JN.*

[115] S. Goodwin, *PM,* (Childhood), F 2.

[116] S. Goodwin, *PM,* (Rice family), F 2.

[117] S. Goodwin, *PM,* (Servants), F 8.

[118] S. Goodwin, *PM,* (Childhood), F 2.

[119] Brighton, *TCTF,* I, 119. The toll bridge between Portsmouth and Kittery extended from Rindge's wharf in the North End of town to Nobel's Island and on to the Kittery shore.

[120] Ingmire, 2, 27, 92. Alexander Rice was a bridge builder, and he helped to build the new toll bridge in 1819. He had earlier built the bridge between York and Kittery, still known as the Rice Bridge.

[121] S. Goodwin, *PM,* (Childhood), F 2.

[122] Stackpole, *OK&HF,* 272-273.

[123] S. Goodwin, *PM,* (Childhood), F 2.

[124] Rice family genealogy. On file, Maine Room, Rice Library, Kittery, ME. In 1824 Alexander's son William, who had entered the Navy in 1813 as a midshipman, was given his first command on the *Perseverance,* a ship built by William Badger and owned by Samuel Coues and John Rice. On its maiden voyage, along with another Portsmouth ship, it was destroyed off the coast of the Bahamas, and all but one of the ship's crew were killed, including its young captain.

[125] Ibid.

[126] Fenwick, 24 Jan. 1959.

[127] Bruce Ingmire, "The Industrialization of the North End of Portsmouth" (*Portsmouth Press,* 5 May 1992), 17-18.

[128] Brighton, *POPS&CT,* 21.

CHILDHOOD STREETS

[129] S. Goodwin, *JN.*

[130] Brewster, II, 208-209.

[131] Ibid., II, 24-29. Henry Sherburne, an ancestor of Sarah's, once owned the Portsmouth Hotel. This pier, along with the hotel, was said to be superior to anything in Boston during this time.

[132] Ibid. Before 1826, when windows and tight doors were added, these arches were kept open during the hours of operation to let in needed light. Of course the open arches also let in the cold during the winter days.

[133] Ibid., II, 29-35. One year, Sunday school classes were held at Jefferson Hall; at the start of the Civil War, it was used for military barracks.

[134] John Garraty, *The American Nation* (New York: Harper & Row, 1966), I, 180.

[135] Saltonstall, 128-129.

[136] Brighton, *TCTF*, I, 81.

[137] Ibid.,101. However, not all of the plans for expansion were successful. About this time completed plans were on paper for a huge commercial center to be built at the bridge's northern terminus between the Oyster and Bellamy Rivers, where it could tap into some of the overland trade from Concord, as well as handle a portion of the shipping trade. It was to be called Franklin City. Even though many planning meetings were held, and quite a few lots were sold, the center never materialized.

[138] S. Goodwin, *PM,* (Servants), F 8.

[139] Fenwick, 24 Jan. l959.

[140] Brighton, *POPS&CT,* 45.

[141] S. Goodwin, *JN.*

[142] Brighton, *TCTF*, I, 92-93.

[143] Brewster, II, 28.

[144] Beth McDermott, *Shaping the Neighbor-hood: Portsmouth's History with Fire* (unpublished notes on file at Strawbery Banke, Portsmouth, NH, 1999). One of a set of matching chairs that George Washington sat in during his 1789 visit, a 1717 copy of the rare "Vinegar" Bible, and an organ, said to be the oldest in America, were saved.

[145] Brewster, I, 349-353.

[146] Ibid., II, 209-210. Buck Street is now State Street.

[147] Ibid., II, 204-207.

[148] Saltonstall, 151.

[149] Membership list, Federal Fire Society Members (unpublished, on file at the Moffatt Ladd House).

[150] S. Goodwin, *JN.*

[151] McDermott. These engines held up to two hundred gallons of water, and were filled by volunteer bucket brigades of men, women, and children. The tubs were pulled to the fire by firefighters, or carried there by horse drawn wagons, and water was then pumped out and discharged in a steady stream aimed at the fire. It wasn't until the 1830s that a reliable flexible canvas hose came into use.

[152] Ibid.

[153] Ibid.

[154] Ibid.

CHILDHOOD FAMILY
[155] S. Goodwin, *PM,* (Childhood), F 2.

[156] Richard M. Candee, *Building Portsmouth*, (Portsmouth, NH: Portsmouth Advocates, Inc., 1992) 22-23. Hart came from a family that produced several of Portsmouth's finest joiners during the eighteenth century.

[157] S. Goodwin, *PM,* (Childhood), F 2.

[158] Saltonstall, 180-183. Gundalows were indigenous to the area, having first been built by some of Portsmouth's earliest settlers to convey passengers and goods across the rough cross currents of the Piscataqua River. By the time of Sarah's childhood they were used mainly to transport rough cargo such as stone, lumber, brick, and ballast. They were propelled by pole, but many were rigged for sailing. Some were even painted.

[159] S. Goodwin, *PM,* (Childhood), F 2

[160] Karin Calvert, *Children in the House* (Boston: Northeastern University Press, 1992), 59-60. While Rousseau's promotion of total freedom with no early formal training conflicted somewhat with American standards, for the most part child experts of that day advised giving children more freedom to develop their natural tendencies.

[161] S. Goodwin, *PM,* (Childhood), F 2.

[162] Ibid., (Servants), F8.

[163] Ibid.

[164] Letter from Sarah Goodwin to Rev. Alfred Putnam, May 23, 1895.

[165] S. Goodwin, *PM,* (Childhood), F 2.

[166] Estes & Goodman, *The Changing Humors of Portsmouth* (Boston: Francis Courtway Library of Medicine, 1986), 59-65. The botanist was Samuel Thompson. He founded

the "Friendly Botanic Society," in Portsmouth sometime between 1808 and 1812.

[167] Ibid., 7, 22. Consumption was the number one cause of death in North America from Colonial times until the latter part of the nineteenth century.

[168] *Portsmouth Oracle*, 22 August 1812.

[169] S. Goodwin, *JN*. It was not uncommon for children of this period to know their Biblical phrases well enough to quote them in everyday conversations.

[170] Rice Family transcript.

[171] S. Goodwin, *PM,* (Childhood), F, 2.

[172] S. Goodwin, *JN*.

[173] Jane Nylander, *Our Own Snug Fireside,* (New York: Alfred Knopf, 1993), 144-147.

[174] Brighton, *TCTF,* I. 101. The bathhouse was run by the Moses family, and was open daily from sunrise to ten in the evening between the months of May and October. Mrs. Moses attended the female customers, and Mr. Moses attended the males, for a cost of twenty-five cents per visit or five visits for a dollar.

[175] S. Goodwin, *PM,* (Thanksgiving), F6.

[176] Mary Beth Norton et al., *A People & A Nation,* (Boston: Houghton Mifflin, 1990), I, 219.

[177] S. Goodwin, *JN*.

AUNT FLAGG

[178] Saltonstall, 93.

[179] Brighton, *TCTF,* I, 88.

[180] S. Goodwin, *PM,* (Aunt Flagg), F6.

[181] *Encyclopedia Britannica, Micropaedia,* (Chicago: Encyclopedia Britannica, Inc., 1974), 1X, 923. Unfortunately he was a loyalist as well as a spy for the Crown prior to the Revolution, and returned to England after the Revolution.

[182] S. Goodwin, *PM,* (Aunt Flagg), F 6.

[183] Ibid.

[184] Nylander, 139-140.

[185] S. Goodwin, *PM,* (Aunt Flagg), F 6.

[186] Ibid.

[187] Brighton, *TCTF,* II, 142.

[188] S. Goodwin, *PM,* (Aunt Flagg), F 6.

WAR OF 1812

[189] S. Goodwin letter to Rev. Putnum, 23 May 1895.

[190] Brighton, *TCTF,* 11, 84-85.

[191] Ibid.

[192] Ibid.

[193] Brighton, *TCTF*, I, 84-86.

[194] Ibid. 199.

[195] Saltonstall, 134-139.

[196] Ibid., 133-139.

[197] Norton, I, 223. Even then the rest of the Barbary States demanded tribute from Americans until 1815.

[198] Saltonstall, 137.

[199] Brighton, *POPS&CT,* 7-9.

[200] Ibid. 8-10.

[201] Saltonstall, 145.

[202] S. Goodwin, Putnum letter.

[203] Norton, I, 225.

[204] S. Goodwin, Putnum letter.

[205] Saltonstall, 143.

[206] Brighton, *TCTF,* I, *100.*

[207] Brighton, *POPS&CT*, 35.

[208] S. Goodwin, Putnum letter.

[209] Ibid.

[210] Saltonstall, 149-150.

[211] S. Goodwin, *PM,* (Grandfather Parker), F 2.

[212] Pillsbury II, 24.

[213] Brighton, *TCTF, I,* 113.

[214] Saltonstall, 153.

[215] Ibid.

[216] S. Goodwin, Putnum letter.

[217] Pillsbury, 2, 25.

[218] S. Goodwin, *PM,* (History), F 1.

[219] Pillsbury, 2, 24.

[220] Saltonstall, 154.

[221] Brighton, *TCTF* I, *105.*

[222] Saltonstall, 159.

[223] Brighton, *TCTF*, I, l05.

[224] Saltonstall, 159.

[225] Mrs. Marston Fenwick, "William Rice's Give-A-Way Program" (*Portsmouth Herald,* 4 Jan. 1959).

[226] Saltonstall, 165.

[227] Winslow, *W & H,* 186.

[228] Fenwick, *WRGP.*

[229] Norton, I, 256-257.

[230] Saltonstall, 155.

[231] S. Goodwin, Putnam letter.

[232] Brighton, *TCTF,* I, 106.

[233] Saltonstall, 166.

234 Brighton, *TCTF,* I, 105-106.
235 S. Goodwin, Putnum letter.

ASSEMBLY HOUSE
236 S. Goodwin, (Music Lessons), F 1.
237 Ibid., (History), F 1.
238 Elwin Page, *George Washington in New Hampshire* (Portsmouth NH: Portsmouth Marine Society, 1989 reprint), 68. Washington's chief objection to the homes was that they were primarily wooden structures, as opposed to the brick, clay, or stone structures commonly found in southern states. He also noted there were about seventy-five ladies present at a ball in his honor, and deemed many of them *"handsome,"* but he wondered why such a greater proportion of the ladies in New England had darker hair than in the southern states.
239 S. Goodwin, *PM,* (Assembly House), F 3.
240 Ibid., (Music Lessons), F 2.
241 Ibid., (History). F 1.
242 Ibid., (Music Lessons), F 2.
243 Ibid.
244 Ibid., (History), F 1.
245 Ibid., (Music Lessons), F 2.
246 Ibid., (Looking Back), F 2.
247 Ibid., (Assembly House), F 3.
248 R. Candee, 22.
249 S. Goodwin, *PM,* (Assembly House), F 3.
250 Ibid.
251 Ibid., (History), F 1.
252 Ibid.
253 *Encyclopedia Britannica,* 1V, 639.
254 Brighton, *TCTF,* 11, 161.
255 S. Goodwin, *PM,* (History), F 1.
256 *The Portsmouth Herald*, 23 Aug. l958.
257 S. Goodwin, *PM,* (Assembly House), F 3.
258 Brighton, *TCTF,* 11,185-186. Although Sarah is generally quite accurate in her memories, local historian Ray Brighton reports the ball held that night in his honor was at Jefferson Hall, and Sarah noted that by this time most of the balls were held at Franklin Hall.

THE DRESSMAKER
259 Norton, I, 254-257. Pre-made clothing was available as early as the 1820s, but it was primarily worn by males and consisted of poorly fitting garments such as baggy suits, cut in bulk in standardized patterns, and hand sewn by women who worked at piece rates out of their own homes. It wasn't popular with the majority of women until the end of the century.
260 S. Goodwin, *PM,* (Dressmaker), F 7.
261 Saltonstall, 150.
262 S. Goodwin, *PM,* (Dressmaker), F 7.
263 *Encyclopedia Britannica,* 3,528.
264 S. Goodwin, *PM,* (Dressmaker), F 7.
265 Pillsbury, II, 314-315.
266 Ibid.
267 David K Nartonis, *"The New Divinity Movement and its Impact on New Hampshire's Churches 1769-1849." (Historic New Hampshire,* Spring Summer 2000, 55) 25.
268 Norton, I, 98-99.
269 S. Goodwin, *PM,* (Dressmaker), F 7.
270 Nartonis, 26.
271 Ibid., 206-208.
272 Nartonis, 29. Along with the traditional Congregationalists and Presbyterians, the list included Methodists, Calvinist Baptists, Free Will Baptists, Christian, Episcopalians, Unitarians, Universalists and Quakers, and Shakers.
273 S. Goodwin, *PM,* (Dressmaker), F 7.

NORTH END NEIGHBORHOOD
274 S. Goodwin, *PM,* (Kennards), F 2.
275 Nylander, 118-119.
276 S. Goodwin, *PM,* (Kennards*),* F 2.
277 Brighton, *POPS&CT,* 205.
278 S. Goodwin, *PM,* (Kennards), F 2.
279 Ibid.
280 Ibid.
281 Brighton, *POPS&CT.*
282 Ibid., 193.
283 S. Goodwin, *PM,* (Kennard), F2.
284 Ibid.
285 S. Goodwin, *PM,* (Misses Hart & Misses Slade), F 7.
286 Brewster, II, 270-274. Spring Market was open to all who could manage to find a spot spot beneath the sprawling cover of the open market place. When the new market was built a certain amount of business was diverted to the inner city, but the old Spring Market was still quite a lively spot during Sarah's youth.

Eventually a new market building was built and the old market was moved to Nobel's Island.

[287] S. Goodwin, *PM,* (Misses Hart & Misses Slade), F 4.

[288] Brighton, *TCTF,* 11, 106.

DINAH & BOSTON

[289] S. Goodwin, *PM,* (Rice Family), F 2.

[290] Constance Ward, "Negro Slavery in Colonial Portsmouth" (unpublished thesis on file in Portsmouth, NH, Library Archives, 1969), 1-3.

[291] Ibid., 46-47. By 1776, there were six hundred and thirty-three slaves in the state of New Hampshire. This was the highest number ever recorded in the state, and Portsmouth had the most slaves.

[292] C. Ward, 5-7. Most of the slaves brought to New England were not considered prime, but they were also not subjected to the heavy workload common in the southern or West Indian plantations. However, some of the more desirable slaves were set aside for wealthy Portsmouth merchants on request.

[293] Ibid.

[294] S. Goodwin, *PM,* (Dinah Gibson), F6.

[295] Ibid.

[296] Ibid.

[297] Ibid.

[298] Brewster, I, 210. Some slaves were contracted out to work for others in the community, and it was not unusual to find slaves working on the docks or on board ships.

[299] S. Goodwin, *PM,* (Assembly House), F 4.

[300] Brewster, I, 177.

[301] C. Ward, 28.

[302] Brewster, I, 210-213.

[303] Ibid. This form of peer pressure helped to maintain order within the slave community, as well as to minimize overly harsh or severe treatment of slaves.

[304] Sherman, 18.

[305] Brewster, I, 154-156. Prince's name does appear as one of the members of this fighting force. He was also said to be the black soldier who was immortalized in the famous Revolutionary War painting of George Washington crossing the Delaware by Emanuel G. Leutze,

though recent research has been able to place Prince in Philadelphia with his master the night of the crossing. John Blunt, another Portsmouth man, is depicted in the portrait as the pilot of the boat.

[306] Sherman, 18-19. They were led by Peter Frost of Durham, slave of George Frost, and Nero Brewster, slave of William Brewster of Portsmouth, as well as the chosen "king" of the city's slave community.

[307] *The Boston Sunday Globe*, 21 Feb. 1999.

[308] Norton, I, 164-166.

[309] C. Ward, 46.

[310] Stackpole, *HONH,* I, 264.

[311] Ibid.

[312] S. Goodwin, *PM,* (Dinah Gibson), F 6.

[313] Ibid., (Rice Family), F 2.

[314] Wibird Penhallow, *Portsmouth City Directory* (Portsmouth, NH: 1821).

[315] S. Goodwin, *PM,* (Dinah Gibson), F 6.

[316] Ibid.

[317] Penhallow, *PCD.*

ALMS HOUSE RESIDENTS

[318] S. Goodwin, *PM,* (Alms House), F 4.

[319] Coquillette, David, *Law in Colonial Massachusetts* (Boston, MA: The Colonial Society of Massachusetts, 1984), 154. During most of the seventeenth century there was not a great deal of poverty in most New England towns, and what poverty did exist was taken care of by a combination of church and town charity.

[320] Robert Kelso, *The History of Public Poor Relief in Massachusetts* (Boston: Houghlin Mifflin, 1919), 109-112.

[321] S. Goodwin, *PM,* (Alms House), F 4.

[322] Brewster, I, 127-129. Taxpayers were unwilling to support vagrants from other districts, and during the seventeenth and eighteenth centuries most New England towns had laws that were designed to discourage settlement within the town limits. On the average there was a residency requirement, and a required waiting period of at least three months before benefits were paid out. The sheriff or other town officials had the right to issue official warnings to vagabonds, gypsies, and other undesirables against remaining

within the town limits for an extended period of time. The local history books record several instances when Portsmouth selectmen issued warnings to some residents, who were ordered to either send the guests away or give security to the town to insure that they would not end up on the town welfare rolls. One widow with no relatives to back her with security was given a fortnight to remove herself from the city limits.

[323] S. Goodwin, *JN.*

[324] Coquillette, 166. It wasn't until 1735 that Boston built an adequate workhouse for those able to work, but the rest remained in substandard combinations of prison/asylum/pauper houses.

[325] Ibid., 153-155. This surge was due to several convergent factors that occurred within the colonial society of this time. First there was an increase in the overall population, with a corresponding decline in available land. There were also a series of minor wars, in particular the French and Indian War, and these were followed by period inflation. All of these factors contributed to a growing unemployment problem and an increasingly transient population.

[326] Ibid., 168-169. Though the practice of farming out some of the poor continued, many who applied to the towns for relief under the poor laws were institutionalized in these work farms.

[327] S. Goodwin, *JN.*

[328] Brewster, *Rambles,* I, 127-131. Charles Brewster touched on the dreadful conditions that existed in this second house in his *Rambles,* citing the recollections of the grandson of the man who was overseer of this almshouse for thirty-six years. It seems Clem March was a giant of a man, feared by the residents, who were kept in line by just the sight of his cane.

[329] S. Goodwin, *PM,* (Alms House), F 4.

[330] Estes, 182-189. In New England, public care for those deemed insane was not available until some time after the 1840s, when social reformer and humanitarian Dorothea Dix exposed the intolerable conditions suffered by the mentally ill in Massachusetts, who were put

into prisons alongside criminals of both sexes.

[331] S. Goodwin, *JN.*

[332] Estes, 182-189.

[333] Ibid. There was some outrage at the appointment of the young doctor, as he was fresh out of school and inexperienced, but he was given the newly created position of City Physician the following year.

[334] Ibid.

[335] S. Goodwin, *PM,* (Alms House), F 4.

[336] S. Goodwin, *PM,* (Esther Benson), F 5.

[337] S. Goodwin, *PM,* (Alms House), F 4.

[338] Ibid.

[339] S. Goodwin, *PM,* (Esther Benson), F 5.

[340] S. Goodwin, *PM,* (Alms House), F 4.

[341] S. Goodwin, *PM,* (Esther Benson), F 5.

[342] Estes, 183-184. Esther's story is not an unusual one. Although extreme, it is reminiscent of the treatment that abused wives have endured through the ages. However, today women do have recourse through the courts and access to safe shelters for themselves and their families. When Esther lived in Portsmouth married women had no legal rights and those who left their homes because of abusive husbands and intolerable conditions lost all legal claim to their children, and were left to fend for themselves.

[343] S. Goodwin, *PM,* (Alms House), F 4.

[344] Ibid., (Ester Benson), F 5.

[345] Ibid., (Phebe). F. 5.

[346] Ibid.

[347] Ibid.

[348] Ibid. The Seaman's Home was a combination temperance and boarding house, and also served as a hospital facility for seamen from 1832 to the Civil War.

[349] Chas. Brewster, *Portsmouth Directory* (Portsmouth, NH: C.W. Brewster & Son, 1861), 152.

SCHOOLS

[350] Catherine Fennelly, *Town Schooling in Early New England* (Meredin, CT: Meriden Gravure Pub. Company, 1962), 5.

[351] Brewster, I, 78-81.

[352] Pillsbury, 2, 331.

[353] Ibid.

[354] Johnson, 2-4.

355 Fennelly, 11. The study of Greek and Latin was mandatory for entrance into Harvard at this time so these schools taught these subjects.

356 Brewster, 1, 298-302. Dearborn built a schoolhouse behind his own house, complete with a large hall to teach dancing, a skill considered to be an important part of a young woman's education.

357 Ibid.

358 Brewster, I, 304. It was reported that those students who attended the first teacher's classes learned in one year more than most would have in five.

359 Clifton Johnson, *Old Time Schools & School Books* (New York: Dover Publications, 1904), 31.

360 S. Goodwin, *PM,* (Schooling), F 2.

361 Ibid.

362 Ibid.

363 Brewster, I, 303-306.

364 S. Goodwin, *PM,* (Schooling), F 2.

365 Ibid.

366 Ibid.

367 S. Goodwin, *JN.*

368 S. Goodwin, *PM,* (Schooling), F 2.

369 S. Goodwin, *JN.*

370 S. Goodwin, *PM,* (Schooling), F 2.

371 *Cambridge Historical Society Assoc.* 11, No.9. (Cambridge, MA: Cambridge Historical Society, Oct. 1916), 9-19.

372 Ray Brighton, *Rambles About Portsmouth* (Portsmouth NH: Portsmouth Marine Society, 1991), 151-153. President Monroe was in Portsmouth for three days. During that time he toured the harbor, the forts, and the Naval Yard. On his last night he was entertained at a concert held by local musicians in Jefferson Hall.

373 Mrs. Marston Fenwick, *Portsmouth Herald,* 26 July 1958.

374 Brighton, *RAP,* 151-153.

375 Cambridge Historical Association. Willard letters, letter Mary to Joseph Willard, 9-19.

376 Ibid., II, 22.

377 S. Goodwin, *JN.*

378 Fennelly, 30.

THE "OLD THREE DECKER"

379 S. Goodwin, *PM,* (North Church), F 4.

380 Brewster, I, 332. After much discussion it was resolved to employ every possible means to prevent any ship carrying tea from the East India Company from coming into the Port of Portsmouth. It was also agreed that anyone caught aiding or abetting the importation or sale of this tea was considered an enemy of the country.

381 Brighton, *TCTF,* 1, 6. Today twelve of those acres comprise the hub of the city's commercial district, bounded by the present day Congress, Court, Chestnut, and Pleasant Streets. The remaining thirty-eight acres at the head of Islington Creek are currently valuable commercial and residential properties.

382 Ibid. The Episcopalian minister left town under a cloud of accusations made by the Puritan Council in Massachusetts that he had illegally performed marriages and baptisms under the rites of the Episcopal Church, a crime under Puritan law.

383 Candee, 67. In 1731 this group built a new meetinghouse a little further north on Marcy Street on a rise now known as Meetinghouse Hill.

384 Brewster, I, 331. However, the vane was never gilded until 1796. In the 1850s a steeple clock donated to the parish was put on the right side of the bell tower.

385 S. Goodwin, *PM,* (North Church). F 4.

386 Ibid.

387 Brewster, I, 326-331.

388 S. Goodwin, *PM,* (Servants), F 8.

389 S. Goodwin, *PM,* (North Church), F 4.

390 S. Goodwin, *JN.*

391 S. Goodwin, *PM,* (North Church), F 4. The parishioner with the red cushions mentioned below was Edward Cutts, according to historian Charles Brewster.

392 Ibid.

393 S. Goodwin, *PM,* (North Church), F 4.

394 Brewster, I, 210-211.

395 S. Goodwin, *PM,* (North Church), F 4.

396 Brewster, I, 352.

397 Ibid. I, 262-3. President James Monroe sat in this same pew almost three decades later during his 1817 visit to Portsmouth.

398 Brewster, 1, 352. During the service it was said that Washington never took his eyes off of Reverend Buckminster, who wore a tri-cor-

nered hat and long canonical robes. The venerable minister used this auspicious occasion for an opportunity to address his congregation and his distinguished guests with a sermon that was both patriotic and religious in nature. At the end he was filled with high praise for the country's first President and all he had done to free America from the bonds of tyranny.

399 Nartonis, 25. Although the First Amendment called for the separation of church and state as early as 1791, New Hampshire remained one of three New England states that continued public support for this church until the Toleration Act was passed in 1819.

400 S. Goodwin, *PM,* (North Church), F 4.
401 Brighton, *TCTF*, II, 118.
402 Brewster, *TCTF*, I, 327.
403 S. Goodwin, *PM,* (North Church), F 4.
404 Ibid.
405 Brighton, *TCTF,* II, 8.
406 S. Goodwin, *PM,* (Wedding Journey), F 2.
407 Thomas O'Connor, "Changing Times At Harvard," (*The Boston Globe*, 16 August 1999), A15. With an emphasis on intellectual reasoning, moral uprightness, and the possibilities inherent in social reform, Unitarianism attracted a large following of intellectuals during this time.
408 S. Goodwin, *PM,* (North Church), F 4.
409 Ibid., (Wedding Journey), F2.
410 Brighton, *POPS&CT,* 68.
411 Candee, pp.83-84.

MARRIAGE AND WEDDING JOURNEY
412 S. Goodwin, *PM,* (Music), F. 2.
413 Brewster, 1, 163-165. In his first *Rambles*, Charles Brewster, wrote that prior to the Revolution, Colonel Boyd became the wealthiest man in Portsmouth almost overnight, when he came into the possession of all the property and silver of a very successful businessman, who mysteriously disappeared on the eve of his wedding to a daughter of the prominent Scheafe family. The groom was never heard from again.
414 S. Goodwin, *PM,* (Music Lessons), F 2.
415 Brighton, *POPS&CT,* 44. Parsons specialized in the importation of coffee, and was for a

short time part owner of the ship *Olive & Eliza.*
416 *Encyclopedia Britannica*, I, 885.
417 S. Goodwin, *PM,* (Assembly House), F 4.
418 Ibid., (Music Lessons), F 2.
419 Ibid., (North Church), F 4.
420 Ibid., (Music Lessons), F 2.
421 Ibid., (North Church), F 4.
422 Ibid., (Music Lessons), F 2.
423 The Political Graveyard of Politicians: politicagraveyard.com/bio/smith/2.htlm/, 3/30/03.
424 S. Goodwin, *PM,* (North Church), F 4.
425 Brighton, *TCTF,* 11, 182.
426 Brighton, *POPS&CT,* 45, 65.
427 S. Goodwin, *PM,* (History), F 1.
428 Ibid., (Servants), F 8.
429 Ibid., (History), F 1.
430 Ibid., (Wedding Journey), F 2.
431 Ibid., (Looking Back), F 2.
432 Ibid., (Wedding Journey), F 2.
433 Page Smith, *The Nation Comes of Age* (NY: McGraw-Hill, 1981), IV, 793. Tudor also created Malois Gardens, the first amusement park in the United States. Located in Nahant, MA, it featured, amongst other things, a dance hall, an ice cream parlor, a shooting gallery, Indians, two tame bears and a bowling alley. At the time Nahant was a popular summer resort for the elite and literary set of Boston; the park was not well received by the summer regulars.
434 S. Goodwin, *PM,* (Wedding journey), F 2.
435 "A Visit to the Catskill Mountain House 1826." Author unknown, published in a Boston paper, 1826. www.catskillarchive.com/misc/boston1826.htm.
436 Ibid. Although the carriage road was a good wide one, it was such a steep incline that the angle was quite uncomfortable, and many opted to walk alongside the carriages rather than ride.
437 S. Goodwin, *PM,* (Wedding Journey), F 2.
438 Ibid., (NY 1827).
439 Ibid. It was the conclusion of the essayist of 1826 that the host was "uncommonly polite," and a true gentleman. The rooms were well furnished and comfortable, and in his opinion the Mountain House provided almost every luxury found in the first class city hotels of the day.

440 Ibid., (Wedding Journey), F 2.

441 1826 Boston newspaper.

442 Ibid.

443 S. Goodwin, *PM*, (New York, 1827), F 3.

444 Ibid.

445 Edward S. Martin, "Domestic Manners of Americans, 1831 by Mrs. Trollope," *The Wayfarer in New York* (NY: McMillian Co. 1909), 33-36.

446 Ibid.

447 Ibid.

448 S. Goodwin, *PM*, (New York 1827*)*, F 3.

449 Ibid.

450 Smith, IV, 1085-1090. Though a southerner, Scott remained with the Union throughout the Civil War. He died at the age of eighty, one year after the war's end.

451 S. Goodwin, *PM*, (New York, 1827)., F 3.

452 Lloyd Morris, *Incredible New York* (NY: Random House, 1951), 46, 294. In later years Broad Street was home to the New York Stock Exchange, and parts of Canal Street where Sarah "took tea" became New York's red light district.

453 E. Martin, 31-37. An abundance of marble topped tables, handsome chiffonniers, elegant mirrors, and French porcelain displayed in tasteful decorations brought to mind the interiors of some of the finest homes in Europe.

454 Ibid.

455 Morris, 48-53. Chatham Street later was part of New York's "red light district.

456 S. Goodwin, *PM*, (NY 1827), F 3.

457 Ibid., (Wedding Journey), F 2.

458 Ibid., (New York, 1827), F 3.

459 Ibid.

460 Ibid., (Wedding Journey), F 2.

461 Ibid., (New York, 1827)., F 3.

462 Ulysses Hedrick, *A History of Horticulture in America* (NY: Oxford University Press, 1950), 204. The store Sarah visited was Thornburn's second store; the first burned down and as it wasn't insured he was put into debtors' prison for a period. This was one of the first shops of this kind, and eventually he was very successful.

463 S. Goodwin, *PM*, (Wedding Journey), F 2.

464 Ibid., (Looking Back), F 2.

465 S. Goodwin, *PM*, (Wedding Journey), F 2.

466 Brighton, *POPS&CT*, 178. The *Sarah Parker*, built by William Badger in 1827, was jointly owned by the counting houses of Goodwin & Coues and Ferguson & Jewett.

467 S. Goodwin, *PM*, (Wedding journey), F 2.

468 Brighton, *TSOTP*, 31. He spent his summers in Portsmouth for many years, and his ties to the city were so strong that in 1842 he was granted membership into the Federal Fire Society.

469 S. Goodwin, *PM*, (Wedding journey), F 2.

470 *The Savannah Press*, 5 Nov. 1919. The *Savannah Press* once noted that it had such a momentous history as a hostelry it was "almost as well known as the city itself."

471 *Ibid.*, 14 Jan. 1956. It was named in honor of Count Pulaski, a Polish nobleman killed during the siege of Savannah in 1779, but not before he saved his adopted city from certain destruction.

472 Ibid. At the end of the Civil War Jefferson Davis and his wife were confined there for several days under the guard of northern troops before he was imprisoned in Virginia.

473 Ibid.

474 Ibid. On the upper levels there was a cage elevator, with an ornate hand wrought iron design, that probably would not have been there when Sarah was there in 1828.

475 S. Goodwin, *PM*, (Wedding Journey), F 2.

476 Ibid.

477 Ibid.

478 *The Savannah Evening Press*, 14, Jan. 1956.

479 S. Goodwin, *PM*, (Wedding Journey), F 2.

480 *McMillian Encyclopedia* (NY: Simon & Schuster, 1995), 651.

481 S. Goodwin, *PM*, (Wedding Journey)*,* F.2.

482 Ibid.

483 *Encyclopedia Britannica*, X, 1275-78.

484 S. Goodwin, *PM*, (Wedding journey), F 2.

485 Ibid.

486 Ibid.

487 http//www.chestercathederal.com.3/30/04.

488 http://www.eeo.co.uk/grosvenor-estate/ brief-history.asp, July August 2004. The title of Duke of Westminster was not yet created at the time of Sarah's visit. Robert Grosvenor, the second Earl of Eaton, who was named

the Marquis in 1831, lived there then. His grandson Hugh was made the first Duke of Westminster in 1875.

489 S. Goodwin, *PM,* (Wedding Journey), F 2.

490 http:www/bwpics.co.uk/grosvenor. bridge. htm/. 30 March 2004. By the time of Sarah's visit plans were underway for a second bridge that was laid out by the Marquis of Westminster, named the Grosvenor Bridge in honor of his family. This bridge was completed by 1832, and it was the largest stone bridge in the world at the time.

491 S. Goodwin, *PM,* (Wedding Journey), F 2.

492 Ibid.

493 http://www.manchester2002ukcom/history/ victorian1//.html. 19 January 2004. These conditions caused a terrible stench of waste, which filled the air, and since coal was used to heat the homes and factories, a cloud of soot and smoke also hung over the city at all times.

494 S. Goodwin, *PM,* (Wedding Journey), F 2.

495 Ibid.

496 *Encyclopedia Britannica,* XII, 435-7.

497 S. Goodwin, *PM,* (Wedding Journey), F 2. Originally an ascetic mystical religion based on communal living, by the nineteenth century their focus was on social reform. The argument over the alphabet may have been related to mystical tenets.

498 Brighton, *POPS&CT,* 178.

CHILDBIRTH

499 Richard and Dorothy Wertz, *Lying In* (New Haven: Yale University Press, 1977), 79-81. This practice of shielding pregnant women from the view of others was evidence of the ambivalence Victorian society felt towards the birth process. While motherhood was revered in America during this time period, so was purity and modesty. Since pregnancy was necessarily contingent on a sexual act, it was a subject infused with embarrassment and shame for many women, and was not spoken of in polite society or openly acknowledged by many.

500 Letter to Sarah Goodwin from Ichabod Goodwin, January 1, 1829.

501 Brighton, *POPS&CT,* 178-179. Arriving on March 28, 1829, the ship got caught up in the strong current of the Piscataqua River and became temporarily grounded upon a rock on Noble's Island.

502 S. Goodwin, *PM,* (Wedding Journey), F 2.

503 S. Goodwin, *PM* (Servants), F 8.

504 Estes, 69. Yet in the city of Portsmouth existing records indicate that male physicians often attended deliveries during the last half of the eighteenth century, but these physicians did not provide any systematic care prior to or following birth.

505 Ibid., 37-44. They were either trained to avoid all eye contact with the patient during exams, or to maintain constant eye contact to assure the patient that he was not looking at any other part of her body. In addition women were generally reluctant to discuss female complaints or problems with male doctors, as they had done in the past with midwives. Therefore many infections or injuries that were incurred before or during the birth process were left unattended.

506 Ibid., 44-49. Within a few more decades the majority of American women would come to rely solely upon male physicians to deliver their children. By mid-century midwives had been driven away from the profession of childbirth. Considered unfit for a woman's delicate sensibilities, the field of childbirth became strictly a male domain.

507 Ibid. 114-118. At the time it was believed that pain brought on the maternal instinct.

508 Estes, 45-52. Dr. Cheever also practiced dentistry. In addition he was noted for his progressive lectures at the Portsmouth Lyceum, and his articles in the prestigious *New England Journal of Medicine.* He was in favor of such avant-garde subjects as sulfur bath cures, as well as the science of phrenology, which taught that a person's mental capacity could be determined from the size and shape of their skull. He also enjoyed the distinction of being the very first person in Portsmouth to make daguerreotypes.

509 Wettz, 80-81. By the time Sarah's children were born, a woman attended by a male physician was likely to give birth in bed lying on her side in a lateral position known as the

Sims position, while female attendants made sure she was properly covered by a sheet for modesty's sake.

[510] S. Goodwin, *PM,* (Servants), F 8.

[511] Sally Kevill Davies, *Yesterday's Children* (Suffolk, England: Antique Collectors Club, 1991), 40-48. The underlying reason for the high mortality rate amongst these babies was that clay and pewter bottles, along with cow's milk, were perfect breeding grounds for bacteria. About this time Louis Pasteur discovered bacteria, and pinpointed them as the primary culprits in these infant deaths. However, pasteurization was not introduced until the latter part of the century when bottle-feeding became a popular alternative to breast-feeding.

LETTERS FROM THE EARLY YEARS OF MARRIAGE

[512] Ichabod Goodwin letter to Sarah Goodwin dated June 16,1829.

[513] S. Goodwin, *PM, (Wedding Journey),* F 2.

[514] Sarah Goodwin letter to Ichabod Goodwin dated October 30, 1830.

[515] Sarah Goodwin letter to Ichabod Goodwin dated November 2, 1830.

[516] Brighton, *POPS&CT*, 23-24.

[517] Sarah Goodwin letter to Ichabod Goodwin dated November 14, 1830.

[518] Sarah Goodwin letter to Ichabod Goodwin dated November 22, 1830.

[519] Sarah Goodwin letter to Ichabod Goodwin dated November 30, 1830.

[520] Sarah Goodwin letter to Ichabod Goodwin dated December 7, 1830.

[521] Sarah Goodwin letter to Ichabod Goodwin dated December 17, 1830.

[522] Sarah Goodwin letter to Ichabod Goodwin dated December 25, 1830.

[523] Sarah Goodwin letter to Ichabod Goodwin dated January 14, 1831.

[524] Sarah Goodwin letter to Ichabod Goodwin dated February 10, 1831.

[525] William Rice letter to Ichabod Goodwin dated January 1, 1831. Thayer Cummings Library, Box F33.

[526] Brighton, *POPS&CT*, 178.

[527] Sarah Goodwin, *JN.*

CHILDREARING

[528] S. Goodwin, *PM,* (Wedding Journey), F 2. This home was patterned after an architectural design of the well-known Boston architect Charles Bullfinch. Constructed right before the War of 1812 by James Hazelton and a group of investors, it was the first home ever built on Islington Street, which had been known as the rock pile up until then. It was about twenty years old when the Goodwins bought it, and there were other houses on the street by the time the Goodwins moved there. Eventually Islington Street became a main thoroughfare of the city.

[529] Goodwin Family Bible.

[530] S. Goodwin, *JN.*

[531] Smith, IV, 871-875.

[532] Catherine Beecher and Harriet Beecher Stowe, *American Woman's Home* (Hartford, CT: Harriet Beecher Stowe Center, 1975, reprint. Original by J.B. Ford Co., 1869), 276-286.

[533] S. Goodwin, *PM,* (Unkind neighbor), F 5.

[534] Ibid., 117-118, 155.

[535] Karen Calvert, *Children in the House* (Boston: Northeastern University Press, 1992), 97-102.

[536] Ibid.

[537] Ibid.

[538] Ibid.

[539] Ibid., 112-113.

[540] S. Goodwin, list of child raising rules found amongst papers. Author may or may not be SPRG.

[541] Fennelly, 38-40.

[542] Brewster, I, 79-80. This school, which still stands, was built on the land given to the city a century and a half earlier to be used for a public school house.

1830-1840: WHALING, WHIGGERY AND RAILROADS

[543] Kenneth Martin, *Heavy Weather & Hard Luck* (Portsmouth, NH: Portsmouth Marine Society, 1998), 12-14.

[544] S. Goodwin, *PM,* (Servants), F 4.

[545] Martin, 18-23.

[546] Ibid., 57-63. The two other whaling companies formed about this time met with some success.

[547] Letter, George Cummings to Ichabod Goodwin, August 14,1835, Saratoga Springs. Box F33, Thayer Cummings Library.

[548] Ray Brighton, *The Tall Ships of the Piscataqua* (Portsmouth, NH: The Portsmouth Marine Society, 1989), 21-22, 37-38.

[549] Brighton, *TCTF,* I, 125. Insurance was a relatively new business at that time. Small insurance companies, like the ones Goodwin and Coues were involved with, were quite profitable. Those who entered the business first were granted charters by the state legislature giving them the right to insure their fellow businessmen against fire loss, maritime loss, and even the loss of life.

[550] *Encyclopedia Britannica*, 478-9. In October of 1829, this railroad ran a contest judging trial runs of various locomotive prototypes to determine which would be the best design to launch the line. The winner was the *Rocket*, powered by an engine fired by a system of multiple burning tubes.

[551] S. Goodwin, *PM,* (Wedding Journey), F 2.

[552] Norton, I, 246-247.

[553] Pillsbury, 516.

[554] S. Goodwin, *PM,* (Wedding journey), F 2.

[555] *Portsmouth Daily Evening Times*, 5 July 1882.

[556] Undated letter, Theodore Jewett to Ichabod Goodwin, circa 1830-40s. Box F33, Thayer Cummings Library. Jewett's wife was a sister of William Rice's, and he was the father of Sarah Orne Jewett.

[557] Pillsbury, 171.

[558] Norton, I, 356-357.

[559] David Walker Howe, *The Political Culture of the American Whigs* (Chicago: University of Chicago Press, 1979), 88.

[560] Ibid., 18-20.

[561] Brighton, *TCTF,* I, 129-130.

[562] S. Goodwin letter to Rev. A. Putnam, May 23, 1895.

[563] Ray Brighton, *TCTF,* II, 182. Goodwin was also a charter member, and for many years president of the Portsmouth Marine Society, president of the Howard Benevolent Society, and a long-standing member of St John's Masonic Lodge No. 1. In addition, Goodwin was a board member of the Mechanics Reading Room, as well as the Portsmouth Lyceum, which sponsored lectures on important issues of the day. Samuel Coues was president of the Lyceum in 1840.

THE SERVANT PROBLEM
[564] S. Goodwin, *PM,* (Servants), F 8.

[565] Ibid.

[566] Ibid.

[567] Ibid.

[568] Nylander, 121-127. Because there were no screens on the windows at this time, homes were subjected to an infestation of ants, flies, mosquitoes, and other unwelcome pests each summer. Therefore it was necessary to cover or remove items that might be damaged by flyspecks such as oil paintings, mirrors and other gilded items. Homemade remedies were used in an attempt to control these seasonal pests, but were not always effective.

[569] S. Goodwin, *Waste Book.*

[570] Nylander, 139-140.

[571] S. Goodwin, *WB.*

[572] S. Goodwin, *PM,* (Servants), F 8.

[573] Ibid.

[574] Ibid., (History), F 1.

[575] Ibid., (Servants), F 8.

[576] S. Goodwin, *JN.*

[577] S. Goodwin, *PM,* (Servants), F 8.

[578] Nylander, 205. Prior to the introduction of tin ovens, near the turn of the eighteenth century, fresh meats were roasted by hanging them on a rope over the open-hearth fire or by putting them on a spit either turned manually or by a clock jack. These jacks were clock-driven mechanisms that drove a series of wheels and ropes to turn the spit.

[579] S. Goodwin, *PM,* (Servants), F 8.

[580] Ibid.

[581] Ibid.

[582] Pat Riley, *Servants in Nineteenth Century Portsmouth* (unpublished essay on file Strawbery Banke, 1984), 2.

[583] S. Goodwin, *PM,* (Servants), F 8.

[584] Faye E Dudden, *Serving Women: Household service in Nineteenth Century America* (CT: Wesleyan Press, 1983), 65. The position offered the opportunity for the young female immigrants to settle in as Americans, save

their wages, and assimilate into the culture by observing the social customs, manners, and mores prevalent in average American families.

585 Hasia Diner, *Erin's Daughters in America* (London, England: John Hopkins Press), 95.

586 Riley, 4.

587 S. Goodwin, *PM*, (Servants), F 8.

588 Riley, 4.

589 Diner, 93.

590 Campaign letter, circa 1960, for Governor Wesley Powell with bibliographical sketch on Mary Gosse Powell, undated.

591 S. Goodwin, *JN*.

592 S. Goodwin, *WB*.

THANKSGIVING HOLIDAYS

593 S. Goodwin, *PM*, (Thanksgiving), F 6.

594 Ibid.

595 Nylander, 270-271.

596 S. Goodwin, *PM (Thanksgiving), F6.*

597 Ibid.

598 Ibid.

599 Ibid.

A CANADIAN HOLIDAY

600 Malone, XX, 380-382. At the time his own father, Levin Winder, an anti-war Federalist, was mayor of nearby Baltimore. Because of this, Winder's troops focused more on protecting that city than the seat of the federal government.

601 S. Goodwin, *PM*, (Prince of Wales, Montreal), F 2.

602 *Encyclopedia Britannica*, 111, 850. He was of the Scottish peerage. His wife was the daughter of the first earl of Durham.

603 Ibid.

SARAH'S GARDEN

604 S. Goodwin, *PM*, (Garden), F 2.

605 S. Goodwin, *JN*.

606 S. Goodwin, *PM*, (Garden), F 2.

607 Ann Leighton, *American Gardens of the Nineteenth Century* (Amherst, MA: University of Massachusetts Press, 1987), 85.

608 S. Goodwin, *PM*, (Garden), F 2.

609 Ibid.

610 S. Goodwin, *JN*.

611 S. Goodwin, *PM,* (Misses Hart & Slade), F 6.

612 S. Goodwin, *JN*.

613 S. Goodwin, *PM*, (Garden), F 2.

614 S. Goodwin, *JN*.

615 Leighton, 228-240.

616 S. Goodwin, *JN*.

617 S. Goodwin, *JN*.

618 Leighton, 241-248.

619 Ibid.

620 Ibid.

621 S. Goodwin *JN*.

622 Ibid.

623 S. Goodwin, *PM*, (Garden), F 2.

624 S. Goodwin, *JN*.

625 Hedrick, 270-273.

626 S. Goodwin, *JN*.

627 Hedrick, 230-231.

628 S. Goodwin, *JN*.

629 Hedrick, 263.

630 S. Goodwin, *JN*.

631 Ibid.

632 Ibid.

633 S. Goodwin, *PM*, (Garden), F 2.

634 S. Goodwin, *JN*.

635 Ibid.

636 Ibid.

637 Ibid.

638 S. Goodwin, *PM*, (Garden), F2.

639 S. Goodwin, *JN*.

640 S. Goodwin, *PM*, (Garden), F 2.

641 S. Goodwin, *JN*.

642 Ibid.

MRS. ABC

643 S. Goodwin, *PM*, (Mrs. ABC), F 6.

644 Ibid.

645 Ibid.

646 Ibid.

THE WIDOW'S MIRACLE

647 S. Goodwin, *PM*, (An Experience), F 4.

OLD THINGS

648 Stackpole, *OKHF,* 38-39.

649 S. Goodwin, *PM*, (Old Things), F 6.

1840-1850: FACTORIES, BANKS & POLITICS

650 Norton, I, 256-262.

[651] Brighton, *RAP*, 144.

[652] C.W. Brewster & Son, *PCD,* 1861. The machinery was driven by 300 horsepower high-pressure steam engines that consumed 1,900 tons of anthracite coal annually. A total of 26,128 spindles and 412 looms consumed over 375,000 pounds of cotton, with an annual production of over 3.5 million yards of lawn, a thin cotton or linen fabric.

[653] Brighton, *RAP*, 144.

[654] Ibid.

[655] Brighton, *RAP*, 145.

[656] Ibid., 231-233. Most agreed that this fire was not as devastating to the town as the three fires at the start of the century had been. By then insurance covered much of the losses; damage was contained because of fire fighting equipment.

[657] Brighton, *TCTF,* II, 129.

[658] Goodwin, 295.

[659] Ray Brighton, "Goodwin Was New Hampshire's First Civil War Governor." (*Portsmouth Herald*, 15 April l990), 4A.

[660] Smith, IV, 1059-1060.

[661] Brighton, *TCTF,* I, 139.

[662] Brighton, *Portsmouth Herald, GNHFCWG*, 4.

[663] Ibid., IV, 1066-1067.

[664] Norton, I, 382.

[665] Smith, IV, 1084.

[666] Howe, 225-237.

[667] S. Goodwin, *JN*.

[668] Smith, IV, 1040-43.

[669] S. Goodwin, *JN*.

[670] *Encyclopedia Britannica*., IV, 1086.

[671] Ibid., 1081.

FRANKLIN PIERCE

[672] S. Goodwin, *PM,* (Franklin Pierce), F 2.

[673] Roy Nichols, *Franklin Pierce* (Philadelphia, PA: University of Pensylvania Press., 1931), 29-32.

[674] Ibid., 34-35.

[675] S. Goodwin, *PM,* (Franklin Pierce, F 2.

[676] Pillsbury, 489.

[677] S. Goodwin, *PM,* (Franklin Pierce, F 2.

[678] Ibid.

[678] Ibid.

[680] Nichols 76-77.

[681] Ibid., 257.

[682] Ibid., 203.

[683] Smith, IV, 1010.

[684] Nichols, .224-226.

[685] Norton, I, 381.

[686] S. Goodwin *PM,* (Franklin Pierce), F 2.

[687] Brighton, *RAP*, 156-160.

[688] S. Goodwin, *PM,* (Franklin Pierce), F 2.

[689] Nichols, 527-532.

THE FAMILY 1850s

[690] Ovid L. Futch, *History of Andersonville Prison* (Gainsville, FL: University of Florida Press, 1968), 26-28.

[691] Fenwick. 5 January 1959.

[692] S. Goodwin, *JN*.

[693] S. Goodwin, *PM,* (Thanksgiving), F 2.

[694] Ibid., (Gorham House*), F 3.

[695] Georgina Barnhill, "Depictions of the White Mountain in the Popular Press," *Historical New Hampshire,* 54, 111&IV (Concord, NH: New Hampshire Historical Society, Fall/Winter 1999), 115.

[696] Pillsbury, 170.

[697] S. Goodwin, *PM,* (Gorham House), F 3.

[698] Pillsbury, 170.

[699] S. Goodwin, *PM,* (Gorham House), F3.

[700] Ibid.

[701] Ibid.

[702] Ibid.

[703] Ibid.

[704] Ibid.

[705] Elton Hall, "The White Mountain Photography of Francis Blake," *Historical New Hampshire,* 54, 111 &IV (Concord, NH: New Hampshire Historical Society, Fall/Winter 1999), 135-140. The Glen House in the White Mountains was destroyed by fire in the winter of 1884 and then it was rebuilt.

[706] S. Goodwin, *PM,* (Gorham House), F 3.

[707] Hall, 54, 111 &1V. Many years later in 1885 Cherry Mountain in nearby Jefferson was the site of a terrible mountain slide, much like the one that killed the Willey family in Crawford Notch during the 1830s.

[708] Barnhill, 107. About this time the early promoters of daguerreotypes added to the lure of the mountains.

[709] S. Goodwin, *PM,* (Gorham House), F 3.

[710] Ibid., (Peotone Ill.), F 2.
[711] Garraty, 1,221. The importation of slaves had been illegal since 1808, and both the United States and Britain were committed to stopping illegal traders.
[712] S. Goodwin, *PM*, (Trip to Concord), F 2.
[713] Letter, Samuel Storer to Admiral Storer, May, 1859.
[714] Ibid., June, 1859.

1850-1860: CLIPPER, GASLIGHTS AND ELECTIONS
[715] Brewster, *PCD*, 1861-1871.
[716] *PJL&P*, 13 Dec. 1851.
[717] S. Goodwin, *W B*.
[718] Brighton, *C0PP&MWBT*, 13.
[719] Brighton, *TSOTP*, 159.
[720] Brighton,*COPP&MWBT*, 78-95.
[721] Saltonstall, 211-212.
[722] Brighton, *COPP&MWBT*, 129-130.
[723] Brighton, *COPP&MWBT*, 152-153.
[724] S. Goodwin, *PM*, (Gardens), F 2.
[725] Brighton, *TSOTP*, 175-76.
[726] Pillsbury, 500.
[727] Ibid., 503-4.
[728] Charles Penrose, *Ichabod Goodwin: Sea Captain, Merchant, Financier, Civil War Governor of NewHampshire,* Newcomer Society Pamphlet (Philadelphia, PA: Day & Zimmerman Pub., Aug 1956).

THE GOVERNORSHIP
[729] Pillsbury, 515-16.
[730] Brighton, *Portsmouth Herald, GNHF-CWG-PH,* Part II, April 22, 1990.
[731] S. Goodwin, *PM*, (Governorship), F 2.
[732] Pillsbury, 7.
[733] Ibid.
[734] Pillsbury, 517.
[735] S. Goodwin, *PM*, (Governorship), F2.
[736] Ibid.
[737] Pillsbury, 11.
[738] S. Goodwin, *PM*, (Mr. Dexter), F 8.
[739] S. Goodwin, *PM*, (Governorship), F 8.
[740] Ibid.
[741] John Kouwenhoven, *Adventures of America 1857-1900* (NY: Harper Bros., 1938), 44.
[742] S. Goodwin, *PM*, (Governorship), F 8.

[743] Benton, *EB-Micro.* 1V, 283.
[744] S. Goodwin, *PM*, (Governorship), F 8.
[745] Hedrick, 264.
[746] Norton, I, 426-427.
[747] Elwin Page, *Lincoln in New Hampshire* (Boston: Houghton Mifflin, 1929), 12-13, 50-51.
[748] Pillsbury, 517.
[749] Richard Winslow III, *Constructing the Munitions of War* (Portsmouth NH: Portsmouth Marine Society, 1995), 16.

CIVIL WAR BEGINS
[750] *PJL&P,* 6 April 1861.
[751] Geoffrey Ward, *The Civil War* (NY: Vintage Books, 1990), 38.
[752] *PJL&P,* 6 April 1861.
[753] Rev. Stephen G. Abbot, *The First New Hampshire Regiment* (Keene, NH: Sentential Publishing, 1890), 58-59.
[754] Rev. Stephen G. Abbot, p. 56.
[755] Brighton, *TCTF*, I, 159.
[756] Pillsbury, 522.
[757] *PJL&P*, 4 May 1861.
[758] Pillsbury, IV, 8-9.
[759] *PJL&P*, 4 May 1861.
[760] Pillsbury, 1V, 8-9.
[761] Goodwin, 296.
[762] *PJL&P,* 4 May 1861.
[763] Pillsbury, 521-522.
[764] Major Otis F.R. Waite, *New Hampshire in the Great Rebellion* (Claremont, NH: Tracy Chase & Co, 1870) 67-68.
[765] Ibid., 115.
[766] Ibid., 108.
[767] Waite, 34-136.
[768] Ibid., 84-86.
[769] *PJL&P*, 27 April 1861.
[770] Winslow *CMOW*, 285-291.
[771] Ibid., 40.
[772] Ibid., 61.
[773] G. Dewey, 116.
[774] S. Goodwin, *JN*.
[775] Futch, 26.
[776] *PJL&P,* 14 March 1903.
[777] Robert Kirsch & William Murphy, *West of the West*, (New York: E.P. Dutton & Co, 1967), 364-37.
[778] S. Goodwin, *JN*.

A TRIP TO THE PRAIRIE

[779] *The History of Peotone* (Centennial booklet, on file at Peotone Library, Peotone, IL, 1956). After the treaty was finalized, approximately five thousand Native Americans left Illinois and moved westward to Missouri.

[780] Ibid.

[781] Garraty, I, 348-350.

[782] *History of Peotone.* 7.

[783] Garraty, I, 346-350.

[784] *History of Peotone*, 10.

[785] Samuel Storer, Letter to father, December 1863. On file, Thayer Cummings Library .

[786] Will Ichabod Goodwin. On microfilm file, State Archives, Brentwood, NH, #3784, July 14, 1883).

[787] Norton, I, 266.

[788] Samuel Storer, Letter, May 1859. On file Thayer Cummings Library, May 1859.

[789] John Clayton, *The Illinois Fact Book and Historical Almanac, 1673-1968* (Carbondale, IL: Southern Illinois University Press, 1970), 223.

[790] S. Goodwin, *PM,* (Peotone, Ill), F 2.

[791] S. Goodwin, *PM,* (Servants), F 8.

[792] Clayton, p. 312.

[793] S. Goodwin, *PM,* (Peotone, Ill), F 2.

[794] *History of Peotone,* 12-14. In later years corn and oats became the primary crops.

[795] S. Goodwin, *PM,* (Peotone, Ill), F 2.

[796] Norton, I, 327.

[797] S. Goodwin, *PM,* (Peotone, Ill), F 2.

[798] Paul Angle, *Prairie State: Impressions of Illinois, 1673-1967* (Chicago: The University of Chicago Press, 1968), 331.

[799] S. Goodwin, *PM,* (Peotone, Ill), F 2.

[800] Angle, 74.

[801] Ibid., 162.

[802] S. Goodwin, *PM,* (Peotone, Ill), F 2.

[803] S. Storer, letter to Admiral Storer, 16 Nov 1862. On file, Thayer Cummings Library.

[804] *Boston City Registry,* 1863.

[805] Ibid., 1864.

[806] S. Goodwin, *PM,* (Garden), F 2.

THE WAR YEARS

[807] Winslow, *CMOW,* 6, 78-79.

[808] Ibid., 58-59.

[809] Ibid., 117-121.

[810] Ibid., 115-117. Seavey island residents held out for a higher price than the government was willing to offer and the island was not totally owned by the government until 1866.

[811] *PJL&P,* 27 April 1872.

[812] Winslow, *CMOW,* 131-133. Even after their ship was ready to return to duty, most of them remained behind doing guard duty, as they wanted to take advantage of this welcome opportunity to receive an education.

[813] Ibid., 181.

[814] Ibid., 183, 192-193.

[815] Brighton *TCTF,* I, 160-162.

[816] Winslow, CMOW, 197.

[817] Ibid., 229-230. A trial was set to determine charges. However, the matter was eventually settled with the payment of a small fine by the miscreants. The federal draft was eventually enacted in Portsmouth, as well as in the rest of the North.

[818] Ibid. 229.

[819] Ibid., 243-249.

[820] Estes , 142-143.

[821] Ibid.

[822] McDermott.

[823] S. Goodwin, *PM, (*Susie in NY), F 2.

[824] Brighton, *RAP,* 29-31.

[825] Dewey, George, Letter, , 2 Feb 1864, on file at Thayer Cummings Library.

[826] Mark Caldwell, *The Last Crusade of the War on Consumption* (NY: Athenaeum Press, 1985*)*, 95.

[827] G. Dewey, Letter, 10 April1864, on file at Thayer Cummings Library.

[828] Ibid., 17 July 1864, on file at Thayer Cummings Library.

[829] *Harvard Alumni Magazine,* Sept 1912.

[830] G. Ward, 273.

[831] Page Smith, *Trial By Fire* (NY: McGraw Hill, 1982) V, 524.

[832] S. Goodwin, *PM,* (Salmon Chase), F 2. Samuel Hooper, who accompanied Supreme Court Justice Salmon Chase to Portsmouth, was a congressman from Massachusetts. The lights which gave off so much heat would have been gaslights.

[833] Garraty, I, 402.

[834] S. Goodwin, *PM,* (Salmon Chase), F 2.

[835] Pillsbury, 502.

THE END OF THE WAR

836 Lauren Healey, *The Admiral* (Chicago: Ziff & Davis, 1944), 88-89.
837 Winslow, *CMOW,* 300.
838 *PJL&P,* 15 April l865.
839 Ibid.
840 Ibid.
841 Ibid.
842 *PJL&*P, 22 April 1865.
843 Ibid.
844 Ibid.
845 *PJL&P,* 18 July 1865.
846 Waite, 167.
847 Dewey, G, 122.
848 Healey, 88-89.
849 *PJL&P, 27* April l872.
850 Wm. Davis, *The Civil War* (NY: Black Dog & Leventhal, 1994), 404-406.
851 Ibid.
852 Ibid., 409.
853 Winslow, *CMOW,* 304.
854 Ibid., 304.
855 *PJL&P,* 7 Dec 1865.
856 Winslow, *CMOW,* 331.
857 *PJL&P,* 8 July l865.
858 *Ibid.,* 11 November l865.
859 Brighton, *COPP&MWBT,* 127-33.
860 Winslow, *CMOW,* 288-291.
861 *PJL&P*, 11 November l865.
862 Ibid., 14 October l865.
863 Ibid., 9 May 1906.

THE FAMILY IN THE 1860s

864 Kirsch & Murray, 401 & 413.
865 S. Goodwin, *JN.*
866 Garraty, II, 83-87.
867 Ibid., II, 92-93.
868 *Boston Globe,* 19 Jan l903.
869 Robert Nylander, note on Whitney House for Cambridge Historical Comm. rev., July 2, l979.
870 Cambridge Historical Society Association 17:73 (Cambridge, MA: W.A. Greenaugh & Co., 1881).
871 Ibid., 32:36.
872 S. Goodwin, *PM,* (Trip to Concord), F 2.
873 Alan Emmet, *So Fina a Prospect* (Hanover, NH: University Press of New England, 1996), p. 85.
874 Ibid.

875 S. Goodwin, *PM,* (Trip to Concord), F 2.
876 Emmet, 85-86.
877 Hedrick, 269.
878 *Boston Globe,* 27 Jan. 2000, C1-4.
879 Emmet, 86-87.
880 S. Goodwin, *PM,* (Trip to Concord), F 2.
881 Emmet, 89.
882 S. Goodwin, *PM,* (Trip to Concord), F 2.
883 Hedrick, 265
884 S. Goodwin, *JN.*
885 Emmet, 91-2.
886 S. Goodwin, *PM,* (Trip to Concord*), F 2.*
887 Ibid.
888 Eleanor Early, *And This Is Boston!* (Boston: Houghton Mifflin, 1930), 154-163.
889 *Encyclopedia Britannica,* V111, 680.
890 Ibid., I , 211. Alcott eventually moved to Boston. Although she suffered from ill health most of her adult life after she contracted typhoid fever while working as a nurse during the Civil War, she outlived all of her family, dying just two days after her father in March of 1888.
891 Early, 158.
892 S. Goodwin, *PM,* (Trip to Concord), F 2.
893 S. Goodwin, *PM,* (Looking back), F 2.
894 G. Dewey, 18-24.
895 Ibid., 126.
896 Letter from S. Storer to S. Dewey, 31 Oct. l867. On file, Thayer Cummings Library.
897 Ibid., 10 Nov. 1867.
898 Genealogical sketch of Rice family. On file, Thayer Cummings Library.
899 Clause M. Naske, *An Interpretative History of Alaskan Statehood* (Anchorage: Alaska Northwest Pub. Co., 1973), p 1.
900 A.W. Greeley, *Handbook of Alaska* (Port Washington, NY: Kennikat Press).
901 Genealogical sketch on Storer Decatur family. On file, Thayer Cummings Library.
902 Naske, 1-4.
903 G. Dewey note to S. Dewey, 3 March l968. On file, Thayer Cummings Library.
904 S. Goodwin , *PM,* (Looking Back), F 2.
905 G. Ward , 65.
906 Ibid.
907 Michael Kraus, *The United States* (Ann Arbor: The University of Michigan Press, 1959), 57-458.
908 G. Ward, 151-153.

ADMIRAL FARRAGUT
[909] Smith, 5, 285.
[910] George Dewey, *Autobiography of George Dewey* (NY: Charles Scribner's Sons, 1913. Reprint. Annapolis MD: Naval Institute Press, 1987), 52-53.
[911] G.Ward, 105-10.
[912] Dewey, 52.
[913] Ibid., 75-78.
[914] Smith, 5, 286.
[915] Dewey, 76.
[916] Ibid., 81-85.
[917] S. Goodwin, *JN.*
[918] G. Ward, 267-268.
[919] Dewey, 109-111.
[920] S. Goodwin, *JN.*
[921] Dewey, 124-125.
[922] S. Goodwin, *PM,* (Admiral Farragut), F 2.
[923] Winslow, 318.
[924] S. Goodwin, *JN.* Sarah often wrote about the same subject twice. There is another version of Mr. Winthrop's visit in *Pleasant Memories,* very similar, but not as detailed.
[925] Ibid.
[926] S. Goodwin, *PM,* (Admiral Farragut), F 2.
[927] Robert C. Winthrop Jr., *Memoirs of Robert C. Winthrop* (Cambridge: John Wilson & Son, 1897), 6-8.
[928] Ibid., 171-172.
[929] Ibid., 326. Winthrop publicly expressed great disdain for what he considered to be the ridiculous insertion of a women's suffrage clause in the 1872 Republican platform.
[930] Wendell.
[931] S.Goodwin, *PM,* (Looking Back), F 2.
[932] Winslow, *CMOW 318.*

THE FAMILY IN THE 1870s
[933] G.Dewey, 144.
[934] S. Goodwin, *PM,* (NY with Susie), F 2.
[935] Morris, 1-10. These hotels were home to many well-to-do New Yorkers because they provided such needed services. Guests were assured of a busy social schedule and proper contacts, as well as a good address within the city.
[936] Ibid., 100-105.
[937] Ibid., 182.
[938] S. Goodwin, *PM,* (NY with Susie), F 2.
[939] Morris, 66-67. Thomas Bailey Aldrich, a well-known writer and Portsmouth native, was a close friend of Booth and is credited with helping him overcome his problems and return to the stage following the assassination of Lincoln.
[940] Ibid., 65.
[941] Morris, 7, 11.
[972] Ibid., 101-102. Despite Stewart's financial success, this Irish immigrant was never accepted by the city's high society, and was always looked down on for being a tradesman. He was noted for being cold and aloof, and remained somewhat of a friendless introvert to the end of his life
[943] Ibid., 111.
[944] S. Goodwin, *PM,* (NY with Susie), F 2.
[945] Ibid., 4, 27-28, 147-148.
[946] S. Goodwin, *PM, (*NY with Susie), F 2.
[947] Brewster, *Rambles* II.
[948] Sarah Waxman, *The History of Central Park,* www.ny.com.
[949] Morris, 91-97.
[950] S. Goodwin, *PM,* (NY with Susie), F 2.
[951] G. Dewey, 144.
[952] Healey, 94.
[953] *PJL&P,* 27April l872.
[954] Healey, 94-97.
[955] S. Goodwin, (NY with Susie), F 2.
[956] *PJL&P,* 4 Jan 1873.
[957] *Encyclopedia Britannica,* XV1, 529.
[958] Healey, 94-95.
[959] Brighton, *RAP,* 31.
[960] Healey, 94-95.
[961] Delbert Dewey, *The Life and Letters of Admiral Dewey* (NY: Wolfhall & Co. Pub, 1899), 184.
[962] S. Goodwin, *JN.*
[963] *1870-80 US Census Records.* On microfilm, Portsmouth, NH, Public Library.
[964] Brewster, *PCD,* 1861.
[965] *Portsmouth Herald,* 9 May l906.
[966] *PJL&P,* 14 March l903.
[967] S. Goodwin, *JN.*
[968] S. Goodwin, *PM,* (Servants), F 8.
[969] *Portsmouth Evening Times,* 7 October 1886.
[970] S. Goodwin, *PM,* (General Grant), F 3.
[971] Brighton, *RAP,* 160-163.
[972] *PJL&P,* 8, July 1882.

973 Brighton, *TCTF,* I, 154.
974 Ibid.
975*Harvard Alumni N*ews, 1912 (Frank Good-win file, B2150. Harvard School archives Cambridge, MA).
976 Cambridge City Records, 1874-75. (Town Hall, Cambridge, MA).

THE FAMILY IN THE 1880s
977 F. Goodwin, 291-297. Frank was justifiably proud of all of his father's accomplishments. He also lauded his father for his willingness to aid younger men in the business world, with both advice and monetary support. And he noted that Goodwin was always willing to help others in time of need.
978 City Death Records , 1870-90. (Town Hall, Cambridge, MA).
979 Death certificate, Ichabod Goodwin. 4 July 1882 (State of NH Dept. of Human Services, Archival Library, Concord, NH).
980 *PJL&P,* 8 July l882.
981 *PDC,* 6 July l882.
982 *The Daily Evening Times*, Portsmouth, NH, 5 July 1882.
983 *PJL&P,* 8 July l882, p.2 col. 4.
984*TPC,* 10 July l882.
985 State of NH marriage certificate. On file at NH Vital Statistics Archives, Concord, NH.
986 John Hayes Goodwin, 137.
987 *The Boston Sunday Herald*, 2 June l918, E1.
988 *Encyclopedia Britannica,* 422.
989 *BSH,* 2 June l918, E1.
990 Healey, 124.
991 *Harvard Alumni Magazine,* 1912.
992 S. Goodwin, letter to Molly Goodwin.
993 S. Goodwin, *JN.*
994 Molly Punderson Rockwell, "Sarah Storer Goodwin,*" Milton Bulletin*, Milton Academy Publication. June 1965.

GOODWIN PARK
995 Leighton, 186-195.
996 Brighton, *TCTF,* 1, 183-184.
997 Brighton, *RAP,* 32-38.
998 S. Goodwin, *JN.*
999 Ibid.
1000 Ibid.

1001 Ibid.
1002 Ibid.
1003 Ibid.
1004 Brighton, *RAP,* 32-38.
1005 S. Goodwin, *JN.*
1006 *PJL&P,* 7 July 1888.
1007 Ibid. The paper nominated the cadets as "the brightest and prettiest" part of the parade. This was probably a group of young ladies. They also credited the police for having the " the most tak-ing features" of the parade, but failed to go into detail as to what the features were.
1008 Brighton, *RAP,* 35-36.
1009 S. Goodwin, *JN.*
1010 *PJL&P,* 7 July 1888.
1011 Ibid.
1012 S. Goodwin, *JN.*
1013 *PJL&P, 7 July 1888.*
1014 Ibid.
1015 S. Goodwin, *JN.*
1016 Ibid.
1017 Ibid.
1018 Ibid.
1019 Ibid.
1020 Ibid.

19TH CENTURY SOCIAL AND RELIGIOUS REFORM
1021 Pillsbury, 482.
1022 Lilene Cooper, *Susan B. Anthony* (NY: Franklin Watts Pub, 1984), 84-87.
1023 Pillsbury, 561.
1024 S. Goodwin, *JN.*
1025 Ibid.
1026 Cooper, 84-87.
1027 S. Goodwin, *JN.*
1028 Samuel Goodwin letter to Ichabod Good-win, dated October 10, 1831. On file, Thayer Cummings Library.
1029 S. Goodwin, *JN.*
1030 Ibid.
1031 Smith, 4, 248, 987.
1032 S. Goodwin, *JN.*
1033 Ibid.
1034 Ibid.
1035 Ibid.
1036 Ibid.
1037 Anne Braude, *Radical Spirits* (Boston:

Beacon Press, 1989), 15-30.
[1038] S. Goodwin, *JN*.
[1039] Sylvia Cranston, *H.P.B.* (NY: G. Putnam & Sons, 1933), 43.
[1040] Ibid., 504-520.
[1041] S. Goodwin, *JN*.
[1042] Ibid.
[1043] Alex Owen, *The Darkened Room* (Philadelphia: University of Penn Press, 1990), 20-25.
[1044] S. Goodwin, *JN*.
[1045] Braude, 4-5.
[1046] S. Goodwin, *JN*.

SARAH 1890s
[1047] S. Goodwin letter to Molly Goodwin, May 22, 1895.
[1048] Punderson Rockwell, 12.
[1049] S. Goodwin to Molly Goodwin, November, 1895.
[1050] Letter from S. Goodwin to Rev. Putnam, May 23, 1895.
[1051] *Portsmouth Journal,* 17 Oct 1896
[1052] Ibid.

EPILOGUE
[1053] Garraty, II, 215.
[1054] Brighton, *RAP,* 29.
[1055] *Columbia Encyclopedia* (New York: Columbia University Press, 1964) 6, 1798.
[1056] Healey, 287.
[1057] Ibid., 256-260.
[1058] *PJL&P,* 24 September 1898.
[1059] *The Boston Sunday Herald*, 2 June 1918.
[1060] *PJL&P,* 14 March 1903.
[1061] Ibid.
[1062] *Boston Globe*, 19 Jan 1903.
[1063] *Portsmouth City Directory,* 1910 (Boston, MA: W.A. Greenaugh & Co., 1910), 76.
[1064] *PH,* 9 May 1906.
[1065] *PH,* 3 July 1909.
[1066] *Bostonia,* Boston University news Magazine, 15 November 1912, X11, 76-77.
[1067] Healey, 93.
[1068] *PH,* 8 October 1922.
[1069] Will of William Winder, December, 1921. State of NH Probate Court Archives, Rockingham County, Brentwood, NH.
[1070] *PH,* 7 January, 1926.

[1071] Will and addendum of Ichabod Goodwin, filed with State of NH. Probate Court Archives, Rockingham County, Brentwood, NH.
[1072] *PH,* 16 January 1932.
[1073] Ibid., 12 February 1963.
[1074] Healey, 314.
[1075] *The Washington Post*, 7 May 1933.
[1076] Punderson Rockwell, 22-24.
[1077] *Boston Herald Traveler,* 29 July 1971.
[1078] *Boston Globe,* 13 March 1903.
[1079] *Harvard Alumni Bulletin,* 14 October 1914.
[1080] *Boston Herald Traveler,* 29 July 1971.
[1081] Ibid.
[1082] *PJL&P,* 14 May 1906.
[1083] *The Boston Sunday Herald,* 2 June 1918.
[1084] Ibid.
[1085] John Hayes Goodwin, 137.
[1086] Ibid.
[1087] Candee, 19-23.
[1088] Gerald D. Foss *Images of America* (Dover, NH: Arcadia Publishing,1994), 45.
[1089] *Portsmouth Herald*, 12 Nov 2000.
[1090] Brighton, *POPS&CT,* 178.
[1091] Stackpole, *HONH,* 111,170-174.
[1092] *Savannah Evening Press*, 14 January 1956.
[1093] Hall, 135-140.
[1094] *The Boston Globe,* January 27 2000, C 1 & C4.
[1095] *The Portsmouth Press,* March 5, 1992.

BIBLIOGRAPHY

Abbot, Stephen G. *The First NH Regiment.* Keene, NH: Sentinel Publishers, 1890.

Angle, Paul. *Prairie State: Impressions of Illinois, 1673-1967.* Chicago, IL: The University of Chicago Press, 1968.

Beecher, Catherine and Harriet Stowe. *American Women's Home.* Hartford, CT: Harriet Beecher-Stowe Center, 1975 reprint; original 1869 by J.B. Ford Company.

Benton, William, ed. *Encyclopedia Britannica, Micropaedia, and Macropaedia.* Chicago, IL: Encyclopedia Britannica, Inc, 1974.

Braude, Ann. *Radical Spirits.* Boston, MA: Beacon Press, 1989.

Brewster, Charles. *Rambles About Portsmouth.* Portsmouth, NH: C.W Brewster & Son, Publisher, 1859.

_____. *Rambles About Portsmouth.* Portsmouth, NH: Lewis W. Brewster, Pub., 1869.

Bridgewater, William, Ed. *Columbia Encyclopedia.* New York, NY: Columbia University Press, 1963.

Brighton, Raymond A. *They Came To Fish.* 2 Vols. Portsmouth, NH: Randall/ Winebaum Enterprises, 1979.

_____. *Tall Ships of the Piscataqua.* Portsmouth, NH: Portsmouth Marine Society, 1989.

_____. *Port of Portsmouth Ships and the Cotton Trade, 1783-1829.* Portsmouth, NH: Portsmouth Marine Society, 1986.

_____. *Clippers of the Port of Portsmouth and the Men Who Built Them.* Portsmouth, NH: Portsmouth Marine Society, 1985.

_____. *Rambles About Portsmouth.* Portsmouth, NH: Portsmouth Marine Society, 1994.

Caldwell, Mark. *The Last Crusade of the War on Consumption.* New York, NY: Athenaeum Press, 1985.

Calvert, Karin. *Children In the House.* Boston, MA: Northeastern University Press, 1992.

Clayton, John. *The Illinois Fact Book and Historical Almanac, 1673-1968.* Carbondale, IL: University of Southern Illinois Press, 1970.

Candee, Richard. *Building Portsmouth.* Portsmouth, NH: Portsmouth Advocates, 1992.

Coquillette, Daniel R., Ed. *Law in Colonial Massachusetts 1630-1800.* Boston, MA: Colonial Society of Massachusetts, 1984.

Cooper, Lilene. *Susan B. Anthony.* New York, NY: Franklin Watts Publishers, 1984.

Cranston, Sylvia. *H.P.B.* New York, NY: G. Putnum & Sons, 1933.

Davis, William. *The Civil War.* New York, NY: Black Dog and Leventhal, 1994.

Dewey, Delbert. *The Life and Letters of Admiral Dewey.* New York, NY: Wolfhall Publishing, 1899.

Dewey, George. *Autobiography of George Dewey.* Annapolis: Naval Institute Press, 1987 reprint; original, 1913 by Chas. Scribner's Sons.

Diner, Hasia. *Erin's Daughters in America: Irish Immigrant Women in the Nineteenth Century.* London, England: John Hopkins Press, 1983.

Dudden, Faye E. *Serving Women: Household Service in Nineteenth-Century America.* Middletown, CT: Wesleyan Press, 1983.

Early, Eleanor. *And This Is Boston.* Boston, MA: Houghton Mifflin, 1930.

Emmet, Alan. *So Fine A Prospect.* Hanover, NH: University Press of New England, 1996.

Estes, J. Worth and David M. Goodman. *The Changing Humors of Portsmouth.* Boston, MA: The Francis Countway Library of Medicine, 1986.

Fennelly, Catherine. *Town Schooling in Early New England: 1780-1840.* Sturbridge, MA: Old Sturbridge, Inc., 1962.

Foss, Gerald D. *Images of America.* Dover, NH: Arcadia Publishing, 1994.

Futch, Ovid. *History of Andersonville Prison.* Gainsville, FL: University Press of Florida, 1968.

Garraty, John A. *The American Nation.* 2 Vols. New York, NY: Harper & Row, 1966.

Greeley, A.W. *Handbook of Alaska.* Port Washington, NY: Kennikat Press, 1970.

Healey, Lauren. *The Admiral.* Chicago, IL: Ziff and Davis.

Hedrick, Ulysses. *A History of Horticulture in America.* New York, NY: Oxford University Press, 1950.

Hobo, Paul. *Tarnished Expansion.* Knoxville, TN: University of Tennessee Press, 1983.

Howe, David Walker. *The Political Culture of the American Whigs.* Chicago, IL: University of Chicago Press, 1979.

Johnson, Clifton. *Old Time Schools and School Books.* New York, NY: Dover Publications, 1963.

Kelso, Robert. *The History of Public Poor Relief in Massachusetts.* Boston, MA: Houghton Mifflin, 1919.

Kevill-Davies, Nancy. *Yesterday's Children.* Woodbridge, England: Antique Collectors Club, 1991.

Kirsch, Robert and William Murphy. *West of the West.* New York, NY: E.P. Dutton & Company, 1967.

Kouwenhoven, John. *Adventures of America, 1857-1900,* New York, NY: Harper Brothers, 1938.

Kraus, Michael. *The United States to 1865.* Ann Arbor, MI: The University of Michigan Press, 1959.

Leighton, Ann. *American Gardens of the Nineteenth Century.* Amherst, MA: University of Massachusetts Press, 1987.

Malone, Dennis, Ed. *Dictionary of American Biography.* New York, NY: Scribner's, 1936.

Martin, Edward. *The Wayfarer in New York.* New York, NY: The Macmillan Co., 1909.

Martin, Kenneth R. *Heavy Weather and Hard Luck: Portsmouth Goes Whaling.* Prtsmouth, NH: Portsmouth Marine Society, 1998.

Morris, Lloyd. *Incredible New York.* New York, NY: Random House, 1951.

Naske, Claus M. *An Interpretive History of Alaskan Statehood.* Anchorage, AK: Northwest Publications, 1973.

Nichols, Roy. *Franklin Pierce.* Philadelphia, PA: University of Pennsylvania Press, 1931.

Norton, Mary Beth et al. *A People & A Nation.* 2 Vols. Boston, MA: Houghton Mifflin, 1990.

Nylander, Jane. *Our Own Snug Fireside.* New York, NY: Alfred Knopf, 1993.

Owen, Alex. *The Darkened Room: Women, Power, and Spiritualism in Late Victorian England.* Chicago, IL: University of Chicago Press, 1990.

Page, Elwin. *Abraham Lincoln in New Hampshire.* Boston, MA: Houghton Mifflin Co., 1929.

_____. *George Washington in New Hampshire.* Portsmouth, NH: Portsmouth Marine Society, 1989 reprint.

Pillsbury, Herbert. *New Hampshire: A History.* New York, NY: Lewis Historical Publishing, 1927.

Saltonstall, William G. *Ports of Piscataqua.* Cambridge, MA.: Harvard University Press, 1941.

Smith, Page. *The Nation Comes of Age: A People's History of the Ante-Bellum Years.* New York, NY: McGraw Hill, 1981. Volume 4.

_____. *Trial By Fire: A People's History of the Civil War and Reconstruction.* New York, NY: McGraw Hill, 1982. Volume 5.

Stackpole, Everett. *History of New Hampshire.* New York, NY: The American Historical Society, 1919.

_____. *Old Kittery and Her Families.* Lewiston, ME: Lewiston Journal Company, 1903.

_____, Lucien Thompson and Winthrop Meserve. *History of the Town of Durham.* Somersworth, NH: New Hampshire Publishing Company, 1973, reprint; original, 1923.

Ward, Geoffrey. *The Civil War.* New York, NY: Vintage Books, 1994.

Wertz, Richard E. and Dorothy C. *Lying-In.* New Haven, CT: Yale University Press, 1977.

Windsor, Justin. *Memorial History of Boston.* Boston, MA: James R. Osgood and C., 1880.

Winslow, Richard E. III, *Constructing Munitions of War: The Portsmouth Navy Yard Confronts the Confederacy, 1861-1865.* Portsmouth, NH: Portsmouth Marine Society, 1995.

_____. *Wealth and Honor: Portsmouth During the Golden Age of Privateering.* Portsmouth, NH: Portsmouth Marine Society, 1988.

Winthrop, Robert C. Jr. *Memoirs of Robert C. Winthrop.* Cambridge, MA: John Wilson and Son, 1897.

JOURNAL AND NEWSPAPER ARTICLES

Barnhill, Georgia. "Depictions of the White Mountain in the Popular Press," *Historical New Hampshire.* Vol. 54. NH Historical Society (Fall/Winter, 1999).

Bostonian. University of Boston News Magazine, X11, 12 (Nov. 1912).

Brighton, Ray, "Goodwin was New Hampshire's First Civil War Governor," *Portsmouth Herald* (15 April 1990).

Clark, Charles. Introduction to *Historical New Hampshire.* V. 55. Concord, NH: New Hampshire Historical Society (Spring-Summer 2000).

Fenwick, Mrs. Marston. "William Rice's Give A Way Program," *Portsmouth Herald* (24 January 1959).

Goodwin, Frank. "Honorable Ichabod Goodwin," *The Granite Monthly,* 111, No 8 (May, 1880).

Hall, Elton. "The White Mountain Photography of Francis Blake," *Historical New Hampshire*, Vol. 54. New Hampshire Historical Society (Fall/Winter, 1999.)

Harvard Alumni Magazine (Sept., 1912).

Harvard Alumni News Clipping, 1912 Frank Goodwin file. B2150 Harvard School
        Archives, Cambridge, MA.
Nartonis, David, K. *"The New Divinity Movement and its Impact on New Hampshire
        Churches 1769-1849"*, *Historical New Hampshire,* Vol. 55. Concord Historical
        Society (Spring Summer 2000).
O'Connor, Thomas. "Changing Times at Harvard," *Boston Globe* (16 August 1999).
Penrose, Charles. *"Ichabod Goodwin (1794-1882) Sea Captain, Merchant, Financier, Civil
        War Governor of NewHampshire."* Newcomen Society pamphlet. Philadelphia,
        PA: Day and Zimmerman, Pub., Aug. 1956.
Preble, Robert. *Britannica World Language Dictionary.* New York, NY: Funk and
        Wagnall's, 1954.
Rockwell, Molly Punderson. "Sarah Storer Goodwin*," Milton Bulletin*, Milton, MA:
        Milton Academy Publication, June 1965.
Strawbery Banke Guidebook. Portsmouth, NH: Strawbery Banke, Inc.1971.

UNPUBLISHED TRANSCRIPTS AND LETTERS

Barrett, Wendell. *Recollections of Wendell Barrett.* Unpublished transcript. Portsmouth
        Athenaeum, Portsmouth, NH.
Cambridge, Massachusetts, death register, 1881. Archival Department, City Hall,
        Cambridge, MA.
Dewey, George. Letters from George Dewey to Susan Goodwin Dewey from 1864-
        1868. Thayer Cummings Library, Strawbery Banke Museum, Portsmouth, NH.
Federal Fire Society Membership list. Mofatt Ladd House, Society of the Colonial Dames
        of New Hampshire, Portsmouth, NH.
Goodwin, John Hayes. *The Goodwins of Ancient Kittery Maine.* Berwick, ME,
        photocopied, 1985.
Goodwin, Ichabod. Letters to Sarah Goodwin, circa 1829. Thayer Cummings Library,
        Strawbery Banke Museum, Portsmouth, NH.
Goodwin, Sarah, *Common Day Books,* circa 1880s-1890s. Thayer Cummings Library,
        Strawbery Banke Museum, Portsmouth, NH.
Goodwin, Sarah, *Pleasant Memories,* unpublished memoirs, circa 1870s-1889s. Thayer
        Cummings Library, Strawbery Banke Museum, Portsmouth, NH.
Goodwin, Sarah, *Waste Book,* circa 1870s to 1880s. Thayer Cummings Library,
        Strawbery Banke Museum, Portsmouth, NH.
Goodwin, Sarah, letters to Mary Buttrick, circa1894-1895. Thayer Cummings Library,
        Strawbery Banke Museum, Portsmouth, NH.
Goodwin, Sarah, letters to Ichabod Goodwin, circa 1830-1831. Thayer Cummings
        Library, Strawbery Banke Museum, Portsmouth, NH.
Goodwin, Sarah, letter to Alfred Putnum, circa 1890s. Thayer Cummings Library,
        Strawbery Banke Museum, Portsmouth, NH.
History of Peotone, The. Centennial booklet. Peotone Library, Peotone, IL,
1956.McDermott, Beth*, Shaping the Neighborhood: Portsmouth's History with Fire.*
        Unpublished transcript. Education Department at Strawbery Banke Museum,
        Portsmouth, NH.

Nylander, Robert. Note on Whitney House in Cambridge, Mass. For Cambridge
    Historical Commission, rev. 2, July 1979.
Parker Family Genealogy. Transcript. Archives, Tucker Memorial Library, Concord, NH.
Powell, Governor Wesley. Campaign literature, vintage1960s, undated.
Rice Family Genealogy. Transcript. Maine Room, Rice Library, Kittery, ME.
Riley, Pat. *Servants in Nineteenth Century Portsmouth.* Unpublished transcript,
    Education Department, Strawbery Banke Museum, Portsmouth, NH.
Sherman, Ernest L. *A Study of the Slavery and Anti-Slavery Movement in New
    Hampshire to 1850.* Unpublished thesis. Tuck Memorial Archives, Concord, NH.
Sherburne Family Genealogy. Transcript. Tucker Memorial Library, Concord, NH.
Storer, Samuel. Letters to Rear Admiral George Washington Storer, circa 1860s. Thayer
    Cummings Library, Strawbery Banke Museum, Portsmouth, NH.
Storer, Sarah Goodwin. Two letters to Susan Goodwin Dewey, circa 1860s. Thayer
    Cummings Library, Strawbery Banke Museum, Portsmouth NH.
Ward, Constance. *Negro Slavery in Colonial Portsmouth.* Unpublished thesis, 1969.
    Portsmouth Public Library, Portsmouth, NH.
Waxman, Sarah. *The History of Central Park.* www.ny.com.articles/centralpark.html.
Unknown author. *"A Visit to the Catskill Mountain House 1826,"* published in a
    Boston newspaper in 1826. www.catskillarchive.com/misc/boston1826.

NEWSPAPERS

Boston Globe, The. 19 January 1903, 13 March 1903, 21 February 1999, 16 August 1999,
    27 January 2000.
Boston Herald Traveler. 29 July 1971.
Boston Sunday Herald, The . 2 June 1918.
Portsmouth Daily Chronicle. 6 July 1882.
Portsmouth Daily Evening Times. 5 July 1882, 7 October 1886.
Portsmouth Herald, 9 May 1906, 3 July 1909, 7 January 1926, 16 January 1932, 23 August
    1958, 24 January 1959, 12 February 1963, April 1990, August 10 2000, 12
    November 2000, *Spotlight* 15 February 2001
Portsmouth Journal of Literature and Politics. 13 December 1851, 9 June 1860, 6 April
    1861, 4 May 1861, 27 April 1861, 15 April 1865, 22 April 1865, 8 July 1865, 14
    October 1865, 11 November 1865, 7 December 1865, 27 April 1872, 4 January
    1873, 8 July 1882, 7 July 1888, 24 September 1898, 14 March 1903, 9 May 1906,
    14 May 1906.
Portsmouth Oracle. 22 Aug 1812.
Savannah Evening Press, The. 14 January 1956.
Savannah Morning News, The. 26 August 1947.
Savannah Press, The. 5 November 1919.
Washington Post. 7 May 1933.

STATE AND TOWN RECORDS

Boston City Registry, 1863-64.

Bradford family certificates. Georgette, Joseph. State of NH Dept. of Human Services Archives, Concord, NH.

Brewster, Charles. *Portsmouth Directory, 1856-7, 1861, 1869.* Portsmouth, NH: C.W. Brewster & Son.

Cambridge City Death Records, 1870-1890. Cambridge City Hall, Cambridge, MA.

Cambridge City Records, 1874-1875.

Cambridge Historical Society Association, 1816, 1881. Cambridge, MA: W.A. Greenaugh and Co.

Decatur family marriage and death certificates – Mabel and Stephen. State of NH Dept. of Human Services Archives, Concord, NH.

Edmond, Joseph. *Portsmouth City Directory, 1834.* Joseph Edmond Pub.

Goodwin family Bible. Copies of family records. Thayer Cummings Library, Strawbery Banke Museum, Portsmouth, NH.

Goodwin, Ichabod will. Rockingham County Probate Court, Rockingham, NH.

Goodwin family death certificates – Sarah, Ichabod, Frank and Hope. State of NH Dept. of Human Services Archives, Concord, NH.

Portsmouth Town Records, 1831. NH State Library, Concord, NH.

Portsmouth City Directory, 1910. Boston: W.A. Greenaugh & Co.

Penhallow, Wibird. *Portsmouth City Directory, 1821.* Portsmouth, NH.

Storer family death certificates – Sarah and Samuel. State of NH Dept. of Human Services Archives, Concord, NH.

United States Census figures 1870-80. Portsmouth Public Library, Portsmouth, NH.

Winder family death certificates – Abby. State of NH Dept. of Human Services Archives, Concord, NH.

Winder, William will. Rockingham County Probate Court, Brentwood, NH.

Index

MARGARET WHYTE KELLY, a native of Lancaster, NH, was raised in Laconia, NH. She has a Bachelor's degree in the History of American Culture from the University of New Hampshire, and a dual Masters degree in Creative Writing and English Literature from Simmons College in Boston. She is a former newspaper reporter and feature writer, and wrote a history column on the town of Warner, NH, for several years. For twelve years she worked as a researcher, interpreter, role-player and public speaker at Strawbery Banke Museum, in Portsmouth, NH.

Ms. Kelly has participated in a New Hampshire-based oral history project, and has taught as an adjunct teacher at a local community college. Currently she runs her own tour guide company in the Maine and New Hampshire Seacoast region. Ms. Kelly splits her time between Wells, ME, and the Lake Sunapee Region of New Hampshire. This is her first published book. She is currently working on a book with a focus on New Hampshire during the 1940s.

INQUIRIES can be directed to MeKelly@maine.rr.com.